35-

D1019987

THE SOCIAL CREDIT MOVEMENT IN ALBERTA

SOCIAL CREDIT IN ALBERTA

ITS BACKGROUND AND DEVELOPMENT

A series of studies sponsored by the Canadian Social Science Research Council, directed and edited by S. D. Clark.

The Social Credit Movement in Alberta

JOHN A. IRVING

Professor of Ethics and Social Philosophy
Victoria College, University of Toronto

->>>->>><<<-<<<-

UNIVERSITY OF TORONTO PRESS

Toronto, 1959

Copyright, Canada, 1959
University of Toronto Press
Printed in Canada

London: Oxford University Press

To

SIR FREDERIC CHARLES BARTLETT

for his teaching, writings, and friendship

Foreword

IT IS POSSIBLE that television, had it been available to the Alberta resident of the early nineteen thirties, would have permitted Mr. Aberhart to exploit even more than by radio his great powers of oratory, but it is difficult to imagine how it or any other instrument of communication could have brought him any closer to the people of Alberta. Long before they had ever seen the man, thousands of persons throughout the farm and urban areas of Alberta had become his devoted followers, prepared to accept his every word and to support him in whatever he proposed to do. For someone who believed that political action was the outcome of a rational process of discussion and deliberation, the observation of political developments in Alberta in the years 1932–5 would have been a disillusioning experience. The people truly appeared to have taken leave of their senses, and nothing but disaster, it seemed, could result from the election to office of persons who had so little understanding of the economic and political world as Mr. Aberhart and his Social Credit colleagues.

Yet to the social scientist who has learnt not to be shocked by the conduct of his fellow humans, whether on an isolated island of the South Seas or in a fashionable residential district of a big city, there are no actions of people which do not make sense if viewed within the social context in which they occur. This clearly was the case with respect to Social Credit. Indeed, it might well be suggested that any other kind of conduct would not have made sense on the part of the people of Alberta in the early 1930's. The debt-ridden farmer, unable to sell what little he was able to produce, could scarcely be expected to behave like a bank president, church bishop, or even a professor of economics.

It is the great merit of Professor Irving's study that he takes the people of Alberta as they were and seeks to discover the reason why, in such great numbers, they turned to Social Credit. The contribution of this study to an understanding of the Social Credit movement scarcely needs to be emphasized. No less significant, however, is its contribution to the sociology of collective behaviour. There are few books in the field of sociology or social psychology which come near this one in documenting the rise of a social movement. Professor Irving, it is true, could scarcely have found anywhere more interesting material with which to work. The social scientist might well be grateful to the late Mr. Aberhart for displaying, in his conduct, manner of speech, and indeed in his very appearance, all the qualities of the charismatic leader. And few movements could have conformed more fully to the stereotype of the social movement than Social Credit. But much skill was required, and much patience and industry, to uncover the sources of data relating to a movement such as this which had lived so completely in the minds of people, and skill of a high order and a great deal of industry have clearly gone into the making of this book.

S. D. CLARK

Preface

ALTHOUGH THE PHILOSOPHY of Social Credit has been systematically and extensively promoted throughout many parts of the British Commonwealth and the United States for nearly forty years, it was in Alberta that there first emerged a Social Credit movement sufficiently strong to win and maintain political power. During the past twenty-four years Social Crediters have not only retained control of the government of Alberta but have also achieved political power in British Columbia. If they have been much less successful east of Alberta, they have at least felt sufficiently strong on occasion to contest provincial elections in Saskatchewan, Manitoba, Ontario, Quebec, and New Brunswick. They have also contested the last seven federal elections. Between 1935 and 1958 the Social Credit party was continuously represented in the House of Commons by members who, at various times, were elected from constituencies in four provinces.

The development of the Social Credit party in Canada now extends over a quarter of a century in time and from the Pacific to the Atlantic oceans in space. This book is restricted to an analysis of the rise of the Social Credit movement in Alberta during the formative years between 1932 and 1935. After its first electoral victory the movement became institutionalized as a political party. The study of the development of the Social Credit party in Alberta as well as in Canada at large after 1935 requires a different conceptual framework than is appropriate to the analysis of a social movement. By limiting the investigation in time and space, this study becomes manageable, thereby making it possible to present a more detailed analysis and a more comprehensive interpretation of the psychology of a social movement than has hitherto been available.

The importance of the study of collective behaviour is immediately apparent to most psychologists, psychiatrists, and social scientists. It should be equally apparent to moral and political philosophers. The rise of the Social Credit movement in Alberta illustrates, in eminent degree, the social context in which democracy functions under stress. The functioning of the democratic process in Alberta during the rise

of the Social Credit movement provides a much needed corrective to
the abstract concepts of the classical philosophers of democracy from
John Locke to John Dewey. No interpretation of democracy which
ignores the phenomena of collective behaviour can hope to stand. In its
wider implications this book may therefore be envisaged as a contribution to the democratic philosophy of society and the state.

In the twentieth century several large-scale movements based on
philosophies such as socialism, communism, fascism, or Naziism have
sought to transform society through the attainment of political power.
Owing to its more limited objectives, the Social Credit movement provides an unusual opportunity for a study of the formative role of ideas
in the process of social development. Further, the multivalent interpretation of the movement which has been possible in this book casts a
revealing light upon the highly simplified and schematic models that contemporary philosophers of science have devised to explain the nature
of social causation. Whatever may be their value as intellectual games,
a detailed and careful analysis of the Social Credit movement in Alberta
indicates that such abstract models have little reference to the actualities
of social change. A realistic understanding of social causation cannot
be attained without such extensive empirical analyses of social
movements.

This book is based mainly upon interviews with people in Alberta,
but private papers, private collections of newspaper and other files,
mimeographed materials, leaflets, pamphlets, government brochures,
newspapers, articles, and books have also been used. In nearly every
instance, people have not wished their names identified with interviews,
private papers, or private collections. Every effort has therefore been
made to protect the identity of informants and owners of private papers
and files.

References to printed materials available in the Legislative Library
in Edmonton have been documented either in the text or in the footnotes.
Documentation of interviews in research of this type could have involved thousands of references in footnotes to interviews, most of
which would have had to remain anonymous. After careful consideration,
it was decided to keep footnotes to a minimum by restricting them to
references to printed materials (except for references to certain type-
written and mimeographed reports and minutes in the Head Office of
the United Farmers of Alberta Co-operative in Calgary, which have
been made fully available for this investigation through the kindness
of the president of the organization).

Material based on interviews has been quoted directly, rather than
paraphrased, when it is especially controversial (as in chapter II), or
especially illuminating (as in chapters VIII, IX, X).

I wish to express my thanks to the people of Alberta, especially to
many members and leaders of both the U.F.A. and the Social Credit
movements and governments, who have been generous with their time
and records, as well as to Mrs. Frank Gostick, formerly Provincial
Librarian of Alberta, for her helpfulness on many occasions.

It is a pleasure also to record my indebtedness to Professor S. D. Clark,
the editor of the series, for many valuable suggestions; to the anonymous
committee of readers for sound and constructive criticisms; to Dean
John Macdonald and Professors Leonard W. Doob, Morris Ginsberg,
J. D. Ketchum, Otto Klineberg, and Malcolm G. Taylor for stimulating
discussions during the preparation of the book; to Miss E. Pearl Shepherd
for her skill and patience in typing the manuscript; to Miss Francess
Halpenny and Miss Barbara Ham of the University of Toronto Press
for editorial advice; to the Social Science Research Council of Canada
and the Publications Fund of the University of Toronto Press for
financing the expenses of research and publication; and to my wife, who
realized that a single arch of intention spanned the hours and miles.

The influence of Dr. Hadley Cantril on my analysis of the Social
Credit movement in Alberta is so important as to merit special mention.
Without attributing responsibility to him for the interpretations contained
in this book, I should like him to think of it as a continuation of the
discussions we have had during and since our years together as
colleagues at Princeton.

J. A. I.

May, 1959

Contents

THE SOCIAL CREDIT MOVEMENT
IN ALBERTA

CHAPTER ONE

The Social Credit Movement
and its Setting

ON THE NIGHT of August 22, 1935, as Canadians listened to their radios, they heard, with amazement and incredulity, that the first Social Credit government in the world had been elected that day in the province of Alberta. Throughout Alberta, of course, everybody was waiting by the radio, whether in family groups, house parties, or political gatherings at party headquarters. Before the tabulation of votes was completed, telephone calls from New York and London, headlines in newspapers, spot news in broadcasts, had confirmed the slogan of Social Crediters, "The Eyes of the World are on Alberta." The morning after the election a number of people lined up at the city hall in Calgary to collect the first instalment of the Social Credit dividend of $25 monthly, which, they confidently believed, would be immediately forthcoming from their new government.

When William Aberhart, who had led the Social Crediters to their spectacular victory, became premier of Alberta on September 3 his supporters numbered 89 per cent of the members of the new Legislative Assembly. The United Farmers of Alberta (or U.F.A., to give the movement its more usual name), who had governed the province since 1921, had been permanently eliminated as a political force. The Liberal party, which had held office from the formation of the province in 1905 until 1921, had been so crushed that it remained disorganized for over a dozen years. The Conservative party, which had never held office in the province, was so shattered that its prospects remained negligible for another twenty-five years.

The suddenness (as it seemed) of the new movement's rise to power and the magnitude of its victory aroused world-wide comment. Most of the commentators in 1935 were more or less aware that the doctrines of Social Credit had been systematically and extensively promoted in various parts of the British Commonwealth and the United States for nearly twenty years. Why, they asked, had a movement that had failed so hopelessly elsewhere achieved political domination so rapidly in Alberta? How, they continued, could a democratic electorate be so misled as to give such overwhelming support to a movement whose politically inexperienced and economically illiterate leaders had promised dividends of $25 monthly to each person over the age of twenty-one? The spirit of much of the comment on the Social Credit victory may be summed up in the attitude expressed by the editor of the *St. Catharines* (Ontario) *Standard* on the day following the election: "The whole thing is a chimera, a nightmare that passeth all understanding."

In this book it is proposed to offer a systematic and comprehensive analysis of the rise of the Social Credit movement in Alberta as a phenomenon of mass psychology. We shall investigate, in multiple perspectives, how the movement originated, how it spread, how it rooted itself, and how it flourished in the province from its inception in the autumn of 1932 to its achievement of political power in the summer of 1935.

Social movements tend to appear during periods of widespread social unrest, when profound dissatisfaction with the existing social order arises. No conditions could have been more favourable for the development of such unrest than those which existed in Alberta in the autumn of 1932. The farmers of the province had experienced every possible agricultural ordeal; they had been made the playthings of the high tariff manipulators; they had built up markets in the United States only to have them ruthlessly cut off; they had suffered drought and every agricultural pestilence from root-rot to grasshoppers; they had seen prices drop to such incredibly low levels that sometimes it did not pay to haul their produce to market. Under such circumstances, they found it well-nigh impossible to keep up the payments on their heavily mortgaged farms. The discouraged farmers, looking for some tangible cause for all their miseries, focused their resentment and hate upon the banks and loan companies. In the cities, towns, and villages the masses of the people were no better off. Unemployment was general: thousands were living on relief; still other thousands came close to lacking adequate food, clothing, and shelter. Thousands of people were socially perplexed, frustrated, and angry. They were caught in a steel web from which there seemed no escape. Their social environment, their feeling for the process of life, their hope for the future, all became meaningless. Amid such desperate social and economic conditions, William Aberhart appeared as the prophet of a new social order based on the philosophy of Social Credit.

In its most developed and complex form, the philosophy of Social Credit includes a monetary theory which both "explains" the inner workings of the capitalistic financial system and offers a remedy for its unsatisfactory functioning in periods of depression and inflation, a political theory which redefines the role of the individual in the democratic state, and an interpretation of history in terms of a long-existing Judaic plot or conspiracy to secure control of and dominate the world. Underlying these three basic doctrines of Social Credit is a moral-religious theory of the fundamental rights of man, which has been variously expressed in terms of elusive conceptions such as Cultural Heritage, Political Liberty with Economic Security, and the Struggle of the Powers of Light against the Powers of Darkness in the World. At no time has Social Credit advocated the overthrow of the capitalistic system or of private enterprise.[1]

Social Credit owes its origin to a Scottish engineer, Major Clifford Hugh Douglas (1878–1952), who was impressed by the fact that many developments *physically* possible from the engineer's point of view are *financially* impossible. As assistant director of the Royal Aircraft Works in England during the First World War, he made comprehensive studies of cost accounting which led him to the conclusion that, in over 100 industrial establishments, the weekly sum-total of wages and salaries was continuously less than the weekly collective price of the goods produced. It was upon this conclusion that he formulated his now famous "A plus B Theorem." In this theorem, A equals the flow of purchasing power to the masses (as represented by wages, salaries, and dividends), and B equals bank charges, overhead costs, taxes, and the cost of raw materials. If A plus B represents the cost of production under the financial system, the rate of flow of purchasing power to the masses will be less than the rate of flow of prices in the same period of time. There will thus be a discrepancy, which Douglas maintains must be permanent, between A (the purchasing power of consumers) and A plus B (the total cost of production). The "A plus B Theorem" became the key conception of Douglas's economic theories, and provided him and his followers with one of their principal slogans, "Poverty in the Midst of Plenty," a paradox which clearly has very great propaganda value in a period of widespread social unrest fostered by an economic depression.

On its negative or critical side Social Credit maintains that a permanent deficiency of purchasing power is inherent in the capitalistic financial system in the Machine Age; on its positive or constructive

---

[1]The literature of Social Credit is voluminous. The following three books were widely read in Alberta: C. H. Douglas, *Social Credit* (London: Eyre & Spottiswoode, 1924, 1933); Maurice Colbourne, *Unemployment or War* (New York: Coward-McCann, 1928); C. Marshall Hattersley, *This Age of Plenty* (London: Pitman, 1926). For a brilliant exposition and critical analysis of the doctrines of Social Credit see C. B. Macpherson, *Democracy in Alberta* (Toronto: University of Toronto Press, 1953), chapters IV, V, VII.

side it seeks to solve the problem of distributing the abundance of goods produced, as well as to increase production. It is maintained that other proposals for social reconstruction suffer from three fallacies: that there is a limit to production; that work is the only just prior condition of industrial income; and that there is magic in state ownership. Further, other reformers have not realized the significance of the distinction between financial credit, which is based upon gold, and real credit, which is based upon such factors as raw materials, power, and labour. Under the existing system, financial credit has fallen into the control of bankers who, through its manipulation, exploit the community for purposes of private profit. A functional financial system should be concerned with the issue of credit to the consumer up to the limit of the productive capacity of the producer, so that the consumer's real demands may be satisfied, and the productive capacity of the industrial system may be utilized and developed to the fullest extent.

The present political system of democracy, according to the Social Credit theory, has led to the development of economic slaves: money has become the master rather than the servant of man. The people, who should be the sovereign authority, have lost their control over the monetary system; their sovereign authority has been usurped by bankers who have set up a financial dictatorship, and who use their control of credit to render ineffectual the voting power of the people. The economic system no longer fulfils a moral purpose: instead of economic security and freedom from want, the individual is faced with "poverty in the midst of plenty," misery, and unhappiness.

Social Credit argues that, if the economic system is to function successfully, the state must make at least three fundamental changes: it must recover its control over the monetary system; it must issue social credit in the form of a *national dividend* (based upon a survey of the real wealth of the nation) to every person; and, to prevent the possibility of inflation, it must establish a *just price* for all goods. The evils in the existing economic system can be remedied by supplying the people with credit based upon the potential goods and services of society. This is the people's right, their *cultural heritage*. Only in this way will the individual be freed from wage slavery, be able to choose the work he likes best, be in a position to claim those goods which are rightfully his so that he can enjoy more leisure time. There was, from the beginning, a moral foundation for the changes in the monetary system proposed by Social Credit—the financial system must be reformed to enable the individual to achieve the fullest measure of self-realization.

As a political theory, Social Credit is presented as a "Way of Life": human nature is essentially good, and the individual, as the most important fact of society, is an end in himself, not a means to an end. Personal freedom is the most precious possession of life, and every individual should therefore have political freedom, at the same time that he enjoys economic security. The state exists solely to promote the individual's welfare, freedom, and security. The Social Credit Way of Life is compatible with both Christianity and democracy, but its philosophers are extremely critical of the existing form of political democracy as well as being opposed to socialism and communism. It is asserted that there exists today only constitutional democracy, not functioning democracy. Parliament should be under the direct and continuous control of the electors; in actual practice, the people's representatives are controlled by the party machine. In place of the present system of limited state dictatorship, it is proposed to restore sovereign authority to the people: they must be organized in a "Union of Electors" through which the individual can directly express his aims and desires to his representatives in Parliament.

It is as an interpretation of history that the theories of Social Credit are curiously familiar and at the same time most elusive. As the constant criticism of "Finance" wore somewhat threadbare, there gradually evolved the colourful doctrine that national and international events can only be understood in terms of the machinations of a select group of bankers (most of whom bear Jewish names) who are indissolubly linked with the Judaic conspiracy, working through the Masonic Order, as well as through both international capitalism and international communism. The wars, depressions, and revolutions of our time can only be understood if it is realized that they are one and all the result of the activities of world conspirators or world plotters who will stop at nothing in their efforts to destroy both democracy and the system of free enterprise, and who are especially malicious in their attempts to ruin the British Empire.

The emphasis that has been given in Alberta to each of the three aspects of the philosophy of Social Credit has varied with the time, the occasion, and the person. But there can be no doubt that, during the years of the rise of the Social Credit movement, this philosophy was interpreted essentially as a theory of monetary reform, which had its moral foundation in the conception of the cultural heritage. In Alberta, however, the philosophy was presented within a context of Christian fundamentalism and Bible prophecy that remained quite foreign, and indeed incomprehensible, to the mind of Douglas.

CHAPTER TWO

The Prophet

WHILE THE WRITINGS of Douglas must be considered the ultimate source of the Social Credit movement, it is impossible to think of that movement in Alberta without thinking of William Aberhart, who established it, developed it, and brought it to political power. Until his fifty-fourth year, he devoted himself almost entirely to education and religion. During a quarter of a century in Calgary as teacher and preacher he acquired great prestige in certain quarters; he perfected highly efficient techniques of exposition and organization; and he built up a personal following of hundreds of thousands of people through his radio broadcasts on Bible prophecy and pre-millennial fundamentalism. These factors were influential in determining the nature and course of the Social Credit movement; and an interpretation of Aberhart's significance as social and political leader involves, therefore, an analysis of his career as educator and radio evangelist. In discussing his earlier activities, however, it is important to remember that we are here concerned primarily with the psychology of a social movement rather than with the psychology of a personality; and we shall emphasize, accordingly, those aspects of the life and thought of this remarkable man which will enable us, as far as possible, to visualize him as he would appear to various groups of people in Alberta in the autumn of 1932 when he launched the Social Credit movement.

William Aberhart was born near Egmondville (a village which was attached to Seaforth, although not incorporated into it), Huron County, Ontario, on December 30, 1878, the son of William Aberhart, of German origin, and Louisa Pepper, an Englishwoman. The elder Aberhart had been brought to Canada at the age of seven by his parents who, according to tradition, had emigrated in the 1840's to escape, like so many others, from the oppressive military service regulations of Prussia. The younger William Aberhart grew up on his father's small dairy farm with three brothers and one sister. His father and mother were phlegmatic and thrifty; they were remembered by the townsfolk of Seaforth as honest, dependable people and as exacting bargainers in business dealings. They took little interest in the life of the community apart from their membership in the Presbyterian Church, the only religious institution in Egmondville at that time. Although the discipline in his unpretentious home was strict, the work hard, and the hours long, in later years Aberhart frequently spoke with gratitude of his parents' influence. Proud of being a farmer's son, he would refer in his radio addresses to the sayings of his father and the experiences of his boyhood days. In his last lecture at the Calgary Prophetic Bible Institute, delivered on April 4, 1943, seven weeks before his death, he repeated a favourite illustration which had obviously made an indelible impression on his life: "My father used to tell us boys on the farm, in our younger days, that we could never plow a straight furrow if we did not focus our attention on a particular post or tree or other landmark away at the end of the field. He warned us again and again not to allow a big stick or clump of brush or a tree to distract us as we passed along."[1] In his public addresses, Aberhart acknowledged also his obligation to his mother, to whose training may be attributed his capacity for hard and prolonged work.

He received his elementary education at the Egmondville Public School during the period when Richard Hicks, a stern disciplinarian, was principal. From 1892 to 1896, he attended the Collegiate Institute in Seaforth, a bright, progressive town with a population of some three thousand. At that time this school had a staff of six to eight teachers under the principalship of Charles Clarkson, who enjoyed a considerable local reputation as an organizer. While at high school Aberhart was interested in all subjects, but mathematics was his favourite, and the teacher of that subject, William Prendergast, B.A., made an unforgettable impression upon him. He used to tell him, "You will make a better job of sawing wood if you know Euclid than if you don't." Prendergast used the method of making his pupils "work out" mathematical problems, and he would sometimes, when they were baffled, even refuse to show them how to achieve the solution, a teasing technique which his clever and impressionable pupil was later to apply so successfully to questioners and critics in Alberta during the stormy period of the rise of the Social Credit movement. Giving of his best to each subject in the curriculum, Aberhart never had a failure in any of the rigorous departmental examinations which characterized the Ontario educational system in the late nineteenth century. In class he always had unbounded confidence, and was invariably the first to answer questions. His teachers noticed that, in addition to his studious habits, he combined exceptional powers of concentration with amazing powers of retention.

[1] *A Tribute to William Aberhart* (memorial brochure published by the Calgary Prophetic Bible Institute, 1943), p. 3.

For a boy who had to walk several miles to and from school each day, as well as deliver milk to Seaforth homes from his father's dairy farm, Aberhart's participation in extracurricular activities was phenomenal. Although never a good mixer, his outstanding characteristic was an ability to organize his fellow students for various projects, and in this he was greatly encouraged by Principal Clarkson. Aberhart was very fond of sports such as skating, tennis, and badminton, and he achieved fame in Huron and the adjoining counties as a formidable football player. In those days, Seaforth had one of the best teams in Western Ontario, and Aberhart was considered its best player: it is said that for years members of other teams were terrified at the prospect of encountering the bulky and indomitable centre half from Egmondville on the field. But it was also noticed that although he excelled as an individual player by sheer physical prowess, Aberhart was not a good team player: even in his youth a desire to dominate or to be constantly in the spotlight caused him to experience certain psychological difficulties in that co-operation with others which membership in a football team demands. Apart from sports and organizing his fellow students, his main relaxation was music, to which, although he had received no formal training in it, he remained devoted throughout his life. He played, in an indifferent manner, the piano, the guitar, and the violin, and he passionately loved to sing; his fondness for music was inherited by his two children, and in later life he derived great pleasure from the accomplishments of his daughter Ola, who became well known in Alberta and British Columbia as a vocalist.

On graduating from the Seaforth Collegiate Institute, Aberhart spent a year at the Chatham Business College, from which he received a diploma in 1897, and a year at the Hamilton Normal School from which he received a teaching certificate in May, 1898. During the next few years he was awarded diplomas from the Province of Ontario Art School in geometry, advanced drawing, etc. (1899) and in advanced geometry (1904); a diploma as High School Cadet Instructor from the Toronto School of Infantry (1901); and a Commercial Specialist's certificate with honours from the Ontario Department of Education (1905). He was proudest, however, of the degree of Bachelor of Arts which he obtained in 1910 from Queen's University by extramural study during a period when he was married, with two children, and when, in addition to his teaching duties, he was actively engaged in church, Sunday school, and Y.M.C.A. work in Brantford. That a love for study persisted throughout his life is shown by his purchase, about 1941, of a linguaphone, with complete courses of lessons in French, German, and

Spanish: at the time of his death he had already made considerable progress in learning to speak French and Spanish.

From 1899 to 1901, Aberhart taught successfully in a rural school, S.S. No. 7, Morris, near Wingham. In a letter written in June, 1901, D. Robb of Brussels, then Inspector of Public Schools for East Huron, recommended to the Ontario Department of Education that he be granted a first class professional certificate, and commended him highly for the discipline, order, management, and progress of his school.[2] Owing to the possession of a business college diploma, Aberhart was then enabled to become established quickly in Brantford, where he remained for the next nine years. From 1901 to 1902 he had charge of the public school Leaving and Commercial Diploma class of the city, a position in which his capacities as a disciplinarian and organizer were speedily noted by his superiors. In recommending Aberhart for advancement in June, 1902, William Wilkinson, Principal of the Central Public School, commented also on his unusual gifts as a teacher.[3] When Wilkinson died, Aberhart succeeded him as principal, continuing to teach, during the next few years, book-keeping and other commercial subjects. As principal of Central School, he was a strict disciplinarian but extremely just in his judgments. He was well liked by the members of the staff and the pupils in spite of his severe treatment of offenders.

Early in 1910, certain friends who had gone to Alberta wrote to Aberhart and asked if he would join them in Calgary if a suitable teaching position were offered him. On receiving a specific offer, and lured by the prospect of greater opportunities in the "last best West," Aberhart went to Calgary in the spring of 1910 at the age of thirty-one, at the height of the pre-war boom days, and at the very time when the United Farmers of Alberta, whom he was destined to overthrow politically a quarter of a century later, were beginning to build up a strong organization.

During his youth, Aberhart's religious interests were apparently stimulated much more by itinerant evangelists than by his parents or by participation in the life of the Egmondville Presbyterian Church. When nearly sixty years of age, with the prestige of a successful high school teacher and principal of long standing, and with hundreds of thousands of religious followers who had contributed hundreds of thousands of dollars to his religious enterprises, he revealed one night to a small study group in a private house in Calgary the secret of his religious motivation. While giving an earnest address on Social Credit, he persistently pounded

[2]Mrs. William Aberhart, papers.
[3]Ibid.

the flimsy table the hostess of the group had placed before him, and as if by way of an aside said:

Excuse my pounding this table. It reminds me of the fact that when I was a boy we had protracted revival meetings in our district. I sat in those meetings night after night and marvelled at the power of the preacher over the people. The preacher was very emphatic and he pounded the pulpit heavily. I was so impressed that I went out into a woodlot, day after day, and practised speaking and pounding a pine stump with my clenched fists. I had discovered the power of words and gestures over people, and I have never forgotten the power of that preacher to dominate those people.

The second important factor in Aberhart's religious development was his membership, about 1906, in a men's Bible class conducted by Dr. William Nichol, in Zion Presbyterian (now United) Church, Brantford. The teacher of this class, who was a well-known physician, has been variously described, in the recollections of those who knew him, as "a grand old man," "a fine Christian gentleman," "a pre-millennialist," "popular, but opinionated," "an excellent Bible scholar." Dr. Nichol's class was not strongly organized, and there was none of that insistence on individual responsibility for various activities which Aberhart was later to make so prominent in the Calgary Bible Conference. Greatly stimulated by Dr. Nichol's interpretation of Bible prophecy, which was based upon the pre-millennial doctrines of the Reverend Dr. S. J. Schofield, Aberhart soon outstripped his teacher in zeal for study and research, and organized a Bible class in the Central Public School, on a voluntary basis, for the members of his staff. The principal study of this class, which met after four o'clock, was the Book of Revelation, and one of its members recalls that she read many manuscripts which Aberhart prepared by way of commentary on this perplexing book, with a view to suggesting corrections and checking grammatical constructions. During the pastorate of the Reverend Dr. W. G. Martin, who succeeded the Reverend Dr. R. B. Cochrane, Aberhart had his own Bible class in Zion Church. His method differed from that of Dr. Nichol in certain respects, particularly in his introduction of charts, but the content of his teaching remained essentially that of Schofield. It now became evident to Aberhart's associates that he hoped to qualify as a minister in the Presbyterian Church, but, as one of his contemporaries in Brantford has remarked, "He got in wrong with the ministers and officials of the Church because of his high-handed methods and his tendency to condemn all who were not of his opinion. Just prior to his departure for the West, there was increasing evidence of this intolerance." Another and less critical account, widely circulated by his disciples in Alberta, explains that his failure to enter the ministry was due to the reluctance of the Presbyterian Church to finance the necessary training period in Knox College of a married man with two children.

In spite of the difficulties which Aberhart was beginning to encounter owing to his dominating personality, his departure for the West was considered a distinct loss to the educational and religious life of Brantford, and the mayor of the city, William B. Wood, wrote to him appreciatively in March, 1910:

I am more sorry than I can express that you have decided to leave Brantford. Everybody admits that you have done first class work as Principal of our Central School and you have surrounded yourself with a large circle of friends who esteem you very highly for your moral worth and Christian character. I know that you have been the instrument through which God has spoken to many a heart and no greater honor than that can come to any man in this world. No one can blame you for seizing the wider opportunities of our growing West. I sincerely hope that your fondest hopes may be fully realized and that Mrs. Aberhart, yourself, and the children may enjoy life in your new home.

All the same, I must again express my great regret that you should leave Brantford and I think it was a great mistake to allow you to go.[4]

This letter would tend to cast serious doubts on the story, assiduously circulated in later years by political opponents, that Aberhart was forced to resign as principal of Central School after he had lost his temper and disciplined an offending pupil much too brutally. A letter of recommendation from E. E. C. Kilmer, B.A., Inspector of Schools, also refers to his excellent character and to the confidence and respect he enjoyed in Brantford.[5]

Although the pattern of Aberhart's future development both as educator and as religious leader had been very largely determined in Ontario, no one could have foreseen what tremendous energies, hitherto latent in the man, were to be released by the challenge of the greater opportunities of the rapidly growing province of Alberta. From his arrival in Calgary at Easter, 1910, until the summer holidays, he taught at the Victoria Public School, and the following autumn he became principal of the Alexandra (later the Mount Royal) School at a salary of $1,400 per annum. In 1912 he was promoted to the principalship of the King Edward School, where his salary rose from $1,850 to $2,100 during the next three years. The turning-point in his career occurred in 1915 when, by a close vote and with some misgivings, the Calgary School Board appointed him principal of the newly organized Crescent Heights

4Ibid.
5Ibid.

High School at an initial salary of $2,250, which was gradually increased to $4,200 by 1935.

The development of Crescent Heights School in the North Hill district of Calgary was a great venture during the darkest years of the First World War; and the difficulties that Aberhart must have encountered are apparent when one realizes that instruction had to be carried on in the cramped quarters of the old Balmoral School for thirteen years. Situated in a prosperous middle-class district and surrounded by handsome, comfortable residences with well-kept lawns and boulevards, the present imposing building was finally completed in 1928 at a cost of $275,000. The school, which is of Collegiate Gothic design, contains twenty-one class-rooms (each of which will seat forty students), four science laboratories, two gymnasiums, dressing and shower rooms, three special rooms for office staff and teachers, steel lockers in the corridors, and a library study room large enough for eighty students. The gymnasiums, one for boys and one for girls, are equipped with side galleries and are so arranged that they can be converted into an auditorium that will seat between seven and eight hundred. On a bright summer day the view from the third-floor windows of the school is beautiful and expansive in all directions. Immediately below the cliffs of the North Hill one may see the busy city of Calgary, rich in the legends of the old West, nestling with an European compactness at the confluence of the swiftly flowing Bow and Elbow rivers. The eye travels over the heights of Mount Royal and across the foothills of the Rockies to the jagged snow-capped peaks of the Banff gap, eighty miles away. Rolling ranch-lands, treeless and often parched, stretch southwards to the American border and eastwards to the plains of Saskatchewan. Northwards runs the branch line of the Canadian Pacific Railway to Edmonton, linking the numerous towns and villages which serve the rich farm lands of central Alberta. It is such incomparable vistas that give to Western Canada its challenge and its charm.

Aberhart will always be a legendary figure at the Crescent Heights High School, over which he presided as principal for twenty years until he assumed, in 1935, the premiership of Alberta: his teaching experience in Ontario and his first five years in Calgary may be regarded as preparatory for this last and greatest phase of his career as an educator. What manner of man was Aberhart as teacher and principal at Crescent Heights? The bitter political controversies and the intense hatreds which developed during the early years of the Social Credit movement have made it difficult, if not impossible, to answer this simple question directly and unequivocally: the social investigator must, in assessing Aberhart's reputation as an educator, sift fact from legend and penetrate, if he can, beneath both the glowing approval and the hostile criticism.

The altogether favourable report of what was really happening at Crescent Heights during Aberhart's principalship has nowhere been stated more clearly than by one of his teachers who was also a religious disciple, and long a member of the congregation of the Calgary Prophetic Bible Institute:

To the thousands of graduates of Crescent Heights High School in Calgary, his name will always bring memories of a genial principal, who, while he was a hard worker himself, and expected everybody else to be a hard worker, was, nevertheless, a very human sort of person, with a sense of humor which could be relied upon to enliven every interview. He was held in the very highest esteem by his fellow teachers, who early recognized him as a leader among them. Students, too, respected and admired their principal. He was always eminently fair in his dealing with young people, and former pupils recall that he was never too busy to listen patiently to both sides of a story. It is given to few principals to enjoy the respect, loyalty and genuine affection of staff and student body, which was accorded Mr. Aberhart in the Crescent Heights High School.

He won, too, the highest approbation of the parents of his students. His genius for organization made the Crescent Heights Parent-Teachers' Association the largest and most active association of its kind in the Province. Much of the success of the later Home and School Association in Alberta can be traced to the influence of that group.

In short, Mr. Aberhart was one of the most talented and distinguished teachers that Canada has ever produced. This teaching ability of his was destined to prove a highly contributory factor in the achievements of his later life.[6]

Today only a small percentage of Aberhart's former students and colleagues would accept uncritically such a laudatory estimate of his capacity as a teacher, although there would be more general agreement among them regarding his outstanding ability as an organizer.

The more critical attitude to Aberhart as a teacher has been stated by a well-informed and thoughtful member of his staff who knew him intimately at Crescent Heights School:

Aberhart was a good dog-trainer, or perhaps we should say a good drillmaster. He wanted his students to learn their tricks mechanically, and never

[6]*A Tribute to William Aberhart*, p. 5. Although no author's name is given in this brochure, Miss Mabel C. Giles, B.A. (McMaster), was responsible for writing most of it, but it was afterwards revised by certain officials of the Bible Institute.

mind the *reason* for them. His rule-of-thumb approach which led him to use charts in teaching arithmetic, got them through the examinations, but when it was all over they hadn't the faintest idea *why* they had answered the questions that way. He insisted on mechanical memory, without thought or reasoning behind it. "Never mind why," he would say to his students. Any of them who learned to think for themselves, like ———, and ———, say that he was a drillmaster, not a teacher at all. Others, who have never learned to think, will tell you that he was fine teacher. If education consists merely in having facts and procedures drilled into you, the latter group is right.

That Aberhart's approach to the educational process was persistently mechanical finds confirmation in the attitude of another colleague who worked with him for many years:

With Aberhart, everything had to be cut and dried, like the charts he developed for teaching arithmetic. The student was never given a chance to develop his own ideas in his own way. Everything was tabulated and pigeon-holed, so Aberhart was considered efficient. He was a great disciplinarian; for example, when he was here there was no noise in the halls. But he didn't give his students a chance to express their opinions if they differed from him. In his educational ideas he was a reactionary of the first water, and he simply wouldn't fit into a modern progressive scheme of education.

Some students liked him, and others detested him. He frightened students half to death in his office. A great number of them respected him, but most of them feared him. I could never regard him as a real educator, for he stultified the growth of students. Clever students always felt cramped by his methods.

The attitudes of the more intelligent of Aberhart's students are very similar to those of his colleagues. The comment of a brilliant lawyer is typical:

Aberhart was an excellent teacher if the result you want is rote memory displayed in answering examination questions. A large percentage of his students passed. He taught me writing, grammar, and arithmetic. He was an excellent penman himself and made a pretty fair job of teaching writing; in his teaching of grammar we were always amazed that a man who knew all the rules would himself make so many grammatical errors in speaking. He wanted to be known mainly as a teacher of arithmetic, and his charts of this subject were his especial pride.

He taught arithmetic in a purely mechanical fashion, and he never got any of us to the point where we were imbued with a real love of knowledge. But we passed the examinations and our parents were naturally pleased with the results. He was a born organizer, and he applied his great ability in this area to the organization of the rules of arithmetic. We were all in awe of the old man, and so we always did *his* home-work. Night after night I have copied things down and memorized them, so that he wouldn't bellow at me the next day.

Even those among his students who are favourably disposed to Aberhart suggest that his methods did not wholly appeal to them, as is indicated by the attitude of a prominent business man:

I was under Aberhart for the four years from 1919 to 1923. He taught us a sort of commercial arithmetic, and everything was always very explicit, and was illustrated by the use of charts. He would put a type solution of a question on the black-board and say, "All questions of this type are solved this way." He appealed to me perhaps more than to many others in the class because I could follow his rules, and this made arithmetic easy. But he didn't appeal to my pal who was more independent than I and who wanted to express himself in his own way. I would say that the main characteristic of Aberhart's teaching, as of his whole life, was simply this: if you were willing to do what he said and follow the rules he set up, you would get along splendidly with him.

I was in his office within six weeks of my entering his school. I had let off a pistol cap in the classroom. He roared at me and said I was trying to burn down the school. Although he threatened to expel me, I was finally let off with a terrible warning. Before I left his office, he put my name down in a black book. I decided then and there that I'd better get on with him or I'd be kicked out of the school. After this storm blew over, I found him very approachable. My later relationships with him were quite pleasant, and as my parents attended his religious services, I came to have a great respect for him.

The attitudes of his colleagues and students alike indicate that Aberhart had developed no original methods of teaching: he had merely transplanted to the West the nineteenth-century techniques of instruction which Egerton Ryerson had introduced, from Prussia, into the Ontario school system. It is noteworthy that charts, which played so prominent a part in Aberhart's expositions of both pre-millennial and Social Credit doctrines, had already been highly developed as a pedagogical device for inculcating the principles of arithmetic.

Aberhart's greatness as a teacher has been proclaimed tirelessly by his religious and political followers, but long before they set to work on his behalf he himself had used various devices to create in the public mind a belief both in his school's and in his own superiority. At meetings of the Parent-Teachers' Association, for example, he would impress the mothers by showing slides of all the scholarship winners at Crescent Heights. Perhaps his most successful technique, and one which was certainly responsible for developing favourable attitudes towards him, was the extensive newspaper publicity he secured for scholarship winners at Crescent Heights, until in time the public came to believe that this school easily led every other in Alberta. Actually, a statistical analysis of the record cards of the students of Crescent Heights School would not substantiate either the claim that Aberhart had more scholarship winners than other schools, or the belief, so widely held, that he was a phenomenal teacher and principal. The percentage of successful students at Crescent Heights from 1915 to 1935 was not outstanding. Aberhart publicized those students who were successful in such a way as to build up the impression that they were typical. When one examines the record in terms of the whole group of students who came to the school, there are indications that Aberhart sought, as far as possible, to eliminate everyone who was troublesome, slow, or backward, a procedure which was, of course, in accord with both educational philosophy and industrial practice in his time. It is also clear that he had no awareness of emotional maladjustments among his students, and in dealing with their problems he would not consider extenuating circumstances: to him, a student was simply either intelligent or unintelligent. Visitors always noticed a general air of industry and well-being among the students, but such conditions were surely to be expected in a school situated in a prosperous middle-class district of Calgary.

While most of Aberhart's former students and colleagues are inclined to question his superiority as a teacher, none of them would seem to doubt his eminence as a principal. He was intensely loyal to the members of his staff, and in any difficulties that might arise between them and the higher school authorities or the public, they knew that he could always be depended upon to give a fair statement and defence of their position: to the outside world, no matter what he might say privately to individual teachers, his staff was perfect. Several of them felt that, at times, he was inclined to be something of a bully, but they knew how to deal with him on such occasions. "He would roar at us," one of his teachers has reported, "with his tremendous voice, and the walls of his office would seem to shake. But if you stood up to him, and yelled back, in a moment or two he would sit down in his chair and burst into laughter. The incident was over." In his official relations with teachers he was usually not autocratic; they all felt that they could freely discuss the problems of the school with the principal, and that he was amenable to suggestions. At the same time they realized that he was watching their work closely for, like every other Calgary principal, he had to be concerned with the scholarship average of the school: each teacher was required to furnish in the autumn a statement of the number of students who had written departmental examinations in his subject the previous term, together with percentages of successes and failures. In arranging classes, Aberhart invariably did his best to discover an individual's preferences with a view to assigning him the subjects he wished to teach. He also took care to distribute the teaching load as evenly as possible, including the super-vision of extracurricular activities, such as sports, music, dramatics, Hi-Y, the school paper, etc., for which the staff members were respon-sible. There can be no question that he worked his staff harder, and got more effort from them, than any other principal in Alberta, without the teachers realizing what he was doing. Staff meetings were conducted in a thoroughly formal manner: minutes were kept by a secretary, and debatable issues were decided by majority vote, to the outcome of which the principal always strictly adhered. He never interfered with an individual's teaching methods if the results were satisfactory, but there is evidence that the theory of evolution caused the principal no little mental anguish. On one occasion he is reported to have said to a teacher, "I hope you aren't teaching evolution. I don't approve of that theory." When the teacher replied in a firm tone, "*I'm* teaching biology," Aber-hart made no further comment.[7] In his public addresses, however, he often attacked universities for teaching evolution, and he could always get a laugh by referring to philosophy as "fool-osophy," but such stric-tures were considerably weakened by his constant flaunting of the Queen's extramural B.A. Although he dominated women (who flocked to his religious and political meetings), it was noted that Aberhart was always more lenient in his treatment of female than of male members of the staff, and that he never entered the men's common room except to issue an order. He was not given to mixing with other men, and his fellow principals regarded him as an outsider. The fact that he was not a member of the Alberta Teachers Alliance from about 1923 on aroused much unfavourable comment; as one well-known Alberta principal has drily remarked, "We realized, of course, that the fee of twelve dollars per annum, together with his inability to dominate the organization, would naturally keep Aberhart from joining our association." Most of

[7]Aberhart also mistrusted the nebular hypothesis of the origin of the universe. On April 20, 1931, in reply to a rural teacher who had attended his religious services when she lived in Calgary, and who had asked him how certain statements in the geography text could be reconciled with the Bible, he wrote: "You have mentioned the nebular hypothesis of the world's creation. The latest encyclopaedia Britannica gives a number of reasons why this theory cannot be held as scientific to-day. Were I in your place, I would use that fact to show how progressive and unreliable science is. I would teach the nebular theory carefully to them and then tell them that the latest science refutes this theory. If you wish to point out that this is entirely contrary to the teaching of the Bible you can do so then.

I believe it is wise for the teachers to present these theories and show the children wherein they are wrong, then if they face an examination at which they are requested to state the theory they can do so. I would warn them that it is not necessary, if they are asked to state the theory, to show wherein it is wrong unless they are definitely asked to do so."

his colleagues resented, too, the Puritanism which prohibited them from smoking in the school (except in the boiler room, and even that was sadly secretive) and the students from having organized dances under official auspices, although he was finally forced to yield on this latter point.

While they respected him as a principal, most of Aberhart's staff members were critical of him as a person. On social occasions they were often embarrassed by his ungrammatical and flamboyant speech, boisterous laugh, and uncouth manners. Although the theories of Social Credit carried a wide appeal for rural teachers, it has been estimated that, at the most, only three of Aberhart's colleagues would have supported him politically in 1935. His dramatic expositions of Bible prophecy made most of the Crescent Heights teachers shudder, but, with a tolerance that Aberhart himself found it impossible to exhibit towards those with whom he differed, they felt that he had every right to devote his spare time and energy to religious activities if he so wished. About 1929, when the Calgary School Board had developed a certain antagonism to his Bible Institute work, to which he was obviously devoting time during school hours, all the teachers rallied to the cause of their principal, and the issue was settled on the general understanding that he would thereafter limit his religious activities to out-of-school hours. But these same teachers had no illusions about the quality of Aberhart's intellect.

He seemed [one of them has said] to have a mind like a cabinet, full of little drawers opening and closing. Consequently he never had a philosophy of education, and his outlook was essentially compartmentalized. He had a perfectly marvellous mechanical memory; he could go into a room and teach a class only once, and the next time he could call every student by name. He could read something and remember it almost exactly, but he couldn't *think* about it or *analyse* it. He either accepted ideas completely or threw them out completely—consequently it is not surprising that he became a hopeless fundamentalist and a Social Crediter.

At the same time, they could not but admire the dynamic energy and high colour of the man. "Aberhart was," a brilliant and discerning colleague has reported, "one of the three unforgettable persons whom I have known—the other two are Paul Robeson, and Dr. —, of the University of —. He was a great noise and a great light. In his presence one felt as if one were in a magnesium flare."

Colleagues, students, and the general public were dazzled by Aberhart's capacity as an organizer, and it is undoubtedly his unusual gifts in this direction which have made him a legendary figure in Albertan education circles. Teachers who worked with him still feel that, without exception, he had the finest capacity for organization of any principal in Canada. Within a few days after it opened each September, Crescent Heights would settle down to serious work, although class personnel was rarely stabilized for weeks. Each student would be presented with an individual time-table which had been carefully worked out by the principal in terms both of the previous year's examination results and of what courses the student wanted to take. The bulletin board in the principal's outer office has become legendary and is often cited as a paramount example of the clock-work precision on which Aberhart always insisted: every teacher had to consult it daily at 8:45 A.M., and again at 1:45 P.M., for instructions. As a somewhat hostile colleague has put it, "The majority of times there was nothing on the board for you, but heaven help you if you didn't look. Aberhart might have something planned for the whole school, and your individual negligence would throw the whole organization out of gear. Crescent Heights was run just like a machine, and if one cog slipped, the whole machine stopped." The insistence that a minor omission of duty constituted a major catastrophe naturally led to the criticisms that the school was too mechanically organized, that it was run like a factory, and that human relationships were almost entirely neglected.

Aberhart's infinite interest in detail, which enabled him to organize both students and teachers in an unparalleled manner, extended to the school's extracurricular activities, all the details of which were observed closely from his office. If a play were being produced, for example, he would personally supervise the publicity and the sale of tickets. He attended rugby games, encouraged debating, arranged theatre parties (though the play had to be something "worth-while," like, for example, *She Stoops to Conquer*), and organized the annual school banquets. Crescent Heights commencements, at which the public saw the principal in action, and at which the presentation of departmental certificates took place, became glamorous occasions for publicizing the power and the glory of the school—and of its principal—throughout southern Alberta. Public occasions, such as banquets and commencements, were always given headlines in the newspapers, partly owing to Aberhart's connection with the press through his religious activities, partly owing to his foresight in securing outstanding speakers whose presence turned a routine social or academic function into a major event in the city. It was generally admitted that the Crescent Heights Parent-Teachers' Association, which Aberhart had helped to organize, was the largest and most successful in Calgary, with a regular attendance of over two hundred. But, at the same time, certain parents felt that the principal over-dominated, especially in later years when he refused to allow the group to unite with the Federation of Home and School, mainly, it is said, because he knew that he could not control the latter organization. There can be no question, however, that most parents supported him loyally as school principal (however dubious they may have been of his religious and political beliefs), although it must be conceded that their attitudes towards him were sometimes quite unfavourable. The statements of two prominent citizens of Calgary, both university graduates, are typical of those parents who take a hostile view:

My son was at Crescent Heights, and I consider that Aberhart had a complete disregard of other persons' rights. Students were almost always afraid of him, and I believe his teachers were half-afraid of him too. His work in the P.T.A. was successful because he did have a fine method with women, whom he always held in the hollow of his hand. But his idea of education was simply, "drill things into people mechanically, make them memorize." My fundamental criticism of him is that he wasn't humanitarian enough. He was much too domineering, and he didn't treat people as human beings: they were just pawns in his scheme of things.

On one occasion, Aberhart struck down a boy for refusing to admit he had been impudent to a lady teacher. In considering Aberhart, you must never forget that his was the most violent temper it is possible for a human being to have, and the students at Crescent Heights suffered from that terrible temper for twenty years. Ask his admirers about the ——— ——— story, and see if they can explain away his treatment of that boy!

Although they might sometimes criticize him bitterly, students, teachers, and parents alike were universally impressed by Aberhart's energy and ingenuity in devising schemes for maintaining and improving the morale of Crescent Heights. Each spring, for example, after the Easter examination results were known, he would organize home-work campaigns, in which the students were asked to sign pledges that they would devote a certain extra number of hours a week to study, in addition to their regular schedule. No coercion was used to induce them to sign, but most of the students would support the plan: the mere fact that the principal had originated it was sufficient to ensure its success. One of Aberhart's most memorable morale-building schemes has been described by a teacher, who refers to the story as "The Inception of Social Credit, or the Birth of a Great Idea":

During the school year 1920 to 1921 when I was in Grade X and small motion picture projectors were a rarity, Aberhart organized the children of Crescent Heights into a company, and sold them shares of one dollar in value. With the proceeds he purchased a motion picture projector. He then exhibited pictures after four, at five cents admission fee, in the assembly hall of the school. These pictures were obtained from the Extension Department of the University of Alberta. He would bring in pupils from different Calgary schools, but he never mixed high school with public school. There would be, on an average, two showings weekly.

From time to time, with a great deal of ceremony, the shareholders were presented with the interest on their investment. Eventually, as with all well-managed stock-companies, the shares were redeemed at par, plus a twenty-five cents bonus. At each occasion on which a share was redeemed, there would be a ceremony with appropriate pomp, and the master's hand would pat the brow of the young investor. To succeeding generations of students these original shareholders were a race apart, because they received a special rate for performances. By 1927 the projector had passed into the limbo of forgotten things. It had gone round and round, and the students had got their money back—but Aberhart kept the projector.

During the next year, 1921 to 1922, the Calgary *Albertan*, as part of an advertising campaign to increase its circulation, ran a musical competition in which prizes were offered both to schools and to individuals. Each week the newspaper published the life history and picture of a composer, and these items were collected into scrap-books: at the end of the competition, each contestant had to write an examination based on the life histories. Aberhart was particularly interested in the school prizes, of which the first was a piano, and the second a phonograph with records. So he involved the whole school, including its teachers, in a contest with the community at large: each teacher had to review a life history in class and not a few students were immensely amused when one of their most unmusical masters gave a magnificent ten-minute discourse on Schubert. But such enterprise has its just rewards, and it is said that Crescent Heights won not only all the school prizes but all the individual prizes as well.

Aberhart's experiments in morale-building at Crescent Heights did not, however, always have such a happy outcome. Shortly after the school opened in September, 1922, for example, he announced that during the summer, while visiting in the United States, he had heard of a new plan for student self-government. He proposed that all problems concerning discipline in the class-room, as well as recreational activities like athletics, social functions, and entertainment, should be turned over to the control of an executive elected by the students from among their number. Following a period of campaigning, elections were held about mid-November. The most popular students were naturally elected, but they also turned out to be the most irresponsible. Without any preliminary period of training these students suddenly found themselves possessed of considerable power. As the winter wore on the discipline of the school progressively deteriorated, and the teachers were in an almost constant turmoil. But the school struggled on somehow to the spring of 1923, when the experiment was abolished as suddenly as it had been introduced the previous autumn. Aberhart, who would never admit that he had made a mistake, insisted that the idea would have worked if the right people had been elected. As a result of his disillusionment, however, he became firmly convinced that mere popularity was an insufficient criterion of an individual's ability to perform the duties of an elected office. It is said that this ill-fated experiment in democracy was responsible for his decision to use a technique of selection, as well as election, in the nomination of the Social Credit candidates in 1935.

As far as can be discovered, Aberhart has left no publications bearing on his educational ideas or experience. In response to invitations of successive editors, he wrote introductions to the *Bugle*, a magazine published annually by the students of Crescent Heights. But these prefaces contain no more than the conventional advice regarding the conduct of life that most school principals manage to grind out for such occasions: a careful perusal of their contents casts no further light upon Aberhart's mind and personality.

Even Aberhart's cruellest critics are prepared to admit that as a high school teacher and principal he was one of the most efficient educators and administrators in Western Canada during the period from 1910 to 1935. More detached observers, including most members of both the Calgary School Board and the provincial Department of Education, felt that the province was fortunate to have attracted to its teaching profession such a powerful personality and tireless worker. However they might view his religious activities, they considered that his professional training was so thorough and so ingrained as to save him from any cheap notions concerning education. Finally, both his teaching staff and his students, although they may criticize what they consider to be his weaknesses, usually express a respectful admiration for the authoritarian personality who dominated Crescent Heights for so many years. Some of them add that they were also very fond of him.

For twenty-five of his thirty-three years in Alberta, Aberhart earned his living as a school-teacher and principal, but in the opinion of many who knew him religion was the major passion of his life. No sooner had he arrived in Calgary than he resumed, in the old Grace Presbyterian Church, the work of Bible teacher which he had carried on in Brantford. Although he was ordained as an elder in this church in August, 1911, it was not long before he became involved in a controversy with both the Irish superintendent of its Sunday School, a Mr. Humphries, and its Scottish minister, the Reverend Alexander Esler, M.A., D.D., who had been inducted in October, 1910, a few months after Aberhart arrived in Calgary. The Bible class, which met on Thursday nights, aroused such interest owing to Aberhart's powerful teaching that the minister himself began to attend. But while the ordinary members enjoyed the class immensely Dr. Esler disagreed violently with Aberhart's interpretations of scripture and also, it is said, disapproved of his attempt to dominate policy by insisting on a separation of the finances of the Bible class from those of the church. As the minister's outstanding preaching ability was attracting large audiences, Aberhart, outmatched, transferred his religious activity to Wesley Methodist Church. Here, too, the desire to dominate led to friction, and he soon moved on to Trinity Methodist Church. For the third time a controversy arose and the overbearing Bible teacher, who could lead but never follow, then dissociated himself for a period from institutional churches.

The dates of the next phase are somewhat obscure, but during the years between 1912 and 1915 Aberhart co-operated with "Professor" W. T. Broad in giving Bible instruction at the Eagle Hall which used to stand on First Street West. Broad, then on the faculty of Mount Royal College, a Methodist secondary school, had formerly been in charge of Cliff's College, near Carlisle, England, and had originally come to Calgary in the boom days to promote oil companies. An ardent pre-millennialist, he had been strongly influenced while in England by the teachings of Ethelbert W. Bullinger, in whose writings, which he introduced to Aberhart, may be found one of the sources of the latter's particular interpretation of Bible prophecy, especially the doctrines of the Second Coming and the Rapture.[8] By 1915 serious differences had developed between Broad and Aberhart, and their partnership, which had attracted a great many people to the study of the Bible, broke up. It is said that one of the main sources of irritation was Broad's objection to the holding of classes during the same hours as regular church services. Broad confided, in 1919, something of his experience with Aberhart to a friend who had been absent from Calgary on war duty for five years previously: "Mr. Aberhart's doctrine is absolutely sound, but he simply doesn't know how to work, or co-operate, with others, and he doesn't know the meaning of the word 'love.'" About the time their partnership dissolved, the Eagle Hall was demolished to make way for a new building, and Aberhart then attached himself, in 1915, to

---

[8]Two of Bullinger's books have been reprinted in recent years. See especially, *Number in Scripture* (London: Lamp Press, 1952), and *The Witness of the Stars* (London: Lamp Press, 1954). The Preface to the First Edition of the latter is dated August 31, 1893.

Westbourne Baptist Church, named after London's Westbourne Park Church (made famous by the preaching of one of Britain's great religious reformers, the Reverend Dr. John Clifford), and founded in 1905 with funds contributed by the London church and the First Baptist Church in Calgary. In this small and financially embarrassed east-end conventicle, the members of which were devotees of Christian fundamentalism, Aberhart during the next dozen years stumbled upon the road to glory.

For the first few years after his decision to work with the Baptists, Aberhart created little stir in Calgary: he was busy consolidating his new position as principal of Crescent Heights School; and the energies of the community were being fully devoted to the First World War. But he began to come into public notice almost as soon as the war ended; and by 1920 he was recognized as the leader of the Westbourne Church. Shortly before he came to it, this Church had suffered a serious loss of membership to the much more strongly established First Baptist Church. Taking advantage of this situation he volunteered to do most of the preaching for the congregation, which had become so weak that it was barely able to maintain a regular minister, if it would allow him the use of the building for his additional religious enterprises: it was not long before certain members felt that he was practically using their church as a personal chapel. The deed to the Westbourne property was, at that time, still in possession of the officers of the First Baptist Church, which as we have noted had contributed to its building fund. The then pastor of the latter Church has described the characteristic manner in which Westbourne's champion shortly proceeded to deal with this situation:

Being an astute man, Aberhart wanted to get control of the Westbourne property. So he came to the First Church officials and claimed that Westbourne Church should have the deed to its own property. A committee was appointed to meet with the Westbourne officials, who were assured that, if they would run Westbourne as a Convention Baptist church, and support our missionary enterprises in the West, including Brandon College, it would approve the handing over of the deed. The Westbourne officials agreed to our committee's proposal, and the title-deed was handed over. But within a year or two after securing the deed, they discontinued their support of our missionary enterprises. We protested, and they said they were sorry but they could no longer support our missionary projects as Brandon College was too modernistic. But they kept the property. Technically, Aberhart obtained it for them through legal channels, but morally he stole a church.

However critical the officials of First Baptist Church may have been regarding Aberhart's methods, there can be no doubt that his leadership and powerful Bible teaching revitalized Westbourne. The energy that he now began to devote to religious work is astonishing: on Sundays he would teach a Bible class at 10.00 in the morning, preach at 11.00, give an exposition of Bible prophecy in the afternoon, preach again in the evening, and take the monthly Communion service at the close of the day's work; in addition, he directed week-night prayer meetings, deacons' meetings, and numerous committees. It is not surprising that the Church increased considerably in membership, and that a number of enthusiastic, if somewhat minor, business men were attracted to its support.

In 1918 a group of earnest men of different denominations, who had been strongly influenced by Aberhart's Sunday afternoon addresses, formed under his guidance the Calgary Prophetic Bible Conference. Meetings were held at first on Thursday nights, in the spacious lecture room at the Public Library, for the discussion of fundamental Biblical doctrines and especially those connected with the Second Coming of Christ. Within a few weeks the attendance became so large that the Conference was moved to Westbourne. In 1919 the group secured the Paget Hall and took up the study of the Book of Revelation, to the gratification of a large audience. By the following year the lectures had become so popular that they were transferred to the Grand Theatre, and meetings were held thereafter every Sunday afternoon from October to the end of May. In 1923 the Conference moved to the Palace Theatre, which was more convenient to street-cars and had better facilities for musical programmes, as well as a seating capacity of 2,200. The account of a business man, long a member of the Conference's executive, affords glimpses of the growing enthusiasm for Bible prophecy as well as of the type of inner organization which Aberhart developed during the post-war years:

In the autumn of 1917 I noticed an advertisement of a meeting, to be held in the Public Library, at which William Aberhart would discourse on Bible Prophecy. My father had always been interested in pre-millennial studies, and had sent me a copy of *Our Hope*, a book by Gabilene. So I went to the meeting, and was very much impressed by Mr. Aberhart's exposition of the Bible. I attended quite a number of similar meetings which he held on Thursday nights during that winter, and his lectures fascinated me. Then for a period of a year I was in ———. As soon as I returned to Calgary, in 1920, I inquired if Mr. Aberhart were still giving lectures on the Bible, and discovered that he was now speaking in the Grand Theatre on Sunday afternoons. I attended these meetings and met quite a number of the men behind Mr. Aberhart. I found they were mostly members of Westbourne Baptist Church. From 1920 to 1929 I would say that Westbourne and Mr. Aberhart were one, and that he was put where he was finally by that Church, which was then included in the Western Convention of the Baptist Union.

As a result of Mr. Aberhart's teaching, my brother and my wife and I all joined the Westbourne Church, and before long I was made an officer of both the church and the Calgary Prophetic Bible Conference. The latter organization, which was composed of young fellows, not all of whom were associated with Westbourne Baptist Church, looked after the organization and promotion of the Sunday afternoon lectures. Friction developed between those who were not Baptists and the members of the church. Aberhart insisted that the Bible Conference must be a part of and under the jurisdiction of the Board of Deacons of Westbourne, with the result that a number of independents, who did not believe in total immersion, withdrew. But the Bible Conference from then on had an authentic church sponsorship behind it; and if any trouble developed in the Conference committee, Aberhart could always refer the problem to an inner group, the Board of Deacons, which thus put him in almost absolute control at all times. As the members of its executive were also members of Westbourne Church, and as this executive was elected by these church members, the Calgary Prophetic Bible Conference was definitely a Baptist institution, and not a sectarian group, as many journalists who have written up Aberhart have mistakenly thought. Aberhart always insisted on our being Baptists. He was very keen on respectability. He himself became an immersed Baptist when he joined Westbourne.

By the middle 1920's Aberhart had built up an enthusiastic personal following that numbered several thousands, and the Prophetic Bible Conference was well established as a strong, and somewhat spectacular, religious institution. But he was not, as yet, very influential beyond the city of Calgary although he had already begun to develop certain techniques for reaching a wider public, of which the most important was probably the printing and sale of pamphlets containing his interpretations of prophecy.

As we have seen, he had prepared commentaries on the Book of Revelation during the Brantford years; and as early as 1912 he established a lifelong connection with the Franklin Press of Calgary, then operated by Abe Shnitka, a warm friend and admirer who was himself keenly interested in the Hebraic scriptures. Of Aberhart's earlier writings, the most widely circulated was a series of fourteen lectures bearing the general title *God's Great Prophecies*. Each of these pamphlets contained from one to three lectures, a set of test review questions, and statements for the further guidance of students, of which the following is typical:

Any Reader, who cares to write the answers to the above questions carefully, on one side of the paper only, and mail the same to the Lecturer—

WILLIAM ABERHART, B.A.,
1216 Thirteenth Avenue West,
Calgary, Alberta, Canada,

will receive his personal supervision and correction of the same if One Dollar is enclosed to cover postage, etc. This also advances the privilege of any three other Bible questions that you may desire.

The extensive correspondence (all of which he himself answered in his own handwriting) that resulted from the circulation of his printed lectures convinced him of the necessity of systematically propagating his doctrines beyond Calgary.

By the winter of 1922, the various enterprises of the Church and Conference had become so prosperous, and the burden of his extra activities so excessive, that Aberhart found it necessary to consent to the calling of the Reverend E. G. Hansell (who had been trained at the Bible Institute of Los Angeles) to the pulpit of Westbourne, on the distinct understanding that the new pastor would be under his jurisdiction. The procedure by which the eventual departure of Mr. Hansell was assured has been related by the then secretary of the Conference:

Aberhart said to the executive Committee, "Let us get Hansell in and guarantee him a salary. We'll create a pastor's salary fund. I'll write to him and tell him we have six months' salary ahead." (We had already raised $750.) The pastor came and Aberhart said to him, "Now Mr. Hansell if we have to break into this fund, you'll realize you're not wanted." Aberhart was a liberal contributor to our Church funds, but when friction developed between Mr. Hansell and himself he diverted his offering to general expenses, with the result that the pastor's salary fund went down and down. This was the push and Mr. Hansell had to leave. Aberhart had no regard for human personality. His objectives were primary, and everybody had to fall in line or be disposed of.

To meet the growing demand of his following for religious literature, a bi-monthly magazine, the *Prophetic Voice*, was established in October, 1924. The objective of this publication was stated on the front cover (which was designed by Hansell, and which bore in the upper left-hand corner the expression MARANATHA!) as "the Cause of Evangelical Christianity and the Faith, Once for All Delivered Unto the Saints." Each issue usually contained one of the lectures given by Aberhart during the season, or one for which there had been a special request; and also included were numerous shorter articles and comments by his more literate disciples. "The printed page," an editorial in the second issue announced, "is the most potent and extensive way of broadcasting God's GREAT TRUTHS. If we can express in our Journal ideas that are fundamental to the best in life, we feel sure you will find it to your advantage to secure a share in the work by your moral and financial support." Readers were urged to avail themselves of further opportunities for study by borrowing books from a library which the Bible

Conference was also developing. "We want," said the editor in the issue of December, 1926, "to keep in close touch with all those interested in the prophetic news of the day, in order that, through our joint co-operation, we may keep posted on the striking features of current events. . . . You may want a certain kind of tract to send to some one. Perplexing questions will be answered. What a splendid opportunity to improve yourself will be given in our magazine!" Through his pamphlets and correspondence regarding Bible questions, and the circulation of the new journal, Aberhart now began to build up a loosely organized following in southern Alberta, and he was occasionally invited to give prophetic lectures in villages and towns near Calgary.

A second innovation in 1924 was the organization of what were later called Bible Institute Study Classes. These grew out of Aberhart's restless desire to have some kind of religious activity going on every night in Westbourne. It was not sufficient to devote Monday night to a young people's meeting, Wednesday night to prayer meeting, and Friday night to choir practice. To fit Tuesday and Thursday nights into the schedule, Aberhart developed the idea of an institute for training Bible students systematically, in the manner of theological seminaries. During the session of 1924–5, he offered lecture courses on Biblical Exegesis and Systematic Theology; and one of his few religious disciples among the staff of Crescent Heights gave a course of lectures for Sunday School teachers. These intensive classes were entirely voluntary on the part of both instructors and students.

The following year Aberhart announced the opening of a Bible Institute at Westbourne. He assumed the title of Dean, and the staff was drawn from among the abler students who had taken his lecture courses the previous year. The curriculum bore many resemblances to that of fundamentalist Bible colleges. Instruction was carried on in the manner of regular schoolroom classes. Each student took notes of the lectures; and from time to time Aberhart distributed mimeographed outlines of his courses. Periodic tests were carefully marked and returned with appropriate comments. In the beginning the students were drawn mainly from the Westbourne congregation and supporters of the Bible Conference but within two years the Institute was attracting a steady stream of students not only from various regions of Alberta but also from Saskatchewan and British Columbia. The rapid expansion of the work of the Bible Institute was, indeed, an important factor in the decision to launch a campaign for funds to erect the large building known as the Calgary Prophetic Bible Institute.

If the success of the new Bible Institute surpassed Aberhart's expectations, another development during the autumn of 1925 had more far-reaching implications not only for his own future but also for that of Alberta. Significantly enough, it was one of the leading officials of the Bible Conference, rather than Aberhart himself, who conceived the idea of broadcasting the latter's Sunday afternoon lectures. This official, who was then employed by an electrical company, approached W. W. Grant, one of the pioneers of radio in Calgary and founder of the station CFCN (known as "The Voice of the Prairies"), with the suggestion that Aberhart should go on the air.

When this proposal was put to Aberhart he is said to have immediately remarked, "If I broadcast, people won't come to the theatre, and there will be no collection. Where will we obtain the money to meet expenses?" The same official then suggested that a radio club could be organized, through which those who listened to the broadcasts might each contribute one dollar to assist with expenses. Aberhart still strongly opposed the idea, but the official finally persuaded him to allow Grant to put on one broadcast as an experiment. In those days there were still technical difficulties connected with broadcasting from a place other than a studio, but the ingenious Grant had a telephone line installed from the Palace Theatre to the studio of CFCN, to which a microphone was then hooked up. The details of this experimental broadcast were so carefully worked out that even a few of Aberhart's followers who were in Calgary's General Hospital at the time were provided with earphones by the Bible Conference. To his followers it was an unforgettable scene when, one fateful Sunday afternoon in November, 1925, with the stage of the theatre strung with wires and with technicians looming in the background, Aberhart, with extreme reluctance, went on the air. "He trembled," one of his followers has said, "at the thought of broadcasting. Indeed, he was in abject terror as he faced the microphone."

In spite of Aberhart's emotional difficulties, the initial broadcast was an overwhelming success: he was amazed at both the contributions of money and the many enthusiastic letters that flowed in. Before long 500 people had become paying members of the radio club, a large number when one considers that only crystal sets were being used. As the broadcasts continued, it quickly became apparent that Aberhart had an exceptional radio appeal, and within a year it was realized, in the words of one of his officials, that "nothing could stop him." And nothing did: at the height of his fame, CFCN estimated that 350,000 people were listening to the Sunday afternoon broadcasts, which were then being heard throughout the three prairie provinces, as far west as the Okanagan valley of British Columbia, and in the American mountain states. Aberhart may have been terrified when he first went on the air but he became one of the great broadcasters of his time.

The introduction of Sunday afternoon broadcasts, together with the circulation of the magazine, led people in rural districts to press for the organization of a Radio Sunday School. Early in 1926 the work of the Bible Conference was expanded to include this new department, through which boys and girls, from the ages of six to sixteen, could secure a free correspondence course of fifty-two lessons designed to provide "a general knowledge of the stories of the Bible with their value to the present day." Children were invited to make application for lessons, either through themselves or through their parents; and the first two lessons with *questionnaires* attached would then be sent immediately. As each lesson was completed and returned to the Bible Conference, another lesson was sent out. Examinations were held every three months, or after every thirteen lessons, to see that the pupil had mastered the work and prizes were given to pupils making honours on term examinations. Supporters of the Bible Conference were urged to contribute to the financing of the Radio Sunday School, which was described in the appeal as "a real, essential missionary work in this western land." Within a year of its inauguration, the enrolment of the Radio Sunday School had increased to over 1,000; and its number eventually reached 8,000. It continued to function throughout the worst years of the depression and is still being carried on vigorously.

During the winter of 1926 further developments in the affairs of Westbourne prepared the way for that solution of Aberhart's problem of religious organization which, when followed up relentlessly some three years later, placed him in an exceptionally advantageous position during the 1930's as the founder and leader of the Social Credit movement. There had been, from the beginning, no lack of financial support from either seen or unseen audiences for the broadcasts of the Bible Conference, but the high rent of the Palace Theatre was a considerable strain on the budget. In addition, Westbourne Church itself, although crowded at the Sunday morning and evening services, was falling into disrepair; and accommodation for its Sunday School was quite inadequate. As it was realized that a fairly large sum would be required to rehabilitate the church, a building fund was established. With support from Aberhart's radio audience, this fund grew so rapidly that the deacons of Westbourne and the Executive of the Bible Conference called a special meeting in the Church in March, 1926, to discuss the advisability of building a new Church and Bible Institute, large enough to house all their activities and with up-to-date equipment and modern conveniences, in a downtown location. A Building Campaign Committee was organized, an excellent central location was secured on Eighth Avenue West, and an architect was invited to work out a design.

In a letter and eight-page prospectus sent out on April 2, Robert W. Scrimgeour, chairman of the Building Campaign Committee (he was also treasurer of the Church), proposed the formation of the Westbourne Prophetic Bible Institute Church Association for the purpose of building a combined Church and Bible Institute at a cost of approximately fifty thousand dollars. The building was to contain (1) an adjustable auditorium capable of seating 1,200 to 1,500 people for church and lecture purposes; (2) a Bible Institute or School Assembly Hall with movable partitions to accommodate 300 students; and (3) residence accommodation for 50 students. The prospectus stressed repeatedly the urgent need of a Bible Institute for the sake of the rising generation:

For some time now, it has been felt by many lovers of the TRUTH ONCE DELIVERED, that there is a great need, in this Western Country of ours, of an Up-to-date Bible Institute or School of Learning where our young people, especially, and any others who wish it, can secure a good training in Bible Knowledge without having their faith undermined by atheistic, skeptic, and modernistic teaching, too often found in many of our present day theological colleges and universities. The cry of young people, who have had their faith shipwrecked, is to be heard on every side. Has it reached you where you live yet?

Did you ever stop to consider where you would send your boy or girl when you desired them to learn something of the Bible? Have you ever pondered over this question in regard to your own faith? Do it for a moment or two, right now—and the problem will soon be apparent to you.

We want to help you solve this problem. You cannot do it alone. You will need to co-operate with others.

Among the subjects to be taught in the Institute were listed Bible Knowledge, Personal Evangelism, Homiletics, Public Speaking, and Bible Teaching. The proposed centre, it was suggested, would also serve its supporters and people generally in five other ways: (1) a Fundamental Baptist Church would be established "where the pure doctrines of the Word of God will be regularly upheld and the Sacred Ordinances of the Christian Church will be properly administered"; (2) there would be a regular Sunday afternoon or evening broadcast of Fundamental and Prophetic doctrines; (3) the Staff of the Institute would be available for part of the year to hold evangelistic services or to give lecture courses throughout the West; (4) religious literature, lectures, and a monthly magazine would be published and distributed; (5) Bible correspondence courses might be arranged for those unable to attend the

Institute. It will be seen that it was proposed to integrate in one building, and under central control, the various enterprises which Aberhart had been building up in Calgary during his previous sixteen years of religious activity.

The techniques which Aberhart and his followers devised for raising money to build the Institute have become legendary in Alberta. It was proposed, at first, to raise $50,000 by issuing 500 certificates of donation, each valued at $100 and representing one sod. The Executive Committee and the Deacons' Board of the Conference and Church appealed for the co-operation of approximately five hunderd vitally interested people.

Each must dig down and turn up a $100 sod. Some may take two certificates. Others may take ten or fifty, according to their means and as they realize the importance and value of the Institute to their loved ones and the West in general. A few may band together and get one certificate.

Now, tell us: How many sods can you turn over? Remember you can turn one or two now and plan to complete the job within, say, six months.

Beginning with the latter half of 1926, dramatic appeals for funds were made through the media of radio, letters, pamphlets, and newspapers. Later, the actual building of the Institute was also dramatized and the public was kept constantly informed of work in progress: the foundations had been laid; the basement was almost completed; the second story was begun; the roof was being put on! Once a specific type of appeal for money no longer brought results, the emphasis was shifted. The campaign for sods resulted in 132 contributions at $100 each, with many others contributing part of a sod. When the basement was assured, Aberhart launched a brick and rafter campaign; and towns, villages and post-offices struggled to win favourable mention in his Sunday afternoon broadcasts by contributing twenty-five bricks, or more, at $5 a brick! In the end, when all other devices seemed exhausted, people were simply asked to help liquidate the building debt of the Institute. Financial support for the campaign was heaviest, of course, in southern Alberta, but contributions came from Saskatchewan and British Columbia, and even a small number from Manitoba, Ontario, Quebec, Great Britain, Alaska, and the northwestern states.

In spite of public enthusiasm, however, Aberhart's supporters did not immediately raise the full $65,000 which was required to complete the Institute. Foreseeing this situation, he and his Executive, even before a building lot was secured, had arranged through a Calgary trust company for the sale of $30,000 worth of bonds at 8 per cent. It appears that his followers were the principal subscribers to this issue, which was taken up within three weeks, and which constituted a first mortgage on the building. Subsequently, when these bondholders periodically received their interest cheques, Aberhart would put on a special drive to persuade them to drop their cheques on the collection plate. It was found that nearly 90 per cent of the bondholders donated their interest to the Institute. Further, under the terms of the mortgage, a bondholder could be paid off annually. Aberhart paid off as soon as possible all those who cashed their interest cheques, and thus secured most of the bonds practically interest-free. A considerable number of people were even persuaded to give or bequeath their bonds to the Institute, and in a relatively few years the building was free of debt.

The formal opening of the Institute took place with considerable ceremony and publicity in October, 1927, when the Reverend Dr. W. B. Riley, B.A., of Minneapolis, preached the inaugural sermon and held a series of revival meetings. Shortly afterwards the Executive appointed Aberhart as President and Dean, and regular instruction began in the various courses offered by the Institute. The first bulletin, issued in the summer of 1927, contained a summary of the doctrinal basis of the Institute which stressed, among other articles of faith, the divine verbal inspiration, absolute supremacy, infallibility, and efficiency of the Bible in all matters of faith and practice; the Immaculate Conception, Virgin Birth, absolute Deity, and physical resurrection of Jesus Christ; the sacrificial, substitutionary theory of the Atonement; the physical resurrection of the dead, "both of the just and the unjust, the Christians at the Lord's appearing, the Israelites at His coming, and the unbelieving dead at the end of the millennium"; "the everlasting happiness of the righteous and the awful and everlasting misery of the unbelieving wicked, in a literal lake of fire, prepared for a real, personal devil and his angels"; and the pre-millennial doctrine of "the visible bodily return of our Lord in flesh and bones (*a*) At His appearing in the air for his Church. (*b*) At his coming to the Mount of Olives to establish the millennial reign of righteousness upon the earth." The bulletin also announced that the Institute would use every legitimate, Christian means of combatting and resisting modernism, higher criticism, scepticism, evolutionary interpretations of man's origin and nature, and "sectarianism in all its forms." Positively, it would bring together and instruct Fundamentalists in "the faith once for all delivered unto the saints"; it would train Sunday School teachers, personal workers, colporteurs, home and foreign missionaries, evangelists, evangelist singers, pastor's assistants, and pastors; and it would regularly broadcast the "Word of Truth" over the air for old and young alike.

Educational qualifications for admission to the Institute were purposely kept low: Aberhart and his Executive laid down the principle that "no man or woman should be excluded simply on educational grounds, but that they should possess a common school education or its equivalent"; and it was recommended that no student under the age of sixteen or seventeen should seek admission. There was no charge for tuition in Bible courses, but students were required to pay for courses such as shorthand, typewriting, music, sewing, millinery, domestic science, and motor mechanics. Among the subjects of instruction for the regular three-year course were listed Apologetics and Bible Introduction, Systematic Theology and Bible Doctrine, Biblical and Sacred History, Bible Geography and Oriental Customs, Personal Evangelism and Field Work, Bible Exegesis and Interpretation, Homiletics and Effective Expression, Bible Teaching and Sunday School Organization, music, and a literary and general English course. For those who could not attend the regular sessions, there were available Aberhart's printed lectures, the *Prophetic Voice*, correspondence courses, Radio Sunday School lessons, and, most important of all, the Sunday afternoon broadcasts.

To teach its imposing curriculum, the educational staff of the Institute in 1927 consisted, for the most part, of persons whom Aberhart had trained at Westbourne in the preceding years. Among the instructors were the Latin teacher at Crescent Heights, a dentist, a book-keeper, an accountant, two mechanics, an insurance agent, and several housewives, all of whom enthusiastically gave their services during part of the day, at nights, or on Saturdays and Sundays, without remuneration other than that peculiar ego enhancement which the privilege of working for the Lord—and Aberhart—seemed to bring to so many of the latter's associates over the years. An outsider, Westbourne officials of that day often declare, can form little or no conception of the long and hard hours that Aberhart and his Executive spent in teaching students, attending committee meetings, supervising routine affairs, and planning for the future. But, no matter how much he demanded of them, his devoted disciples were always full of admiration for his ingenuity and receptivity to new ideas, and always prepared to assist him in the use of new techniques of salvation.

The first student to graduate in the regular three-year Bible Institute course was Ernest Charles Manning, who had been attracted from his parents' farm near Rosetown, Saskatchewan, by the Sunday afternoon broadcasts, and who lived for several years in Aberhart's home, almost as a member of the family. A remarkable sympathy and understanding developed between the older and the younger man; and Aberhart often said that if he had had a son, he would have wished him to be like

Manning. But most of Manning's teachers at the Bible Institute apparently had no reason to suspect, during his student days, that his career would become inseparably linked with that of Aberhart, the future of the new Calgary Prophetic Bible Institute, and the evolution of the Social Credit movement.

The enthusiasm engendered among Aberhart's followers by his success in building the Institute obscured for most of them the changing pattern of his relationship to Westbourne which had in April, 1926, a membership of less than 200, drawn from approximately one hundred homes, under the pastoral care of the Reverend E. G. Hansell. For a time after Hansell's arrival all had gone well, but eventually, as might have been expected, he found himself in difficulty with Aberhart. The friction finally developed to the point where the pastor, although he had gained a certain personal following, felt compelled to move to another church. Aberhart's tactics immediately after Hansell's departure have been described by a then member of the Executive of the Bible Conference:

Mr. Aberhart then called a meeting of his Conference committee and said, "Look, fellows, a group favouring Mr. Hansell has pulled out. Has it ever struck you that one man could sway a democratic group of Baptists, and this whole building fund could go to another group. Here's what we should do: we should build this proposed church, not as a church, but as a Bible Institute and allow the Westbourne congregation to occupy it as a church home, but the title to the property would remain in this little group here" [the Executive of the Bible Conference]. So we incorporated our little group under the Church Holdings Act of Alberta, and membership was limited to those members of the Executive Committee who were *actively* engaged in the work of the Calgary Prophetic Bible Conference. If you didn't keep up activity, you were out!

In accordance with this plan, the Executive of the Bible Conference, some of the members of which were also deacons of Westbourne, incorporated the Institute in 1927 under the Church Holdings Act of Alberta (later known as the Religious Societies' Act), thus providing for its right to own property and legally receive or disburse funds voluntarily subscribed by its supporters. The articles of incorporation did not provide for any active voting membership other than membership in the Executive of the Bible Institute. To comply with the requirements of the Act, the Institute was designated as a church organization, with the members of its Executive designated as its "congregation," the legal term used to refer to the active voting membership of a religious organization incorporated under the statute.

The position of Westbourne under this arrangement was curious and difficult to define, owing to the absolute confidence which the inner circle of Aberhart's followers reposed in him. At a church meeting held in the old building, the new corporation formally invited the congregation of Westbourne to occupy the Bible Institute as their church home. The invitation was accepted and the Board of Deacons of Westbourne *voluntarily* offered, on motion of the brothers Harry B. and Robert W. Scrimgeour, treasurers of the Conference and the Church respectively, to contribute approximately $600 monthly to the Bible Institute for necessary upkeep, interest payments, and bond redemption—an excessively large amount, it would seem, for less than 200 members, practically all of whose incomes were something less than modest. On the completion of the new building, the congregation of Westbourne closed their church and moved to the Institute, where three different types of activity were now carried on: (1) the teaching of students; (2) regular church services and meetings; and (3) Aberhart's Sunday afternoon broadcasts; but the Executive of the Institute and the deacons of the Church controlled, in actuality, all these enterprises.

For a few months, the arrangement worked happily. The congregation, under the pastorate of the Reverend Wilburn W. Silverthorne, who had succeeded Hansell, was able to maintain its promised contribution. But trouble was brewing. Silverthorne turned out to be unsatisfactory and left. Aberhart then took over completely again. Although he filled the Institute at church services, there was little or no pastoral visiting. The deacons felt that they should obtain a regular clergyman, but prospects who preached for a call feared Aberhart's domination. By January, 1929, the Church's finances were beginning to slip badly and considerable dissatisfaction was rising among its people. The report of the treasurer showed that the Church was no longer raising $600 monthly for the Bible Institute. The then treasurer of the Institute and superintendent of the Sunday School has given a revealing account of Aberhart's tactics **during the next few fateful months:**

After Mr. Kepler (the church's treasurer) had read his report, Mr. Aberhart got up and said: "Is no one going to take note of the fact that you are falling behind in your obligation to pay $600 a month to the Institute." I arose and said: "Mr. Aberhart, that isn't an obligation, it's a free will offering." He then said "I can't carry on; if these people are going to use this as their church home they've got to be prepared to pay for it." This started a rift. As I pointed out again and again that it was merely a free-will offering, a group rallied around Mr. Aberhart and another group around me. I didn't want to be a leader of a group. I concluded that a lease should be entered into, and it would stop all this bickering. So I asked for a meeting of the Bible Institute members and made this proposition: "Suppose the Westbourne Baptist Church members agree to pay the light, telephone, heat and stenographic bills of the Institute, and pay the interest on and retire its bonds as well." Mr. ——— and I had worked out these monthly charges from an accounting standpoint and they came to $328 monthly. Mr. Aberhart said, "Your figures are all wrong," and he added, as he threw the sheet of paper down the length of the table, "the interest alone is more than that." I then had to explain to him that the interest charges decreased as the bonds were retired. The controversy then got quite hot— there were some people who were for Mr. Aberhart first, last, and all the time, no matter what he did. At another meeting of the church members, it was pointed out that we had an empty building on which we were paying taxes. A motion was put that we should go back to our own church. Mr. Aberhart then proposed an amendment that if the Westbourne congregation returned to its old building, he should be given the right to form his own Baptist Church. But no one voted for the amendment. The main motion was then put and lost. Mr. Aberhart got up and said, "That's fine, folks. You stay here and pay $600 a month, and the question can't be raised again." After legal consultation, we called another meeting, re-raised the issue, and voted to return to our old church. Sixty-five per cent of the Westbourne membership then left the Institute and returned to our original building. It was the month of June, 1929. I never spoke to Mr. Aberhart again, except once during his political campaign when he stopped me on the street and offered me the post of Provincial Treasurer if I'd come in on Social Credit.

As a last Christian act, and at Aberhart's request, the deacons of Westbourne returned one night to the new Bible Institute Baptist Church to conduct an ordination service for its new Board of Deacons. In later years, members of Westbourne were sometimes heard to remark, thankfully and without a trace of rancour, that the Peace of God had once more come to their old church. They were not impressed by the tumultuous meetings held in the Calgary Prophetic Bible Institute during the years when the Social Credit movement was at its height.

Thus it came about that in June, 1929, the Principal of Crescent Heights High School was left, for all practical purposes, in undisputed control of the Bible Institute and its property. Those members of the Executive who had returned to Westbourne resigned that month, but the articles of incorporation were so framed that the remaining members were legally able to make new appointments; and they proceeded likewise to replace various other officials who had resigned with younger men. The most important of these was Manning who, some months previously, at the age of twenty, had been made secretary of the Institute, and whose loyalty and devotion were so unquestioned that he shortly became Aberhart's right-hand man.

Although he benefited immensely from it, this upheaval was a severe shock to Aberhart, who had not anticipated that he would become involved in such difficulties when he had arranged, two years previously, for the Executive of the Bible Institute to have complete legal control of its property. As security for the future, the legal control of the property of the Calgary Prophetic Bible Institute was now vested in a Board of Management, the members of which constituted an inner group of the Executive, and who had, like Manning, manifested unquestioning loyalty and devotion to Aberhart and his religious work. During the fourteen years from 1929 to Aberhart's death, there was inevitable friction between him and various pastors of the Bible Institute Baptist Church, elaborate and gleeful accounts of which are preserved in the files of Calgary newspapers. But the settlement of 1929 was so effective that no internal crises since that time have seriously threatened the future of the Bible Institute.

Scarcely four months after Aberhart achieved control of the Institute, the New York stock market collapsed and the depression began. But the consolidation and expansion of the Institute's various activities seem to have continued unabated during the years between 1929 and 1932. During this period Aberhart organized Bible study groups throughout southern Alberta. Some of the stronger and more active of these developed into congregations, as at Red Deer and High River, under the Institute's jurisdiction. The interest of such groups was sustained not only by Aberhart's Sunday afternoon broadcasts but also by the personal visits of vigorous young preachers like Manning. But Aberhart's showmanship constantly demanded new techniques of promotion. During the winter of 1931, for example, he wrote a drama entitled "The Branding Irons of the Anti-Christ," designed the costumes and scenery, and coached a cast of young members of the Institute in its production. It was subsequently presented in numerous towns and villages where there were Bible study groups, much to the edification of the faithful. It is said that this play's success gave Aberhart the idea of dramatizing the theories of Social Credit for stage and radio presentation some three years later.

Aberhart's supervision of and participation in the numerous activities centred in the Institute necessarily involved him in an incredible schedule of working hours. During the school year, his duties as principal required his presence at Crescent Heights for five days a week from 8.30 A.M. to at least 4.15 P.M. As soon as school was out, he would usually hurry off to the Institute where, it is said, he often worked until midnight, and sometimes until 2.00 A.M. Those who knew him best declare that he could not have long survived such a schedule without the sympathetic and understanding co-operation of his charming wife, the former Miss Jessie Flatt of Galt, Ontario, whom he had married in 1902. Mrs. Aberhart, who was totally devoid of worldly ambition, devoted herself whole-heartedly to the welfare of her husband and two daughters. If she did not participate actively in the social life of Calgary or the religious activities of the Institute, her husband's friends and enemies were well aware of her strong and guiding presence behind the scenes.

In addition to an exceptionally happy home life, Aberhart's amazing capacity for work was made possible by his robust physique and excellent health. He was a man of size and stature, heavily built and tall, with the reddish-blond colouring of his Germanic ancestors, full lips, and clear blue eyes. His followers believed that his large head, which had only a fringe of hair at the sides and back, was of the shape and type that inevitably houses brains. Although large, he was agile; and he seemed to have an inexhaustible supply of physical energy to back up his relentless drive. Like most large men, he had a mild and courteous manner (except when he was replying to his severest critics), a ready smile, and a genial, jovial personality. A *pince-nez* added to his general appearance as a man of distinction, and made him readily identifiable in newspaper caricatures. His voice, which was perhaps his greatest asset as a public man, was clear, pleasant, sonorous, and capable of great range and volume; and he had learned to manipulate its curious undertones with highly dramatic effect.

As Aberhart always wanted to be doing something, he had no time to sit for a portrait. The two paintings of him by Nicholas de Grandmaison, the versatile Banff artist, were both done posthumously from photographs, but they exhibit him in considerably different lights. In the portrait that looks down from the right front wall of the Bible Institute's auditorium, Aberhart is depicted in warm, soft colours as a serene, greathearted, humanitarian, deeply spiritual, profoundly sympathetic personality, without the slightest suggestion of claws beneath the velvet. In the portrait that hangs in the Legislative Building at Edmonton, the external equipment that made his career possible looms in the foreground on the desk at which he is seated—the old-fashioned pen, the ink-well, the Bible, the telephone, the microphone. Here Aberhart himself is painted in cold, harsh colours as callous, cruel, hard-driven, scheming, deceptive: the blood is almost oozing from the pallid skin and the horns are almost sprouting from the head. His enemies gloat over the latter portrait, while his admirers wonder why it was accepted for public display in Alberta's Legislative Building.

In the light of Aberhart's pedagogical and religious activities, it is not surprising that he played little or no part in the social and cultural life of Calgary. Society leaders in the city considered him a shy man, and noticed that whenever possible he would avoid participation in ceremonial functions by sending a personal representative. Nor would he accept invitations to serve as honorary president of athletic clubs at Crescent Heights or elsewhere, preferring to have such offices filled by members of his staff. Before leaving Ontario, he had joined the Masonic Order, but he seems to have ceased active participation in its affairs when he went West. Although he might indicate on occasion his membership to fellow Masons, he never used this connection to arouse public support for his various enterprises. In the middle 1920's, he served as the first secretary of the Calgary Branch of the League of Nations Society, when R. B. Bennett was its president. It is said that Bennett, whose memory for names and faces was legendary, loved to embarrass Aberhart at public meetings of the Branch by pretending to have forgotten his name. But no matter how often he was asked, Aberhart always gave his name to Bennett with a smile, and carried on loyally and efficiently his duties as secretary.

Despite Aberhart's activity on behalf of the League of Nations, those who knew him well claim that until he took up Social Credit he had no real interest in public affairs. He was, it is true, preoccupied with the politics of the Israelites and the economics of the New Jerusalem; but his concern with the contemporary scene was wholly in terms of its relationship to the prophecies of Daniel. Thus he knew the exact location of Armageddon, but nothing of Czechoslovakia. Dates were meaningless, unless they referred to, say, the Second Coming. The educated classes of Calgary might be exercised over the economic and political consequences of the First World War or the titanic struggles between Capital and Labour, but Aberhart showed not the slightest interest. When asked during a conversation for his views on national or international events, he would invariably reply that his mind was on higher things.

He could give a detailed account of Noah's Ark or of the Great Pyramid, but modern art and architecture had no existence for him. He belonged to no clubs and attended no lectures or concerts. The more worldly kinds of recreation, such as cards, smoking, drinking, dancing, and the theatre, were inventions of Satan which a prudent man would avoid like the plague. Yet he was not unduly censorious, and he had become reconciled to a world full of sinners, many of whom might even be accepted as fairly decent people. If he was narrow, he was not ascetic, for he loved good food, good clothes, and good cars. Such concessions to the flesh-pots redeemed him from fanaticism. Then, too, he had a sense of humour. If it was of a somewhat primitive, custard-pie variety, it was generally kept within bounds by his sense of decorum.

Although he had played football, badminton, and tennis in his earlier years, Aberhart took no exercise during the last twenty years of his life. His recreational activities in Calgary seem to have been confined to checkers and chess. From all accounts he was an excellent checkers player. But he was especially fond of chess, which he had taught himself to play by reading a great variety of books, and from which he derived immense pleasure and relaxation. He was a decisive or "flash" player: his own thought processes were rapid, and he disliked slow, deliberate plays or prolonged thinking-out of possible moves. Much as he liked to divert opponents by conversational devices, there was no spuriousness about his game: those who played with him speak respectfully of his skill.

His interest in chess, as well as his methods of playing, are reflected in several unpublished manuscripts he wrote on the game. These include both short papers on general openings in chess and elaborate analyses in which long and complicated games are worked out on paper. One quite sizable manuscript is entitled, significantly enough, "Conversational CHESS—How to talk your opponent out of the GAME: A simple form of Salesmanship to Kill the Monotony of These Slow Games." The preface reads: "By the conversation Method the purpose of each move is hidden by the player, and the tricks and traps are revealed by the counter repertoire as the game proceeds. . . . We hope that the readers will enjoy the battle of words, and will be able to remember the games by the talk which takes place." There follow fifteen pages of amusing dialogue designed to accompany moves in a game of chess.

The circumstances under which Aberhart decided to promote the cause of Social Credit have become legendary in Alberta. However dramatic that decision may have been, a careful investigation of its background suggests that it was influenced by considerably more factors than have hitherto been supposed.

When the depression struck, Aberhart was in his fifty-first year and suffering from a certain restlessness not uncommon to middle age. The previous spring he had attained undisputed control of the Institute and its property. But about the same time he had reluctantly and finally abandoned an ambition of long standing to qualify as a lawyer by completing a correspondence course in law under the auspices of the American Extension University of Spokane, Washington.

The malaise occasioned by the realization that he was now irrevocably committed to a teaching career was not wholly assuaged by the fervour with which he plunged into the task of consolidating and expanding the work of the Institute. Had he been assured of financial security he might, indeed, have abandoned teaching and devoted his life entirely to religious activities. But he had already made his decision on this possibility several years previously: the officials of Westbourne had suggested to him after Hansell left in 1926 that he give up his principalship and become their full-time pastor at a yearly salary of $5,000, but he had chosen the security that went with the considerably smaller salary of the principalship instead of the more lucrative but insecure pastorate. It was, in fact, well known that he was inordinately careful in avoiding any move that might jeopardize his position—and salary—at Crescent Heights. While the amount of time he devoted to religious activities had occasioned some discussion among its members, especially after he assumed full control of the Institute, the Calgary School Board had decided not to interfere with his outside work, on the distinct understanding that it would not be carried on during regular school hours. But, in the minds of some of the Board's members, there was little doubt that during the early 1930's Aberhart's career as religious leader had taken precedence over his career as educationalist. They decided, however, to let him go his own way, fearing a charge of interference with freedom of speech.

During his long career as religious leader in Calgary, Aberhart had periodically experimented with new ideas and new techniques to arouse public interest. It is true that, up to 1932, he had shown no concern in public with economic questions, although one of his officials had given a lecture in the Institute on "Economics and Religion" as early as the spring of 1929. Holding an important educational position, on a fixed salary with security of tenure, Aberhart was not personally affected by the depression during its early years. But, as economic conditions worsened, his religious following became increasingly restless. Then the teaching profession itself began to suffer and Aberhart gradually became aware of the impact of the depression upon the people of Alberta in general. The activities of the Bible Institute were bound to be affected. In a very significant sense, the introduction of Social Credit ideas into his Sunday afternoon broadcasts during the autumn of 1932 may be interpreted, in its inception, as another of the new techniques by which Aberhart sought to arouse interest in the work of the Bible Institute. At the same time, it must be emphasized that the decision to promote the philosophy of Social Credit was influenced by other factors in addition to the exigencies with which the Bible Institute itself was confronted in 1932.

There is evidence, from Aberhart's correspondence with religious associates and friends on the Pacific coast, that as early as 1930 "the going was getting harder at the Institute." As the depression developed, it became more and more difficult to fill the Institute's auditorium on Sunday afternoons, and there can be little doubt that Aberhart was seeking a fresh approach to this problem. His critics assert that his radio audience was also falling off drastically. But such a claim has been denied categorically by the then officials of station CFCN, who have suggested, however, that contributions from radio listeners may very well have diminished considerably as the depression worsened. Here, again, certain letters indicate that Aberhart was insisting that he needed, more than ever before, preaching assignments during his summer vacations in cities like Vancouver, B.C., or Portland, Oregon, to bolster his prestige and work as a fundamentalist religious leader in Alberta.

An event that occurred in the autumn of 1931 suggests that Aberhart was becoming aware of the magnitude of the depression. During the previous year-and-a-half even the best recent graduates of Crescent Heights High School had been experiencing considerable difficulty in securing jobs, and many of the older graduates had lost jobs they had held for years. As the winter of 1931-2 approached, a former student who had been hard hit by the depression begged his old principal to "assume the responsibility of doing something to deal with the serious economic situation caused by the depression." At the conclusion of the interview Aberhart said, "The Gates of Hell shall not prevail against it," an unusual use of a famous scriptural reference which the desperate young man never forgot. On several other occasions during the winter and spring of 1932, this same man urged Aberhart repeatedly to do something about "the plight of youth," but he felt that he was getting nowhere with his former principal. His persistence was finally rewarded, however, in the autumn of 1932, when Aberhart invited him to take up the cause of Social Credit.

At the very time that his former student was needling Aberhart to do something about the plight of youth, the salary scale of the teachers of Calgary became a subject of public discussion. In that city the collapse of the oil boom of the 1920's had been added to the débâcle of the depression. The development of the Turner valley oilfield had encouraged much reckless speculation: nearly everybody who had had a dollar, or could borrow one, had been in the oil game: terms like "margin buying," "selling short," and "pyramiding," had been on nearly everybody's lips. When the crash came, sizable fortunes had disappeared overnight, and thousands of "penny-ante" investors lost heavily. As a result, the general business recession produced by the depression was probably felt more acutely in Calgary than in any other city in Western Canada. It is small wonder that the city's taxpayers, particularly the larger ones, began to consider ways and means of reducing taxation. It is no wonder at all that to accomplish this they attacked Calgary's education budget. Under such circumstances the salary lists of teachers are obviously intended to be cut!

The economy-minded business men and industrialists of the city were fortunate in that the chairman of the School Board, the local manager of an internationally known company with headquarters in Eastern Canada, was quite prepared to carry out their wishes with regard to the education budget. Indeed, he made it no secret that his aim was not merely to reduce salaries but to "put the fear of God into those Reds"—some of the Calgary teachers having actually joined the Canadian Labour party! This man was not a public relations expert for nothing, and he soon had the enthusiastic support of both the city's newspapers, but more particularly of the *Calgary Herald*, in his campaign.

Throughout the winter and spring of 1931–2 the campaign to reduce teachers' salaries was carried on relentlessly. Editorials appeared criticizing the enormous cost of education and stressing the poor quality of public and high school graduates. Suggestions were even made that the schools might have to be closed owing to lack of funds. "Vox Pop" and "Mother of Ten" wrote letters to the newspapers discussing the shortcomings of the school system, even of particular members of the staff.

The teachers, of course, did not suffer in silence. They had their friends, and so had the cause of education. It is said that many letters on behalf of the teachers were written to the *Herald*, but that few appeared in print. A mass meeting was held in protest against the action of the press and School Board, but it was ineffective as far as immediate results were concerned. Teachers' salaries were drastically cut, in some cases, it is reported, by about 30 per cent. "Vox Pop" then ceased his epistolatory diatribes.

Aberhart took no prominent part in this controversy. Under the circumstances, he considered that activity on behalf of his profession was bound to be ineffective. But he brooded over the situation, both as it involved his own salary and as it affected the whole cause of education.

By the spring of 1932 the people of Alberta were being seriously affected by the depression. Bread-lines became common, and citizens who had never imagined themselves in such a humiliating situation had to go on relief. Growing numbers of unemployed began going from place to place, riding on the top of freight trains. Aberhart had a reputation of being very tender-hearted with people in trouble. Dozens of working men now came to him with their problems; and he frequently gave money to those who were down and out. Many others, in deep distress, wrote personal letters to him, urging him to try and do something positive about the depression.

No one in touch with schoolchildren could fail to be keenly aware of the hardships through which most families were passing. Distress was most evident in ragged and patched clothing and lowered nutrition standards. Aberhart expressed concern for the pupils of Crescent Heights, and the members of his staff felt that his concern was inspired by genuine humanitarian sentiments. Not, however, until the salaries of teachers were drastically cut did he begin to wonder seriously whether something was not definitely out of joint in the economic system. During the late spring of 1932 he wondered often and openly, but as yet had no plan of salvation.

As the school year drew to its close, a Grade XII student at Crescent Heights committed suicide, owing to his family's wretched circumstances. Shaken to his depths by the tragic death of one of his favourite and best students, Aberhart went up to Edmonton, early in July, 1932, to mark matriculation examinations. There he engaged in long discussions concerning the problems of the depression and their possible solution with a friend and fellow examiner, Charles M. Scarborough.

A university graduate in engineering and teacher of chemistry at the Victoria High School in Edmonton, Scarborough had become interested in Social Credit in 1925. While crossing the Atlantic to England, he had occupied a deck-chair next to a British engineer who was returning from the Orient. During his years in India this engineer had known Major C. H. Douglas, who had been for a time the representative of the Westinghouse interests there. From Douglas he had imbibed the doctrines of Social Credit, and he made a convert of Scarborough during the voyage. The latter was so enthusiastic that immediately after his arrival in London he purchased Douglas's books and studied them intensively all summer.

On returning to Alberta, Scarborough began to discuss Social Credit not only with his friends but also with his students. Under his guidance, study groups were formed in Edmonton for the systematic reading of Douglas's works. From time to time he also gave talks on Social Credit to various urban and rural groups. He was especially interested in the mathematical side of Social Credit, and derived considerable amusement from working out schemes for the application of Douglas's principles. Within a year or two after his conversion, Scarborough became convinced that Social Credit was the solution to the problems of Western Canada. Having no taste for leadership himself, he began "to look around for someone who would really take hold of Douglas's ideas and put them across." He was aware of an interest in monetary reform among the U.F.A. Members of Parliament, but concluded that they were receptive to so many theories that none of them could be counted on to give whole-hearted devotion to Social Credit.

While engaged on an engineering project in southern Alberta during the summer of 1926, Scarborough heard one of Aberhart's Sunday afternoon broadcasts over CFCN. "It struck me at the time," he has recorded, "that Aberhart would be the man who could launch an educational programme on monetary reform. Anyone hearing him in those days would certainly agree that he could sway his audiences. One could not help but recognize his dynamic personality and gift of oratory."

Scarborough had met Aberhart personally for the first time in the summer of 1929, when both were marking examination papers at the King Edward School in Edmonton. During several weeks' association, the former tried repeatedly but vainly to interest the latter in Douglas's theories. Thenceforth, however, whenever the two met, Scarborough would force a discussion of political and economic questions. They nearly always found themselves on opposing sides. At the close of such conversations Aberhart would sometimes concede, under pressure, that monetary reform might be urgently needed (as Scarborough was insisting) but he decidedly would not agree that Social Credit was the method of bringing it about.

When Scarborough met Aberhart at the Edmonton Normal School early in July, 1932, he noticed at once that the latter had been deeply shocked by the suicide of the Crescent Heights' student, and that the economic distress occasioned by the depression was preying on his mind. Encouraged by these symptoms, he redoubled his efforts to arouse Aberhart's interest in Douglas's theories. But he had such little success that one day when he was in the midst of an exposition of Social Credit Aberhart told him he was crazy.

That night Scarborough concluded that Aberhart's lack of interest in Social Credit hitherto was due to the technical character of Douglas's theories. "Perhaps," he reflected, "something simpler might turn the trick." Before he gave up badgering Aberhart, he decided to make one more try. The following evening, armed with a copy of Maurice Colbourne's *Unemployment or War*, which presented Douglas's theories in highly popular form, Scarborough closed in on Aberhart at his room in St. Stephen's College, on the campus of the University of Alberta.

The period of marking examination papers was drawing to a close and Scarborough realized that this was his last chance. He sat down in Aberhart's room and the two of them spent several hours reading aloud and discussing sections of Colbourne's book. At long last, to Scarborough's great joy, Aberhart became intensely interested. Before Scarborough left, around midnight, he loaned the book to Aberhart on condition that he promise to read it through.

Several hours later, as the summer sun rose over the prairies and bathed the university campus in dazzling light, Aberhart had fulfilled his promise. As he laid down the book, he decided that Social Credit was exactly what the people of Alberta needed to redeem their province from the depths into which the bankers and financiers had plunged it.

CHAPTER THREE

➤➤➤·➤➤·᠊᠊᠊᠊᠊᠊᠊᠊᠊᠊᠊᠊᠊᠊᠊᠊᠊᠊

Strategy and Tactics: I

To ITS DEVOTEES in Alberta the early years of the Social Credit movement will always remain its heroic period. In the absence of an authentic history, the activities of the years from 1932 to 1935 have been invested with such a legendary halo that today even those most deeply involved in the movement sometimes find it difficult to distinguish fact from fiction. For an understanding of the movement, it is essential, therefore, to provide as detailed an analysis as possible of the strategy and tactics by means of which it was initiated and developed. The materials for such an analysis include field interviews, mimeographed and printed leaflets, pamphlets, and newspaper reports.

It must be emphasized, also, that the Calgary Prophetic Bible Institute was the unique headquarters of the movement, and that every activity was personally supervised, if not always inspired, by William Aberhart. It is doubtful whether there could have been a successful Social Credit movement without Aberhart; it is equally doubtful whether he could have provided effective leadership without the resources of the Institute, over which he had undisputed control. Nor would the movement have grown so rapidly had it not been rooted in the religious following which he had built up during the previous twenty years. Further, the techniques used in developing the movement did not represent a departure from, but were rather continuous with, the methods of indoctrination for which he had long been famous in Alberta.

In its inception, the Social Credit movement may be best understood, therefore, not as a new movement but rather as an extension of an already well-established fundamentalist and prophetic movement. That Social Credit activities were considered from the outset as merely an extension of religious interests is evident from Aberhart's first move in publicizing his recently discovered idea. Sometime during the early autumn of 1932 (the precise date cannot be established), at a meeting of the Institute's Board of Management in the T-Kettle Inn on Eighth Street, he asked for and received permission to introduce Social Credit doctrines into his Sunday afternoon broadcasts. Those present on that half-remembered occasion seem to have viewed such a request as merely routine business of the Institute: did not Bible prophecy deal with certain aspects of man's economic needs? It was implicitly understood that any references to Social Credit would be religious and economic and not political.

Gradually, and with cautious reservations, Aberhart now began to weave Social Credit ideas into his addresses. The radio scripts are not available, but those who remember the broadcasts were apparently not aware of a sudden shift in the emphasis to which they had been accustomed. Social Credit ideas, Aberhart insisted from the beginning, offered a fulfilment of fundamentalist and prophetic Christianity. As his thoughts evolved during the autumn of 1932, his listeners noticed a gradual shading-off of a purely religious emphasis and a growing reference to economic problems. Then he began to throw out challenging questions: Isn't the root of our economic troubles a shortage of purchasing power? Why couldn't Social Credit be applied to the solution of the problems of the depression, which was then entering its fourth grim year? He urged the people to decide *for themselves* after careful study of Social Credit ideas. Within a few weeks the new appeal began to interest even those who had scant respect for Aberhart's religious doctrines. Late in the fall, in response to an invitation, he held a public week-night meeting in the Canadian Legion Memorial Hall for the discussion of Gessell Scrip. At this, his first non-religious meeting in Calgary, Aberhart informed his audience that the Gessell plan was entirely unsatisfactory. He announced, further, that Social Credit alone offered hope. As a result of this meeting, at a time when both the prices of farm products and the wages of urban workers were falling to new low levels, and when thousands of families in Calgary were on relief, the idea that the depression might be due to a shortage of purchasing power began to be discussed in secular circles in Calgary, and especially among such groups of intelligentsia as the Knights of the Round Table and the Open Mind Club.

Towards the turn of the year interest in Social Credit had increased to the point where Aberhart, in response to numerous requests, announced that early in 1933 he proposed to offer at the Institute a series of public week-night lectures devoted to a systematic exposition of the writings of Major Douglas. It was emphasized that the enterprise would be strictly educational. As these lectures developed it was noticed that the content of Social Credit material in the Sunday broadcasts was increased and presented with more urgency.

By the end of January requests for lectures or addresses on Social Credit began to come from groups and organizations in both Calgary and nearby towns and villages. To meet this demand, and without realizing the importance of the step he was taking, Aberhart organized a class or study group (as it soon came to be called) in which potential speakers were given systematic instruction in Social Credit theory. Although in after years Social Crediters were to vie with each other for the honour of having been the first to enrol, this group seemed at the time to be merely part of the routine activity of the Institute. Such an impression was only natural. In offering week-night lectures on Social Credit, and in forming the study group, Aberhart was merely extending to his new interest the techniques for training workers which had long proved so successful in his strictly religious activities. Looking back, however, the institution of the first study group may be considered a crucial stage in the development of the Social Credit movement. During the following years most of the volunteers whom that group attracted and inspired became dedicated to the propagation of Social Credit.

At the organizational meeting of the original study group in the Institute's lower auditorium, the thirty students who turned up received a lasting impression that they had gone back to school. Certainly their teacher's methods were calculated to inspire such an attitude. After a deacon had registered the students, Aberhart informed them that he proposed to use class-room techniques for teaching them Social Credit. At the next meeting, a series of mimeographed lessons would be available for one dollar, which would be returned to those who attended the full course. Weekly, thereafter, throughout the remainder of the winter, the spring, and the early summer this group received systematic instruction in the fundamental principles of the saving philosphy. As a good school-teacher Aberhart methodically, and somewhat ponderously, made ample use of black-board and chart to illustrate his points. Within a few months his charts were synthesized into expository masterpieces which aroused the interest of almost everyone in Alberta: the most famous were those depicting the A plus B Theorem and the flow of credit as the blood-stream of the state.

With the growth of the movement, Aberhart began to build up a supply of printed materials, following a policy he had long practised in connection with the religious activities of the Institute. His original black-board demonstrations, mimeographed leaflets, and charts formed the nucleus of a long series of four-page white leaflets, called "Study Group Features." These leaflets bore such titles as "The Present Methods of Business," "The Social Credit Concept," "Purchasing Power in the Hands of the Consumers," "The Necessary Flow of Credit or Where Will all the Money Come From?" and "The Perfect Cycle." Roughly two-thirds of each leaflet was devoted to what purported to be Aberhart's own exposition of Social Credit, followed by eight or ten questions designed to test the student's grasp of that exposition. The last part of each leaflet contained a brief summary of a chapter of Douglas's book, *Social Credit* (in the third leaflet Aberhart switched from the 1924 to the 1933 edition of this work). Owing to their schematic form, these leaflets met the need of Social Crediters for slogans, catch-phrases, and facile summaries. Widely distributed for the use of study groups, they gradually became an influential factor in the diffusion of Aberhart's doctrines throughout the province.

The "white leaflets" (as they were popularly called) were supplemented in the spring of 1933 by a series of six four-page coloured leaflets. These were devoted entirely to brief summaries, also highly schematic, of Douglas's book *Credit Power and Democracy*. Used at first solely in the Institute for the training of speakers, the coloured leaflets were later demanded by study groups everywhere; and many reprintings were necessary during the following two years.

The fourth phase in the development of Aberhart's expository materials was marked by the publication in May, 1933, of the celebrated "Yellow Pamphlet." Although it was unsigned, everybody knew who had written it. Destined to arouse bitter controversy in future years, it was entitled *The Douglas System of Economics*. Its front cover also carried the words: "Credit Power for Democracy"/ a system of State Credit / which will supply / Purchasing Power to the Consumer / This is a brief outline of the above system as applied to our Western Provincial needs."

The printed page could never adequately convey the impact upon audiences of Aberhart's manner of speaking. Nevertheless, these four sets of materials—mimeographed lesson sheets, while leaflets, coloured leaflets, and the Yellow Pamphlet—do indicate what he was teaching during the months when the Social Credit movement emerged. He was unquestionably expounding Social Credit doctrines as they could be found in Douglas's principal works. At the same time he was deliberately adapting those doctrines to the Alberta situation.

This double emphasis existed from the beginning. In his first mimeographed lesson sheet, distributed at the first meeting of the first study group in the Institute, Aberhart wrote: "Our First Duty is to distinguish carefully The Douglas System declaring the principles of Social Credit and The Douglas plans of adaptation." The principles, he continues, are axiomatic and self-evident, but the plans need careful revision and discussion. The plans are dependent upon the physical features, products, national characteristics, and financial condition of the country

involved. A close study of his earliest printed materials indicates that
Aberhart continued to emphasize his initial distinction between principles and plans. The failure of both his friends and his foes to appreciate
the bias he gave to his interpretation of Social Credit, coupled with his
extreme sensitivity to criticism from Simon Pure disciples of Douglas,
led to much bitter controversy inside and outside the movement during
the next two years.

The four most controversial aspects of Aberhart's adaptation of
Social Credit to Alberta revolved around his teaching with regard to basic
dividends, the flow of credit, automatic price control, and the claim that
his monetary proposals could be implemented at the provincial level.
That his views on all four issues were clearly defined by the winter of
1933 is evident from the mimeographed and printed materials he circulated during that period.

Aberhart's doctrine of basic dividends was expounded, in the third
white leaflet, as the only real remedy for Alberta's economic ills:

(1) Through the agency of basic dividends granted to every bona fide
citizen we shall give purchasing power sufficient to buy the bare necessities of
food, clothing, and shelter, without basing the same on work, but the unearned increment of Social Credit.
(2) This will be distributed through Credit Houses at which monthly, a
credit pass book will be presented by each citizen and an entry of $25.00
will be made. The citizen will then be able to pay for purchases by a non-
negotiable certificate ordering the transfer of Credit to another. The process
will be largely a matter of book-keeping.
(3) For travelling in other parts of Canada and small purchases at home,
Dominion currency will be supplied by the Credit House, upon the
presentation of a non-negotiable certificate for the amount.
(4) No citizen will be allowed to overdraw on his account without special
arrangement for same.
(5) Salaries, wages, and commissions, etc. are in addition to these basic
dividends.

An exposition of Aberhart's interpretation of Douglas's doctrine of
the continuous flow of credit is given on the first page of the Yellow
Pamphlet.

By the Douglas System of Credit Power, the flow of credit automatically
adapts itself to the business to be done, and no one can prevent its flow. By
this system, all payments for goods and services are made by cheque on the
Provincial Credit House. This will ultimately reach the House and a cross
entry will be made. E.g.—Citizen A wishes to pay his grocery bill. He writes
out a cheque for $20.00 and gives it to his grocer, who deposits it at the
Provincial Credit House. The Clerk then credits the grocer's account with
$20.00 and debits the Citizen's account with the same sum, and the cheque
is filed. The Citizen's credit in the Provincial Credit House has given him

the right to draw the cheque which acts as a medium of exchange for the groceries. Hence the Credit System and cheques would easily take the place of Bank Notes and Bank Cheques. In case of Citizens requiring small sums to buy goods, the province could issue scrip or coins for this purpose.

This credit system will keep the province in close touch with all business transactions and would enable it to extend credit to Farmers and other producers in accordance with their needs.

With the exception of his addresses on basic dividends, no aspect of Aberhart's exposition of Social Credit aroused more public interest than his definition of the flow of credit as the bloodstream of the state. Just as the blood flows to every part of the body, feeding, clothing, and sheltering every cell, so, he argued, must credit flow to every individual and every productive enterprise of the state for the same purpose. Nothing must be allowed to interfere with this flow of credit. But it was perfectly clear that finance *was* interfering with this flow of credit. By granting or withdrawing overdrafts or loans finance could stimulate or retard the flow of credit. Finance benefited by stimulating when it should retard and by retarding when it should stimulate. "Thus the State," wrote Aberhart, "has periodic attacks of anaemic conditions." Unless the amount of purchasing power distributed during any period equates the total production available during that period, a surplus of goods will pile up, production and purchasing power will both be reduced, and pernicious anaemia of its bloodstream will make the state sick unto death.

Aberhart emphasized that the Social Credit remedy for the state's pernicious anaemia consisted in the regulation of the *amount of purchasing power, not the amount of money or of credit*. As he saw it, the amount of purchasing power was dependent upon (1) the amount of real credit available (2) the rate of flow of credit. To enable his listeners to visualize his solution, he then argued, in the fourth white leaflet, as follows:

In 1930 the grand total of internal activities in Canada was $4,800,000,000, (Official Hand Book 1933 p. 139). On page 130 we are told that total imports for 1930 into Canada were $1,248,273,582. That makes a total trade of about $6,000,000,000.

The money in circulation in 1930 was:

Dominion notes $174,616,015
Bank notes $159,341,085
                                                              ─────────────
                                                              $333,957,100

(Official Hand Book 1933 page 155.)

Thus we see that six billion dollars of business was done with 350 million dollars of currency, or that is one dollar had $17 purchasing power.

When we finally grasp the principles enunciated above we are able intelligently to answer the question—"Where will all the money come from, to give $25 a month to every adult in the Province of Alberta?"

1. In 1931 at the last Canadian Census, the population of Alberta was 731,605. The number of persons under twenty was 416.36 per 1000. The total number of Alberta's population over 20 would therefore be about 427,000.

If each of these received $25.00 a month we would require $10,700,000 a month to feed, clothe, and shelter all our people.

2. That the Province of Alberta can care for all her citizens is evident from the statistics of tangible wealth given (Official Handbook 1933 p. 47.)

(*a*) Alberta has total wealth of $2,406,000,000 or i.e. $3,724 per capita. ... (*c*) If we can make our capital wealth produce 8%, each man, woman, and child could receive $25.00 a month without decreasing our capital wealth. . . . (*e*) on the basis of production figures in Alberta for the three years 1929, 1930, 1932, we could have given our adult bona fide citizens $300 each and would have had 109 million dollars to distribute for industrial enterprise. But the Flow of Credit would decrease the quantity of credit required by at least twelve times. Instead of 128 millions we should not need 20 millions.

In Aberhart's interpretation of Social Credit, Douglas's conception of a just price was expounded in terms of an automatic price control system. Such a system would be necessary if production and consumption were to be equalized and the hoarding of foodstuffs prevented. In the Yellow Pamphlet, Aberhart outlined it as follows:

The Government, through their economic officials, will fix and declare the price of all necessities for food, clothing and shelter on the basis of a fixed ratio, viz:

$$\text{Market Price} = \frac{\text{Total Consumption}}{\text{Total Production}} \times \text{Total Cost}$$

E.G. If 50,000 pairs of shoes costing $6 a pair should be produced or imported and only 40,000 pairs were purchased by the Consumers, then the price would automatically be reduced by the Officials to 4/5 of $6.00 = $4.80 a pair, to increase the Consumption.

This means that only when consumption equals production will the price at which goods are sold be adequate to cover the total cost of production. In other words, the principle of profit on necessities is abolished.

The Government will be obliged to cover the deficiency in price in two ways: (1) By sales to foreign countries at a profit. (2) By granting additional Credit to the Distributors.

The most controversial issue revolving around all of Aberhart's Social Credit proposals was unquestionably their constitutionality under the British North America Act. Aberhart discussed the constitutional aspect in his second mimeographed lesson sheet, but it is not mentioned in the white or coloured leaflets. In the Yellow Pamphlet he merely stated that "in no way should the introduction of this system be allowed to interfere with the relationship between Alberta and Canada or any of the other provinces. Owing to the schematic character of the second mimeographed lesson sheet, it is not possible to discover his precise attitude towards the constitutional aspect at the time he initiated the first study group. In this document he did, however, list three exceptions to the federal control of currency and credit under "An Act Respecting Banks and Banking," chapter 12, section 138, viz.:

(a) A cheque on some chartered bank paid by the maker directly to his immediate creditor; or (b) a promissory note, bill of exchange, bond or other undertaking for the payment of money made or delivered by the maker thereof to his immediate creditor; and (c) not designed to circulate as money or as a substitute for money. 1923, c. 32, s. 136.

Nothing more concerning the constitutional aspect is indicated in the second lesson sheet except the comment that the Bank Act would be reconsidered in June, 1934. But among the members of the first study group there is general agreement that Aberhart definitely assured them that the Social Credit proposals could be implemented at the provincial level. The movement was, in fact, already well established before the constitutional aspect became a controversial issue.

Aberhart's early study group materials have been quoted at some length because they constitute our only documentary sources of information regarding his interpretation of the technical doctrines of Social Credit at the time he initiated the movement. But it must not be supposed that he presented his doctrines in radio addresses or on the public platform in anything like the restrained form in which they appeared in writing. His speeches on Social Credit, as recalled by his devotees, were interlaced with much emotional rhetoric about the impact of the depression on the people of Alberta, coupled with impassioned moral and religious exhortations and frequent references to Bible prophecy.

It is claimed by those who were closest to Aberhart that no copies of his Sunday and week-night broadcasts given during 1933 have survived. Until January, 1934, newspaper reports of his Social Credit activities are rare: the journalists were, quite naturally, unaware that a new social movement was emerging. One early newspaper report, published in the *Calgary Herald* in February, 1933, conveys an impression of the type of public address he was giving as the movement took shape. Entitled "Decent Standard of Living For All Seen in Douglas Plan Applied in Alberta," the meeting was reported (in part) as follows:

Income for everybody, sufficient for food, shelter and clothing, regardless of occupation or lack of it; the competitive system retained but with its worst features removed; private enterprise permitted but not allowed to expand beyond the public good, such were some of the results seen in application of the principles of the so-called Douglas system to the conditions of Alberta.

William Aberhart explained the principles to a meeting of the Home and School Federation which overflowed the assembly hall of Victoria School Tuesday evening. Lively questioning followed the address, and discussion led by C. E. Burchill of Mount Royal College. Dr. G. W. Kerby presided.

Three principles are essential to the plan, but would be applied differently according to the circumstances of the country which adopted them. Mr. Aberhart said.

The basic idea is that all citizens of a country own its natural resources and are entitled to a share in their distribution, instead of permitting a few financiers to exploit them. From this it follows that a government must function for the benefit of all the citizens instead of favoring privileged classes, whether manufacturers, producers, or bankers. Every citizen is a consumer and so the consumer must be the first consideration of a government.

On the security of the natural resources the government would credit every man and woman each year with enough to feed, shelter and clothe them during the year. In payment for the necessities of life everyone would give non-negotiable notes on his account in this government credit house, which would then be transferred to the credit of whoever presented them. Such credits would have to be spent each year for any unspent remainder would be eliminated yearly. . . .

An automatic price control would be maintained by the government which would make hoarding of products impossible. For as the amount of goods increased the price would have to decline, thus keeping a balance between production and consumption. The producer would be guaranteed the cost of his product but there would be no profit allowed, only a commission. Those who wished to engage in production of a certain kind, against the advice of an advisory board, would be at liberty to do so, but would not be furnished with loans from the government credit house as would those who followed advice.

The result of these measures would be to keep up a constant purchasing power; to prevent alternate inflation and deflation at the will of the banks; to keep a constant flow of credit available for the productive industries and for the distribution of their products. . . .

Answering questions, Mr. Aberhart thought it no use whatever to appeal to Ottawa to introduce some such system. The financial control of government is too well known to need discussion, the speaker said. Nor can a political party be counted on, for they are out of date, and the speaker prophesied the end of all political parties shortly.

During the winter and spring months of 1933 Aberhart held a number of public meetings in schools and halls scattered throughout Calgary. It is recorded that five study groups were established outside the Institute during this period, but at this time the activities of these groups seem not to have been well directed. Until the autumn the

Institute remained the only regular centre for the systematic study of the new economics. Outside Calgary, an interest in Social Credit was developing in southern Alberta as a result of the Sunday afternoon broadcasts, which were devoted more and more to the exposition of economic theories. Aberhart soon began to receive invitations to give addresses on Social Credit in other cities and towns. He accepted as many of these as his duties permitted during the school term. In the late spring the demand for personal appearances became so persistent that from May throughout the summer of 1933 Aberhart and Manning were engaged in what amounted to an organized speaking tour of southern Alberta. During the vacation months of July and August, when this tour was at its height, the Social Credit group in the Institute was left in charge of an able group of ardent Douglas students, including Gilbert McGregor, C. G. Palmer, A. J. Logan, Archie Kennedy, and Mrs. H. Jarvis, who had emerged from the initial studies.

The interest that Aberhart had aroused, after only eight months' activity on behalf of Social Credit, is evident from his strenuous itinerary during the summer of 1933. For one month he and Manning were on the road five days a week, holding two meetings daily, and visiting some forty centres. The last meeting of the week was usually held on Friday night and the pair then spent the week-end in Calgary, fulfilling their regular duties at the Institute on Sunday, and leaving again on Monday. Announcements of addresses for the coming week were always made over the radio during the Sunday broadcasts. As Aberhart was swamped with invitations to speak, he could afford to choose the points for personal appearances to suit his convenience and advantage. All the advertising for the meetings was handled by radio; the educational nature of the tour and the economic conditions under which the people were living assured co-operation from many other quarters. People often drove fifty to sixty miles to attend these meetings, which drew such large audiences that every available seat was always occupied in the largest building the community possessed.

From the beginning Aberhart employed at these meetings a technique widely used by Social Crediters in Britain and the United States. A devoted follower would circulate through the audience, at a certain stage of the programme, petition blanks with attached pencils. Signatures would be obtained for the purpose of demanding of the government of Alberta that it should, at the earliest possible moment, proceed with a thorough investigation of Social Credit. If the Douglas proposals were found feasible, the government should implement them by legislative action immediately. The majority of those present always signed these petitions. Collections, which averaged about four cents per person, were taken to help defray the expenses of the work. In addition, there was a heavy sale of Yellow Pamphlets at the close of each meeting. A number of Douglas's books were carried for reference purposes and people were urged, if financially able, to purchase these for careful study during the winter months.

With two such efficient and experienced platform speakers as Aberhart and Manning giving addresses and answering questions, the people, if not always convinced, were inevitably stimulated to think anew about the problems of the depression. In every community visited, people were impressed by the self-sacrifice of the speakers. "Here were two men," one who heard them during that period has related, "not taking their much-deserved holidays in the hot summer weeks, and spending the entire time travelling and lecturing day and night, without one cent of financial remuneration. The collections did not meet the out-of-pocket expenses by a long ways. All for the cause of the common people for whom relief was long overdue! What a stimulus those lectures supplied!"

If the people were eager to hear Aberhart, he was just as eager to meet them. This was his first tour of the provincial towns. He had long dreamed of seeing his radio listeners face to face and at last Social Credit had supplied the opportunity. Manning, who acted as chauffeur during the tour, has estimated that 95 per cent of those who attended the meetings during that first triumphant summer were members of Aberhart's radio audience. It must have been most gratifying to Aberhart to find at every point he visited such a large number of people who had listened regularly to his broadcasts as far back as the commencement of his radio work in 1925. Hundreds had hoped for so long for the opportunity of shaking his hand and voicing personally their appreciation of his religious work. "How the faces of his radio Sunday School scholars did beam," an admiring observer has reported, "as they met Aberhart at these lectures. I am certain he never realized before just how far his work was reaching and its great accomplishments. It was these very people who had learned to know and trust him through his religious work who now threw off their coats to aid in advancing this new economic movement which he sponsored. At the larger places these followers provided curling rinks and hockey arenas with full seating accomodations requiring many days' work in preparation."

In a very significant sense the tour was localized: with few exceptions (of which such a distant point as Wainwright should be mentioned) the meetings were held south of a line drawn from Red Deer to Hanna. There was a marked tendency to focus the appeal around towns in southern Alberta such as Granum, Macleod (now Fort Macleod), Lethbridge, and Medicine Hat. Wherever they existed, branches of the Bible Institute were of course used for promotion purposes. The rise of the Social Credit movement in Alberta provides strong support for the view that, in Canada, monetary experiments "have tended to be closely related to religious experiments in means of salvation."[1] The vast majority of Aberhart's religious followers lived in southern Alberta, where drought and depression were experienced most severely: the Social Credit movement found its earliest enthusiasts among these religious followers: among these same people the movement has maintained its solidarity longest and most surely. The first tour, during the summer of 1933, gave the movement begun the previous autumn in the Institute such an impetus that its future was assured.

During Aberhart's summer tour the group of ardent Douglasites in charge of the week-night meetings at the Institute had worked enthusiastically and effectively. When the prophet returned to full control early in September he expressed surprise and pleasure at the crowds from all over Calgary who were surging into the Institute, clamouring for instruction in Social Credit. Requests for lectures on the new economics were also pouring in from nearby towns and villages. Faced with demands that he himself could not possibly meet, it became clear to him that the response of the people required new operating tactics. The value of the systematic indoctrination to which the members of the original study group in the Institute had been subjected for some eight months was now apparent. Aberhart appealed for volunteers from this group to spread the new gospel.

With their teacher's blessings most of the members of the group went forth from the Bible Institute. Under their aggressive leadership study groups were formed all over Calgary during the remaining months of 1933 and dozens of lectures were delivered in surrounding centres. These activities may be taken to mark the birth of the Social Credit movement as a social movement. But at the time its proponents were not conscious of the nature of the enterprise they were launching. As far as they could see they were merely meeting a need which had arisen as a result of the impact of Aberhart's activities upon the masses of the people. But had they been fully aware of the future of their movement they could hardly have proceeded more energetically or efficiently to their objectives. The

[1]See S. D. Clark, "The Religious Sect in Canadian Politics," *American Journal of Sociology*, vol. 51, no. 3, November 1945, pp. 207–16; "Religion and Economic Backward Areas," *Papers and Proceedings, American Economic Review*, vol. 41, no. 2, May, 1951, pp. 258–65.

dynamic quality of the movement from the autumn of 1933 until the provincial election of 1935 was largely due to this lack of clearly defined goals.

By the end of 1933 the conquest of Calgary was well under way. Study groups, based at first on school districts but later expanded in many other directions, were organized over the entire city. Systematic organizer though he was, Aberhart could not have succeeded so rapidly without the competitive zeal of his followers, some of whom were overcome with a desire to do nothing else but organize and lead study groups. The enthusiasm of Mrs. Donald L. MacCulloch, who had been the first to enrol in Aberhart's original study group, was characteristic of many others: "I went around myself," she relates, "to people's doors, talked Social Credit like a salesman, got them interested, and then called meetings in their homes to organize groups. I got the use of the Labor Temple for meetings of working people. Mr. Aberhart said of this, 'You're going into the Lion's Den.' I held meetings every week, on Tuesday nights, for over three years, in the Labor Temple. There was always a big placard on the door with my name, as president of the new group, and my telephone number. I was the first to begin the organization of groups outside the Institute. I formed twelve groups altogether." Such devotion to the movement became characteristic of many of Aberhart's followers throughout the whole of Alberta.

The winter of 1933–4 saw study groups organized in every quarter of Calgary: at the height of the enthusiasm during the spring and summer of 1935 there were sixty-three groups actively functioning in this city alone. Meetings were held the first four nights of each week in any kind of hall that could be obtained for little or no cost, and frequently in private homes. Friday nights were reserved for mass meetings in the upstairs auditorium of the Bible Institute, into which over 2,000 people regularly crowded. In the spring of 1934 Social Credit theories were the subject of universal and continuous discussion among the adult population of Calgary.

The conquest of Calgary proceeded almost simultaneously with the organization of study groups over a large area of southern Alberta. During 1934 groups were established in nearly every rural area south of Edmonton. But the Bible Institute remained the nerve-centre of all such activities: radio announcements of seemingly innumerable meetings for the forthcoming week would be made each Sunday afternoon from its pulpit. Such meetings were usually arranged through Manning (the secretary of the Institute) by local citizens who would almost invariably have been influenced by Aberhart's religious doctrines. The prophet was always especially gratified on the rare occasions when a former pupil of the Crescent Heights High School took the initiative in organizing a local meeting in some rural town or village on behalf of Social Credit. Efforts would always be made to secure Aberhart himself as the speaker for every meeting, but the group would be prepared to accept Manning or, indeed, any of the other accredited speakers sent out from the Institute. The hope would always remain, however, that Aberhart himself would come eventually. For the people of Alberta were definitely not satisfied at the opportunity merely of hearing him twice weekly on the radio. They had an overwhelming desire to meet him personally.

The religious background of the Social Credit movement was never far to seek, but during the autumn of 1933 it became apparent that not everyone who had become enthusiastic over Douglas's proposals was equally well disposed towards Aberhart's specifically religious doctrines. In fact the original study group in the Institute had contained a number of intellectuals who had little or no interest in religious matters. Among these were the leaders who had conducted the group during Aberhart's absence in the summer of 1933. Inspired by Charles G. Palmer, a university-educated business man to whom the depression had been far from kind, this secular group organized the New Age Club, easily the most intellectual and colourful of the 1,500 study groups that emerged in Alberta. Using Palmer's office as its headquarters, the New Age Club (which continued its activities until the early months of the Second World War) was destined to become the centre of the first of three serious schisms which have appeared within the Social Credit movement. From the first its leaders considered themselves at least the intellectual equals, if not the superiors, of Aberhart. Unlike all the other Social Credit groups inspired by the activities of the Bible Institute, the New Age Club followed the orthodox Douglas line and became officially affiliated with the Social Credit Secretariat in London.

Shortly after obtaining recognition from London the New Age Club published an extensive pamphlet entitled *The Douglas Proposals—Social Credit Principles Elucidated*. This pamphlet, which carried a large photograph of Douglas on its cover, contained in condensed form twelve articles written by David Warren Ryder in 1933 and published in the *San Francisco News*. It also listed the aims and policies of the New Age Club:

What we are primarily concerned with is: (1)—To spread the doctrine of social credit as devised by Major Douglas; (2)—To retain our affiliation with the Social Credit Secretariat of London, England, of which council Major Douglas is chairman, the function of which body is that of a service organization, acting as a critical and advisory body on the literature of the movement, and as a body receiving and giving suggestions for activities connected with social credit in all its aspects, political and technical, whilst maintaining a register of affiliated associations and groups throughout the world. It is not a directive organization, except upon request, for, in accordance with the social credit philosophy, it is left to the individual to decide upon his own activity, and for groups to determine the form of propaganda most suitable to their situation and personnel; (3)—To seek co-operation to the fullest extent with all who are social credit minded; (4) —To advance, by educational methods through the study groups and public meetings, the Douglas proposals, looking to their application in the province of Alberta and elsewhere; (5)—To render assistance to all social credit crusaders; (6)—To finance by membership fees and private and public contributions the above activities.

This statement indicates that, while the London Secretariat had no check on Aberhart at all, it had strongly influenced the directors of the New Age Club.

The Club became such an active centre in distributing literature and in sponsoring speakers for meetings both within and without Calgary that, in secular circles, and among the middle and upper classes of the city, it began to take on something of the prestige of the Institute itself as the centre of the new movement. Its leaders solicited funds without the prior consent of Aberhart, undertook speaking tours without his authorization, organized subsidiary study groups, and published pamphlets offering the orthodox Douglas interpretation of Social Credit. But the crowning personal indignity which the New Age Club inflicted upon Aberhart was the refusal of its members to submit to his censorship of their speeches.

In spite of growing friction, however, the New Age Club continued, until the spring of 1934, in close association with the personnel and activities of the Institute. Among its members were numbered some of the best minds, if not quite the best speakers, that the movement has attracted in Alberta. Within Calgary its secular approach appealed to professional people who, owing to religious indifference, had remained unmoved by Aberhart's activities. Its office, located in the Board of Trade building, served as a strategic centre for the distribution of Social Credit literature. In fact many of Aberhart's most zealous followers in later years, including Mrs. Edith Gostick, were first introduced to the new economics through the New Age Club. Its chief speakers, though not sought after as eagerly as Aberhart and Manning, were in great demand. One of them has estimated that he must have addressed at least 250 meetings in or beyond Calgary. There can be little doubt that the New Age Club had considerable appeal for the better educated person, but its philosophers were too analytical and unemotional to compete successfully with Aberhart for a large following among the masses of the people.

The New Age Club was especially active in selling pamphlets written by its own members. The most widely circulated of these pamphlets, written by Charles G. Palmer, the Club's secretary, was entitled *Are We Poor and How? Why the Douglas System of Social Credit Principles for Alberta.* After devoting several pages to an analysis, in terms of Douglas's doctrines, of the situation created in Alberta by the depression Palmer wrote:

The Douglas School of Economics lays the axe to the belief that in order to right ourselves we must have:

1. WORK.
2. CHANGE OF GOVERNMENT.
3. REVOLUTION BY FORCE.

or all three simultaneously combined. These, as will be shown, are vital fallacies and do not offer even a faint hope of fundamental help. The first two have often been tried out with disappointing results, while the third named recourse is unthinkable in this commonwealth of enlightened peoples.

Answering the first—LABOR-SAVING DEVICES have paved the way to human progress and being our cultural inheritance, should be used for the benefit of all, rather than a select few. They are like so many keys to unlock the doors to a GOLDEN AGE and a LEISURE (meaning unenforced activity) STATE.

To the second—A CHANGE OF GOVERNMENT is simply a change of bosses. What is proposed in Social Credit Principles is a change of Economic System. Cancer is not cured by a General Election but by a remedy.

As to REVOLUTION BY FORCE—Nowhere in the proposals of social or community credit, Real (not financial) Credit being vested in the consumer and based on the power to consume, do we find room or necessity for confiscation of rightfully owned property or repudiation of honest debt. Persuasion rather than force and education than coercion are the prompters. On our banner is not emblazoned the motto, "make the rich, poor," but "MAKE ALL RICH."

DIVIDENDS—CREDIT FLOW—
JUST PRICE

Since Purchasing Power in the hands of the consumer has become the vexed question of the day and since there is not lack of will to produce and consume, it is high time that our men of affairs became seized of the idea that the only way to put purchasing power into the hands of the consumer is to PUT purchasing power into the hands of the consumer, not by restricting or speeding up production or by re-dividing the too little of the means of exchange which we now possess, but by making new tokens and giving them away for nothing. Not BLUE EAGLES on your lapel but WHITE EAGLES in your pocket, not the Dole of Pity, the Hand-out of charity or the Gesture of Mock-Magnanimity, but the Dividend on your citizenship share in your country's Limited Liability Company, which is your right. In this sense the old rule is reversed—Every Country DOES owe its bona-fide citizens a living.

Away, says the Douglas System of Economics, with this lie of poverty. Let us equate consumption to production by a free, unrestricted and auto-matic flow of credit (the blood-stream of the nation) without interest and for the whole period of production, rather than by short-term, interest-bearing loans subject to call at inconvenient times.

Finally, let us by the distribution of a STATE DIVIDEND and the operation of a JUST PRICE FACTOR, cut the fungus-growth of finance from the tree of civilization.

Again we were wrong to call this inflation. There can be no inflation until there exists more than enough money with which to purchase consumers goods, as the Just Price obviates the usual fiasco attendant upon inflation.

LAWS, NOT PERSONNEL TO BLAME

Lest any of the foregoing statements be misconstrued, nothing herein contained is intended to reflect adversely on the personal character of our local bankers who are merely carrying out duties, having little or nothing to do with origination of financial policies. They in turn, who direct the performance of such tasks, disagreeable though they may be, are themselves the victims of their own devices and they too must profit by such economic changes as will shift from their minds the responsibility of longer operating and upholding a system resting on powder kegs of public discontent. The powder-train is already laid, the fuses are ready for lighting, with the public as the Guy Fawkes in the piece.

Operating under laws made for them by legislators of former generations, they are but playing the game of finance according to the rules. Shall we not forthwith change the rules?

Hardly any other study group that emerged from the activities of the Bible Institute followed the lead given by the New Age Club in placing itself under the supervision of the Douglas Secretariat. If Aberhart did not exactly prohibit close ties with London, he certainly did not en-courage them. Whatever central organization the Social Credit movement had during its early months was directly under the auspices of the Bible Institute. As each study group was formed it had the right to send two delegates to a Central Council which functioned as a third unit under the charter of the Bible Institute, the Bible Institute Baptist Church, which held morning and evening church services, constituting the second unit. The Central Council was a purely advisory body, whose executive (of which Aberhart was president, Palmer the vice-president, A. J. Logan the secretary) was elected by the members of the Bible Institute and not by Social Crediters as such. This arrangement was maintained until the spring of 1935, although hundreds of groups outside Calgary had sprung up during the previous eighteen months. It would be fair to say that, until the decision to go into politics was taken, no group challenged the paternalistic authority of the Bible Institute, with the exception of the New Age Club. For two-and-a-half years the organization of the Social Credit movement was maintained in the closest association with the Institute. But, until the spring of 1934, the key figures on the inner executive of the Central Council were also, with the exception of Aberhart and Manning, leading members of the New Age Club. Aberhart saw to it that the Central Council dealt almost entirely with group affairs. Although it had little policy-making power, it was, nevertheless, the germ from which the Southern and Northern Alberta Social Credit Leagues developed prior to the election of 1935.

If the Central Council had slight control of general policy, it seems to have had no jurisdiction whatever over the finances of the movement. From the beginning Aberhart stressed the need of contributions to promote Social Credit activities. Mimeographed lessons, leaflets, and pamphlets had to be paid for, and collections were always taken at meetings. Even when members of the New Age Club went out speaking, the collections always found their way to the Institute. Apparently it never occurred to Aberhart to pay either himself or anyone else for making speeches; speakers received only the barest allowance for necessary expenses. The prophet, presumably with the assent of the Institute's Board of Management, is said to have managed all the money that was sent in to the central office by the followers of Social Credit until the formation of the Social Credit Leagues in April, 1935. His reputation for honesty was such that no person dreamed of questioning him. In any event, the movement had the free use of the Institute and was thereby saved great expense. It may be that all general contributions went into the treasury of the Institute; even the members of the New Age Club, with few exceptions, felt that this procedure would have been quite proper as the movement was operating under the Institute's charter. It should be noted that certain of the original members of the Central Council, who later became bitter critics of Aberhart, were never prepared to assert publicly that he derived the slightest personal profit from Social Credit activities.

Although hundreds of speeches expounding Social Credit were made during 1933, the movement attracted very little newspaper publicity. Suddenly, in January, 1934, Social Credit activities began to receive almost daily notice in the Calgary press. In accounting for this remarkable change at least four factors must be considered. First, the movement had now gained such momentum that it could no longer be ignored: it had begun to have real news value. Second, the New Age Club contained a number of professional and business men who contrived to arouse fresh interest among journalists for whom Aberhart's strictly prophetic enterprises had long since ceased to be good copy. Third, the hot debate over Social Credit at the annual convention of the U.F.A. held at Edmonton in January attracted the attention of farmers all over the province. Fourth, through the conversion to Social Credit of a number of leaders among women of the middle class in Calgary, of whom the most active were Mrs. Edith Rogers and Mrs. F. G. Grevett, invitations for lectures on the new economics began to pour into the Institute from women's groups in every quarter of the city.

Aberhart was quick to realize that exploitation of the rapidly developing interest among farm and women's groups required the development of techniques of organization and promotion apart from the Institute's religious activities, with which Social Credit had hitherto been intimately linked. The early months of 1934 marked a turning-point in the evolution of the movement. Henceforth, while the religious appeal was never far beneath the surface, the secular emphasis became more and more prominent. The impact of the four factors mentioned above was cumulative: increased excitement and publicity led to thousands of new converts in both urban and rural areas: the increased momentum led, in turn, to still further excitement and publicity. By the spring of 1934 the movement had broken through the barriers hitherto imposed upon it by prophetic fundamentalism and was sweeping through southern Alberta like a prairie fire. But no matter how many secular circles might propagate the theories of Social Credit, it must not be forgotten that the brown-faced Bible Institute remained the undisputed headquarters of the movement.

On routine tours late in 1933 officials of the U.F.A. had already begun to feel the groundswell of the movement in rural Alberta. But they attached no political significance to the penetration of Social Credit ideas into the rank and file of the U.F.A. The movement was first invested with political implications on January 6, 1934, when four candidates in a provincial by-election in Calgary appeared before the executive committe of the Central Council to give their views on Social Credit.[2] On January 11 Aberhart was reported as urging Social Crediters to support only those candidates who promised to press for an early governmental enquiry into the merits of Social Credit.[3] The following night, speaking on "Social Credit and the By-election" before a capacity

[2]*Calgary Herald*, January 8, 1934.
[3]*Ibid.*, January 13, 1934.

audience in the Institute, he reiterated the slogan "Vote for Social Credit." On January 17 a mass meeting of 700 women in the Institute voted unanimously to wire a resolution petitioning the United Farm Women of Alberta, then in convention in Edmonton, to give its support to an investigation by the Alberta government of the Douglas system.[4] Under such pressures a debate on the feasibility of Social Credit for Alberta could not be kept off the agenda of the U.F.A. convention which met in Edmonton concurrently with the U.F.W.A.

During this debate, the hostility that developed between the Co-operative Commonwealth Federation and monetary reform factions revealed the extent of the internal strife within the U.F.A. When it was over the socialists had scored at least a technical victory. The outstanding resolution of the convention was a motion for the adoption as far as "are practicable and applicable to provincial affairs" of the policies of the C.C.F. in a provincial political platform to be prepared by the Board of Directors for submission to the convention in 1935. But the wide divergence of opinion is evident from another resolution that called for "an investigation by the C.C.F. executive into the Douglas Social Credit proposals and their careful consideration by the provincial government with a view to their introduction if found feasible." Faced with such resolutions, the harassed U.F.A. premier and his Cabinet felt justified in postponing a decision as to what to do about Social Credit until at least the meeting of the legislature in February.

Their delay enabled the Liberals, who were deriving new hope from the growing schism within the U.F.A., to seize the initiative. On February 10, W. R. Howson, the provincial Liberal leader, filed a resolution in the legislature demanding an enquiry into Douglas Social Credit with Aberhart and Douglas as the principal witnesses.[5] Not to be outdone in the federal field, William Irvine (who had long been partial to theories of monetary reform), the U.F.A. Member of Parliament for Wetaskiwin, asked a committee of the House of Commons to call Aberhart and Douglas before it to explain the new economic theory.[6]

The enthusiasm for Social Credit developing in rural areas was accompanied by a sudden outburst of interest among women's organizations in Calgary. From the middle of January accounts of Social Credit lectures given to women's groups appeared nearly every day in the *Calgary Herald* and the Calgary *Albertan*. These accounts indicate that socially prominent converts were constantly engaged in organizing lec-

[4]*Ibid.*, January 18, 1934.
[5]*Ibid.*, February 10, 1934.
[6]*Ibid.*, March 8, 1934.

tures and study groups in women's circles. "Women generally," Mrs. Grevett announced on January 11, "are taking a greater interest in economics, and are endeavoring to find a system which will put purchasing power into the hands of the consumer. Women are anxious, in the interest of the home, that our high standard of living shall be preserved."[7] On January 17 Mrs. W. E. Callbeck, the principal speaker at a meeting of 700 women in the Institute

gave a lucid picture of the life of the individual, the home and the state under the present system. She claimed that since manual labor is being displaced consistently by mechanization, work can no longer be the medium by which purchasing power may be distributed. "Shall we scrap the modern machinery of production or shall we adopt a more adequate system and keep pace with modern science and invention?" she asked.[8]

At the same meeting Manning dealt with the fundamentals of the Douglas system, C. H. Wilmott appealed to the audience to study that system, Mrs. W. W. Rogers outlined her work as women's organizer, and Aberhart spoke briefly.

The systematic indoctrination and organization taking place among women's groups is well indicated in an announcement, typical of scores of others, that appeared in the *Calgary Herald* on January 27:

A meeting for women who are interested in economics will be held at the Prophetic Bible Institute, 516 Eighth Avenue west, next Monday evening at 8 o'clock.

Mr. Ernest Manning will discuss the Douglas System of social credit. Members of the economics groups of the University Women's Club, the Business and Professional Women's Club, and the women school teachers of this city are especially invited to attend.

Monday evening's meeting is the first of a series of four lectures on economics. Discussion will be invited. These classes are in charge of Mrs. W. W. Rogers, the women's organizer.

Such meetings were always relieved by the inclusion of musical numbers. When the size of the gathering permitted, there would be a social hour at which tea would be served.

Whenever the newspaper publicity given to lectures and group discussions showed signs of decreasing, the women's leaders organized bazaars, mass teas at the Institute, and picnics. Social Credit doctrine was advanced in terms of any and every activity in which women might be interested. An account of a meeting of the Women's Christian Tem-

[7]*Ibid.*, January 11, 1934.
[8]*Ibid.*, January 18, 1934.

perance Union in February illustrates the techniques of penetration that were constantly used:

> Economics and social reform were so closely interlocked that any attempt to separate them would result disastrously for both, Mr. William Aberhart told the quarterly meeting of the Calgary WCTU branches, lecturing to them on the Douglas plan and social reform.
> At the present moment all social workers found their efforts blocked by economic distress. He proposed the Douglas System of economics as a way out for both economic distress and social reform.
> Taking in turn the four pillars of society, namely: home, school, church and state, Mr. Aberhart pointed out the increased power to efficiency, which would come to each under the Douglas System.
> Quoting President Wilson, the speaker said, "Poverty and famine have never been known to breed reform, but increase debauchery." By guaranteeing food, clothing, and shelter a healthy atmosphere would be created, which in itself would do much toward eradicating many present social evils.[9]

At still other meetings the Douglas system was related to the peace movement, to the financial problems of working class women, to housing, and, of course, to scriptural teaching concerning a new social order. For those interested in mental health a series of meetings was held in the public library on "Psychology and the Douglas System," a course which included a lecture entitled "Mind and Its Functions." No interest was too remote, no group too inconsequential for the Social Crediters to argue their doctrine before it.

The barrage of meetings and publicity within Calgary during the winter months profoundly impressed the villages, towns, and other cities of southern Alberta, all of which were served by the metropolis's newspapers. With initial assistance from Aberhart's speakers, the Douglas system was presented to organized groups in every direction. Beginning as a big-city enterprise, the Social Credit movement was transferred to the small towns within a year of its inception. Control of the Institute's radio facilities enabled Aberhart to give efficient, even though remote, supervision to organizational work outside Calgary. Each newly organized study group was admonished to listen to the Institute's Sunday afternoon broadcasts, to write in for speakers, literature, and guidance. By the summer of 1934 the small-town character of the Social Credit movement had been definitely established.

Nor were the rural districts far behind the small towns in their enthusiasm for the movement. If the leaders of the farmers were cold to Aberhart's ideas from the beginning, the rank and file of the U.F.A.

[9] *Ibid.*, February 16, 1934.

membership were much more receptive. As we shall explain more fully in later chapters, considerable sentiment for monetary reform had long existed within the ranks of the U.F.A. In nearly every local there would generally be at least one person to whom monetary reform had become the best hope for the future. Inspired anew by Aberhart's mission, these devotees within the U.F.A. locals actively promoted his cause as their own. Under their influence, the locals, in ever-increasing numbers, requested speakers and literature from the Institute. The U.F.A. leaders were tireless in their efforts to halt the spread of Social Credit. They were seriously handicapped, of course, by court actions which were hanging over the heads of the Premier and his Minister of Public Works. The importance of the scandals in providing fuel for the Social Credit movement can be over-estimated. Undoubtedly, the scandals weakened the U.F.A. cause but the strength of the Social Credit movement in rural areas was derived essentially from a positive rather than a negative appeal. During the winter of 1934 some U.F.A. locals in southern Alberta had already become Social Credit study groups, a process which was greatly accelerated throughout the whole province during the following year.

In accounting for the rapid expansion of the movement during the winter of 1934 the activities of the New Age Club should not be underestimated. Its speakers were as tireless as those of the Institute itself in spreading doctrine and in promoting the organization of study groups not only in Calgary but in small towns and rural areas as well. This Club originated one technique in particular which caught the imagination of Alberta, and from which Aberhart himself learned an instructive lesson in the art of propaganda. Following the debate on Social Credit at the U.F.A. convention, the New Age Club circulated a petition on behalf of the Douglas System. Entitled *For the Good of Each and All*, the petition contained four clauses:

Whereas our country lies in the throes of severe economic depression, and many of our loyal bona fide citizens are in dire need of the bare necessities of food, clothing and shelter which they are unable to obtain for lack of purchasing power:

And whereas our granaries, warehouses and elevators are full to overflowing, of the necessities required, to such an extent that much of our products are being wantonly destroyed or wasted:

And whereas there seems to be no prospect of deliverance from any source within our Province in spite of the fact that three years have elapsed and conditions are growing steadily worse:

Be it therefore resolved that we petition our provincial Government Representative to take into careful consideration, the method of solution known as *The Douglas System* and after investigation, if he finds this system feasible, that he press for action to inaugurate it at as early a date as possible so that it may be given a fair trial.

As presented to the six Calgary M.L.A.'s the petition contained a type-written list of the names of 12,000 citizens, whose signatures indicated that they must have been influenced, in greater or less degree, by the new movement. Such tangible evidence of the popularity of Social Credit ideas seems, for the first time, to have startled political leaders in all parties.

At the very period when the publicity attending the successful circula-tion of the petition was at its height a bitter controversy arose within the inner circle of the movement. This controversy may be interpreted as a struggle between Aberhart and the New Age Club for control of the movement. In its essence it was, however, the opening battle in a contest concerning the correct interpretation of Douglas's doctrines which has continued intermittently for the last quarter of a century.

There were at least four contributory causes of the controversy of February, 1934: the interpretation of Social Credit given in Toronto by C. V. Kerslake, then secretary of the Douglas Credit League of Canada; an attack on Aberhart's version of Social Credit by Larkham Collins during a press interview in Vancouver; the growing hostility between Aberhart and the New Age Club in Calgary; and, finally, the attitude of the Douglas Secretariat in London. Some understanding of each of these factors is necessary for an assessment of the total situation with which Aberhart was faced at that time.

As we have seen, Aberhart had not been the first to introduce Social Credit ideas into Canada or even into Alberta. But his group at the Institute seems to have been the first organized study group, formed, as it was, in January, 1933. But other groups soon sprang up in various provinces, mainly through the influence of Englishmen coming out to Canada, or through readers of *New Age*, the *New English Weekly*, and Douglas's books. The Douglas Credit League of Canada was organized in April, 1933, with headquarters at Toronto. During the next ten months the League's secretary, C. V. Kerslake, sought to locate and coalesce all the Douglas supporters in Canada. Kerslake (who con-sistently maintained that the League was an educational association, and not interested in any political party) seems to have received no co-operation whatever from Aberhart. During the visit of the Royal Commission on Banking to Toronto, Kerslake, in a private conversation with one of its members, Premier John Brownlee, stated that, owing to the B.N.A. Act, Social Credit could not be introduced at the provincial level. Shortly afterwards, in November, 1933, the *Ottawa Citizen*, edited by Charles A. Bowman, an old friend of Douglas, embarked on a long crusade for Social Credit. The Douglas Credit League, which had obtained official recognition from London, now appointed provincial organizers in British Columbia and Quebec and began to make arrangements for organizers in Alberta, Saskatchewan, and Ontario. But in Alberta it received no co-operation except from a few groups that had officially affiliated with the London Secretariat. Of these the strongest and most active was, of course, the New Age Club. It is highly probable that Kerslake reported Aberhart's intransigence to London and that he also used the New Age Club as a lash to bring the Alberta movement into line.

Apart from organized groups there were also a number of independent students of Social Credit. Of these, the most prominent in Calgary was Larkham Collins, a leading accountant, who had prepared an elaborate analysis of Douglas's theories for the Open Mind Club. In an interview given to the *Vancouver Sun* during a visit to the Pacific coast, Collins assailed Aberhart's understanding of Social Credit in no uncertain terms. This attack, which was widely publicized in Alberta, came at the same time as the New Age Club and the London Secretariat were also closing in on Aberhart. Engaged as he was in two major activities, in addition to his duties as high school principal, it is small wonder that Aberhart's resolution began to weaken under the strain of constant criticism.

Although the evidence is not conclusive, there can be little doubt that the leaders of the New Age Club encouraged the mounting criticism of Aberhart's interpretation of Social Credit during the winter of 1934. Such keen and independent students of Douglas as Palmer, Gilbert McGregor, and W. D. MacLean had concluded that, under the B.N.A. Act, monetary reform could not be achieved at the provincial level. With the support of Kerslake, Collins, and the London Secretariat they became more and more outspoken. They were also becoming extremely dissatisfied over the close association of the movement with the Institute: at one point the question of obtaining an alternative headquarters was actually raised. But it was probably Aberhart's insistence on supervision of speeches, lecture schedules, and finances that most irked the proud intellectuals of the New Age Club. As these men were as passionately devoted to Social Credit as Aberhart, they always thought of themselves as working for the movement rather than the Institute. At this stage it was still impossible for Aberhart to think of his Social Credit following apart from his religious following. He could, therefore, afford no criticism which imperilled his position as Dean of the Institute. There is some evidence, difficult to evaluate objectively, that the leaders of the New Age Club were considering the chances of a successful challenge of Aberhart's leadership. The controversy may best be understood as a struggle for control of the movement, in which both ideological and administrative issues were involved. Towards the end of February the intervention of the London Secretariat gave the New Age Club, for two months at least, the upper hand.

The immediate cause of the Secretariat's intervention was the Yellow Pamphlet, *The Douglas System of Economics*, which we have reviewed above. A copy of this pamphlet had apparently been shown to Douglas by a friend of Aberhart's who was visiting in England. Douglas, presumably without reading the pamphlet completely, autographed it, "C. H. Douglas, with Kind Regards." In due course, it found its way back to Aberhart, who contended thereafter that Douglas's autograph amounted to an endorsement of its contents. Early in 1934, however, the pamphlet came to the attention of the London Secretariat, to whom it was apparently forwarded by Kerslake, presumably at the instigation of the secretary of the New Age Club. The Secretariat then wrote a letter to Aberhart (of which Charles G. Palmer, as secretary of the New Age Club, also received a copy) informing him that they could not officially endorse his movement and requesting that the name "Douglas" be removed from his pamphlet. Both Aberhart and Palmer received this letter on February 23. Few Social Crediters, of course, were aware of the sequence of events which lay behind an advertisement appearing on the church page of the Calgary newspapers the following day. But, over the week-end, hardly anything else was discussed among either the inner circle or the mass following of the movement.

In this advertisement Aberhart announced that he would give his last address in Calgary on the Douglas System the following Monday night in the Institute.[10] On the day scheduled for the meeting, the advertisement was confirmed by a news item: "William Aberhart will give what is announced as his last address on the Douglas system this evening in the Prophetic Bible Institute, speaking on 'The Douglas System and Peace.' "[11]

At this crowded and memorable meeting, with many of his followers weeping as he spoke, Aberhart claimed he was being persecuted and posed as a martyr. He told the audience he was being accused of presenting his own views of Social Credit and this he denied. He recounted that he had been attacked by Kerslake and Collins, and referred to the

[10]Calgary *Albertan*, February 24, 1934.
[11]*Ibid.*, February 26, 1934; *Calgary Herald*, February 27, 1934.

literature he had prepared for his followers. But he did not tell the meeting that the Secretariat had made it plain that his version of Social Credit could not be given official approval. At the climax, when he announced his resignation as President of the Social Credit movement, an impassioned disciple dashed madly to the platform and defended him in an incoherent and frenzied speech. A resolution protesting Collins's accusations, as reported in the *Vancouver Sun*, was passed unanimously and forwarded to that newspaper's management.

The following day the newspapers announced that Aberhart had resigned because of criticism by one faction of the movement in Toronto. Declining to give details of the criticisms to the press, Aberhart said he had stepped aside until the arrival of Major C. H. Douglas, for whom a visit to Alberta was being projected by a special committee of the legislature for the purpose of considering various plans of credit management. One newspaper added that "followers of Mr. Aberhart claimed Tuesday that manuscripts of their leader's pamphlets on Social Credit had been approved by Major Douglas himself before they had gone to press." But it was also made clear in the news items that Aberhart's resignation was the result of a long controversy over the correct interpretation of Social Credit with the members of the New Age Club, some of whom had "criticized from public platforms the interpretation placed upon the theory by Mr. Aberhart." Questioned concerning the future of the movement, Charles G. Palmer, vice-president of the Central Council, announced that Social Credit activities would be continued as vigorously as ever after Aberhart's retirement.[12] Shortly afterwards Gilbert McGregor was elected president of the Central Council or (as it was now coming to be called) Social Credit League, not by its members but by the officials of the Institute. The New Age Club seemed to have emerged victorious from the bitter controversy, even though Palmer, its moving spirit, had failed of election to the leadership of the movement, owing to the Institute's stand on alcoholic beverages.

Under the new leadership no diminution of popular interest in Social Credit seems to have occurred. If Aberhart's resignation was a play for absolute power, as his opponents have suggested, he must have been disappointed at the immediate returns. For the movement continued to roll along with crowded mass meetings and enthusiastic study groups as before. Nor did Aberhart adhere to his statement that he would give no more public addresses in Calgary on Social Credit. Although withdrawing from the Friday night meetings, he continued to weave the new economics into the Sunday afternoon broadcasts. Within three weeks his

[12]Calgary *Albertan*, February 28, 1934.

appearance before the Agricultural Committee of the legislature made him front page news again throughout the province. In the small towns and rural districts, many adherents of the movement seem either not to have known of his displacement as leader or to have attached no significance to it. This was perhaps not surprising, for his religious broadcasts were still heard every Sunday whereas McGregor had no radio facilities.

If Aberhart's resignation had no apparent effect upon the response of the people it influenced the future of the movement in two important respects. First, the dissension encouraged opponents of the movement to attack Aberhart much more vigorously than previously. Under this severe criticism Aberhart was forced to consolidate his interpretation of Social Credit to the point of no return. Second, the first visit of the author of the Social Credit theories to Alberta came during McGregor's tenure of office. In every way possible the opponents of Social Credit used the controversy with the New Age Club to confuse, if not actually to mislead, Douglas concerning Aberhart's real position in the movement. Their tactics were successful in so far as the future personal relationships between Aberhart and Douglas were concerned: the misunderstanding engendered between these two men had far-reaching effects upon the movement in Alberta and, indeed, in Canada at large.

Three important events in the development of the movement occurred during McGregor's régime: Aberhart's testimony before the Agricultural Committee of the legislature; Douglas's testimony before the same committee; and Douglas's appearance at a mass meeting in Calgary. It is significant that McGregor himself had no part in the legislative hearings; if he influenced certain circumstances attending Douglas's Calgary appearance, Social Crediters at large remained unaware of such activities.

As the legislative hearings represent a transition from the first or educational phase of the movement to its second or semi-political phase, they are considered in the next chapter. But Douglas's Calgary visit, as distinguished from his participation in the hearings at Edmonton, was a very important event in the earlier phase of the movement. Considering the attitude of financial and business leaders to Social Credit, the circumstances under which that event was arranged constitute a remarkable example of the evolution of the unintended.

Shortly after the government's announcement on February 22 that Douglas would come to Alberta in April as its "reconstruction advisor," certain members of the Open Mind Club conceived the idea of inviting him "as a lark" to address a public meeting in Calgary. As the plan matured, they realized that Douglas might well be used to discredit Aberhart and designed their arrangements to that end. Inspired by

Larkham Collins, a keen student of Douglas's writings and a severe critic of Aberhart, they succeeded in inducing the Calgary Canadian Club to act as joint sponsor of the meeting, and to arrange that Douglas's speech should be broadcast. It was carefully planned that Aberhart would not be invited to join leaders of the sponsoring organizations and civic officials on the platform the night of the meeting. They expected that Aberhart would be so humiliated at such treatment that he would not even attend as a member of the audience.

When Social Crediters read in the newspapers that Douglas would speak in Calgary, they were puzzled that no mention was made of Aberhart's part in the arrangements (though McGregor was the titular leader of the movement at that time). They were infuriated when it became known that Aberhart was being deliberately snubbed by Douglas's sponsors.

Aberhart never divulged to his followers that he himself had also been rebuffed by Douglas. Shortly after Douglas arrived in Vancouver (following a triumphant tour of Australia and New Zealand), Aberhart telephoned, offering him a Sunday afternoon broadcast at the Institute, promising a large listening audience. Douglas declined this invitation, stating that he had already accepted Larkham Collins's invitation to address a public meeting in Calgary. During Douglas's first visit to Alberta, Aberhart had other opportunities of realizing the extent to which Douglas had been prejudiced against him both by C. V. Kerslake in Toronto and by the leaders of the New Age and Open Mind Clubs in Calgary. It is reported, for example, that on Douglas's arrival at Edmonton from Vancouver, to participate in the legislative hearings on his theories, he brusquely elbowed Aberhart out of his way on the station platform and went off with Collins.

If Aberhart suffered such indignities in silence, it was quite otherwise with his followers. Prominent women leaders in the Social Credit movement, as well as many men, made sharp protests to Collins and his associates regarding their shabby treatment of Aberhart. At first the Open Mind and Canadian Club leaders attempted to side-step the issue; finally, under great pressure, two days before Douglas's meeting, they invited Aberhart to be a guest of honour on the platform. At first he declined. When it became known that he would not attend, public feeling ran high in Calgary. Rumours circulated that the railway workers at the Ogden Shop, a strong Social Credit centre, were determined not to let Douglas speak unless Aberhart were on the platform. Aberhart still insisted that he did not wish to attend the meeting. Then, it is said, the Ogden Social Crediters told him once again, in no uncertain terms, that he had better go to the meeting or Douglas would not be allowed to speak. Faced with the determined stand of his followers, as well as to prevent an uproar at the meeting, Aberhart reluctantly agreed to accept the invitation to appear on the platform. Having been forced by the public outcry to accept Aberhart's physical presence, Collins and his associates now carefully arranged that he should have no other role at the meeting.

Although Douglas's appearance at the Calgary Armouries had been arranged by Aberhart's critics and opponents, Social Crediters considered it one of the most notable and dramatic events in the history of their movement. To many outside the movement, who were unaware of the intention underlying the meeting, it seemed as if Douglas's ideas had finally received recognition from the *élite* of the city. The chairman of the meeting, who was a prominent alderman as well as president of the Canadian Club, was loudly applauded for his introductory remarks that "if Major Douglas can propound a plan applicable to this province to bring a feeling of order and security out of the chaos existing at the present time . . . he will be the greatest human benefactor this country and this world has ever seen."[13] As an especially high honour, Douglas was welcomed and introduced enthusiastically by the Mayor of Calgary himself.

When Aberhart mounted the platform, the crowd had yelled repeatedly, "We Want Aberhart!" The brass band played more loudly, as it had been instructed, in an effort to quell the disturbance. But during the preliminaries the crowd kept demanding "When is Aberhart going to speak?" They became quieter when the chairman gave the impression that Aberhart would be allowed to speak—after Douglas. During his address, which lasted for nearly two hours, Douglas remained unperturbed although some of the audience left, others frequently broke the thread of his discourse by prolonged applause, and still others continued to demand Aberhart. When Douglas finally concluded, without having once referred to Aberhart, the crowd gave a very rough time to another prominent alderman who attempted to offer a vote of thanks. Shouting frantically, "We Want Aberhart," a large section of the audience staged a football rush from the bleacher seats to the centre of the hall. The chairman, realizing that the meeting was completely out of hand, cut short his fellow alderman and signalled the band to play "God Save the King." The uproar was so great that, even with the band playing its loudest, the music of the anthem could scarcely be heard. So ended the only public meeting that Douglas ever addressed in Alberta.

[13]*Calgary Herald*, April 9, 1934.

The memorable evening concluded with an episode that, while it seemed not to shake the phlegmatic Douglas, casts a revealing light upon Aberhart's subsequent attitudes to and relationships with him. With the meeting ending in a tumultuous uproar, Aberhart accompanied Douglas to quarters in the Officers' Mess which were being used as a cloakroom. Here, impeccable witnesses have reported, an altercation developed, almost accidentally as it were, between the two men. Stung by the success of the official effort to ignore him, even in the face of the crowd's imperious demands, the emotionally overwrought Aberhart accused Douglas, it is said, of sabotaging the Yellow Pamphlet and of generally failing to support the Alberta Social Credit movement. Douglas, it is reported, replied to these accusations by suggesting that Aberhart's knowledge of Social Credit theory, and especially its application, was inadequate and that the Yellow Pamphlet should be withdrawn. Instead of a discussion of basic principles the conversation degenerated into a violent quarrel: others present, it is said, were astonished at Aberhart's rough language as well as by the childlike bickering between the two men. "It was," one of the witnesses has stated, "really an awful quarrel and quite a disgraceful thing to happen to men in their positions." This unfortunate encounter was, apparently, one of the only two occasions on which Douglas and Aberhart ever talked to each other personally.

In their relationship to Douglas's visit the women of Calgary fared much more happily than the men. Sponsored by prominent women organizers of the Social Credit movement, a mammoth reception and tea was held in honour of Mrs. Douglas at the city's leading hotel. It was carefully arranged that Aberhart should casually, quite by accident, happen along at an appropriate moment and, by popular demand, be invited to speak, entirely impromptu, of course, to the gathering. Naturally, his talk was enthusiastically applauded, but, more important, it also won Mrs. Douglas's admiration and gave her a different impression than her husband had received of Aberhart's position in the Alberta Social Credit movement. In reporting this social function, the newspapers played up at considerable length Mrs. Douglas's intelligence, charm, career, and interest in her husband's theories, but failed altogether to mention Aberhart's speech.

Douglas's speech, by contrast, received unusually extensive coverage in metropolitan as well as rural newspapers in Alberta. In most of the newspapers it was dramatized with banner headlines, large pictures, and box references to highlights of the meeting. The *Calgary Herald*, for example, devoted twelve columns, or one-and-a-half pages, to a complete report of the speech, thereby giving it the status of a major historic event.[14]

Although the newspapers dramatized the event, Aberhart's followers formed a very unfavourable impression of Douglas both as a speaker and as a thinker. As a speaker, he was stolid and unemotional, he seldom raised his voice above a monotonous conversational tone, resorted to no tricks of oratory, and made no attempt to arouse enthusiasm in his audience by flights of rhetoric. He was obviously no match for the colourful Aberhart.

In his opening remarks, Douglas astonished Social Crediters by his massive ignorance of the Alberta situation. He confided to his audience that he had recently taken steps to obtain democratic leadership for Social Credit in Alberta: he had invited his old friend, Charles A. Bowman, editor of the *Ottawa Citizen,* and one of the very first and very best students of Social Credit in Canada, to preside at an organizing conference of Social Crediters, to be held somewhere in the Middle West. Bowman had accepted this invitation and, Douglas informed his audience, "any further steps will, of course, be entirely in your hands."

Following this naïve opening, Douglas criticized the economic system mercilessly and outlined, in the most general terms, a plan of attack for Social Crediters. Absolute unity of all classes was imperative in the battle for financial freedom. "It is a fight," he asserted, "which is in no sense in the interests of any single class of society." Although the breaking of the monopoly of credit, the money power, would have its greatest physical effect upon the down and out classes, there was no class which did not suffer either physically or mentally from the effects of the present outworn financial system. The groups or organizations which controlled national and international credit would not give up their power "unless made to let go in the nature of something that may be termed a war." The stakes in this struggle were tremendous: they were nothing less than the life or death of civilization, and perhaps the life or death of the major portion of the population. The greatest present danger, apart from war, was the possibility that the power of the financial system might be transferred to the state. The propounding of a perfect plan to break the monopoly of credit was of minor importance compared to the possibility of putting that plan over. There were many plans, including his own; but immediately some simple method of managing the money system was evolved, it was either declared illegal or made illegal within a very short time. As far as Alberta was con-

[14]*Ibid.* The summary of Douglas's speech given below is based on the *Herald*'s complete text.

cerned, the present objective must be the creation of a condition that would make the application of a plan possible. This could be achieved only by bringing pressure to bear on federal representatives until the final movement for reform was made in London!

If Aberhart's followers were disappointed in Douglas as a speaker, they were infuriated by the content of his address. Expecting that he would deal with the more advanced aspects of Social Credit, they considered his presentation to be elementary. He had spoken as if Social Credit ideas were entirely new to them: he did not tell them anything that Aberhart had not already presented more pleasantly and profoundly. They were especially critical of the elusive generalities by which he sought to conceal (as they interpreted it) his inability to offer a detailed Social Credit plan for Alberta.

Douglas's appearance in Calgary on April 7, 1934, made quite a different impact on the development of the Social Credit movement than its promoters had intended. It marked the first attempt of Aberhart's critics to enlist Douglas's support in discrediting him. As far as Social Crediters were concerned, this attempt was a dismal failure. It turned out, in fact, to be a boomerang: Social Crediters were now completely convinced that Aberhart was a much more effective exponent of Social Credit theories than Douglas. After having seen Douglas in action, they refused to accept further criticisms of the adequacy of Aberhart's exposition of Social Credit. Compared to the great Aberhart, Douglas was now perceived as a very little man inded. As a result of Douglas's indifference to him, Aberhart was henceforth encouraged to go his own way, relying entirely on the response of his mass following for the justification of whatever strategy and tactics might be adopted. Nothing more was heard, of course, of Douglas's proposal for a conference of Western Social Crediters to select a democratic leader: nothing serious, that is, but Aberhart's followers had many a laugh over such an inane idea. Finally, the dramatization of Douglas's appearance by the newspapers also benefited the Social Credit movement. Never before had Social Credit ideas recieved such publicity in Alberta. Once the publicity had begun on such a large scale, Aberhart and his followers were quick to seize every opportunity of continuing and expanding it. Douglas's Calgary speech, therefore, launched a new era in the newspapers' attitudes to Aberhart's movement: henceforth Aberhart's activities, as well as the activities of his principal associates, became front-page news. From whatever aspect one considers it, the plan to use Douglas to denigrate Aberhart redounded entirely to the advantage of the latter. Aberhart learned much from this ordeal, but the leaders of the U.F.A. apparently remained oblivious to what had happened.

At the conclusion of the hearings before the Agricultural Committee of the legislature in April the government announced that a report on Douglas's proposals would be prepared and published within a few weeks. This announcement was followed by a lull in the activities of the movement, a calm period that would not occur again for several years, as the people were now expecting that at long last the government would take decisive action. Such a lull was natural, for up to this time the work of the movement had been educational, with no emphasis on political implications. Certainly no suggestion had hitherto been made that the movement should run its own candidates in the forthcoming provincial election. The people had forced the theories of Social Credit on the attention of their elected representatives. It was now up to the government. But it was widely felt that the legislative enquiry had marked a new stage in the evolution of the movement. The people had become convinced that something *must* be done about Social Credit. If the government should refuse to act, more drastic steps than had hitherto been contemplated would have to be taken.

The popular belief that monetary reform could be achieved at the provincial level was not shared by the titular head of the movement. During the legislative hearings McGregor's position had steadily deteriorated. Possessed of an analytical mind, he was essentially the student type. His speeches, although clear and forceful, were incapable of arousing personal devotion among the masses. His determined stand in favour of federal, rather than provincial, action had set him, as well as his companions in the New Age Club, apart from the grass-root sources of the movement. Severely handicapped by his personal financial position, he suffered most of all from the lack of a headquarters with radio facilities. Thus he had no way of keeping in touch with the several hundred organized groups that had developed in the province by the time of his election to the presidency.

By the middle of April it was clear that the people were not responding to McGregor's interpretation of Social Credit. His position as leader of the movement was no longer tenable. Early in May, McGregor, who no longer wished to continue in office, had a stormy interview with Aberhart prior to a meeting of the Central Council in the Institute. He told Aberhart that, immediately following the reading of the minutes, he would propose that he should resume office as president. Aberhart refused this offer, not because he did not want to be head of the movement again, but because he desired a triumphant return by popular demand, and this had not materialized. McGregor resigned that same night and an acting president was appointed.

Early in May an overwhelming demand for Aberhart's return to leadership was heard throughout the movement. Faced with the necessity of organizing a summer campaign, Aberhart enthusiastically resumed the presidency of the Central Council and the leadership of the movement. For the masses of the people he had, in fact, never ceased to be the leader. But his tactics had now left him in a position to gain what must have been his primary objective when he resigned in February—undisputed control of the movement.

His first act was to force the Douglasites of the New Age Club out of the executive of the Central Council and, within a short time, entirely out of the movement proper. Palmer and Logan were displaced as vice-president and secretary respectively and their positions filled by Mrs. Grevett and Manning. McGregor, who continued to address meetings outside Calgary, was informed that his speeches must henceforth be scrutinized by the president before delivery. McGregor naturally refused to accept such censorship and withdrew from the movement. Although invited a month later to return, McGregor refused, feeling that he could never meet the conditions laid down by Aberhart. The break between the two men was so complete that only twice thereafter did they have even a casual conversation together. Thus ended a period in the development of the movement which eliminated the influence of Douglas and elevated Aberhart as the supreme interpreter of doctrine. From May, 1934, Aberhart's followers covered the province with the slogan, "Social Credit for Alberta." Thereafter, the ideology of the movement was advanced as the brain-child of Aberhart. The most devoted and enthusiastic of his followers among the original builders of the Social Credit movement had suffered the same fate as similar followers among the original builders of the Institute itself in 1927. The new group that gathered around him in the inner circle of the movement could be trusted, like the new group that had gathered around him after the Institute was completed, to give the loyalty he required, uncritical, absolute, lifelong.

Driven from the inner circle of the movement, the leaders of the New Age Club carried on their group as a separate organization. They remained as tireless as ever in promoting Douglas's theories, but insisted that monetary reform was a federal concern over which the province of Alberta had no control whatever. They announced that they would enter federal politics but here, again, Aberhart outmanœuvred them. Although greatly handicapped they continued, until the autumn of 1939, to make speeches, write endless letters to the newspapers, publish articles, and distribute pamphlets on Social Credit. Their office also introduced many people to the movement, most of whom subsequently deserted them for the more successful and glamorous Aberhart. Acting under instructions from Kerslake they attempted to co-ordinate the activities of other strictly Douglas students at scattered points throughout the province, such as Norman Jaques at Mirror, George Whicher at Vulcan, Sidney Cliffe at Edson, and Herbert Boyd at Edgerton. Inspired by the New Age Club, these small groups banded together to form the Douglas Social Credit League. In the fall of 1934 McGregor, Logan, and Cliffe (editor and publisher at Edson of a small-town weekly newspaper) established a newspaper entitled *Social Justice Advocate*, later changed to *Douglas Social Credit Advocate*. These activities availed little beyond enabling their promoters to get their pictures in the metropolitan newspapers once again and to publish still more articles on Douglasism. In the face of a mass movement schismatic ventures were bound to fail: the newspaper survived for a few months, the League somewhat longer. But, no matter how embittered they might become through repeated failures, at no time did the leaders of the New Age Club assist Aberhart's political opponents in denigrating Social Credit ideas. Though forced by the response of the people to admit that the whole movement in Alberta centred about the person of Aberhart, the members of the New Age Club never ceased to look back, with nostalgic regret, upon McGregor's régime as "the lost cause."

In future years the mass of Aberhart's followers thought of the activities of the New Age Club as "something that didn't amount to a hill of beans," "a mere drop in the bucket." It was, in reality, an insignificant factor in the tidal wave that swept the province in 1934–5. The new secretary of the central council was, as it turned out, the ultimate beneficiary of the first schism within the movement. To Ernest Manning, then only twenty-five years of age, McGregor and his associates had failed because "they became technical critics of something they didn't understand." Henceforth, his star was in the ascendant. He now had an opportunity of proving his value, first to Aberhart and, ultimately, to the future of the movement.

To the mass following of the movement in the late spring of 1934 the events of the past few months had clearly demonstrated that the movement could have no leader but Aberhart. Whether he was in or out of office had made no real difference: he was indispensable to the movement. He had weathered the storm of bitter criticism provoked by Douglasites and returned as official leader: that was enough for the clamorous masses. As far as Alberta was concerned the future belonged to Aberhart.

CHAPTER FOUR

Strategy and Tactics: II

UNTIL THE SPRING of 1934 it seemed to the people of Alberta that the Social Credit movement was essentially an educational enterprise. But late that spring its possible political implications began to be discussed. The strategy and tactics of the movement now entered their second, or semi-political, phase. The most important single factor in this transformation was unquestionably the government's decision to have evidence taken by the legislature's Agricultural Committee on the Douglas System of Social Credit (popularly called the "hearings").

The government had taken this decision reluctantly, and only under extreme pressure. In response to numerous solicitations from Social Crediters, the monetary reform faction within the U.F.A. movement itself had forced a discussion of Social Credit at the annual convention of 1934; the provincial Liberal leader had called for an investigation of Douglas Social Credit; a U.F.A. federal member had asked the Standing Committee on Banking and Commerce of the House of Commons to call Aberhart and Douglas before it; and the Alberta Federation of Labour had demanded that advocates of Douglas Social Credit should be given every opportunity of stating their views before members of the legislature.

In addition to incessant agitation in political and labour circles, the government had also been faced with insistent demands from newspapers that Douglas's proposals should be thoroughly investigated. The Douglas system, editorials noted, had been the subject of concentrated propaganda and discussion throughout Alberta. It had formed the theme of a long series of Sunday sermon broadcasts which some had received as the authentic interpretation while others had detected distinct variations in several essentials from the real Douglas plan. The government should, therefore, sponsor a thoroughgoing discussion in the legislature, with the object of determining how far the system could be applied to Alberta.

Such editorials frequently included caustic comments regarding the uncritical belief of Aberhart's followers in Social Credit as a magic formula. Douglas, the newspapers pointed out, had been directing the attention of British economists and statesmen to his system for over a decade. Why had he been unable to influence public opinion at home to give it a trial? Four years of depression had offered every new solution for economic ills a glorious opportunity to win converts: if Douglas's system was a cure-all, why had it not been applied elsewhere? Having asked such sharp questions, newspapers would then strongly urge the government to investigate Douglas's complex system from all angles: in view of Aberhart's large following in Alberta nothing was more needed, they emphasized, than intelligent criticism of the Social Credit proposals.

The hearings[1] opened on March 19 with Aberhart's presentation of his system of Social Credit which he said he had prepared as being especially adapted to Alberta. Between March 19 and 21, two enthusiastic students of Douglas, who were critical of Aberhart's interpretation of Social Credit, stated their positions: Herbert Boyd of Edgerton, official delegate of the Douglas Social Credit League; and J. Larkham Collins, chartered accountant of Calgary. The latter, who appeared solely as a private citizen, had declined C. V. Kerslake's invitation to appear as an official delegate (as was Boyd) of the anti-Aberhart faction of Douglasites. In answering a question regarding his status, Collins quoted from one of Kerslake's letters to him: "You can say you do not represent us but are fully acquainted with our policy and that you can confidently assert as our opposition to Mr. Aberhart rises from the fact that he does not understand social credit as propounded by Major Douglas."[2] The two Douglasites were followed by Professor G. A. Elliot, Department of Economics, University of Alberta, who discussed at considerable length the production and distribution of capital goods and the nature of purchasing power, and who also made penetrating comments on the salient features of Social Credit theories, for which he was subsequently mercilessly satirized in Aberhart's stage and radio dramas as "Professor Orthodox Anonymous." On March 21, Aberhart was recalled for further examination, and an opportunity was given to him and the other three speakers to question each other and for the members of the Agricultural Committee to question him. Douglas himself gave evidence on April 6 and was recalled for further questioning on April 10.

As stated by the government, the main object of the enquiry was twofold: first, to elicit the principles of Douglas Social Credit and the

[1]The factual material presented below concerning the hearings is based on *The Douglas System of Social Credit: Evidence Taken by the Agricultural Committee of the Alberta Legislature, 1934*. This booklet which was printed by order of the Legislative Assembly of Alberta, 1934, is referred to in subsequent footnotes as *Evidence*.

[2]*Evidence*, p. 41.

proposals for its application as a solution of economic problems created by the depression; second, to hear evidence concerning the possibility of operating Douglas's plan in Alberta. During the enquiry many phases of the theory and application of Social Credit were discussed: much of the evidence, however, revolved around the details of how a Social Credit system could be operated in Alberta.

During the enquiry, repeated efforts were made to exhibit inadequacies in Aberhart's exposition of Douglas Social Credit, with specific reference to the Yellow Pamphlet. Under close questioning Douglas definitely stated that the publication committee of the Social Credit Secretariat in London, after careful study, had concluded that it was technically unsound, and had, therefore, refused to accept it as an interpretation of his scheme.[3] In response to pointed questions, Collins and Boyd indicated in no uncertain terms that they fully agreed with the decision of the Secretariat and the Douglas Credit League of Canada (of which Kerslake was secretary) to repudiate the Yellow Pamphlet.[4] In spite of these representations, Aberhart defended his pamphlet and resolutely insisted that it *had* been endorsed by Douglas.[5]

The newspapers played up the evidence concerning the technical inadequacy of Aberhart's interpretation of Douglas Social Credit. But, as far as the people were concerned, the central issue of the hearings was the possibility of applying a Social Credit plan in Alberta rather than the technical clarification of principles. Collins, in his evidence, argued that the Douglas scheme could not possibly be operated in Alberta owing to the province's judicial and fiscal situation, but he urged the legislature to memorialize the federal government "to the end that a foundation may be laid for a broad Dominion-wide Social Credit movement." He claimed that his view concerning the provincial applicability of Social Credit was shared by the London Secretariat as well as by the Douglas Social Credit League. Boyd agreed that Alberta's lack of jurisdiction over money was an insuperable obstacle to the adoption of Social Credit in the province. Nevertheless, he said that Alberta had a real interest in seeing Douglas's plan adopted somehow, if only for the reason that it offered immediate relief from debt.

In expounding his theory of Social Credit, Douglas stated that he proposed a system in which the real wealth of the country could be monetized to establish a "national credit," from which money or "tickets" would be distributed to the population to increase purchasing

[3]*Ibid.*, pp. 106, 124.
[4]*Ibid.*, pp. 41, 61–2.
[5]*Ibid.*, pp. 20, 65.

power. To do this, it was essential for the state to recapture the money power or money monopoly now held by financiers and bankers. The provision of employment was not a primary objective of his system: in the Machine Age a continually decreasing proportion of the population was required in the production of goods and services. He insisted repeatedly that his central point was not so much the advocacy of a rigid plan as the necessity of the state's regaining complete constitutional and legal control over the institutions that sell currency or credit. In this connection, he strongly opposed revolutionary methods and favoured only constitutional means of effecting the essential changes necessary to the adoption of his scheme. Pressed for details of his fundamental plan, he denied that he had ever laid down any set of rules or regulations: his books dealt only with the explanation of certain principles. He admitted, however, that he regarded as possible schemes two main principles: the compensated price and the national dividends.[6] Both of these principles were subjected to close examination during the hearings.

As power to control and reorganize the financial system was necessary for the institution of a Social Credit plan, Douglas was inclined to the view that present constitutional difficulties made it impossible to apply Social Credit to Alberta. But he was somewhat canny and elusive on this central issue, rather than unequivocal: at times, he suggested that only general answers to this question could be given at the present stage. To a sharp question on exactly what could be done in Alberta owing to the province's constitutional limitations with regard to monetary affairs, he replied: "If you have no powers, then of course you cannot do anything." When asked whether Social Crediters would not be better advised to concentrate on the federal rather than the provincial field, he said that Alberta should at least find out how far the province should go, and try to get something done.[7] He admitted that no Social Credit plan for Alberta existed to which he had given his authority or approval.

When pressed for practical suggestions as to what Alberta could do, Douglas replied that it was essential, first of all, to determine what the provincial objective should or could be, and then work towards it, eliminating obstacles whenever possible. He strenuously denied a suggestion that, if applied to Alberta, his scheme would not work owing to the limited powers of the province: "I should say it is not a question that my system would not work, but you cannot put it, at the moment, into operation, but I should not like to be quoted as saying that that pre-

6*Ibid.*, pp. 78–127.
7*Ibid.*, pp. 96–7, 103.

vents it from going into operation."[8] Questioners worked in vain, however, to elicit from him suggestions for the institution of a practical, progressive programme in Alberta.

In lieu of such a programme, he attacked the banks, declaring that it was necessary for governing bodies to exert power to bring these institutions to reason. "Singing sweet songs to these gentlemen," he declared, "and putting up schemes of any kind is not going to do the job."[9] It was necessary to put the banks of Canada really "on the spot." Through taxes and restrictions, the banks could be forced to co-operate. "You will have to go to the bank managers," he advised the Agricultural Committee, "and say you are going to make them feel your action." The only real obstacle to economic reconstruction was the power to do it:

Given the power, either I or dozens of other people could provide you in three months with a scheme which would work perfectly and put Alberta, or Canada, depending on the extent to which it is applied, forever outside the range of poverty. But you cannot do it because you won't be allowed and it is your problem to find out how to get the power to put into operation a technically sound scheme.[10]

In striking contrast to the other four men who appeared before the committee, Aberhart stated unequivocally that his Social Credit plan, which he outlined at length, could be applied to Alberta. There was, he insisted, no substantial difficulty in the way of Alberta's adopting such a plan. Strongly defending this claim, he offered seven reasons why his plan could and should be introduced first into Alberta rather than into the Dominion of Canada: it would take much longer to develop public opinion in favour of Social Credit in Canada as a whole than in Alberta; the task of persuading ten legislatures, nine provincial and one federal, seemed insuperable; the plan would encounter infinitely more opposition, both inside and outside Canada, if proposed for the Dominion than for Alberta alone; much more time would be required for introduction in the Dominion; improvement regularly moves from the small to the large—"a farmer usually summerfallows one field at a time—never the whole farm at once"; the problem of federal debt would be a barrier; even if the system were introduced into Canada, each province would still have to look after its own affairs. "Since it is not interfering in any way with the carrying on of Dominion business," he concluded, "why need we wait? Why could not the Dominion say, Go ahead, Alberta, and

[8]*Ibid.*, p. 122.
[9]*Ibid.*, p. 97.
[10]*Ibid.*

try it out?"[11] When Premier Brownlee asked him what his first steps would be if he were asked to organize a plan for Alberta, Aberhart replied that he would have Douglas come to Alberta and organize a scheme.[12]

The hearings marked the first shift in the centre of gravity of Social Credit from Calgary to Edmonton. Though it was only temporary, the attention given to Douglas's theory at the centre of government naturally aroused widespread public interest. On the morning when Douglas himself commenced giving evidence, although the proceedings were broadcast, the galleries and floor of the legislative chamber were packed with visitors. His contributions to the hearings received considerable publicity in the metropolitan newspapers, though nothing like the space and comment that were devoted to his Calgary address. For the Social Credit movement the hearings could not have been held at a more propitious time. Numerous reports and editorials in both urban and rural newspapers kept the issue of Social Credit alive during the very period when, under McGregor's presidency, the movement needed publicity badly.

But in spite of a considerable access of publicity, Social Crediters were not pleased with the conduct of the hearings. They felt that Douglas had contributed nothing to the discussion of Social Credit that Aberhart had not already taught them. In their opinion, Douglas's vague and ambiguous manner of speaking was a definite hindrance to the cause of Social Credit in Alberta. They felt, also, that Douglas had been much too canny regarding his association with Aberhart, especially in connection with the Yellow Pamphlet. What right had Douglas, they asked, to treat a man who obviously had no axe to grind in so disgusting a manner? As a result of this new insight into Douglas's character, many Social Crediters have reported that they "swore off him for life"; others, not so enraged, merely said, for ever after, that Douglas "didn't amount to a hill of beans." They resented also the repeated attempts, as they interpreted them, of Collins, Boyd, and Elliot to trap or "show up" Aberhart by sharp questioning. Collins especially aroused their ire: they felt that he had been extremely vindictive, doing his utmost to discredit Aberhart by emphasizing deviations in the latter's interpretation of Douglas which were negligible.

Then, too, they were irritated by the general conclusion of the newspapers that Douglas had conceded that a thorough inquiry into the

[11]*Ibid.*, p. 19.
[12]*Ibid.*, p. 73.

economic, financial, and constitutional relations of the province to the Dominion would be necessary before any Social Credit plan could be drawn up for Alberta. They felt that enough educational work had already been done on behalf of Social Credit: no further "period of propaganda," as Douglas had put it, was really necessary. Letters poured into the newspapers, asking why a change in the structure of the economic order could not be made immediately. Resentful and restless, Aberhart's followers waited for the publication of the government's report on the legislative hearings. They were convinced that, after all that had happened, the government could not now fail to take action.

No matter how bitterly Aberhart's followers might resent their stand, Collins and the members of the New Age Club interpreted Douglas's attitude during the hearings as a green light to continue their obstructionist tactics. Collins now became more active than ever, broadcasting once a week in a series called "Open Mind," sponsored by "Economics." In his numerous speeches and radio talks, he never failed to make clear his opinion of Aberhart's plan. In a newspaper report of a meeting of the Economic Reconstruction Association in Calgary, for example, he was quoted as having insisted, first, that Douglas believed it unwise to form a Douglas party in politics, second, that Douglas had no plan for the province of Alberta and, third, that the London Secretariat's criticism of Aberhart's Yellow Pamphlet had been "condemnatory in the extreme." In this speech Collins stated that the Secretariat had not merely seized upon negligible deviations in the Yellow Pamphlet, which Social Crediters claimed Aberhart had introduced solely for purposes of clarification. "These criticisms," he declared, "do not speak of any particular error, but in a sweeping statement condemn the whole booklet."[13]

Unlike Aberhart's followers, the U.F.A., Liberal, and Conservative members of the legislature felt that the hearings had yielded everything that could reasonably be expected. If Douglas had not stated unequivocally that Social Credit could not be implemented in Alberta, he had certainly presented no plan, but had merely suggested the strategy to be followed.

Taking their cue from numerous editorials, government leaders emphasized that they had welcomed the opportunity of securing an interpretation of the Douglas plan from its originator. With Albertans showing such an intense interest in monetary policies, any reasonable suggestions for their improvement demanded the closest consideration. The hearings had been all the more desirable because, in recent months,

[13]*Calgary Herald*, May 12, 1934.

there had been such great dissension between professed followers of Douglas. As a result of the careful and respectful hearing that had been given him by the Legislature, the people were now in a position to decide, on the basis of his own exposition, between the two Social Credit factions in Alberta.

Aided by the newspapers, U.F.A. leaders saw to it that extensive and continuous publicity was given to the controversy over the Yellow Pamphlet and Douglas's statements concerning his Secretariat's sweeping condemnation of it. This was only the beginning of a policy, pursued henceforth by U.F.A. leaders, whereby they sought to nullify the prospects of the Social Credit movement by publicizing, in every way open to them, the irreconcilable split in its ranks. Such a policy was, of course, especially encouraged by the socialists within the U.F.A. They hoped that the province-wide publicity given to the bitter conflict between Aberhart and the New Age Club during and after the hearings would result in the collapse of both factions, the end of further agitation for monetary reform, and a consolidation of the C.C.F.–U.F.A. alliance.

The Liberals also stressed the dissension within the Social Credit movement, revealed by the hearings, but with a different emphasis. With the possibility of the rise of two rival Social Credit appeals to the discontented voters, they foresaw a chance of pitting one against the other which, under the single-transferable vote system in use in Alberta, would assist them in defeating the U.F.A. and winning the election. Lulled into a false sense of security by their belief that the hearings had discredited Aberhart, the Liberals formed no conception, until nearly a year later, of the real strength of the Social Credit movement.

Nearly three months elapsed between the conclusion of the hearings and the publication of the Agricultural Committee's Report. While the hard-pressed people waited patiently for an announcement of governmental policy Aberhart, who realized the value of timing, prepared an eight-page pamphlet on *The B.N.A. Act and Social Credit* which was published immediately after the Committee's Report and distributed throughout Alberta by the tens of thousands during the summer of 1934. In this pamphlet (which was prefaced by a cartoon depicting the miserable conditions of life under "Big Boss Finance" in contrast to the abundance of good things offered by "Supervisor of Social Credit"), he argued that the constitution had been honoured more in name than in understanding: some earnest citizens seemed to think the constitution should be constantly used to stultify all freedom and good government. It was not surprising, therefore, to hear from public platforms and private individuals, not an exposure of the fallacies of Social Credit, but a partial admission of all its claims, coupled with moanings that the B.N.A. Act would not permit its introduction at the provincial level. "Are we to conclude from this," he asked, "that it is the function of our Canadian Constitution to prevent any province from solving its problems?" If it was the business of good government to hinder progress towards freedom, especially in an economic crisis, then surely the words "good government" and "constitution" had lost their original import, "meaning to stand together for the good and welfare of each." The introduction of Social Credit into any one province would not interfere in any way with the welfare of any other province or with that of the Dominion as a whole.

Starting from these general principles, Aberhart then presented an analysis of the bearing of the B.N.A. Act and Clause 138 of the Bank Act on his Social Credit proposals. He firmly maintained that nothing in the former could specifically prevent Alberta from embarking on his programme and that the specific restrictions regarding substitutes for money listed in the latter did not apply to the non-negotiable certificates he was advocating for Alberta. Would the people of the province, he wondered, consent to have the will of the majority rendered inoperative "by loosely-jointed constitutional machinery, overstepping its proper functioning through influences of a sordid nature brought to bear upon our good governments?" One thing, he concluded, was certain: with Social Credit offering them a solution, the people would not endure present conditions much longer, especially when the only objection to such a programme was "one of constitutional authority, being intruded into a realm of unnecessary interference." The pamphlet concluded with an analytical parable, the first of many to follow, entitled "Crusoe and Friday," in which contemporary methods of handling unemployment were humorously satirized.

As summer came in, the long-awaited Report on the hearings was finally published. Entitled *The Douglas System of Social Credit*, it ran to 127 large and closely printed pages, in which every shred of evidence taken by the Agricultural Committee was carefully reproduced. "It contains," the committee stated, "much interesting information." The committee had therefore recommended that the evidence "be printed and made available for distribution as a valuable factor for the information of the public on the subject of Social Credit." Well and good, the people felt, but what did the government propose to *do* about Social Credit? In two short paragraphs the committee gave the answer:

Your Committee is of the opinion that while the evidence given disclosed the weakness of the present system and the necessity for controlled Social Credit, it did not offer any practicable plan for adoption in Alberta under the existing constitutional condition.

Major Douglas recognized this and urged that a thorough study be made, first to arrive at a definitive objective, and second, to get a clear idea of the obstacles to be overcome and the limitations to be removed in order to clear the way, and the best method of procedure to secure results.[14]

"This," Social Crediters said to one another incredulously, "is a long-winded way of saying that the government doesn't *really* intend to do *anything* about it." Some, who had been suspicious of the hearings from the beginning, were now convinced that they had been a hoax, perpetrated for no other purpose than the government's desire to discredit Aberhart.

The Report and the government's decision to do nothing marked a crucial stage in the transformation of the Social Credit movement from an educational into a political force. Convinced by Aberhart's pronouncement in his new pamphlet on the B.N.A. Act and Social Credit that the cry about constitutional difficulties was nothing but a red herring, people now began to insist that something *could* and *must* be done to implement his programme. Throughout the Social Credit movement the question was always the same: What are *we* going to do about it? Confronted with the clamour of followers for action, Aberhart now visited the key men of the Liberal and Conservative parties. He was not discouraged by the coldness of the latter, as they were not an important factor in provincial politics. The Liberals seemed evasive: they were torn between a desire to cash in on public opinion and to maintain their traditional position on monetary reform. Aberhart always kept his ultimate moves to himself, but some of those closest to him at this time have suggested that, following the rejection of his proposals by political leaders, he must have begun to think seriously about the possibility of direct political action. Whatever he may have been thinking, there can be no doubt as to the attitude of his followers. They wanted to take the movement into politics.

Public disappointment over the hostile report was deepened by the Court's decision in the Brownlee case. At the conclusion of the trial, late in June, the jury of six found in favour of the plaintiff, awarding large sums not only to her but also to her father.[15] Following the jury's verdict, the premier resigned, although he remained in the legislature. His successor, R. G. Reid, retained all the former Cabinet except the

[14]*Evidence*, p. 2.

[15]On September 22, 1933, the *Edmonton Bulletin* first announced the suit against the premier. Full details of the case were carried by the Calgary and Edmonton papers of this period.

Minister of Public Works, whose continuation in the government had long occasioned considerable dissension within the party and much adverse publicity outside it.

With the U.F.A. faced with dissension within its ranks over affiliation with the C.C.F., the problem of Social Credit, and the moral *débâcle* within the Cabinet, the Liberals and the press clamoured for the government's resignation. Confronted with insoluble problems on every side, the new premier discussed at length with his Cabinet and leading M.L.A.'s the advisability of an immediate general election. As the public outcry over the Brownlee case had reached alarming proportions, the Cabinet urged Reid to stand firm. By the following summer both the moral and the Social Credit storms might have blown over, and the U.F.A. might defeat the Liberals a fourth time. The possibility that Social Crediters might win the election was not even entertained at that time.

Although the U.F.A. leaders did not realize it in July, 1934, the Social Credit movement, not the Liberal machine, was the beneficiary of the scandals that had engulfed Brownlee and his Minister of Public Works and shaken the party to its foundations. Henceforth the Principal of Crescent Heights High School, the President and Dean of the Calgary Prophetic Bible Institute, the President and Leader of the Social Credit movement was presented to the people by his followers, even sometimes by himself, as Sir Galahad. To the public, Aberhart's lofty moral principles and shining character stood in marked contrast to the denigrated U.F.A. leaders. No appraisal of the rise of the Social Credit movement can ignore the significance of the scandals. In the towns and rural districts especially, they became an issue of paramount importance. The leaders of the U.F.A. might affirm again and again that the former premier was innocent of everything except poor judgment, that he had been framed by political foes (a widely current apology), that he was a victim of circumstances. The masses of the people would accept no apology, no defence, no justification. The role played by the scandals was partly evident in the steady falling-off of U.F.A. membership during the summer and autumn of 1934. It was much more evident in the sudden decline or transformation of U.F.A. locals: in many cases their membership deserted almost entirely to Aberhart's movement; in many other cases the local survived only because it had become a Social Credit study group. The leaders of the U.F.A. might continue in office, at every level, for another full year, but they were rapidly becoming leaders who had lost their followers to another movement. This situation was nowhere more apparent than at the grass-roots level of the locals.

The penetration of the Social Credit movement into the rural areas, as well as the resistance of government leaders to it, may be illustrated by an account of a U.F.A. constituency convention held at Hand Hills on August 2:

It was quite evident that the majority of the audience wanted a discussion on Social Credit, and also were in favor of Social Credit. The Provincial Minister of Agriculture at the close of his address, was asked if he did not think Social Credit would alleviate the present financial depression in Alberta. His reply was to the effect that although he had listened to many speakers, and had read numbers of books on Social Credit, he was still very much in the dark regarding the subject and could not give any definite answer or opinion as to the outcome of the success of Social Credit in Alberta. The local member of this constituency gave the opinion that Major Douglas should be asked to come to Alberta again and draw up a plan for Social Credit in Alberta, but it was quite evident from the voice of the meeting that Mr. Aberhart was quite capable of drawing up a plan along Social Credit lines that would ably fill the bill.

A resolution was passed to the effect that the U.F.A. executive be urged to co-operate with Social Credit groups in putting Social Credit into effect. This was passed by the twenty delegates and after the resolution had been recorded a vote of the whole meeting, numbering some 200 people, was taken of those in favor of Social Credit and eighty per cent of those present voted in favor.[16]

Such reports became a characteristic feature of the news columns of the Alberta weeklies during the summer of 1934. The refrain was always the same: the progress of the movement in the rural districts and the growing belief of the people (as one paper put it) that Social Credit was "the only thing to lift the province out of its present quagmire of financial sordidness."

If the infiltration of the U.F.A. locals during the summer and autumn of 1934 was assisted by the scandals, it was due in much larger degree to the strenuous efforts of the Social Crediters. The campaign of Aberhart and his followers during the next fourteen months appears incredible to outside observers; to the participants it was the natural outcome of absolute belief in a righteous cause led by a divinely inspired man. As the crumbling government braced itself for another year of office, plans were made for carrying the gospel according to Aberhart into every populated area of Alberta. Neither the prophet nor his disciples left anything to chance. No opportunity of pressing the case for Social Credit was neglected.

Even the Calgary Stampede, a highly commercialized survival of the

16*Alberta Social Credit Chronicle*, August 17, 1934. This newspaper is referred to hereafter as *A.S.C.C.*

Old West, was used to advertise the movement. In the parade with which this annual event opens study groups entered over fifty floats, gaily decorated with slogans such as "Alberta First for Social Credit." As the procession wound through the streets young men shouted the shibboleths of monetary reform, while thousands cheered from the sidewalks. The New Age Club also participated, bringing up the rear with a car labelled "Douglas Social Credit." This demonstration of strength led to much publicity and favourable comment on the enterprising leadership of the movement not only in the metropolitan papers but in the small-town weeklies as well.

In addition to the Sunday and week-night meetings at the Institute, two meetings a week were held from now on at the Labor Temple with the object of arousing greater support among the working class. During this same period mass teas and bazaars at the Institute became a regular feature of the movement's programme in Calgary. It should be emphasized that however many new ventures might be undertaken, there was no diminution of study group activities which now entered their golden age.

At the end of July a "United Mammoth Basket Picnic" (as the advertisements called it) was held at St. George's Island, a large Calgary park. Even with the thermometer registering one hundred degrees, over 3,000 people listened for hours as Aberhart and seven secondary leaders gave addresses on the principles of Social Credit: "The Woman's Outlook on Social Credit," "Young People and Social Credit," "Depression and War in Relation to Social Credit," and "Current Events and Social Credit." All the speakers emphasized "the efforts being made by old-line parties to discredit Social Credit." Certain psychological aspects of Social Credit gatherings may be illustrated by a news account of the first picnic:

A nice spirit of companionship pervaded throughout the picnic, and many small contributions and offers to join the different Social Credit groups were made during the afternoon. The picnic was a big success, which once again proves that true co-operation will overcome all obstacles and obtain for all that objective which Major Douglas claims should be the aim of all true Social Credit workers.[17]

A new feature of the extensive publicity given to this fore-runner of many similar mass meetings in the open air was the inclusion of a list of Calgary merchants whose donations of goods and services had contributed to its success.

[17]Ibid., August 3, 1934.

Owing to the great success of this picnic two new techniques for promoting the movement were adopted. First, open-air mass meetings were arranged whenever desirable or practicable during the warmer months. Second, the support of business groups in the community was developed in an increasing degree through the solicitation of gifts of goods or services for the promotion of Social Credit activities. Hereafter, an announcement or report of a picnic or tea was hardly complete without a reference to the merchants who were helping it along. This technique was especially significant for the future of the movement in small towns and villages. In such centres the business groups, excluded from membership in the ruling U.F.A. caste, had largely dropped out of provincial politics. Participation in Social Credit enterprises, even if forced on occasion, often revived an interest in public affairs. The support of small-town business men, so marked a feature of the movement, was constantly encouraged by Aberhart's ability to get them working for his cause in a tangible way. As he still insisted that all activities were strictly educational, no political motives seemed to be involved. When the political implications of the movement finally became apparent, these business men were only too willing to assist Social Crediters in attacking the class-conscious U.F.A. The conquest of the small towns, begun by the Institute's religious following, was carried a stage further by business groups. Their support was enlisted initially by Aberhart's challenge to contribute something tangible to a movement that offered new hope of overcoming the depression. By the religious following in small towns the rally of business groups to the movement was not infrequently interpreted as divine judgment on the U.F.A. for the personal misconduct of its leaders.

Despite an overwhelming response from the people, the movement was still suffering, as late as July, 1934, from insufficient newspaper support. The Calgary dailies had attempted to report Aberhart's earliest excursions into Social Credit theory, just as they had previously reported his more sensational religious addresses and broadcasts. Apparently unaware of the real strength of his religious following, they regarded him at first as just another crank in the field of monetary reform. As soon as editorials critical of Social Credit theories began to appear, Aberhart complained, sometimes to the newspapers directly, sometimes over the air, that hopelessly garbled accounts of his speeches had been published. Thinking that something was amiss, the editors assigned their best reporters to cover Aberhart's addresses. When complaints of misrepresentation continued to pour in, the Calgary editors, grown sullen, seem to have agreed to ignore entirely the affairs of the Bible Institute. The silent treatment lasted throughout most of 1933. But, as we have seen, the Social Credit movement had assumed such proportions by January, 1934, that to ignore it longer would have been sheer circulation suicide. Henceforth Aberhart's activities became and remained front-page news until his death over nine years later.

During the spring of 1934 the Calgary *Albertan*, which had been losing circulation rapidly, became impressed with the possibilities of exploiting Social Credit. For several weeks it ran a series of front-page articles on Social Credit, written by W. M. Davidson, a former Liberal M.L.A., who had also been Mayor of Calgary. These articles, which dealt with pure Douglasism, naturally lacked the colourful phraseology with which Aberhart enlivened his expositions of Social Credit at the Institute. Worse still, they criticized Douglas's proposals adversely. Aberhart requested a personal interview with the publisher. To placate Aberhart, whose followers were envisaged as potential subscribers, the *Albertan* undertook to run a series of his own articles on Social Credit, free of charge and without editorial corrections. It is said that the series was abruptly ended after the writer demanded payment for his services. Several months later the *Albertan* made another effort to woo Aberhart's followers by running a third series of articles on Social Credit, this time by the Marquis of Townsend. Until July, 1935, the paper then pursued a twofold policy of giving Aberhart much more than his share of news space and of muting its editorial criticism of his doctrines. It is said that this approach enabled it to continue in operation during a difficult period of financial stress in 1934–5. There is considerable evidence that the *Albertan*'s various series on Social Credit were widely read: even at the present time, both friends and foes of Social Credit, in the country and in cities, proudly display scrap-books containing files, usually complete, of the three series.

Following Douglas's first visit to Alberta, in April, 1934, the *Calgary Herald*, easily the most flourishing of the metropolitan dailies, inaugurated a policy of vociferous opposition to Aberhart and all he stood for that ended only with his death. While it gave reasonable news space to the activities of the Social Credit movement, its editorial columns carried violent attacks on him and his proposals.

By the summer of 1934 Social Crediters could no longer complain of inadequate news coverage of their activities. But only one newspaper in Alberta was consistently giving editorial encouragement to their doctrines. Following the lead of the *Calgary Herald*, the others were constantly criticizing, and even frequently ridiculing, the movement and its leader. The movement's need of its own organ for diffusing information and doctrine was met by the foundation of a weekly newspaper, the *Alberta Social Credit Chronicle*.

This publication was inspired and edited by Charles K. Underwood. Like many others, he had already been reading books on social and economic problems before he began listening to the Sunday afternoon broadcasts from the Institute. Impressed by Aberhart's firm stand that Social Credit was the only remedy for the depression, Underwood decided to offer the movement his talents and experience as a newpaper-man. When first approached in the spring of 1934, Aberhart said he would be interested in having a newspaper for the movement but was unable to finance it. Assured that Underwood would undertake it on his own responsibility, he agreed to recommend the newspaper strongly in his radio talks and to contribute a weekly article on some phase of Social Credit. With the assistance of Frank Hollingworth, another ardent Social Crediter, as business manager, Underwood published his first issue on July 20, 1934.

At the beginning the two men faced almost insuperable difficulties. Seeing no future for such a paper, five Calgary shops refused to print it unless four or five weeks' printing deposit was made in advance. During its first six months the paper was printed by the *High River Times*, whose owner believed in fair play for Social Crediters, until increased circulation made production in Calgary imperative. Once it had made good, the Albertan Job Press, which produced one of Calgary's dailies, eagerly undertook the task of printing the *Social Credit Chronicle*.

Although only $43 worth of advertising was secured for the first issue, 4,000 copies were printed. Assigned the task of selling these copies, eighty unemployed persons, recruited at meetings, managed to dispose of only 800. Of the 2,800 copies of the second issue, which contained $87 worth of advertising, 2,000 were given away free to people known to be antagonistic to Social Credit. Opponents of the movement were now certain that the little paper would die a natural death with its third issue.

But, instead of dying, the paper gained strength and soon became a powerful influence in consolidating and expanding the movement. The policy of giving each study group ten free copies for its members resulted in thousands of readers who became enthusiastic subscribers. Within a few months the paid-up circulation approached 14,000, and some 6,000 additional copies were being sold weekly at Social Credit meetings. During the spring and summer of 1935, 9,000 copies were sent to Edmonton each week for distribution in the northern constituencies. On its first anniversary, it was claimed that the paper had 60,000 readers in Alberta, as well as hundreds of subscribers all over the world.

After the first five issues, its format was enlarged from fifteen inches by ten inches to regular newspaper size, the number of pages was increased, and it carried thereafter a heavy volume of advertising. Within three months it had a staff of eight, which grew to twelve the following year. During this period of expansion it moved from the tiny, single room on the third floor of an old building where it had started to pretentious, well-furnished offices in the heart of Calgary. Much of the paper's phenomenal success was due to its skilful circulation manager, Miss Eva A. Reid, one of Canada's ablest journalists, who had followed Manning as secretary of the Central Council.

From its inception, the *Chronicle* was avowedly and unashamedly an uncritical organ of the Social Credit movement. Its editor believed that the future development of the movement required such a weekly publication to supplement the heroic work of Aberhart and his trusty band of workers in delivering and explaining the "Good Cheer" message of Social Credit to the people of Alberta. The paper was therefore characterized by unremitting and relentless propaganda on behalf of the correctness of Aberhart's proposals, as well as by a constant insistence that no other programme could resolve the paradox of poverty in the midst of plenty. Every effort was made to present simple and readable explanations of the principles and consequences for Alberta of Social Credit. "We wanted," said the editor, "to put Social Credit in ABC form, so that simple folk would understand it, and realize that, if applied to the province, it would remove the soul-crushing menace of the depression and in its place leave happiness and contentment."

Each issue contained, as had been agreed, at least a leading article by Aberhart, usually accompanied by his picture. In addition, items and messages prepared by others not infrequently appeared under his name, including pieces written by the editor himself. An attempt was made to secure a monthly contribution from Douglas, and one every six weeks from Dean Hewlett Johnson of Canterbury, then an ardent Social Crediter. Five articles were contributed by John Drinkwater, two by Sir Oswald Mosley (who approved of Social Credit but said it was fifty years too soon), and even three by Father Coughlin (who praised Aberhart's programme but said he wasn't asking enough). The appearance of articles by such well-known writers and agitators gave prestige to the paper and thereby to the movement, influencing waverers to rally to Aberhart's cause.

While the *Chronicle*'s essential function was the exposition of the principles and application of Social Credit, its role as a purveyor of news concerning the growth and activities of the movement was of almost equal importance. It always carried reports, often quite lengthy, of addresses given at meetings, not only by Aberhart but by many secondary and local leaders as well. It also kept its readers informed of the development of organizational activities in the movement during the periods of transition to political action, involvement in the web of politics, and struggle for power.

As part of its folksy appeal, considerable space was given in each issue to announcements and reports of study group meetings. Through this device, the names of thousands of local leaders appeared in print, and hundreds of minor speeches and talks received favourable mention. Readers of the section devoted to group activities came to feel they were members of a movement whose forward march was irresistible.

In both its editorial and its news columns the *Chronicle* praised Social Credit spokesmen unreservedly. Anyone who opposed the movement, of whatever party or on whatever grounds, was just as surely subjected to ridicule and contempt. During the election campaign, Social Credit candidates were treated as demi-gods, while opposition candidates, and more especially those of the U.F.A., were attacked mercilessly. If its editor's claim that it won the election for Aberhart is an over-statement, it cannot be denied that the paper played a major role in the struggle for power.

Parades, special appeals to the working class, mammoth picnics, mass meetings in the open air, solicitation of support from commercial interests, and the publication of a newspaper were among the new techniques adopted during the summer of 1934 for promoting the movement. But the greatest dynamic of all during that memorable summer was provided by the heroic speaking tours undertaken by Aberhart and scores of devoted followers. Until the winter of 1934 the movement had been huddled around the Institute. Since January the movement had definitely become identified with Calgary as a whole rather than with the Institute alone. The growth of the movement to provincial dimensions was its most spectacular feature during the second summer. By autumn it was established in nearly every smaller city, town, village, and rural area. But it should be noted that during this process of expansion, with its accompanying secularization, the Institute never ceased to be the headquarters of the movement, its unifying and spiritual centre.

The speaking tour of Aberhart and Manning was naturally the most effective of the many tours undertaken during the summer and autumn of 1934. Following the pattern of the previous summer, the pair spent five days on the road, returning to Calgary for Institute activities each week-end. This year the campaign was carried as far north of Edmonton as Barrhead. The meetings were crowded out everywhere. Unlike the previous summer, the secular following now far outnumbered those who were primarily attracted for religious reasons. The scope of the tour is evident from a report on it given by Aberhart at a mass meeting in Calgary on July 28: "In the last month he had travelled over 2,500 miles and delivered thirty-nine addresses to approximately thirty thousand people, and the reception he received in all towns was one of encouragement and enthusiasm."[18]

At the close of each meeting Aberhart challenged those who had been converted to Social Credit to organize a local study group. The decision to form a group was usually made immediately. An account of a meeting at Blackie is typical of the programme in small towns and villages:

On Monday afternoon [July 16] Wm. Aberhart addressed an audience in Blackie on phases of Social Credit operation. Despite inadequate opportunity for advertising the event, and despite the busy season, 350 people gathered to listen with interest and attention to Mr. Aberhart's address. Reeve Sam Brown introduced the speakers, stating, however, that Mr. Aberhart needed no introduction to Alberta audiences as his name was a household word. Mr. Manning of Calgary, also spoke, referring to current conditions of production, and inability to dispose of produced goods. Mr. Aberhart gave a lucid explanation of the various types of credit in our economic structure. Real credit is ability to pay through services or goods; financial credit is possession of bonds or similar security. But social credit is built up on the presence of human beings. Without the human element there would be no social credit, and every individual is a contributor. The speaker illustrated the value of social credit in the functioning of economic life.

ORGANIZE SOCIAL CREDIT GROUP

At an after-meeting it was decided to form a Blackie Social Credit group which will include the surrounding countryside. For the purpose of organization a meeting will be held in the Blackie Co-op. rooms on Monday afternoon, July 23.[19]

Each organized group was encouraged to keep in touch with the central headquarters at the Institute. But groups outside Calgary seem to have had no real representation on the Central Council. This loose organization, which persisted until April, 1935, was actually one of the movement's greatest sources of strength. Enjoying almost complete autonomy, each group was on its own and acted as a rallying centre for the

18Ibid.
19Ibid., July 20, 1934.

movement over a large area. Thus, following the organization of a group at Blackie, "after different schemes were discussed, it was decided to organize groups in each municipal district division, with the president of each group acting on the executive of the central group at Blackie." Representatives were elected to form groups in the various districts. Three weeks later these representatives reported on the progress of their organizational activities to a general meeting.

The organization of new groups was often facilitated by using the existing machinery of the U.F.A., as is illustrated by the tactics in a rural district shortly after Aberhart's visit to Hanna:

A team of three of our Hanna Social Credit groups visited the Lone Butte school on July 31. The school-house was jammed to capacity with people who were anxiously seeking information on the Social Credit plan. Many of them came over twenty miles to hear the glad tidings. The United Farmers local took over the meeting, and also chose U.F.A. officers as officers of the Social Credit group.[20]

With such tactics in use, the movement was rapidly projected beyond the Institute, beyond Calgary, into the remotest areas of the countryside. People found it almost impossible to resist joining a movement that seemed so spontaneous. Numerous observers have commented that everywhere, during the summer of 1934, "groups sprang up like mushrooms." They did not realize that nearly always this seeming spontaneity could be traced to the energy and organizational tactics of Aberhart.

The content of Aberhart's addresses on the second tour may be illustrated from an account, typical of many others, of a mass meeting held on July 30 in the skating-rink at Camrose:

More than 1500 people streamed in from a radius of thirty miles to the Camrose arena and heard William Aberhart of Calgary expound his Social Credit remedy for the economic morass into which the province is sinking. For two hours this large gathering listened with close attention to the one man whose courageous leadership is lifting the heavy hand of despair from the people of the province.

With an oratory unexcelled in Canada, Aberhart asked the citizens of the district to put aside politics and partisanship and co-operate for at least one year. This, he claimed, was the only way to save the country from revolution, war, and economic slavery.

Social Credit is not the socialization of financial credit, said Mr. Aberhart. This so-called panacea was merely putting a different man with a different colored pen in control of financial credit. To the man without real credit, it didn't make the slightest difference.

[20]Ibid., August 10, 1934.

Mr. Aberhart went on to say that the social credit of the people of Alberta was being exploited by the financial powers of today. The introduction of the system would only abolish the abuse of this tremendous power and return it to the hands of the people by whom it is created in basic dividends.

Answering the often asked question: where does all the money come from? Mr. Aberhart, with the able assistance of Mr. Manning, illustrated how he could buy a suit of clothes and pay his grocery bill without the payment of a single dollar. It is merely a cross entry in books, and if it works so neatly under the present system, it should work the same way under the new order. And the beauty of it all, thundered the speaker, is that it does not interfere with the Bank Act or that old bogy, the constitution.

Quoting a member of the Retail Merchant's Association, Mr. Aberhart claimed that the cost of staples would be reduced 15 per cent under Social Credit. This would follow the removal of bad debts, the costs of collections, and a bigger turn-over. Farm machinery would be reduced from 30 to 35 per cent for the same reasons.[21]

The non-political and disinterested nature of Aberhart's tour was emphasized in the report of the Camrose meeting, but at the same time questions concerning the political future of the movement were raised:

This meeting was the second of his fourth week of touring the province. As he explains, it was not a political meeting. The purpose was purely educational. With two meetings a day Mr. Aberhart has spent the entire month of July on the road. He has no axe to grind, nor is he seeking personal favor and when one considers that he is spending his holiday in this strenuous manner, it leaves no doubt as to his sincerity.

The foregoing is typical of all similar meetings, and in this connection we respectfully ask why we will not lead with Social Credit in the next election? There are many reasons for doing so, and none against.[22]

The response of the people of Camrose to Aberhart's leadership, as contrasted with that of the U.F.A., is also made clear. Again political implications are suggested:

Mr. Aberhart has the absolute confidence of Social Credit of Alberta. As one dear old lady said: "I don't claim to understand the fine points of the system, but if Mr. Aberhart says it is so, then I am sure everything will be all right." It is a pleasure to feel the temper of the audiences. There are many, many thousands who will back him to the last ditch. . . . While our self-styled leaders have been philandering, this man has been spending days of concentrated study on problems which are rightly theirs.

His heart burns for the welfare of the common man. It would be refreshing to have a churchman at the head of our government. Who is better fitted to carry out the teachings of Jesus Christ than a believer and doer of Christianity? This may be a novel idea to many of us but is worthy of consideration.

[21]*Ibid.*
[22]*Ibid.*

For the above and for many more reasons than is listed here, may we in Camrose venture to suggest that we voice the desire of thousands when we say "We Want Aberhart."[23]

Aberhart's appeal to the people was so great that many of them would frequently follow him long distances, from one meeting to another, as is evident from an account of two meetings held on the same day in east central Alberta. At Sibbald

a capacity crowd, over 500, listened attentively to the splendid addresses of Mr. W. Aberhart and Mr. E. Manning and each and every one were loud in their praises of talks of these well known social credit pioneers. The meeting was held in the afternoon and in the evening many cars journeyed to Oyen to again hear Messrs. Manning and Aberhart when they addressed a meeting at this point to over 700 people. When you get 1200 people at two meetings it shows what they think of social credit in this district.[24]

As Aberhart moved about the province, all the roads led, on a given afternoon or evening, to the centre in which he had scheduled a meeting.

Though the people were responding enthusiastically to Aberhart's summer meetings, the Simon Pure Douglasites continued their obstructionist tactics, attempting to bedevil the movement even in remote rural towns and villages. Following favourable reports of Aberhart's meetings in the issues of the weekly Consort *Enterprise* of July 19 and 26, for example, C. V. Kerslake protested strongly and at length to the editor, on behalf of the Douglas Credit League of Canada, that he was amazed that an intelligent population could be deceived by such foolish ideas as were being advanced by "local Social Credit workers." The legislative hearings, Kerslake informed the editor, had shown conclusively that Alberta had no power to monetize its real credit; and Douglas himself had agreed with this conclusion. Aberhart's followers were therefore deluding themselves by thinking that Social Credit could be applied to Alberta alone, unless that province was contemplating secession. Were the people of Alberta, Kerslake demanded, thinking of secession? Would it be in the best interests of the province? "Are you," he asked the editor pointedly, "in favour of it?" It was not good citizenship, he continued, to follow an individual who was putting forward a plan that would affect the lives of everybody in the province merely because that individual was "honest, sincere, and self-sacrificing in his efforts." In addition to these qualities, a leader must have a plan that was "right," and be in a position to make it effective. A newspaper editor, Kerslake concluded, had a responsibility to the community; if personal admiration for a sincere,

[23]*Ibid.*
[24]*Ibid.*, August 3, 1934.

hard-working leader interfered with the discharge of that duty, only disillusion and calamity would result.

In commenting on this extended diatribe, which he published in his issue of August 17 for the consideration of his readers, the editor of the *Enterprise* remarked that he had never considered amazement to be an unfortunate affliction; it was, rather often, a healthy symptom, indicating that a person was waking up and becoming aware of conditions which in themselves might be amazing. Secession, he replied to Kerslake, was preferable to starvation:

A drowning man will grasp at a straw. If people here are so deluded, so obtuse, unreasonable and foolish as one might conclude from reading that letter, may we attribute it to malnutrition, to the disconcerting influence of standing helpless while women and children suffer for food and clothing; with the knowledge that granaries are bursting with grain, factories packed full of clothing, and wealthy, influential men standing pat for sound money in order that their bonds and dividends may not be affected.

Are the people in Alberta considering secession? They are asking for a living and willing to work for it.

Am I in favor of secession? No! Do our capitalistic friends in the government believe that bonds and dividends are of more importance than human welfare, even life itself?

Do those who promise Dominion-wide Social Credit, or improvement in conditions in five years, eight years or thirteen years from now realize that this does not appeal to people with empty stomachs?[25]

Everywhere he went Aberhart found increasing support, similar to that extended in the Consort *Enterprise*, for action at the provincial level. As his triumphant tour approached its conclusion with the beginning of the school year in September, the cause of the Douglasites had receded into the background. Overwhelmed by the response of the people to Aberhart, the leaders of the New Age Club reluctantly decided to abandon the unequal contest. Leaving him to his own devices in the provincial field, they now began to explore their chances in federal politics.

During the summer of 1934 Aberhart's activities were, as always, the most spectacular feature of the movement. But his tour was only one of many that were undertaken at that time. Many secondary leaders were on the road for several months, and numerous local leaders were constantly making forays into the school districts in the vicinity of the small towns or villages in which they lived. Of the tours of secondary leaders, the most legendary is that of Mr. and Mrs. W. W. Rogers and J. H. Unwin, who barn-stormed over the whole province south of Edmon-

25Consort *Enterprise*, August 17, 1934.

ton. Other famous tours were those of R. E. Ansley, who covered the constituencies of Ponoka, Wetaskiwin, Camrose, Stettler, Coronation, Innisfail, Olds, and Didsbury; Arthur H. Wray who carried the gospel into northeastern Alberta as far as Lloydminster; and E. J. Poole and A. Reid, who pioneered in the Peace River country. The role of the secondary leaders in the speaking tours is discussed below in chapter VII, and the part played by more local leaders is considered in chapter IX. Visits by secondary or local leaders to any centre might precede or follow a visit by Aberhart. But the sequence never mattered for that summer any Social Credit speaker was sure of an audience. The mass excitement was so great that meetings, conducted by different speakers, might be held for several nights in succession. In the memories of some Albertans the summer of 1934 now appears as one vast blur of meetings.

No objective account of what went on in Alberta that summer can convey an adequate impression of the total impact of Social Credit activities on the people. Tactically and strategically, the tours carried the movement bodily from Calgary into every populated area. In the rural districts, by the end of summer, a new movement, already strongly organized, had arisen on the wreckage of the once powerful U.F.A. In the towns and cities, the people, exhilarated by the decay of the hated farmers' organization, rushed *en masse* into the new movement. In later years, as people recalled that summer, they envisaged the roads as swarming with Social Credit speakers, each of whom seemed to be "out on his own" and self-financing. They retain the impression that every Social Crediter in Alberta had become an evangelist of the new economics, eager to convert anyone he could induce to listen to him. If the memories of the people glow with emotional overtones, hundreds of news items in small-town weeklies provide abundant objective evidence that scores of speakers were on the road, that hundreds of meetings were being held, and that thousands of people were listening to lengthy expositions of monetary reform. Everywhere Social Credit had aroused popular excitement. When Aberhart settled down to his routine as school principal early in September, the movement was sweeping over Alberta like a prairie fire.

Such heightened excitement required a release. As that remarkable summer ended, the demand for political participation, long mooted by the following, long muted by Aberhart, arose in every quarter of the movement. The leader would not or could not come to a decision, but there was no diminution of the organized activities of the movement. Secondary leaders, including the Rogers, Unwin, Ansley, and Wray, continued their relentless speaking tours. The organization of groups continued everywhere. The organization of constituencies begun by Ansley during the summer was continued by him in (apparently) such an unofficial way that Aberhart could still plead, as late as January, 1935, that the movement was "strictly educational, with no political implications whatever." The office of the Institute continued, under ever-increasing pressure, as the nerve-centre of the movement, receiving correspondence about Social Credit and sending out speakers, literature, and information in all directions. The two-hour Sunday afternoon broadcasts, in which Bible prophecy and Social Credit had become indistinguishably mixed, were now heard by an audience estimated at half a million.

While old tactics were continued in full operation during the autumn, new techniques of propaganda were added. First, mid-week radio broadcasts were established as a regular feature of the movement. Second, Aberhart issued appeal after appeal for the names of "One Hundred Honest Men" who could be counted on to represent the true interests of the people. Although it was repeatedly asserted that the movement was educational, and not political in any sense, secondary leaders now began to set up Social Credit constituency organizations. As the autumn of 1934 wore on and Alberta passed into the sixth grim winter of depression, it became increasingly evident that the decision to turn the movement into an active political force could not be delayed much longer. The transformation of the movement into a political party, which will be discussed in the next chapter, was, in fact, already well under way. But at that time most people were more preoccupied with Aberhart's spectacular techniques of propaganda than with the political implications of the movement.

The mid-week radio broadcasts were inaugurated with the famous "Man from Mars" series which was heard from October, 1934, to February, 1935. The scripts were written by Aberhart, with assistance from Manning and other devotees. They grew out of discussions at the Institute concerning the reactions of a stranger from another planet to the economic and political situation in Alberta. A variety of characters were introduced, but the central personality was always the "Man from Mars." Each broadcast followed a similar pattern. Various study groups, whose contributions had financed the affair, would be thanked. Meetings for the coming week would be announced. Then the audience would be informed that a very strange character, known as the "Man from Mars," who had just arrived on earth, was anxious to hear about the political and economic condition of Alberta. Feigning a foreign accent, and speaking in a halting, hesitating manner, the Martian would proceed to question the rest of the cast, which included a C. C. Heifer, Mr. Kant B.

Dunn, and many others. The visitor invariably expressed complete bewilderment at the inability of earthmen to solve their economic problems. A good measure of Social Credit doctrine would be introduced by Aberhart and Manning, who assumed various roles in successive broadcasts. The religious aspect of Social Credit as applied Christianity would always be woven into the discussion. At the close of the interview the Man from Mars would ask pointedly why earthmen weren't intelligent enough to accept Social Credit teachings as the solution to their problems.

Participation in these radio plays has become the most unforgettable event in the career of the individual who played the role of the "Man from Mars". In Alberta, the series is remembered as the most dramatic of all the ingenious devices developed by Aberhart for arousing and maintaining public interest in Social Credit. Tactically, these broadcasts were the opening guns in the most successful political campaign that Canada has ever seen.

While the "Man from Mars" series was at the height of its popular appeal, Aberhart discussed the Social Credit proposals again, and for the last time, with the leaders of the three political parties. Again, the Conservatives were unequivocal in their rejection of his programme. The Liberals, overjoyed at the decay of the U.F.A., were more conciliatory than previously, but still essentially non-committal. Under tremendous pressure from their locals, the U.F.A. leaders were forced, much against their will, to include a discussion of Social Credit on the agenda of their forthcoming annual convention. They were even more irked when popular demand forced them to invite Aberhart to expound his theories before their convention. The battered government was now clinging desperately to the last vestiges of its fourteen years of power, despite a continual challenge from Liberal leaders to call an election immediately.

The rejection of Aberhart's appeals by political leaders called forth a denunciation of political parties generally. Resentful of the scandals, people were saying throughout the province: "Political parties are not interested in a new approach to economic problems"; "politics is rotten"; "political leaders are more interested in philandering than in coping with the depression." Widespread disillusionment with the existing parties was accompanied by an ever more persistent clamour that the Social Crediters should organize at once to contest the election.

But many people had become so embittered as a result of the scandals that they were saying to Aberhart: "You'll never get anywhere because you can't get honest men to represent the interests of the people —you can't find one hundred honest men in Alberta who would be prepared to go into politics." Such remarks, sometimes made in a spirit of sad resignation, sometimes tauntingly, called for an answer. Aberhart was, as always, equal to the challenge. In a series of Sunday afternoon broadcasts, he told the people that he believed there were honest men in Alberta who had shunned politics in the past because they disliked the domination of political machines. He asked his listeners to write in and tell him what they thought about this. How many honest men did they have in their district or constituency? Certain characteristics of honest men would then be announced. Would the people help him by sending in the names of honest men, without telling the man whose name they were sending in, and without mentioning their own names.

As a result of this ingenious device, about 400 names were sent in, mainly from the area south of Edmonton. These names, which were carefully screened, provided Aberhart with a list of key men whom the people themselves seemed to trust. Many of these honest men, as it turned out, were destined to become candidates in the forthcoming election. But during the autumn of 1934 no one was quite sure what future Aberhart had in mind for them. As far as the people were concerned, this appeal kept gossip focused on the personal misconduct of the U.F.A. Cabinet ministers. Apart from its provision of a list of key men and its impact on the scandals, the call for honest men gave additional impetus to the Social Credit movement. It was another indication that the prophet, in striking contrast to the lethargic and discredited government leaders, was a man of action and a man of God.

Public interest in the "Man from Mars" broadcasts and the appeal for honest men was overshadowed, as the New Year came in, by the impending appearance of Aberhart at the annual convention of the U.F.A. The farm leaders were fully aware of the danger involved in permitting him to address their convention, but they had no alternative. By this time such a large number of U.F.A. locals had become nothing more than Social Credit study groups that the executive was simply forced to ask Aberhart to come.

Both sides realized that the debate between Aberhart and the farm leaders, scheduled for January 16, 1935, would determine the future of the two movements. Both sides prepared carefully for the great occasion. The U.F.A. executive was faced with two problems: to keep the delegates in line with the leadership of their movement and party; and to select a suitable resolution for submission to the convention at the close of the debate. How the first problem was solved forms part of the confidential history of the U.F.A. The second problem arose simply because the locals had swamped the Resolutions Committee with recommendations concerning Social Credit. After prolonged consideration the resolution submitted by the Hilda Local was selected because it was the least complicated of the many that had been received.

The night before the great debate Aberhart put on a special reception at the Institute for the delegates to the convention. Scheduled to begin at eight, the meeting attracted such a crowd that the doors of the Institute had to be closed at 7.30 P.M. Hundreds who were turned away quickly made their way to radios and heard the programme over CFCN. With Manning in the chair, the prophet, in sharp contrast to the harassed U.F.A. leaders, played the role of genial host. The visitors from every quarter of the province were welcomed with open arms to the headquarters of the Social Credit movement.

The delegates, as well as hundreds of thousands of radio listeners, were treated to a rich display of the movement's operating tactics. Mrs. Edith Gostick, the first speaker, made a special appeal to the women delegates, stressing the great benefits they would derive from the adoption of Social Credit in Alberta. The "Man from Mars" appeared in person, leaning heavily on a staff and wearing a long white robe, a white beard, and Arab head-dress. His "perplexities" were still uppermost in his mind. He could not understand why people were not receiving enough food and clothing in a land where food and clothing were being needlessly destroyed. Why were some people driving around in big cars, well-fed and prosperous, while others did not have even the barest necessities of life? Aberhart informed the Martian visitor that, if he could stay for the meeting, he would learn that Social Credit was the only way out of the present financial chaos, the only solution of the paradox of "poverty in the midst of plenty." Mr. Kant B. Dunn also managed to leave his farm long enough to appear at the reception. After explaining how he had become an advocate of Social Credit, he insisted on the great good that would accrue to all farmers if they would only give it a trial and vote for it in the next provincial election. High school pupils then portrayed a sad sketch, depicting the poverty and starvation which had become the everyday lot of unfortunate victims of the depression: only Social Credit, the moral ran, could abolish such terrible conditions. The strain was relieved by several comedy numbers, presented by the McDougall study group. At intervals during the evening the orchestra of the Young People's Social Credit groups played instrumental pieces.

The star performer was, of course, Aberhart himself. On arising to speak, he was greeted with prolonged applause. He was feeling very good-natured that evening, owing to the large number of U.F.A. delegates who had come to his reception. He would give them the truth concerning Social Credit. Agriculture was the basic industry and Social Credit was the only solution to farmers' problems. "Your problems are our problems," he assured them, "and we are going to face them together." Three points must be carefully considered: heavy mortgage indebtedness; the prices of farm products; and bank loans on machinery. There followed an analysis and proposed solution of each of these problems. The U.F.A. members were responsible for introducing Social Credit into this country, but unfortunately they had dropped it. That night the delegates were at the cross-roads and must decide which road they were going to take henceforth. He challenged them to take the right road, the Social Credit road. The flaws in the economic system could not be adequately diagnosed in terms of production or consumption:

The fault lies with distribution. It's no good side-tracking the issue, we are just wasting our time looking for any further wrong when we know Distribution is the whole cause. What is the remedy? . . . How are we going to get purchasing power into the hands of the consumer? That's our great problem, that's the problem we have to solve. We are going to see that the people of Alberta are properly cared for, that they are going to be furnished with the necessities of life. There are 731,000 in Alberta and it's our duty to look after them. It's funny in this province of ours there is a law that prevents you starving or illtreating a dog, cow, or any other animal, and yet they allow people to go hungry, illclothed and suffer. Social Credit with its basic dividend to every man and woman of $25.00 per month starts out with the corrective measures at once. It places purchasing power in the hands of the consumer. We have found a scientific way out of our troubles, and if we don't do it, then nobody else will. We have the best brains in the province at our disposal, let us use them and put Social Credit into force. Where does all the money come from? We don't use money. Then where does all the credit come from? Why out of the end of a fountain pen. Social Credit is a scientific principle that can be adopted and can easily be understood. There are some men who don't want to understand it. Wouldn't I like to have some of these M.L.A.'s with me for about five minutes, who claim Social Credit is not workable. . . . "The Federal government won't allow it," that is what they try and tell you, but they cannot stop it, there is nothing whatever in the B.N.A. Act or the Bank Act to stop Social Credit from being operated in Alberta. Some of those so-called learned people claim it will destroy the morale of our people. Will basic dividends stop people from working? Do dividends at the present time stop people from working or looking for work? It has not done so yet, neither will it make our people too independent, but Social Credit will forever remove the fear of poverty, hunger and want. Social Credit is without doubt the solution to our present economic chaos of poverty in the midst of plenty.[26]

[26]*A.S.C.C.*, January 18, 1935.

The reception at the Institute was a memorable experience for the U.F.A. delegates. But the spectacular debate between Aberhart and their leaders on the convention floor in the Central United Church the following day was destined to haunt them forever.

The morning after the reception, groups of delegates, both men and women, could be seen in restaurants or on the streets anxiously talking over Aberhart's challenging address. All were wondering how they should vote that day. Should they please the majority of the members of their respective locals and support Social Credit? Or should they listen to their leaders and vote against it? Wracked with doubt, they assembled in convention.

Aberhart opened the historic debate with an exposition of his doctrines, aided by his famous charts, which lasted for ninety minutes.[27] Reminding the delegates that Social Credit ideas had first been introduced into Alberta by U.F.A. men, he assured them that he was concerned solely for the welfare of the people of Alberta. Why, then, as he had no desire for political office, had U.F.A. leaders been so unco-operative during the past two years? Although he disliked controversy, he had accepted the invitation to address the convention because, at last, the leaders of Alberta's greatest organization had been forced to give him a fair hearing. In view of the hostile attitude of their leaders, however, he expressed grave doubts concerning the possibility of genuine co-operation between the U.F.A. and Social Credit movements. But he advised them strongly to vote only for candidates in the coming election who were 100 per cent for Social Credit.

Following this polemical introduction, he outlined the main principles of Social Credit and discussed their application to Alberta. In his exposition of the distinction between real credit, financial credit, and Social Credit, and in his analysis of the fundamental weakness of the present system in terms of the A plus B Theorem he did not deviate perceptibly from Douglas. But he himself admitted that, in view of Alberta's position as a province, he had found it advisable to speak of basic, rather than national, dividends and, to by-pass constitutional difficulties, to plan for their issue in the form of non-negotiable certificates. To the astonishment of several keen students of Douglas among the delegates, he

[27]The account given below of Aberhart's speech and the debate that followed it is based on a stenographic report of the complete discussion taken down at the U.F.A. convention. The eighty-three-page typescript of this report is entitled "A Discussion of Social Credit at United Farmers of Alberta Annual Convention, 1935, Held at Central United Church, Calgary, January 16, 1935." This important document is on file at the Head Office of the United Farmers of Alberta Co-operative in Calgary.

explained clearly that these dividends would be recoverable through taxation.

Students of Douglas were even more astonished at his exposition of the just price. "The Just Price," he told the convention, "is the price that will be levied by a commission, declared by a commission, as a fair price to the consumer and a fair and just price to the producer and distributor." Such a commission would sit from time to time to ascertain the actual total cost of production and to examine the ratio of consumption to production. If consumption lagged behind production, the commission could allow a discount off the total cost to increase the consumption. This discount would be paid to the retailer by the state credit house or allowed to the consumer on presentation of his invoice at the state credit house. At present, the people of Alberta were suffering from an excessive price spread on consumer goods. Sometimes the price spread average was one to four, that is, an article costing two dollars to produce would cost a consumer eight dollars. The intermediate six dollars was given to those handling the goods between the producer and the consumer. Social Credit proposed to make the profit smaller and the turnover greater.

As no producer could be expected to produce without getting a fair price for his goods, Aberhart promised that farmers would especially benefit by the just price. If the world disagreed and took the view that it would not pay farmers what they deserved for their goods then, said Aberhart, let the rest of the world do what it pleases with its farmers. "But we in Alberta should agree that we will pay our farmers. Agriculture is the basic industry of this province. If we do not solve the problems for the farmers, the province will not soon be ours."

The procedure for determining the just price of a bushel of wheat was then worked out in terms of the actual costs of production for the Alberta farmer. If the just price were fixed at sixty cents a bushel, the farmer would collect that amount. "He will collect that," said Aberhart, "the same as the gasoline tax is collected." To ensure the just price would, of course, require a levy by the state. Although the nature of such a levy was not really explained, he insisted repeatedly that it was not a tax but rather something like wages for services, interest on money, or profit in business. "Everything that is given for services of any kind," he declared, "is a tax, but I like the name levy, for levy is a declaration that you have a right of claiming on some things that are produced. However it does not matter about a term. I am not going to quibble over a term. That is the just price."

He concluded his lengthy address with his striking comparison of the cycle or flow of credit to the bloodstream of the state. As the blood flows out from the heart, it feeds, clothes, and shelters every cell of the body, picks up the impurities of the body, and returns to the heart after purification in the lungs. By analogy, the Social Credit dividends would flow from the state credit house to every consumer, on to the retailer, to the wholesaler, and to the producer, and back again to the credit house to start over again. If anything interfered with the bloodstream, it caused disorder and sickness; if anything interfered with the flow of credit, the state was weakened thereby. Interference with its flow of credit had made Alberta a sick province. But the province could be restored to health by the payment of basic dividends of $25 a month to every adult. For 400,000 people such a payment would mean $10,000,000 monthly, but the additional flow of credit would amount to at least $120,000,000, and probably four or five times this sum. Where would all the money come from? Every hour, Aberhart answered, the heart pumps 135 gallons of blood, making 3,240 gallons a day, 97,200 gallons a month, 1,166,400 gallons a year. "Where am I going to get all the blood," he asked the convention, "will you tell me that? As a matter of fact, I believe I only have four quarts of blood in me, just about four quarts. Will you tell me how a heart can pump 135 gallons an hour with only four quarts of blood? Well, cannot money circulate the same?"

For two hours after his stirring address he answered questions fired at him by delegates. He returned in the afternoon and the debate, now grown bitter, continued for several hours longer. Several important leaders of the U.F.A., including its brilliant vice-president, Norman F. Priestley, spoke strongly against Aberhart's proposals. The rationalists of the farmers' movement urged the delegates not to let their natural concern for the suffering people of Alberta blind them to the economic and constitutional difficulties involved in the application of Social Credit, whether of the Douglas or Aberhart variety. Then a prominent U.F.A. Member of Parliament aroused the convention anew by an impassioned speech on behalf of monetary reform, in which he practically supported Social Credit principles and offered only mild criticisms of Aberhart's deviations from Douglas.

As a result the monetary reformers in the U.F.A., who had already been deeply moved by Aberhart's presentation during the morning, showed signs of getting out of hand. At this point Robert Gardiner, the president of the U.F.A., himself intervened to close the debate. Following a devastatingly critical analysis of Aberhart's proposals, he made a final appeal to the delegates to stand firmly behind their leadership.

But even he had to face sharp questioning from Social Credit sympathizers before the vote could be taken.

In the evening, as the stormy debate concluded, it fell to E. J. Garland, Member of Parliament for Bow River, to present to the emotionally overwrought convention Resolution No. 190, which had been sent up by the Hilda Local:

Whereas, the present financial system has failed to meet the requirements of modern civilization;

Therefore, be it resolved, that a system of Social Credit as outlined by Mr. William Aberhart, of Calgary, be put as a plank in the U.F.A. provincial platform, to be brought before the electorate at the next provincial election.

The official minutes of the convention simply record that: "On the vote being put the resolution was lost by a large majority. In the U.F.W.A. the votes were 3 for and 90 against." It is said that a large number of delegates refrained from voting. The leaders of the U.F.A. had succeeded in keeping the convention in line. The convention was, however, so sadly split that a large number of delegates said: "We're through with the U.F.A."

Utterly exhausted by his long ordeal with the delegates, Aberhart left the convention with halting steps, giving observers the impression of a broken man. That night he dined late with a few close associates at the Mandarin Café. The "Man from Mars," as well as others among the devotees, urged him more strongly than ever before to take the Social Credit movement into politics. He gave them no decisive answer at that time, but they had little doubt as to what the future would reveal. Before leaving for home, they reminded their leader that it was only two years since the first group had been organized in the Institute and the first mimeographed lesson sheets distributed for systematic study. If they did not foresee that the defeat of Aberhart's proposals that day had doomed the U.F.A. to extinction politically, they did feel very strongly that it marked the beginning of an entirely new era for the Social Credit movement.

➤➤》《《‑《《‑

Transition to Political Action

WE HAVE SEEN that the predominant motivation of the people in the Social Credit movement, as well as of its secondary leaders, was personal attachment to the prophet. His requirement of absolute loyalty inevitably made the movement a *following*. To his followers he symbolized the high cause for which they were living and working. Once the New Age Club controversy was settled, the great spellbinder's interpretation of doctrine was accepted without question.

It was otherwise in the designation of the ultimate goals of the movement. Here considerable discussion took place between Aberhart and the secondary leaders, and the response of the people played an all-important role. In this respect the movement provides a remarkable demonstration of a dynamic process of action and reaction. Aberhart's leadership produced a response from the people. That response led him to further action, which, in turn, evoked a further reaction from the people. Thus, at each stage in the evolution of the movement, Aberhart's next step was inspired by the previous response of the people.

The phenomenon of dynamic interaction between leader and led was especially apparent in the process of coming to a decision to go into politics. If Aberhart had said to the people, "Don't go into politics!" they would have accepted his advice. It is significant that he never made such a categorical statement; equally significant that he hesitated for over a year before publicly accepting direct political participation as the goal of the movement. It should be stressed that during most of this period of indecision he was subjected to constant pressure from both the people and the secondary leaders to take the movement into politics. At the same time, like a cat playing with a mouse, he asked the people repeatedly to tell him what to do. Emphasizing the latter type of behaviour, his critics have asserted that he thought of Social Credit in terms of power politics from the first. His admirers, on the other hand, insist that his constant efforts to persuade U.F.A., Liberal, and Conservative leaders to take up the cause of Social Credit provide conclusive evidence that he did everything possible to prevent the movement from becoming a political party.

Whatever Aberhart's motivation may have been, it is clear that the transition from a social movement to a political party was a long-drawn-out process. We have suggested above that, in its inception, the Social Credit movement may be best understood as an extension of an already existing religious movement. Similarly, political participation may be interpreted as continuous with the religious and educational activities of the social movement. The extreme reluctance of Social Crediters to concede that any of their activities are other than religious and educational has always made it difficult to state even the approximate date of the movement's entry into politics. On our interpretation, the struggle for power began with the rejection of Aberhart's proposals by the U.F.A. convention on January 16, 1935.

The acceptance of that date, however, does not preclude a consideration of various earlier activities that may properly be considered political. The earliest public intimation of the movement's political implications came from Aberhart himself during the legislative hearings on March 19, 1934. According to the printed report, he opened his address by saying, rather pointedly, ". . . it is my first appearance in this house of parliament. . . . I hope I do not get the idea of wanting to come back."[1] Subsequently, during the closing period of the legislative investigation, when many of the chief workers and speakers of the movement were in Edmonton, a meeting was held at the Corona Hotel on April 6. With the manager of one of the largest industrial concerns of the city acting as chairman, the group reviewed recent events and discussed whether it was worthwhile to continue their efforts. It was unanimously decided to continue the educational campaign, and (as one of the secondary leaders has recorded), "if no existing party offered its services to the cause, to look forward to having the movement run its own candidates at the next election." This was the first time that such a possibility had received serious consideration, and the thought caused the Social Crediters involved "to return to their respective districts with renewed vigour in their hearts." About the same time Aberhart wrote a letter to Scarborough (who had started him off on Social Credit), gently remonstrating with him for siding with the New Age Club, and intimating that something very big might come his way if he would plunge in and work whole-heartedly for the right cause. McGregor has recorded that in June, about a month after his resignation as leader, one of Aberhart's most intimate associates approached him with the suggestion that his "return to the movement would eventuate in holding a big position some day in the province."

[1]*The Douglas System of Social Credit: Evidence Taken by the Agricultural Committee of the Alberta Legislature, 1934*, p. 11.

Of much greater significance for the political future of the movement than confidential discussions or broad hints to individuals was the highly critical attitude of the people to the government's report on the legislative hearings. During the summer and autumn Social Credit speakers did not hesitate to whip up the people's resentment at the government's seeming indifference to their sufferings. Small-town weeklies began to suggest in their editorial columns that thousands of people were persuaded that Aberhart was the Moses of a new economic deal. It followed that the Social Credit movement should enter politics without further delay. Such newspapers made little effort to answer the charges that "basic dividends" could not be issued in Alberta because of constitutional limitations, and that, if they could be initiated, inflation would result. The prevailing attitude of educated people in the small towns to such arguments was aptly summed up by a local editor: "The hope of the people, long deferred, has made hearts sick. Desperate diseases require desperate remedies. Perhaps people cannot be blamed for accepting unconstitutional and unintelligent prescriptions when constitutional and rational ones are platitudinous."[2] By autumn even such sceptics were coming to the conclusion that "Aberhart might be able to do something if he had political power." With such attitudes becoming widely prevalent outside the movement, Aberhart's followers urged him ever more vigorously to organize for political action.

When confronted with such hints, suggestions, and demands from the people Aberhart would always immediately disclaim any political intentions or ambitions for the movement. In reality, he was discussing participation in the forthcoming election with secondary leaders as early as the first week in July, 1934. R. E. Ansley has recorded one such discussion, which took place on the night of July 3, when he and Aberhart had temporarily joined their speaking tours in the Lacombe-Ponoka area:

It was during our conversation on this trip, that I received the first intimation of the probability that the League would nominate candidates carrying the Social Credit banner in the next Provincial election, which was expected to take place that fall. Previous to that, we had been advising people to keep after their representatives, but such procedure had proven hopeless.

This first "intimation" led to speedy action: on July 20 a representative convention of delegates from nearly every centre of the Lacombe constituency met and formed a Social Credit Constituency Association. In its organization this first Association, like many others that followed it, was modelled after that of the Central Council for Calgary. At the

2Consort *Enterprise*, July 26, 1934.

meeting there was keen discussion regarding the best method of getting Social Credit for Alberta:

Those present realized that the only chance of getting somewhere within the next few years depended upon the results of the next election. A motion was passed to the effect that the organization take political action, connected in no way with any other political party. It was decided that it would not be wise to nominate a candidate until the constituency was better represented, and that an attempt be made to organize as many locals as possible throughout the whole constituency, and also that the organization supply speakers to any district which had not been fully informed on the system as yet.

Early that autumn, the organization of the Red Deer constituency was completed by calling a convention similar to that held at Lacombe. Shortly thereafter Aberhart began emphasizing publicly the need of holding constituency conventions throughout the province.

The steady drift of the movement towards political participation is evident not only from a changing emphasis in techniques of organization but from the content of speeches as well. Early in October, at a mass meeting in Macleod, Aberhart himself

urged the audience to vote "1" for Social Credit, and to give their second choice to any of the other parties they chose; but, he said Social Credit should not become a plank in a party platform. It must not become a political issue, and the old parties will be wise in leaving it out of their platforms.[3]

During that period political leaders, still unaware of the massive strength of the Social Credit movement, were inclined to discount such utterances as bluffs or threats, not to be taken seriously. The first public statement of the political potentialities of the Social Credit movement was made by the secretary of the Alberta Federation of Labour. On the eve of Aberhart's appearance before the U.F.A. convention Elmer Roper announced that Social Credit would be a factor in the next provincial election and predicted that Social Credit candidates would make wild promises.[4]

Such tactics as Aberhart's advice in his Macleod speech and the organization of constituency associations seem to cast doubt on the sincerity of his renewed overtures to political leaders during the autumn of 1934. His state of mind following the highly successful summer tour may be most adequately described as multivalent. The Social Credit movement had obviously turned out to be something much more significant than he had anticipated. Both his friends and his foes often remark that "he had caught a lion by the tail and couldn't let go." But, in spite

[3]*A.S.C.C.*, October 12, 1934.
[4]*Calgary Herald*, January 15, 1935.

of his seeming radicalism, he was in reality a conservative, steeped in the *mores* of capitalistic society. Hence he must have deliberated long and anxiously before deciding to challenge the political status quo. In any just interpretation of his prolonged indecision, a third factor must be considered. He was a consummate actor, capable of becoming deeply immersed in a variety of roles. Thus, in one performance he played the part of prophet of a new movement; in another, the generous presenter of that movement to whatever party would take it up; in still another, the skilful politician of the Macleod speech. Like most actors, he was extremely sensitive to audience reaction. The response of the people finally determined the role he would assume permanently. After three superb performances before the U.F.A. delegates, the great actor was deeply hurt and humiliated by the convention's rejection of his proposals. His wounded ego would ensure that such a rebuff would not be allowed to occur again.

Aberhart had told the U.F.A. convention that "the battle would be fought out at the ballot box." Such a statement must have been made partly as a threat to coerce the delegates. Only two weeks previously, on January 2, Aberhart had informed a great mass meeting in Edmonton: "We hope to have a candidate in every constituency in this province in the next provincial election";[5] but he had added that a decision would depend upon the results of the straw vote which would be taken that month.

This straw vote was designed to test public opinion on Social Credit. It also served as a superb technique of propaganda for the movement from January until early spring, for it not only gave the people a tangible way of expressing themselves during the inactive winter months but also served to keep up the tremendous public interest that had been generated by the summer tours and the autumn broadcasts. Circulated throughout the province on a constituency basis, the printed straw vote ballot carried three questions, which read as follows for towns and rural areas:

1. Have you a vote in the next Provincial Election?
2. Do you wish to see Social Credit introduced into Alberta?
3. Will you vote 1 for a 100% Social Credit Candidate?

For the cities with multi-member representation the third question read:

Will you vote 1, 2, 3, 4, 5, for a full slate of 100% Social Credit Candidates?

Each question had to be answered simply YES or NO.

[5]*A.S.C.C.*, January 4, 1935.

The political implications of the straw vote were emphasized from the beginning: the results of the voting would determine whether a Social Credit candidate would be placed in the voter's provincial constituency. In appealing to the people for a large and favourable vote, four considerations were emphasized. First, Social Credit would help them to unite in common action to secure freedom from financial bondage. Second, by declaring their support for Social Credit the people would encourage the leaders of the movement to go forward. There would be no use nominating Social Credit candidates if the people would not support them. Third, support for the great movement was urgently required *now*. Failure to vote would be counted against it. Fourth, the ballot would be private and secret, and would only be opened at constituency or group headquarters. If preferred, the ballot could even be mailed to the Institute.

Apart from the response of the people, the most remarkable feature of the straw vote was the thorough canvassing of every constituency which was achieved. Local canvassers, usually consisting of group leaders but also including many other interested persons, were organized so efficiently that it is said no city block or rural district was omitted in the big drive. In the effort to give everybody a chance to vote, the canvassers went systematically up and down city streets and country roads, calling at every home. At strategic points merchants loaned their premises for the balloting; one girl covered her particular neighbourhood on horseback; in some districts children wearing clothes made of gunny sacking went around canvassing.

The compilation of returns for the whole province was in charge of the "Man from Mars," who spent two weeks counting ballots at the Institute. When the count for a given centre was completed, the figure was recorded for future use by an ingenious system of ready reference. Numbered pins were driven into a large map of Alberta; a list was then made of the pins, and the number of ballots favouring Social Credit in each district was entered beside the number of the pin. The extent of Social Credit support in a given rural or urban district could then be determined at a glance. As it turned out, such a highly efficient system was actually unnecessary. The results of the straw vote indicated that about 93 per cent of the people were prepared to support a Social Credit political campaign.

By the beginning of February early returns from the straw vote already indicated an overwhelming trend in favour of political action. While still insisting that the movement was entirely educational and that their leader had no political ambitions, Social Crediters now entered a period of feverish organizational activity in both the southern and the northern constituencies. In transforming the movement into a political party they were faced with four major problems, all of which were solved by the end of April: the organization of constituency conventions; the holding of central conventions; the formulation of a platform; and the development of a procedure for nominating candidates.

It is significant that during February and March Aberhart directed the attention of the public and the press, not to the organizational activities of the movement, but to a radio duel between himself and Norman F. Priestley (vice-president of the U.F.A.) and to a spirited interchange between himself and Premier R. G. Reid. These tactics were so successful that the politicians of all opposing camps later expressed astonishment at the speed with which the Social Crediters had developed a political organization capable of contesting the election. They were so fascinated by Aberhart's spectacular public statements against the U.F.A. that they were unaware of the energetic and detailed organizational activity by which a social movement was being swiftly transformed into the most efficient political machine that Alberta has ever known.

The organization of constituency associations, begun during the summer of 1934, had been greatly accelerated the following autumn. In southern Alberta this process was completed early in February, and in northern Alberta early in April. With associations, based on grass-roots study groups, existing in every constituency, the people waited eagerly for Aberhart to call them to political action. The long-expected announcement was first made openly not by the prophet but by one of his women lieutenants. In a speech at Lethbridge on March 4, Mrs. Edith Gostick "made it clear to her audience that a social credit candidate will contest every provincial constituency in the forthcoming election where the straw vote has indicated the interest of the people."[6]

At the time of Mrs. Gostick's announcement, the Central Advisory Board in Calgary was sending out six-page circulars to all study groups and constituency associations. On the cover of this leaflet was printed: "The Alberta Social Credit League / Organization and Discussion of Platform / Constituency and Central Conventions / Preliminary Draft for General Consideration." The leaflet contained a detailed account of the procedures to be followed in connection with constituency convention no. 1, a preliminary statement of the ten planks of the platform, and a brief announcement concerning central conventions.

Acting under authority from the central headquarters at Calgary, Social Credit leaders in each constituency were to call conventions, to

[6]*Ibid.*, March 8, 1935.

meet on or about March 21 at centrally located points. The convention was to consist of representatives from each group or district within the bounds of the constituency. Each study group of twenty or more members was entitled to send three delegates; but groups were warned not to break up into sections in order to gain more representatives. Each delegate must carry a certificate signed by the president and secretary of his group. Any polling division in which there was no group of twenty members might have one representative, but he had to be "approved as a 100 per cent Social Crediter by one of the accredited delegates."

Each convention was to deal with four matters of business, as follows: first, the appointment of a temporary chairman and secretary, if permanent officers had not been elected; second, the appointment of officers for the constituency, to consist of a president (if not already appointed), a vice-president, a secretary, a treasurer, and a number of district directors for each zone of the constituency; third, the election of seven representatives to the central conventions—these could be officers of the constituency convention, but the seven best men should be chosen, and especially those free from party affiliations; fourth, the discussion of the ten planks outlined in the circular and additional resolutions that the delegates thought should be included in the platform. The secretary was to send a report of the convention to the central headquarters in Calgary (the address given being that of the Bible Institute). It was stipulated that no nominations of candidates were to be considered at these conventions; this would be dealt with at convention no. 2, to be held after April 25.

Two general conventions, under the direction of the Central Advisory Board of Calgary, were to be held in Calgary on April 4–5, and in Edmonton on April 25–6. The purpose of these conventions was twofold: to establish the platform which all Social Credit candidates would uphold, if elected; and to formulate procedures for the conduct of the election.

Reports of the constituency conventions indicate that much the same pattern was followed throughout the province. At Hand Hills, for example, despite the bad roads and cold weather, there were present 84 delegates representing 34 groups and polling divisions, and over 200 spectators. "The conference," states the press report, "was a lively one and a fine spirit of co-operation and goodfellowship was shown by the delegates." With Dr. W. W. Cross (later to become Minister of Health and Welfare) presiding, "the provisional platform was discussed at some length. The convention sanctioned it with two minor changes and one additional clause." New officers were elected for the coming year and the seven delegates to the Calgary provincial convention duly appointed. At the Nanton-Claresholm convention, the ten planks of the platform were adopted unanimously without even a suggestion of change. It was also announced that the straw vote indicated 83.9 per cent support for Social Credit in that constituency. These conventions were usually made the occasion for a public meeting in the evening, at which the leading delegates would be introduced to the townspeople and an inspirational address on Social Credit given. Thus, following the convention held in Camrose, which "was crowded to capacity with enthusiastic 100 per cent Social Credit delegates and interested visitors," R. E. Ansley addressed a vast public meeting so eloquently and fervently that the occasion was still being discussed at Camrose some fifteen years later as one of the most memorable events in the history of the community.

The first Social Credit convention held in Canada assembled at the Bible Institute on April 4.[7] Of the twenty-four ridings ranging from Red Deer to the American border all were represented with their full quota of seven delegates, except for one absentee who telegraphed that illness alone prevented him from being in attendance. Following the appointment of Manning as convention chairman, and of Dr. W. W. Cross, of Hanna, as his deputy, the first session was declared open with the singing of "O God, Our Help in Ages Past." The acting mayor welcomed the delegates on behalf of the city and citizens; three leading field-workers spoke briefly in reply and at the same time outlined the progress of the movement throughout the country. A resolutions committee was named by the chair. Then V. W. Green concluded with an illustrated review of the operations of his milling plant at Edmonton and his theories on price spreads. Subsequent sessions were devoted to discussions of the platform and resolutions, and to speeches by Aberhart. It was at this convention that Manning's talents as a leader first became apparent to the Alberta press. Even the hostile metropolitan newspapers were forced to admit that the proceedings of the convention were conducted in a thoroughly business-like manner, and that harmony and good feeling prevailed throughout.

During the two days every seat in the large auditorium not occupied by delegates was filled with spectators from far and near. At various stages of the convention applause was loud and long. Mention of Social Credit, the leader's name, the objectives of the movement, or the passage of a resolution were always the signal for a rousing demonstration. Aberhart himself did not appear on the first day until four o'clock in the

[7]Ibid., April 5, 12, 1935; *Calgary Herald*, April 5-7, 1935.

afternoon. The audience rose in salutation and the building rocked with cheers. He informed his followers that he had just rushed from his classrooms to hear the last speaker of the afternoon. Wishing them well in their deliberations, he stated that he would address them at the close of the convention on Friday evening.

Apart from the adoption of the platform, the business of the convention was mainly concerned with resolutions pertaining to tactics and strategy in the approaching election. Of these, the most important dealt with the appointment of Aberhart as leader, the method of nominating candidates, the attitude to the legislature's invitation to Aberhart to formulate a Social Credit plan for Alberta (this will be considered in chapter VI), the appointment of an advisory committee to assist the leader, and the passage of legislation making it a criminal offence for corporations and organizations to interfere with the political freedom of citizens in their employ.

The devotion which the prophet had inspired in his followers is recorded in the long and flowery resolution demanding that he lead the movement in the forthcoming election campaign:

Whereas, the time has come when it is imperative that the social credit forces of the province be consolidated and systematically directed for definite action; and

Whereas, this can only be accomplished by skilled leadership and supervision which are essential to the success of the social credit movement in the coming provincial election; and,

Whereas, William Aberhart, despite the fact that he has repeatedly declared his personal aversion to political office and has constantly refused to enter the field of political office, is, nevertheless, recognized as the one responsible for the social credit movement in Alberta, and the individual best qualified to lead to victory the thousands whose hopes for economic security have been raised through his educational campaign in the interests of social credit;

Be it therefore resolved that this convention, as representative of the thousands of social crediters in Southern Alberta, demand that Mr. Aberhart complete the work that he has begun by assuming the active leadership of the social credit forces of the province, and furthermore, we insist that he regard this resolution as the mandate of Southern Alberta social credit supporters whose hopes he has aroused.

Be it further resolved that Mr. Aberhart do not stand for a seat in the forthcoming provincial election, and because of this be given a free hand in that he may go wherever he wills within the province for the furtherance of the social credit thought, and that if, as and when the elections occur and sufficient members of the social credit group have been elected to form a government, Mr. Aberhart shall then assume the leadership of the government.[8]

[8]*A.S.C.C.*, April 12, 1935.

It is difficult to believe that such a comprehensive resolution was not officially prepared by the leader himself. In any event, the procedure recommended by the convention was the procedure adopted by Aberhart in the campaign. He himself did not contest a constituency until after the election, when a seat was opened for him in High River by the resignation of the winning Social Credit candidate. By this device, Aberhart was able to maintain stoutly through the campaign, as he had maintained from the beginning, that he had no personal interest in political action and that the Social Credit movement was in no sense a political movement. Apart from its propaganda value, his decision not to contest a seat gave him a decided tactical advantage during the election campaign. He was left free to go into any part of the province at all times, without incurring the risk of personal defeat.

The only hotly debated resolution presented to the southern convention was the one concerning the method of nominating candidates. This resolution grew out of Douglas's theory that the people should be concerned primarily with results, rather than with the means of attaining results. Aberhart interpreted this to mean that in the election the people would not be electing a man, but voting for a set of principles. When the movement entered the political field, he realized that it would be in danger of infiltration by opportunists, eager to climb on the bandwagon. Such persons could easily pack nominating conventions and thereby defeat the purpose for which the movement was entering politics. To short circuit any inclination towards political wire pulling, as well as to assure 100 per cent Social Credit candidates, the following resolution was passed:

Whereas, we must always maintain the fundamental principles of a true democracy; and,

Whereas, there is a tempting opportunity offered under old political lines for candidates to use wire-pulling tactics; and,

Whereas, we believe that it is a fundamental under true democracy that the people directly, or indirectly, through representation are qualified to indicate the general course of their desires but that execution of them must be left to experts,

Be it therefore resolved that in nomination of candidates in each constituency we agree to nominate three or four and that our leader, together with his advisory committee and the seven constituency delegates, be empowered to decide the candidate from those nominated by the constituency convention.[9]

During the debate on this resolution, Aberhart, at the request of the convention, was forced to break his vow of silence. "Mr. Aberhart," the

[9] Ibid.

press report ran, "was urged to express his opinion and (without any desire to influence the voting) he did, concentrating on the potent sentence, 'If you are not going to let me have any say in the choice of my supporters, you will not have me as your leader.' "

As explained to the convention by the chairman, the resolution meant that each riding would name three or four likely candidates. The seven constituency delegates would then appear before Aberhart and his advisory committee to express views regarding the suitability and qualifications of the three or four. Then the leader, in council, would make the selection. An amendment, which would have permitted the seven constituency delegates to act with the leader and advisory committee in collectively passing on candidates was defeated.

As a further safeguard against political opportunism, the convention passed a second resolution regarding the nomination of candidates:

Whereas, there is grave possibility of old line party politicians seeking office through the ranks of social crediters, without being wholly in favor of its introduction into the province; and

Whereas, it is absolutely essential that the most honorable, honest and upright candidates be secured to carry the social credit banner;

Be it therefore resolved that this south central convention urge upon constituencies the importance of nominating only 100 per cent social credit candidates, as sponsored by the Alberta Social Credit League.[10]

Aberhart's control of nominating procedures was further strengthened by a resolution enabling him (and the advisory committee) to delay the announcement of the names of the candidates actually selected to contest the election until after the government's announcement of the election date. It was explained to the convention that this precaution was designed to safeguard Social Credit nominees from "general attacks" for too long a period preceding the election. But constituency conventions for nominating candidates could be held any time after the northern convention.

The convention also suggested, in a resolution, that Aberhart should choose an advisory committee of three or four members (to which he would be empowered to add at any time) to assist him in carrying on the campaign. Such a committee would enable him to secure the best possible advice on all important problems. It would also relieve him of some of the work and responsibility, and would assist him in gathering necessary information.

The resistance which members of the movement were meeting (or thought they were meeting) from employers is revealed by a resolution

[10]*Ibid.*

concerning political interference. In its preamble, this resolution stated that, contrary to British democratic theory and practice, some large provincial employers were not only intimidating their employees by threats, but were also "prohibiting and forbidding" them from taking an active part in, or becoming affiliated with, any provincial or federal political organization, such as Social Credit groups. It was intimated that some employers were resorting to threats of dismissal to gain their autocratic ends. In great indignation at such un-British practices, the convention requested the provincial legislature to pass a law, "making it illegal for any organization or company, or employers of labour, to interfere in any way whatsoever with the political freedom of citizens who are in their employ." Social Crediters insist that such a resolution was grimly necessary, and not merely another technique of propaganda.

The highlight of the convention was, of course, Aberhart's closing address. Although two overflow meetings had been arranged, hundreds of people were turned away. Introduced by Manning, the prophet was greeted with prolonged and deafening applause. Throughout his address (which he announced was being broadcast under the sponsorship of "three or four hundred fellows who know what life means, and are thinking of their boys and girls"), he reiterated his faith in Social Credit as the only alternative to the misery of the depression. Insisting that the payment of basic dividends presented no insuperable problems, he **referred scornfully to his critics:**

A man stopped me in the street the other day and asked me how Social Credit is, and I said it is spreading like wildfire, and he said, "I wouldn't touch it with a ten foot pole, and it is going to throw us all into chaos and confusion," and I said, "Are we not now in chaos and confusion," and I would like to ask you another thing, do you mean to tell me, when I am going to feed, clothe and shelter the people of this province, I am in danger of throwing this province into chaos and confusion, and he said, "Where is the money coming from?" (Cheers). I said, "the thing you want to learn is, we do not pay dividends in money." He asked "Where is the credit coming from?" I said it was coming right out of this country here. He says, "Where are you going to get the money to furnish the first dividend?" Where will we get the money to back the first dividend? Mr., will you tell me one thing, would you tell me where we get the money to issue the bonds we sell in New York? He stopped and pondered very carefully and said, "we do not have to get any money to issue bonds, we sell the bonds to get it, we have the resources of the country," and I said, "You have answered your own question." It is the resources of this province upon which we realize to feed, clothe and shelter the citizens of this province. Do not doubt for one moment we cannot do it. The second richest province in Canada could do that.

It was not long ago I picked up my paper and found someone reporting that social credit is a hair-brained scheme. I said, thank goodness I haven't got any hair. You know it is amusing to hear some of the M.L.A.'s, the men who are leading this province, say that it is a hair-brained scheme—you are being deluded for $25 a month. When anybody says that to you, take a good look at him and you will see he has been getting a thousand dollars a month for a long time. Let us notice these things as we go along. They said it was a disease people have got. They said the people would get over it, and set the election over for six months. But the people have got worse. If you ever get it once in your blood you will never get it out.[11]

During the address, he severely criticized the *Calgary Herald*, his most relentless newspaper opponent, for an editorial attack on his mixing of politics with religion.

I got this out of last night's *Herald*. Boys, it's good. (Editorial). This editor knows what he is talking about. The *Herald* does not believe in the Aberhart social credit scheme, nor do we expect it has been promoted up to the present time. (Editorial read). That surely is a polite way of saying it. We are very religious down here at the *Herald*. We do not believe in mixing our religion with politics. Here is another column I picked out, and they should be put together. Listen *Herald*, get the right quotation next time. (Applause.) I am on the air just a short time so do not stop me. I would just like one minute to say one word. You know I have always believed that a religion that amounts to anything should be practiced in every span of life. I do not think it was a very good crack of the *Herald* to put in about the feeding and clothing of the people. The day is past when religion should be put up on the shelf and taken down on Sundays.[12]

When Aberhart referred to Mr. Brownlee's anti-Social Credit campaign, the ex-premier's name was greeted with boos and catcalls from all over the auditorium.

Ex-Premier Brownlee says it [the Aberhart plan] is blue ruin of the future. Can he prevent confusion and chaos by any means he has at his disposal? Why doesn't he tell the people how he is going to prevent it? Then he comes along and when we say there is a remedy he says it is blue ruin. We are trying to stop it and it is the only remedy suggested to stop it. Basic dividends would total 125 million dollars annually in any province with — people. Can we remain indifferent to the limit it offers? We are in debt nearly 183 million dollars, and all these years they have been receiving 8 or 10 million each year, and how much benefit have the people got; 183 million of money spent. How many have been fed and clothed in the 14 years? Mr. Brownlee attacked the plan of the basic $25 dividend plan. The paper says the government admitted their duty to do this—admitted their duty to put purchasing power in the hands of the people. All I ask is that the bona fide citizens of this province be guaranteed the bare necessities of food, shelter and clothing, and if the government is ready to do that, why have they not gone ahead and done this?[13]

[11]*Ibid.*
[12]*Ibid.*; see also *Calgary Herald*, April 6, 1935.
[13]*A.S.C.C.*, April 12, 1935.

At the conclusion of his address, the prophet warned the delegates that, in taking the movement into politics, they must exhibit the iron determination of soldiers going into a crucial battle. Above all else, there must be perfect discipline: the organization that had been developed must be maintained intact, and they must have absolute confidence in their leader's judgment.

You have your chance at the next election, and if you have ever cast your ballot you will cast it at that time, or you will never need to cast another. There are a lot of things the people should know today. Soldiers are not afraid. We will not run. When the day comes, when they say, now cast your ballot, what do you want, are you going to support the old parties in power. You have to decide what you are going to do. I am looking forward, that I have the right views of the people of this province. I am looking forward to a landslide.

Just a minute. This will be my last time to talk to you. I would just like to say this. Please be careful not to organize again after this. Those groups are going to be mighty important. We will need you after the election is over. We are asking you to do something that has never been done before. Do not reorganize your groups. Do not try to change the delegates. Three members from each group as representatives. Let each member go to the next convention. Remember, you have seven delegates. Keep your same delegates except in the case of one being nominated. When I hear your seven delegates talking about a man, how popular he is, etc, the advisory committee will tell me which is the best to put in the field. Will you let us have one trial at this. If we are successful we want you to get messages consistently from the government. Now you still have to study more. There are some delegates say, I wish Aberhart would leave his religion out. I will never try to make you believe my religion. You will think your problem through. We will be sending those platforms out to you so you can study them out again. If there are any young men speakers who would like to go out to the north constituencies, we need them. The crowds are coming out to hear them in Edmonton, and this is spreading all over the land.[14]

Just before he sat down, Aberhart warned his followers that they would face "political gas bombs and dust." "Are you afraid?" "No! No! No!" the audience roared back. In a last burst of fervour, the prophet asked the delegates' permission to place the hymn that the Social Credit had adopted as their theme song, "O God Our Help in Ages Past," at the top of the platform. Amidst thunderous applause, instant approval was granted. On this note the first Social Credit convention in Canada ended. The delegates returned to their constituencies armed for a political crusade.

Three weeks later, during the Easter holidays, 156 delegates from constituencies north of Red Deer assembled in McDougall United

[14]*Ibid.*

Church, Edmonton.[15] The mayor of the city, in welcoming them, recalled that he had welcomed the U.F.A. delegates to a convention in 1919, on the occasion of their decision to enter politics. He intimated that, like the U.F.A. of former days, the Social Crediters had an ideal to fight for. He urged them to political action now, as he had urged the U.F.A. sixteen years previously. "If you wish to be successful you must see that your own candidates are placed in power. They [the U.F.A.] did that, and it is your duty to do the same."

The business of the second convention was concerned with the same resolutions, word for word, as the first. For a second time these resolutions were given unanimous approval. The highlight of the convention was, again, a great mass meeting addressed by Aberhart.

Again he emphasized the need for absolute discipline and unity. "It is," he insisted, "your last fight for liberty, stay steady and firm and you will then win your first fray in this great contest for economic freedom." He called for the election of sixty-three "honest, honorable, determined" Social Crediters to the legislature. When they were elected, Social Credit with its basic dividends to "every bona fide citizen every month, work or no work, would be assured." As at the Calgary convention, he lashed the critics of his programme. "They say it 'Can't Be Done,' that you cannot do 120 million dollars worth of business on ten million dollars, I say it can."

To clinch his argument, Aberhart then picked out a man in the audience and asked him, "Is it not right that you have done $14,000 worth of business in one year, without any capital to start with, and then paid all your debts and finished up with $1,000 to the good?" The man verified this statement in front of the audience. "Then," said Aberhart, "if this man can do $14,000 worth of business with no capital, why cannot we do $120,000,000 worth of business every year with $10,000,000 capital, what is more we know right here before us tonight are hundreds of people who could do the same thing." As he concluded, amidst tumultuous applause, with his analogy of the bloodstream of the state, hundreds of people flocked to the platform to shake hands with him, and to assure him of their support for his cause.[16]

In addition to clarifying and sanctioning strategy and tactics for the approaching election campaign, the general conventions provided the movement with an official platform (see Appendix i). For several months after the Edmonton convention, the province was deluged with

[15]*Ibid.*, May 3, 1935; *Calgary Herald*, April 23–6, 1935.
[16]*A.S.C.C.*, May 3, 1935.

hundreds of thousands of copies of leaflets entitled, "The Alberta Social Credit League/Issues/the Platform/Accepted by the/Social Credit Supporters/of Alberta." Under the theme song appeared the slogan, "In Unity There is Strength," and "Let Us End Poverty in the Midst of Plenty." In appealing for support, the League emphasized that Alberta must build up an economic system backed by a government that would look after the people so that they would no longer have to suffer. "Let us," the appeal for support concluded, "lead the World in the NEW SOCIAL ORDER." From early May until election day this platform led to interminable discussions throughout the province.

The success of the general conventions emphasized the extent to which Social Credit mass meetings were effecting a transformation of public opinion in Alberta. The conditions of politics in the province were being permanently changed. As the disorganized U.F.A. decayed politically, new social norms were arising. The rise of new norms was being made possible by the emergence of a new consensus, flowing from a new concord at the deepest level of the Alberta community. A majority of the members of that community now desired the same basic goal—a Social Credit government. The new concord was channelled and institutionalized by the decision of the general conventions to contest the forthcoming provincial election.

The general conventions not only committed the movement to political action but also provided the delegates with the dynamic necessary to win the election. Many of these local leaders had worked tirelessly for nearly two years, organizing the movement at the grass-roots level and battling the officials of U.F.A. locals on the constitutional and economic aspects of Social Credit. Assembled in Calgary and Edmonton, the delegates realized, for the first time, the massive strength of their movement, its wide diffusion, the comradeship of its local leaders, and the popular appeal of Aberhart.

Broadcast over the whole province, Aberhart's addresses to the conventions were exceptionally effective techniques of propaganda. In addition to their value in answering his critics and in diffusing doctrine, they provided high drama for the delegates. From these addresses they derived the expanding symbols needed to sustain them in the arduous months between the convention and the election. Before coming to the conventions, they had realized, as one delegate has put it, "that Social Credit under the leadership of William Aberhart was becoming one of the outstanding policies in Alberta." The enthusiasm engendered by Aberhart's passionate speeches convinced the delegates that he was the one man in Canada who had the welfare of the people at heart. Doubt concerning his objectives was now removed, and they went home to work fanatically and unceasingly for a Social Credit victory.

In spite of the fact that they voted with one voice to contest the election, the delegates left the conventions with an unyielding belief that the Social Credit movement had not become, and would never become, just another political party. Throughout the election campaign Aberhart did everything he could to promote this attitude among the people. Even when it was obvious that the movement was in politics, he constantly insisted that his activities were purely religious and educational, and not in any sense political. As he saw it, democracy had been well-nigh ruined by party politics. "Democracy," he told his congregation at the Bible Institute on May 7, "has merely become the arena of wire pulling crookedness. . . . If you want another five years the same as the past five years, then vote against Social Credit." In the same sermon, which was broadcast throughout Alberta, he declared that, once the people had been educated to the new economics, party politics would be no more. "I say to Democracy," he said, "loose democracy and let her go, she's been bound too long by party politics."[17]

Coupled with constant attacks on the party system was Aberhart's repeated declaration that he was not seeking political power. A month after the Calgary central convention he was still insisting, "I have a work in the Bible Institute dearer to me than the Premiership of Alberta, the Premiership of Canada, or the Presidency of the United States. I'm getting up in years. I'm not ambitious." Replying to a charge that he was a dictator, he remarked, "The Spirit of Christ has gripped me. I am only seeking to clothe, feed, and shelter starving people. If that it what you call a dictator, then I am one."[18] Party politicians, in opposing the Social Credit movement, were opposing Christianity.

The efficient conduct of business which had so greatly impressed observers of the proceedings at Calgary and Edmonton was equally apparent in the organization of the movement throughout the province for political action. Following the general conventions, Social Crediters

[17]U.F.A. File of Aberhart broadcasts, May 7, 1935. Following their annual convention, in January, 1935, the U.F.A. monitored and recorded Aberhart's broadcasts. The mimeographed files, which include Norman F. Priestley's criticisms of Aberhart's Social Credit theories, are kept at the Head Office of the U.F.A. Co-Operative in Calgary. The present writer wishes to express his appreciation to Mr. George Church, president of the U.F.A., for placing all the U.F.A. files at his disposal for this research project. With a fine loyalty to her employers, the secretary of the U.F.A. has labelled one set of files "Social Credit Propaganda," whereas the other set is labelled "U.F.A. Information."

[18]U.F.A. File of Aberhart broadcasts, April 28, 1935.

were faced with three major administrative problems: the nomination of candidates; the organization of the constituencies; and the final selection of candidates by Aberhart in consultation with his advisory committee.

In accordance with the resolutions of the central conventions, constituency conventions were held, for the most part during May, for the purpose of nominating not one, but several candidates. At these conventions, it was not unusual for a dozen names to be placed before the meeting. One of these would be eliminated in each successive ballot until only three or four remained. During the next few weeks the seven delegates from the constituency to one of the central conventions investigated each of the prospective candidates. As instructed, they looked into the life history of each nominee with specific reference to his general character, integrity, ability, former political affiliations, knowledge of Social Credit, and personal loyalty to Aberhart.

Reports of these conventions follow a uniform pattern. Nominations, balloting, and discussion of constituency organization took place during the day. Speeches on behalf of Social Credit were given at public meetings in the evening. An account of a nominating convention held in east central Alberta is similar to fifty other reports:

It is doubtful if anything but a Social Credit convention could have brought out such a large crowd as gathered on Saturday afternoon to elect four members for the Coronation Constituency. There were 107 delegates present; representing the whole of the Coronation riding, and about as many more who attended to hear what the candidates had to offer. C. E. Gerhart [later to become a Cabinet Minister] was in the chair and Mr. Hamner the secretary wielded the pen. There were seven persons nominated, namely: (list of names with addresses). At the close of the ballot, Messrs. Gerhart, Stark, Shaw, and MacLachlan [who was destined to be selected by Aberhart as the candidate] were elected. After the intermission for supper, the evening programme was opened with several numbers by the drama club orchestra followed by a solo with a guitar accompaniment by Euron Inmen. The address of the evening was brought by Rev. Derby of Hanna, who gave some very lucid explanations of Social Credit principles.[19]

To the local newspapers, as well as to the general public, the nominating conventions seemed to run like well-oiled machines. Many small-town editors and business men who had been hesitating were so impressed by the enthusiasm and efficiency of local Social Credit organizers that they got on the bandwagon as speedily as possible.

During the nominating conventions, considerable attention was devoted to the organization of constituencies. The basis of such organiza-

19A.S.C.C., May 31, 1935.

tion was, of course, to be found in the study groups. Constituency executives had been elected at the March meetings. The constituencies were now subdivided into "zones," the number of which ranged from four to twelve, depending upon the size, natural divisions, and population of the area. The boundaries of each zone were carefully defined, and arranged so as not to divide provincial polling sub-divisions. The zone assembly was open to all active members of all registered groups, as well as to registered associate members, within the zone, and was expected to meet frequently during the election campaign.

Each zone had a council which consisted of a president (who was also the zone organizer), vice-president, secretary-treasurer, and the president of each study group in the zone. The president of a zone was *ex-officio* a member of the constituency directorate. The president of a zone was expected (i) to render every assistance possible in the organization of new groups throughout the zone, and to maintain the activities of such groups after they were organized; (ii) to see that an active group was established in each polling sub-division of the zone; (iii) to assist the constituency organizer, and to assume with him the responsibility of maintaining and improving the activities of the League within the zone; (iv) to assist in the preparation of material for discussion and study in the groups.

Groups and zones were co-ordinated in the ascending hierarchy by the constituency association. Each provincial constituency formed an association comprised of four delegates and the president from each zone in the constituency. The activities of the constituency association were co-ordinated by a constituency directorate, consisting of a president, vice-president, secretary-treasurer, and the president of each zone in the constituency. Each constituency association appointed an organizer, who held office at its pleasure. It was his duty to supervise the organization and maintenance of Social Credit activities in the constituency and to assist the zone organizers. Immediately responsible to the constituency directorate, he was expected to present a report of his activities at each regular meeting of the constituency association.

Next in the hierarchy were the divisional conferences. In 1935, Alberta was divided into fifty-three constituencies, two of which, Edmonton and Calgary, were multiple-member constituencies electing six members each. The Social Crediters proceeded to group these constituencies into seven divisional conferences of three to eleven constituencies. These were: Peace River, Saskatchewan North, Saskatchewan South, Central Alberta, Calgary Rural, Southern Alberta, and Edmonton-Calgary. The Saskatchewan South conference, for example, met at Edmonton and included the following provincial constituencies: Leduc, Clover Bar, Victoria, Whitford, Vegreville, Alexandria, Vermilion, and Wainwright. The divisional conferences were designed to secure greater co-operative effort from the constituencies concerned. During the campaign of 1935 they functioned mainly as administrative units. The working unit immediately below the two central conventions turned out, in actual practice, to be the constituency association.

As the election approached, the zone organizer selected two members from each group whose duties were (i) to make a thorough canvas of their polling sub-division with the object of obtaining a complete voters' list; (ii) to ascertain the attitude of each voter to Social Credit; (iii) to act as scrutineers on election day. Attitudes to Social Credit were recorded in the Voters' List by the mark $(+)$ for favourable, $(-)$ for unfavourable, and $(?)$ for doubtful. The zone organizer attempted to talk personally with each doubtful voter.

In the early summer of 1935 the organization for political action was so detailed and so complete that to Social Crediters, as well as to thousands who were not members of groups, the movement seemed like an irresistible army, advancing methodically and inevitably to an election victory. This was exactly the impression that its leaders at all levels wished to give.

While his followers were busily organizing the constituencies for political action, Aberhart and his advisory committee began holding hearings at strategic points for the final selection of candidates. Outside the movement, no phase of Social Credit activity received more severe criticism that Aberhart's insistence that the nominating conventions should not be entitled to the final choice of candidates. U.F.A. political leaders, in particular, maintained incessantly that this method of naming candidates proved conclusively that Aberhart was a "dictator."

To this criticism, Aberhart replied that the method had been endorsed unanimously by the two general conventions. Such a justification of the procedure seems to have been accepted by all local leaders with one exception. The delegates to the Calgary convention had barely returned home when the president of the Drumheller Social Credit Constituency Association, A. F. Keys, publicly accused Aberhart of "dictatorship."[20] The prophet, aware of the danger of another split in the movement on the eve of the election, issued a strong appeal for unity and loyalty.

This appeal was immediately effective. Study groups throughout the Drumheller valley called a special meeting to discuss Keys' attack on the leader. The representatives of these groups, assembled in the largest

[20]*Calgary Herald*, April 10, 1935.

hall in Drumheller, affirmed that the Calgary convention's decision, permitting Aberhart to screen the candidates, was entirely orthodox in every way. The procedure at the convention was explained at length and resolutely defended by the delegates. Resolutions from fourteen groups were read, all deploring Keys' action and calling for his immediate resignation as president of the constituency association. The mass meeting thereupon passed a resolution deploring and condemning Keys' action in using the name of the Social Credit organization "to further his own selfish ends." Affirming 100 per cent loyalty to Aberhart, the representatives summarily expelled Keys from the movement.[21] The vice-president of the Drumheller Constituency Association was forthwith elevated to the presidency. Keys returned to the obscurity from which he had briefly emerged. Proclaiming the infallibility of the prophet, Social Crediters in the Drumheller valley closed their ranks, thereafter following without question the procedure laid down at Calgary. No one was surprised when the new president of the constituency association, Herbert Ingrey, was selected by Aberhart and his committee as the final candidate.

The Drumheller incident was given wide publicity by the opponents of the Social Credit movement. But Keys' charge of dictatorship made no impression upon Aberhart's followers: to them the affair seemed merely funny. The people felt that if Keys had really had the true interests of Social Credit at heart he should have registered his complaint at the convention. Why had he waited for three or four days after the close of the convention? Why had he only then published in the daily papers a report stating that dictatorial methods had been used at the convention, including "unfair means and measures in the manner of introducing resolutions"? If Keys had approached Aberhart and other leaders of the movement at the convention, his grievances could have been settled amicably. "He had no right whatever," one Social Crediter has put it,

to try and injure our just cause by publishing articles in the daily papers practically stating that the delegates had no voice in the arrangements, and that everything had been previously "fixed." It was a slur on the intelligence of the other members of the convention who were more than satisfied with the honest manner in which the convention was conducted. Mr. Keys was looked upon as a loyal supporter of Social Credit in the Drumheller district. For many months he had been one of the prominent speakers, and all his addresses were to the effect that Social Credit was for the benefit of mankind and how Alberta would prosper if Social Credit were adopted. In other words, he showed himself as an absolute loyal supporter of Social Credit for

[21]*A.S.C.C.*, April 19, 1935.

Alberta and right behind our leader. If such was the case how could this man give publication to articles in the papers injuring or trying to injure the same cause that he was previously espousing, all because of some trifling grievance at the convention over giving Mr. Aberhart the last word in naming candidates.

Such sentiments, which Social Crediters have expressed over and over again in referring to the affair, indicate that the movement had reached the stage where unquestioned loyalty to Aberhart was well-nigh universal among his followers. They felt that there could be no question that when he had declared he must have 100 per cent Social Crediters behind him,

he knew what he was doing. He wanted to be sure of supporters who had no axe to grind, no political office seekers, no opportunists, but fearless honest men and women who only had the cause of Social Credit at heart, and who were out solely for the benefit of the people to aid in the removing once and for all the stigma of why there should be poverty in the midst of plenty.

The Drumheller incident was of considerable importance for the tour which Aberhart and his advisory committee undertook in order to screen the nominees of the constituency conventions. Whatever the opposition parties might claim, that tour was carried out in a *milieu* in which loyalty and homage to the prophet were paramount attitudes among Social Crediters.

As Aberhart and his advisory committee (whose personnel, with the exception of its secretary, Manning, varied in different sections of the province "to insure impartiality") travelled about Alberta in May and June, their procedure in screening constituency nominees was actually much less autocratic than their political opponents have been prepared to admit. The committee always met jointly with the seven delegates from each constituency. The nominees were interviewed individually and carefully by appointment.

Under the circumstances, the interviews with nominees were naturally surrounded with much secrecy. But sufficient information is available to give a fairly adequate idea of what took place. At each centre the advisory committee's secretary provided the constituency delegates with two sets of questions. One set requested information from the delegates themselves concerning the nominee; the other set constituted a rough guide for the interview with the nominee.

The delegates were expected to answer the following questions about each nominee: Name? Address? Occupation? Religion? Former political affiliations? How long a Social Crediter? Has he been active? Has he held any public office? Has he good platform ability? Is he thought well of in the community? Is there anything that might be brought against him? Is he in the movement for personal gain only, or for the movement principally? Do you know of anything that would disqualify him? During the personal interviews the nominees were grilled on their knowledge of Social Credit theory as expounded by Aberhart. They were then asked two final searching questions: Have you ever said to anyone that if not chosen, you would run as a candidate anyway? If not chosen, will you definitely work for the candidate chosen?

When the interviews for a constituency were completed, the delegates voted by ballot and announced the result to the advisory committee. In most cases, the nominee who had received the highest vote at the con-stituency convention was favoured by the delegates. It is significant, also, that the advisory committee accepted the decision of the local delegates, with four exceptions. It is claimed that the latter were all cases in which the constituency men could not agree or "of obvious collusion." In several instances, where the same man had been nominated by several conventions (as, for example, in the case of R. E. Ansley), the advisory committee had to decide in which constituency he should finally be placed.

The advisory committee had agreed that the names of the candidates selected should not be revealed until the government announced the date of the election. As a result, at least three or four nominees continued to campaign long and hard in each constituency instead of one. Even after long lists of the candidates of other parties had been published, Aberhart still refused to release the names of the Social Credit candi-dates. This policy was criticized bitterly by the metropolitan newspapers as well as by spokesmen of opposing political parties. Although the right of any political party to adopt whatever system it pleased in picking its candidates was admitted, it was pointed out that supporters of the old Alberta parties would make the strongest kind of protests if their leaders attempted such tactics. Cries of "machine politics," it was said, would arise everywhere, for democratic principles required the selection of candidates to be made by constituency organizations. Even those who had hitherto been sympathetic to the Social Credit campaign, it was argued, would surely not countenance Aberhart's system of selecting candidates.[22]

While newspapers and political opponents roared their disapproval, Social Crediters remained unperturbed. They rejected the criticism that Aberhart's policy "smacked of dictatorship," denied that they were

[22]*Edmonton Journal*, July 18, 1935.

subordinating their personalities to their leader, and insisted that the bitter attacks made on Aberhart by his foes were sufficient justification of his superior wisdom.

When the list of Social Credit candidates in the provincial election of 1935 was finally disclosed on July 22, three of the six Calgary selections astonished even some of the most fanatical among Aberhart's followers. At the Calgary nominating convention twenty-seven names had been proposed. Of these, thirteen were approved by the votes of the delegates and their names were sent forward to the advisory committee with the understanding that six of them would be selected as candidates in the election. But the final list of six included only three survivors of the slate of thirteen that had been proposed by the open convention. The advisory committee had substituted one candidate who had not been proposed at all at the convention, and two others who, though proposed, had been defeated in the voting. These three candidates, it appeared, had been brought into the field by the sole authority of the advisory committee.

Opponents of the Social Credit movement now attacked Aberhart with redoubled vigour. Such methods of centralized political control, they insisted, were altogether out of keeping with democratic practice. No other party would consent for a moment to the kind of procedure in nominating candidates that had been employed by the Social Credit organization. Surely such centralized political control must be strange, disappointing, and unpalatable to Social Crediters themselves.[23]

In reply to these criticisms Aberhart maintained that there was nothing unconstitutional, so far as the Southern and Northern Social Credit Leagues were concerned, in the choice of the six Calgary candidates. He stated that, following the nominating convention in Calgary on May 16, a further convention of the Calgary Constituency Association had agreed that the six candidates might be chosen from among any of the twenty-seven preliminary names proposed, and not merely from the thirteen approved by the open convention. Later, still another meeting had given him authority to add the name of any person whom he felt justified in selecting, and this authority had been approved by the Central Council of all the Calgary study groups.[24]

Some Social Crediters were, unquestionably, surprised and disappointed by the final selection of candidates for Calgary. But their feelings were assuaged by the explanation that Aberhart needed the three controversial nominees on the ballot to increase the Social Credit

23Calgary *Albertan*, July 24, 1935; *Edmonton Journal*, July 25, 1935.
24Calgary *Albertan*, July 25, 1935.

party's appeal among the middle and upper classes. Rumours were also widely circulated that some of the candidates who had been dropped would, in due course, be groomed for the federal election, and that Social Credit candidates would be chosen from among their number to contest the three federal ridings of the Calgary district. Other rumours that there might be a break in the Social Credit organization as a result of dissatisfaction with the final selection of candidates were vigorously denied by Aberhart's supporters. They insisted that all decisions that had been taken had been approved by representative groups of Calgary Social Crediters.

While Aberhart's opponents made much of his dictatorial methods in selecting candidates, the explanations of his procedures offered by himself and his supporters were entirely acceptable to the rank and file of the Social Credit movement. A Calgary working man has expressed the general attitude of the mass following at that period:

Mr. Aberhart picked these three men as candidates because he needed them. If he gave them his stamp of approval, that was good enough for me. If they were satisfactory to him, it was sufficient for us working men in Calgary to stand firmly behind the candidates he had chosen. We felt at the time that all we had to do was to see that they were elected by a majority of votes. We had to show the world that Alberta was solidly behind Social Credit.

If Aberhart promised Cabinet posts to two of the three controversial candidates, provided they and the Social Credit party were victorious, he did not disclose it. Such caution was actually unnecessary. By that time his followers were so consumed by the struggle for power that he could do no wrong.

-»»-»»«««-

The Web of Politics

DURING THE PERIOD of transition to political action, the basic ideology of the Social Credit movement naturally aroused violent political controversy. As the new party developed within the social movement, the existing political parties were forced to define their attitude to Social Credit. The entrance of the movement into politics actually produced a crisis within the political structure of Alberta. Douglas himself, as originator of the Social Credit theories, could not avoid becoming deeply involved in that crisis, even though he had long maintained that his philosophy could best serve mankind by avoiding political entanglements. During the winter and spring of 1935, political propaganda in Alberta was more and more dictated by the challenge of Social Credit.

In meeting that challenge, the task of the U.F.A. was, from the beginning, much more difficult than the corresponding tasks of the Liberals and Conservatives. As the party in power, the U.F.A. had to meet the full onslaught of the new Social Credit party. Moreover, in their counter-attack on Social Credit, the U.F.A. leaders were faced with an internal problem from which the old-line Liberals and Conservatives were free. This internal difficulty arose from the fact that for some twenty years various farm leaders, including several of the more dynamic M.P.'s, had themselves been keen students of Social Credit.

These men had long realized that the philosophy of Henry Wise Wood, president of the U.F.A. from 1915 to 1931, had something in common with Douglas's theories. Social Credit had been, in fact, first introduced into Western Canada by Harris Turner, editor of a farmers' newspaper, *Turner's Weekly*, published in Saskatoon. Shortly after the First World War, this magazine (which was sold on news-stands throughout the prairies) published in serial form Douglas's early book, *Economic Democracy*. Among the readers of this magazine were two influential U.F.A. journalists, Norman Smith (editor of the official U.F.A. magazine) and William Irvine (editor, publicist, Labour Member of Parliament for Calgary East from 1921–5 and U.F.A. member for Wetaskiwin from 1925 to 1935). To them must be attributed a large measure of responsibility for circulating Social Credit ideas in Alberta in the 1920's.

For many years Irvine had, through various Labour and farmers' newspapers, been a severe critic of what he called the "banking racket." To him it was outrageous that Alberta's pioneer farmers should be paying from 8 to 12 per cent interest on loans. As an eager student of monetary theory, Irvine visited Douglas in London in 1923, during a visit to England to campaign for the Labour party. Irvine was so impressed by Douglas's abstruse explanations of the monetary system that he arranged for him to come to Canada to give evidence before the House of Commons' Standing Committee on Banking and Commerce. But Douglas, whose expenses to Ottawa were paid by a leading newspaper publisher, failed to impress the Committee favourably. The committee was anxious to secure from Douglas a detailed explanation of his alternative to the Canadian monetary system. But Douglas merely reiterated that he had come "to shoot at our system, not to give the Committee a chance to shoot at him." With the exception of its U.F.A. members, the committee felt that Douglas was talking in another world.

Disappointed in his hope of securing a thorough explanation of Social Credit theory, but still impressed by Douglas's emphasis on the need for financing consumption, Irvine kept up a vigorous propaganda on behalf of monetary reform during the next decade. The economic problems of the prairie farmers, he insisted, were caused by a mal-distribution of purchasing power. As a result of Irvine's and Smith's efforts, several of the ablest U.F.A. Members of Parliament, as well as their official newspaper, became at least part-time exponents of Social Credit monetary reform as an alternative, or at the least as a supplement, to the philosophy of the U.F.A. Then, too, through its educational department, the U.F.A. gave wide distribution to Douglas's books and pamphlets.

The discussion of monetary reform, which had been going on in Alberta since 1898, thus took a new turn in the 1920's. Douglas's theories now became an essential weapon in a long-continuing campaign against domination of the West by the political parties and financial interests of Eastern Canada. At the political level the indigenous philosophy of Henry Wise Wood seemed to meet the needs of Alberta farmers.[1] But from the first there was uncertainty, if not confusion, concerning the economic objectives of the U.F.A. Here was a pioneer province whose farmers, in order to get established, had borrowed large sums of money from banks and loan companies. Faced with foreclosure of his mortgage,

[1]For expositions of Henry Wise Wood's philosophy see: W. L. Morton, *The Progressive Party in Canada* (Toronto: University of Toronto Press, 1950); C. B. Macpherson, *Democracy in Alberta* (Toronto: University of Toronto Press, 1953).

a farmer would frequently estimate that he had more than paid the original loan through an extortionate rate of interest, but he still owed the principal. He would then say, bitterly, that "he had nothing to show for his years of toil and planning."

Agitation for monetary reform was a natural outcome of the financial condition of the Alberta farmers. Having been "talked up" in U.F.A. circles for years, the idea of monetary reform began to gain ground rapidly during the early years of the depression. At a U.F.A. convention it became possible to muster a substantial vote for a provincially owned and managed bank. A section of the U.F.A. believed that such a bank would (1) assist in lowering interest rates; (2) enable the provincial government to control the present uncontrollable investment corporations; (3) nullify the right of a banker to refuse to grant financial credit to a farmer who had real credit or real wealth; (4) wipe out the gold standard; (5) make possible a managed currency; and (6) inaugurate debt-free money. To those among the U.F.A. who believed in a managed currency and debt-free money, the theories of Social Credit became a powerful instrument of propaganda against Eastern financial interests.

The U.F.A. provincial and federal members were especially intrigued by Douglas's A plus B Theorem. A substantial number of those whose primary interest was monetary reform conceived that their essential task was the clarification of this theorem, even though they were not necessarily convinced of its soundness. Apart from that particular question, there had developed within the rank and file of the U.F.A. a widespread belief that Douglas's writings had raised very real issues which it would be worth while to follow up. Thus, when the depression struck Alberta, the U.F.A. locals contained a considerable number of students of Douglas's theories. They were convinced of his significance as an economist, even though the A plus B Theorem remained far from clear in their minds. To them it was important to discover whatever truth there might be in his philosophy as a whole. In 1932, when Aberhart launched his movement, two well-defined factions existed within the U.F.A.: monetary reformers and socialists. To appreciate the full complexity of the problem with which the U.F.A. government was confronted in the face of the Social Credit movement, it is necessary to consider, however briefly, the circumstances attending the foundation of the Canadian socialistic movement, known as the Co-operative Commonwealth Federation.

Inspired by several U.F.A. Members of Parliament, the U.F.A. annual convention of 1932 instructed Premier Brownlee to call a meeting of farm and labour leaders to discuss proposed solutions of the problems created by the steadily worsening depression. The conference, which met at Calgary during the summer, was also attended by a number of Labour leaders and socialist thinkers from British Columbia and Eastern Canada. Owing to the wider outlook brought to it by the socialists, this conference marked a turning-point in the U.F.A. attitude to monetary reform in general, and to Social Credit in particular. As a result of the critical discussions at Calgary, the monetary reformers cut their way through a welter of ideas to a kind of indigenous socialistic theory. It is true that their basic economic and political thought remained far from clear, but they now believed that, at least, they had at long last seen through monetary reform.

During the winter of 1933, the U.F.A.-socialist group actually ran a candidate in a Calgary by-election on the C.C.F. ticket, although that organization had not yet been formally established. Miss Amelia Turner (later the wife of Norman Smith, the U.F.A. editor) barely missed election, and her impressive vote elated the supporting labour and farm groups which had co-operated politically on her behalf.

This near victory for socialism gave rise to a buoyant optimism within U.F.A. circles concerning the future of their movement in Alberta politics. After years of searching, the key to that future had been discovered. It was not monetary reform, as many had long and erroneously supposed. It was socialism. They were now confident that the U.F.A. could be swiftly transformed into the C.C.F., a wider and more comprehensive movement of co-operating farmer and labour groups than Henry Wise Wood, their beloved philosopher and leader, had been able to envisage. The cherished U.F.A., to which they had given years of tireless thought and devotion, would be reborn and live forever as the driving power behind the new socialist movement. Among the U.F.A. philosophers there was an air of expectancy, of something great about to happen, as if the Kingdom of God were almost immediately to appear. They experienced a heightened consciousness. The years ahead were brilliant with the promise of socialism. In this mood the U.F.A. leaders journeyed to Regina in the summer of 1933 to organize the Canadian socialist movement.

The Regina Conference was a direct outcome of the somewhat informal Calgary meeting of the previous year. The Co-operative Commonwealth Federation, which had been conceived at Calgary, was now brought to birth. A majority of the U.F.A. Members of Parliament committed themselves to federal support of the C.C.F., on the understanding that the U.F.A. government of Alberta would be supported provincially by the C.C.F. The U.F.A. federal leaders were actually so deeply involved at Regina that Robert Gardiner, Henry Wise Wood's successor as president of the U.F.A., was considered one of two possible leaders of the national movement. Gardiner withdrew in favour of J. S. Woodsworth, but his acceptance of socialism was clear. The commitment of the U.F.A. to the C.C.F. received no encouragement whatever from the conservative-minded premier of Alberta and his Cabinet. But within a few weeks of the presentation of the Regina Manifesto of the C.C.F., Brownlee's political career suddenly headed into disaster with the announcement of the lawsuit involving his personal conduct. He was henceforth in no position to stay the drift of the U.F.A. towards socialism, a political theory with which he, a corporation lawyer, could have slight sympathy. As the U.F.A. turned to socialism and its premier faced political oblivion, Aberhart and Manning were completing their first triumphant tour on behalf of Social Credit.

Reports of the revival of monetary reform ideas in an unexpected quarter at first only amused the U.F.A. delegates on their return from Regina. But they were soon forced to take the rising Social Credit movement more seriously. As we have seen, the U.F.A. annual convention of 1934 was faced with strongly worded resolutions urging the government to conduct a full enquiry into Aberhart's proposals. Although resolutely opposed to Social Credit, Brownlee saw to it that such an enquiry was duly conducted under the auspices of the Agricultural Committee of the legislature. Forced to resign shortly after the publication of his government's distinctly hostile report on Social Credit, Brownlee was replaced by the less brilliant and less dynamic Reid. The latter was no match for the aggressive and colourful Aberhart.

During the summer and autumn of 1934 the new premier was challenged repeatedly by opposing political parties to call an election immediately. It is believed that Reid himself favoured an election shortly after his elevation to the premiership, but that his cabinet and the U.F.A. caucus advised the longest possible delay, in order to gain time for the ministerial scandals to blow over. The U.F.A. leaders still thought of their real challengers as the Liberals, in spite of the fact that thousands of their supporters in rural areas were already deserting to Social Credit study groups. However ill the former monetary reformers among the U.F.A. might think of Social Credit, it was obvious that their grass-roots followers were finding Aberhart's movement more challenging than the new socialism. The pressure for monetary reform, which had been building up for so many years within the U.F.A. locals, could not easily be drained away from the dynamic Social Credit movement. The decision of the U.F.A. leaders to abandon monetary reform and embrace socialism might have led to successful political action had it not been for the scandals and the Social Credit movement. As it turned out, the clamour of numerous locals forced the U.F.A. leaders, much against their will, to invite Aberhart to expound his version of Social Credit before their annual convention at Calgary in January, 1935. The convention, as we have seen, rejected Aberhart's proposals almost unanimously. But the unity of the convention in the face of Aberhart's threat was much more apparent than real. Within eighteen months of the Regina Conference, symbol of a socialist future, the U.F.A. was well along the way to political destruction.

The uncertainty within the ranks of the U.F.A. concerning monetary reform was brought into the open by a second resolution concerning Social Credit which was passed almost unanimously by the 1935 convention the day following the rejection of Aberhart's proposals:

Whereas, there is a growth of sentiment in the province favorable to the introduction and establishment of Social Credit principles; and whereas, Major C. H. Douglas is the originator of and foremost authority upon the system of Social Credit;

Be it therefore resolved that this convention request the provincial government to engage Major Douglas as consulting engineer in the matter of financial reform and that as such, he will be required to (a) Advise the government to what extent his proposals are practical within the provincial jurisdiction; what helpful initiatory steps might therein be established; these proposals to be submitted to the government for their consideration and not to be regarded as obligatory of acceptance without full examination. (b) Prepare plans for consideration with a view to the possibility of their introduction in the federal parliament.[2]

This resolution was sponsored, significantly enough, by William Irvine, former monetary reformer but now well known as a C.C.F. leader. To Social Credit observers, Irvine's vigorous address practically supported their principles. He congratulated Aberhart on his efforts and the great work he had done in bringing before the people the need for economic reform. He said he had nothing against Social Credit and told the delegates they should get behind it. Personally, he preferred Douglas's plan to that of Aberhart, because he did not think the latter's plan could be successfully adopted in the province. The passage of the motion ensured that Social Credit would remain a live issue among the U.F.A. membership.[3]

The people of Alberta naturally found it difficult to unscramble the

[2]*Minutes*, Annual Convention, U.F.A., 1935.
[3]*A.S.C.C.*, January 25, 1935.

scrambled eggs of the U.F.A. convention. It was clear that Social Credit, and not socialism, had been the main topic of discussion. Everywhere people were asking two questions: "Why had the U.F.A. leaders turned thumbs down on Aberhart Social Credit? Why had Irvine, the C.C.F. leader, turned thumbs up on it?" One baffled citizen has expressed the general confusion in the public mind: "Why was Social Credit with Mr. Aberhart's name attached to it no good, while Social Credit with Major Douglas's name to it, and sponsored by the U.F.A., was fit for the gods?" During the next eight months U.F.A. and Social Credit leaders, by words and deeds, gave a variety of answers to these questions. As the opposing parties engaged in a battle that could end only in political destruction for one of them, the people of Alberta were deluged with speeches, radio broadcasts, sermons, newspaper articles, and even books and pamphlets extolling the merits and proclaiming the weaknesses of Social Credit. Deplorable though it might seem to Douglas, his ideology was henceforth inextricably entangled in the great game of politics.

The debate between the U.F.A. and Social Crediters over the correct interpretation of Social Credit and its applicability to Alberta was opened by Brownlee. At a public meeting at Nanton on February 1, 1935, the former premier vigorously attacked the Aberhart Social Credit plan. He stated that Douglas was most emphatic that Social Credit could not be put into effect in Alberta as a province. Social Credit money would not be legal tender; its issuance would slow down the conduct of business. Any government, Brownlee concluded, that put such a policy in force could not stay in power more than six weeks.[4]

To Social Crediters Brownlee's attack represented merely another phase of the strategy of the money barons, to whom Aberhart was a thorn in the flesh. "The Just Price and Basic Dividends," one Social Crediter has put it, "that guarantee to remove poverty in the midst of plenty and stop exploitation of the people, are naturally nauseating to big, unfair profit makers and exploiters and they are not going to lose this golden egg without a very hard battle." To such thinkers Brownlee, as well as his former colleagues in the cabinet, were merely "tools" of vested interests.

To the charge that Douglas did not believe Social Credit could be applied in Alberta, the editor of the *Chronicle* provided the official reply:

How is it that Major Douglas at Edmonton, before the legislature last year said that if given three months he or any other qualified person could put in

[4]*Calgary Herald*, February 2, 1935.

a successful plan for Alberta? Furthermore, why does Major Douglas only five weeks ago, in a letter written by himself, state: "In regard to the application of Social Credit to Alberta, I have no doubt whatever that the application in a suitable form of the principles would be of advantage everywhere." . . . The statements that we use regarding Major Douglas are bona fide, they are not hearsay, they are not an imagination, and what is more we hold Major Douglas as a man of keen intellect and ability, not given to statements that are contradictory and cannot be relied upon. Mr. Aberhart's proposed Social Credit plan for Alberta is based on the Douglas principles, and what is more we have the assurance from Mr. Aberhart that only after intensive study and careful investigation did he give his ideas to the people of Alberta as a successful solution to the paradox of today, "Poverty in the midst of plenty." . . . There will be every kind of opposition to Social Credit put forward. The false witnesses will be there in their legions, the ninth commandment will be thrown into discard, but if the people will only have the courage of their convictions and give no heed to the ravings of these false prophets of the old political parties and the worshippers of the Golden Calf, but vote solidly for Social Credit candidates at the next provincial election, Alberta will be assured of a bright, bigger and more prosperous future.[5]

For several months this editorial was quoted throughout the province in refutation of the "delectable" (as the Social Crediters called him) ex-Premier Brownlee.

While the long debate between the U.F.A. and Social Crediters concerning the applicability and constitutionality of Aberhart's proposals was still in its early stages, the provincial legislature opened early in February. As it was the last possible session before an election, all the political parties were constantly manœuvring for political advantage. In this process Social Credit, owing to its popular appeal, was used as a pawn both by the Liberals and by the Conservatives. After fourteen years in office, any government is vulnerable. The opposition parties criticized the U.F.A. severely for what it had done, and even more severely for what it had not done. The Liberal and Conservative leaders speedily discovered that the Achilles heel of the U.F.A. was its attitude to Social Credit. Henceforth the government was forced to fight on three fronts.

In attempting to turn Social Credit to their political advantage the Liberals had a tactical advantage over the Conservatives. The federal Liberal leader, in opposition since 1930 and confident of victory in 1935, had already defined his party's attitude to credit when criticizing the federal Conservative government for setting up a privately owned Central Bank of Canada. Speaking in the House of Commons, on June 27, 1934, against the Central Bank legislation, W. L. Mackenzie King had said:

[5]*A.S.C.C.*, February 8, 1935.

The Bank of Canada, as constituted by this proposed enactment, will undoubtedly be the means of vesting in the Bank of England the management and control of Canada's foreign exchange and Canada's internal credit administration. As I said the other evening, once a nation parts with the control of its currency and credit, it matters not who makes the nation's laws. Usury, once in control, will wreck any nation. Until the control of the issue of currency and credit is restored to government and recognized as its most conspicuous and sacred responsibility all talk of the sovereignty of Parliament and of democracy is idle and futile.[6]

If they heard of this speech, Social Crediters in Alberta must have felt that Aberhart himself could scarcely go further in condemning private control of credit.

In formulating their platform during the autumn of 1934, the Alberta Liberals had sought to take every possible advantage of King's declaration. A reform party, feeling themselves more than a match for the Conservatives and the cautious U.F.A., they suddenly realized that the Social Crediters had raised the bidding. To re-enter the game, the Liberals were forced to make concessions to Aberhart's proposals. This they did at their convention on December 3, 1934, when the following planks were included in their platform:

XIV SOCIAL CREDIT: The Liberal party pledges itself when returned to power to employ three of the most expert Social Credit Advocates to carry on a full and complete investigation into the proposed schemes of Social Credit and to evolve and submit a plan of Social Credit for the province, which the Liberal party pledges itself to submit to the legislature for consideration.

XV MONETARY REFORM: Usury once in control will wreck any nation. Until the control of the issue of currency and credit is restored to government and recognized as its most conspicuous and sacred responsibility, all talk of the sovereignty of Parliament and of Democracy is idle and futile. (a) The Liberal party believes that credit is a public matter, not of interest to bankers only but of direct concern to the average citizen. (b) It stands for the immediate establishment of a properly constituted national bank to perform the functions of rediscount and the control of currency issue considered in terms of public need. (c) A central bank is necessary to determine the supply of currency in relation to the domestic, social and industrial requirements of the Canadian people and also to deal with the problems of international commerce and exchange.

The Liberal party stands for a publicly owned national central bank which will, under the control of the government of the nation, issue national currency and credit and manage the monetary system in terms of public need, for the purpose of raising the standard of living of the people and for the further purposes of advancing the economic security of the social system and the stability of the nation.

[6]*Hansard*, June 27, 1934.

Equipped with this platform, the Liberal leader, W. R. Howson, opened his attack on the government at the beginning of the legislative session of 1935. In an amendment to the Speech from the Throne, on February 11, he advocated "a state-owned central bank to control and manage the monetary system in terms of public need." Later, during the Budget debate, he pressed the assault, charging that the government, originally elected to protect the farmers from Eastern financial interests, had become captive to the "money barons" of Montreal and Toronto. He then condemned the government for its opposition to monetary reform, an attitude indicating approval of the existing system. Confident of winning the approaching election, Howson was nevertheless reluctant to antagonize the Social Crediters. He hoped to gain some of their votes for the Liberal party; and he wanted their friendship and support should a coalition government be necessary. Discounting the real strength of the Social Crediters, the Liberal objective was political destruction of the hated U.F.A. Howson attempted, therefore, to use Social Credit to the utmost to harass the U.F.A. without offending Aberhart. The Liberal party, he gleefully announced, had incorporated Social Credit ideas into its own platform.

Much more sensitive than the U.F.A. and the Liberals to Aberhart's criticism of financial institutions, the Conservatives were direct and incisive in their opposition to Social Credit. Their leader, D. M. Duggan, hoped to trap both Aberhart and the U.F.A. in the same pit. In an ironical speech, Duggan urged the government to invite Aberhart and other Social Credit leaders to Edmonton "to submit proposals which, if found practical, and within the legislative competence of the province, the members would desire to have put into effect."

In the face of the tactics of the opposition parties in the legislature, the government faced four factions within the ranks of the U.F.A. The dominant faction, led by the premier and most of his cabinet, believed that the Social Credit proposals, whether advanced by Douglas or by Aberhart, were nonsensical and unconstitutional. Having been very unfavourably impressed by Douglas's intellectual qualities the year before, they were extremely reluctant to invite him again. Although he had been personally congenial, they had been unable to pin him down to any specific programme for Alberta. Feeling that he had a woolly mind, they believed that no more time or money should be wasted on him. They had been irked by Irvine's resolution at the convention and were loath to admit that it tied their hands. But perhaps, some of them reasoned, it might be good politics to invite Douglas to Alberta. He might take their side for he and Aberhart had apparently been far from cordial in their relations during the previous visit. The Irvine faction, ostensibly C.C.F., was rapidly regressing to older ideas of monetary reform. This group now began to argue that monetary reform was the first battle that must be won in a long war for socialism. Irvine believed that he understood Douglas and that Aberhart did not. As the people had become confused by Aberhart's exposition of Social Credit, why not give Douglas another chance to expound and clarify his own theories? Douglas would be in the pay of the government; he might conceivably put a damper on Aberhart and make the latter's movement ineffective politically. Surely everything was to be gained and nothing to be lost by bringing Douglas back to Alberta. The third faction was composed of convinced socialists, who wished no truck or trade with Douglas in any form. Their honest voices were scarcely heard amidst the hullabaloo that the government's indecision had aroused among the people. The fourth faction, not represented among the M.P.'s or M.L.A.'s but numbering thousands among the membership of the U.F.A., was on the verge of going over to the Social Credit movement *en masse*.

The government hoped that delay in following the convention's instructions concerning Douglas would calm the people and halt further defections of its supporters to the Social Credit movement. But during late January and early February it became abundantly clear that the membership of the U.F.A. approved neither of their convention's rejection of Aberhart nor of the government's tactics with regard to Douglas. The impact of the Social Credit movement now began to shatter the U.F.A. organization at its base. The disturbed condition of many locals over the convention's attitude may be illustrated by the following report:

The U.F.W.A. of Delia held a meeting on January 31 to hear the report of their delegates to the recent U.F.A. convention. The meeting broke up in disorder with only three votes supporting the continuation of the organization which had opposed the issue, that the majority of the Delia members were in sympathy with. The result was that a majority of the ladies decided to present themselves in a body and vote for Social Credit as sponsored and led by Mr. William Aberhart, B.A., and the Alberta Social Credit League.[7]

On the same day as the *débâcle* at Delia, with only twenty-four hours' notice of the meeting, crowds flocked from far and near to hear one of Aberhart's secondary leaders speak at Trochu:

In a clear concise manner Mrs. W. W. Rogers showed where Major Douglas only established the underlying principles of Social Credit, but Mr. Aberhart had made definite proposals for Alberta. Mrs. Rogers outlined in detail the Social Credit proposals. The speaker appealed to the people to nominate a

[7]*A.S.C.C.*, March 1, 1935.

Social Credit candidate for the next provincial election and give that candidate 100 per cent support. All questions were ably answered and a very enthusiastic reception was given Mrs. Rogers at the close of the meeting.[8]

Under constant attack in the legislature from the opposition parties, distracted by divided counsels, and increasingly conscious of weakening of its support among the locals, the government still hesitated to follow the convention's instructions. But defections from the U.F.A. membership finally proved too much for it. After long and anxious discussions in caucus, the premier reluctantly announced, on February 22, that Douglas would be brought to Alberta once again to outline a Social Credit plan for the province.

For his services as principal reconstruction adviser to the Alberta government, Douglas exacted a two-year contract, with a fee of $5,000, payable in advance in two equal instalments. He was also to be paid $2,000 for each stay in Alberta not exceeding three weeks. In accepting the appointment Douglas requested assurance of radio and press facilities, which the government promised to the extent of its control. He also requested the "earliest available legal opinion on currency position also limitation on general provincial sovereignty." As he could not reach Alberta before the middle of May, Douglas asked the government to obstruct any hasty changes in the B.N.A. Act![9]

With regard to the powers of the province to legislate on matters relating directly or indirectly to currency or legal tender, Reid forwarded Douglas a memorandum prepared by the counsel in the attorney general's department. The premier then suggested to Douglas:

When you have an opportunity of considering the problem in the light of the information given you on the general question of the right of the province to legislate on matters relating directly or indirectly to currency or legal tender if you will let me have particulars of any suggestions you have to make, we will be glad to give you the benefit of the opinions of the attorney-general with regard to the power to enact legislation provincially to carry out the suggestion.[10]

Any expectations of the U.F.A. leaders that the government's invitation to Douglas would avert a crack-up of the farmers' movement must have been short lived. To its membership the gift of Douglas was too little and too late. The break-up of a local in "next-year country" is typical of what happened throughout the province during the next few months. At a meeting of the Hand Hills Lake U.F.A. local early in

[8]*Ibid.*
[9]*Calgary Herald*, February 22, 1935.
[10]*Ibid.*, March 8, 1935.

March the following resolution was passed and forwarded to the newspapers:

1. We, the members of the Hand Hills Lake Local No. 300 of the U.F.A., believing that the organization has in the past been of great benefit to the farmers of Alberta deplore the stand now taken by our U.F.A. leaders in respect to Social Credit, inasmuch as it must, we believe, inevitably lead to the destruction of our organization.
2. We believe that Mr. William Aberhart sincerely tried to obtain the co-operation of the U.F.A. government last year in a movement that has as its basis the principles that have long been advocated by our organization, that is, public control of finance, a just price, and basic dividends, the last mentioned being merely the logical result of true co-operation within the province. We believe that the opportunity is now offered in our hour of greatest need, to attempt to put into effect that which has been our organization objective and we can no longer support those who, as our leaders, misconstrue a plan that was conscientiously designed to replace an outworn economic system.
3. Therefore we have resolved to discontinue as a local of the U.F.A. and in the meantime carry on as a social organization until such time that another farmers' organization might be formed with leaders in whom we can place our trust.[11]

The officers of U.F.A. locals made strenuous efforts, usually to little avail, to keep the membership in line. As a result, serious dissension frequently developed between the rank and file of a local and their officials. In the Clive area, north of Edmonton, so much dissension developed within the locals over the treatment accorded Aberhart at the U.F.A. convention that it became almost impossible to conduct meetings. The situation that developed in the Eclipse local is typical. Here the members had passed a resolution affirming support of the Douglas Social Credit proposals as enunciated by Aberhart and deprecating the action of the convention in turning down the Aberhart Social Credit proposals for Alberta. The resolution also disagreed "with the unfair argument of the U.F.A. leaders that the Aberhart scheme in any way differs with the principles of the Douglas Social Credit scheme" and strongly protested "the personal political attacks on Mr. Aberhart as made in the U.F.A. publication."[12] Despite the passing of the resolution and another resolution that it be forwarded to the press for publication, the secretary of the local refused to carry out the instruction. As a result of his attitude, the members of the local, at complete loggerheads with their officers, deserted in a body and formed a Social Credit study group.

Defections from the U.F.A. were usually of rank and file membership.

[11]A.S.C.C., March 22, 1935.
[12]Ibid., March 29, 1935.

But that winter even presidents of strongly organized locals were not immune to the appeal of Social Credit, as is illustrated by the following account of a meeting held in the west of the Lacombe constituency by one of Aberhart's touring speakers:

We had not been able to develop any interest in Social Credit there. The district contained a strongly organized U.F.A. Local which had been giving serious study to the socialist programme of the C.C.F. movement. After receiving permission from the local school board to use the school I posted bills announcing I would be there to speak on a certain evening. In the meantime I met the president of this U.F.A. local who took me to task for interfering in a district which already had an organization sponsoring reform. However, he did state that he would attend the meeting.

The local school-teacher acted as my chairman. Having socialistic leanings he took the opportunity to ridicule the efforts of Major Douglas, Mr. Aberhart and myself, and pooh-poohed the whole idea of Social Credit before calling on me to speak. Needless to say, my ire was very much aroused. With a few interruptions which soon disappeared, I spoke for three solid hours, and then was plied with a barrage of questions until about one A.M.

To my amazement our U.F.A. president had remained in absolute silence during the whole evening. But, just at the close, he asked for the floor and proceeded to radically disagree with the performance of my worst critics. He stated that what they had been proposing would never stand the test which the Social Credit principles had received that night. He made it clear that he was through with the U.F.A. In the coming months this chap became our most effective key man for that area.

During the winter and spring the drop in the membership of the U.F.A. was spectacular. On achieving political power in 1921 the organization had a membership of 37,721. By the summer of 1935 this had fallen to 9,838.

While the organization of the U.F.A. rapidly disintegrated, the Social Credit movement steadily gained in strength. On the very day of Reid's announcement of Douglas's visit, Aberhart had bitterly denounced the government's move as "merely a bit of pre-election strategy."[13] The movement's newspaper, in a leading article, dwelt at length upon the utter futility of bringing Douglas back to a province which enjoyed the matchless blessing of Aberhart's knowledge of Social Credit:

Major C. H. Douglas was invited over to Alberta last year, and in spite of the prepared array of questions from the cleverest of Alberta's legislature, he proved conclusively that Social Credit would prove a blessing to the province. Major Douglas also clearly stated that a special plan to suit the needs of this province would have to be drawn up, and that unless he studied conditions in Alberta very closely he could not suggest a plan that could be applied to Alberta.

[13]Calgary Herald, February 22, 1935.

Why bring Major Douglas back on the same trip again? Why pay him $5000 for six weeks advice for that which he has already given?

Major Douglas very clearly states that each and every individual country or state must have a plan to suit their own requirements under Social Credit. Surely these 17 year students of Social Credit that we hear over the air every Thursday night [a reference to radio broadcasts by U.F.A. leaders], after all those years of studying Social Credit should be able, following along the lines laid down by Major Douglas, to suggest a plan for Alberta.

We know, and everybody else knows that until William Aberhart had the courage of his convictions, knowing that Social Credit following along the lines laid out by Major Douglas, would prove a benefit to the people of this province, these old time politicians had no intention whatsoever of sponsoring such a proposal.

Much to their disappointment and in spite of their ridicule during the early stages, they found that Mr. Aberhart's honest appeal to the people was carrying weight, and in such a manner that it spelled absolute defeat in the next provincial election for the government. This must not be allowed. Surely one lone, honest man would not be allowed to destroy the government; we must stop it, but how? With the experience of years of the political game behind them, they came to the conclusion, we'll adopt Social Credit, but we'll have to get rid of that firebrand to our cause—William Aberhart. The best we can do is to gull the people by engaging the services of Major Douglas himself asking for his advice as TO A PLAN OF SOCIAL CREDIT APPLICABLE TO ALBERTA. Not that we are going to put it into operation, but by securing Major Douglas it will show favour in the eyes of the people, in all probability we can split the vote, and our dear old faithful political machine will still be in existence either one way or the other, anything as long as we can stop any new reform party from getting power.[14]

Social Credit speakers on tour of the province insisted that the government's invitation to Douglas could only be understood as another example of the power of wealth. Unless the people of Alberta were unfaltering in their faith in Aberhart, this same wealth would again prove victorious. The speakers emphasized that Douglas himself did not know of conditions in Alberta, and until he did he could not put forward a successful plan. Aberhart, on the other hand, had lived in Alberta for the past twenty-five years, and had been a close student of the province's economic conditions. He was therefore in a much better position than Douglas to suggest a Social Credit plan that could be adopted successfully in Alberta. One Social Crediter's speech sums up the general reaction of the people to Douglas's invitation.

Why do these politicians and financiers try to offset the movement? Why do they try to say Mr. Aberhart's proposals are not sound? Why are they trying to cause a split in the vote of the people? There is only one answer. Social Credit, if adopted in Alberta, is going to be the biggest blow in the world to

[14]*A.S.C.C.*, March 1, 1935.

the racketeering capitalist, and that individual is not going to take this lying down. We all know that money and wealth is a big power, and is going to be a big power from now on until the time of the election. As long as the people of Alberta can close their ears to the lies and misrepresentations that will be profferred them, as long as they can prove themselves steadfast to Social Credit for Alberta, and to its founder, William Aberhart, then there is no question of the result of the election. If Social Crediters win the election, remember this. It will not be a case of investigations for one or two years, but it will mean the adoption of Social Credit principles. If Social Credit is going to be again investigated, and threshed over, then thrown out, then brought back, well, it should take at least another five years, by that time the old parties will still be in power.[15]

The speaker concluded by urging the people to be staunch, faithful, and sincere in their devotion to Aberhart. They must not allow themselves to be led away "by the smooth ponderings of the politician and the capitalist":

They are going to hand you the old-time political "sop" served up on a golden platter; have the courage of your convictions to cast it aside. If William Aberhart tells you his proposals for Social Credit are worth while, if he shows you they are worth while, surely from the lips of a man who has no axe to grind, who is not a politician, but who is only out in a clean, honest manner to help the people, backing his statements on Christian principles, which he himself believes, SUPPORT him.[16]

Instead of calming the people, the government's invitation to Douglas led to an uproar throughout Alberta. Demonstrations on behalf of Aberhart now became so frequent at meetings of U.F.A. locals that the situation was getting completely out of hand. Early in March the government realized that its continuing scorn of Aberhart was proving a boomerang. In desperation, the Cabinet allowed the legislature to adopt, on March 6, a resolution inviting Aberhart himself to submit a Social Credit plan for Alberta.[17] To many this move, which had been recommended earlier by the Conservative leader, seemed a belated recognition of the convention's error in rejecting Aberhart. To many others, it seemed like a frantic political manoeuvre. Shortly after inviting Aberhart, the government arranged for two leading scholars of the University of Alberta, Dean H. R. Weir of the Faculty of Law and Professor G. A. Elliott of the Department of Economics, to give evidence on the constitutionality and economic aspects of Social Credit before the Agricultural Committee of the legislature.

[15]*Ibid.*
[16]*Ibid.*
[17]*Calgary Herald*, March 6, 1935.

The invitation seems to have caught Aberhart unprepared. While he began to think over its implications, the government offered to provide him with a complete staff of accountants, stenographers, and clerks, as well as to compensate him for loss of time and out-of-pocket expenses. The chairman of the Calgary Public School Board announced that Principal Aberhart would be given leave of absence from his duties if he desired to go to Edmonton as Social Credit adviser to the government.[18]

Inclined to the view that the invitation was a trap, the prophet shrewdly waited for the response of the people and sparred for time. His first move was to reiterate, to a mass meeting at Banff, that he had no intention of going into politics or of lining up with a political party.[19] Then, during a provincial-wide radio broadcast, he made public the contents of a letter to Reid. He had asked the premier for answers to the following pertinent questions: What bearing or relationship his services would have upon the duties that had been assigned to Major Douglas; to what extent did the government wish a detailed plan; what was the purpose of having such a plan drawn; did the government have an efficient and comprehensive statistical department; how much time would the government be willing to allow for the preparation of a detailed, comprehensive plan; did the government expect that anyone, with the statistics then available, could draft such a plan within three weeks or two months; if not, would the government reassemble before the election for the purpose of considering the full explanation of the plan?[20]

During the same broadcast, Aberhart disclosed that "a dozen to twenty groups or constituencies" had advised him not to accept the invitation:

The communications had claimed he would be exposed to a number of serious consequences—being made a political football being one of them. "Wait for 100 per cent social credit government," one had said. He said if he could satisfy himself that by formulating a plan—even at the risk of being thrown into "a den of lions"—he would do a service for the people of Alberta, he would do so. Questions in his mind concerned the necessary amount of spade work necessary for a plan. He would be expected to do it "out of pocket." Major Douglas would be given a fee. Furthermore, he understood there was some question in Major Douglas's mind as to the legality and constitutional aspects of a scheme in the province. He, himself, would prefer to see a group of chartered accountants placed on the spade

18*Ibid.*, March 7, 1935.
19*Ibid.*, March 13, 1935.
20*A.S.C.C.*, March 15, 1935.

work before Major Douglas was brought in. Under these conditions of the hiring of Major Douglas, it was apparent those concerned with the invitation do not know much about it.[21]

Throughout this crucial broadcast, Aberhart constantly criticized the government for inviting Major Douglas to Alberta to formulate a plan before the election rather than after it. He insisted that Douglas would be much more useful after a 100 per cent Social Credit government had attained political power. Any plan that Douglas might formulate before the election "would mean little or nothing to those who had been unable to see beyond the present system."

From the beginning, the response of the people to the invitation was negative. They felt that Aberhart had more than done his duty to the legislature the year before. One of his ardent followers has stated the general attitude:

We all know this invitation is only more foolishness just to fool the people. These proposals of Mr. Aberhart's have been so thoroughly gone over during the past year in Alberta, time and time again, that it is safe to say that not one of the outstanding men in the Alberta government today does not know and understand it fully. Why drag Mr. Aberhart before the legislature again for further questioning? Let us wait until the next election. Let us be satisfied in our own strength to offset all these smooth difficulties that are being arranged by the foes of Social Credit. It's another smooth manner of "slipping one over."

On March 18, despite the insistence of hundreds of Social Credit groups that their leader should have no further dealings with the U.F.A. government, the premier wrote to Aberhart, giving straightforward answers to the latter's questions and renewing the invitation to him to come to Edmonton. In reply, Aberhart insisted that he could not "discover the meaning" of Reid's answers to his questions. Nor had the premier indicated either the purpose to which the legislature would put Aberhart's detailed plan or the relation of that plan to the work of Major Douglas.[22] On April 1, Aberhart informed Reid that his school work was too important to allow him to go to Edmonton, even for one day, to discuss a Social Credit plan with the legislature.[23] That same night, he announced in a broadcast that he was not interested in the office of premier; he also indicated that he would not accept the government's offer to act as Social Credit adviser.

Aberhart was now able to adopt a firmer attitude because he was sure

[21]*Ibid.*

[22]The correspondence between Reid and Aberhart was published in full in *A.S.C.C.*, March 22, 1935.

[23]*Calgary Herald*, April 1, 1935.

of the response of the people. Scores of resolutions, advising against his acceptance of the government's invitation, had poured into the Bible Institute headquarters from the constituency conventions and study groups which had been meeting during the previous two weeks to select delegates for the central southern convention. All in the same vein, these constituency resolutions were welded into one resolution, which was passed enthusiastically and unanimously at the Calgary convention:

Whereas, the present government has every opportunity of co-operating with Mr. Aberhart and bringing in a plan of social credit for Alberta; and Whereas the action of the present government of inviting Mr. Aberhart to form a plan of social credit for Alberta at this strategic moment savors of manœuvring for political advantage; and, Whereas, it is our firm belief that the earliest possible introduction of social credit to Alberta can best be assured with a social credit government in power, which is independent of political parties,

Therefore, be it resolved, that this convention strongly urges Mr. Aberhart to refrain from formulating any plan of social credit for the present government.[24]

In a letter to Reid, written on April 12, Aberhart expressed his regret that he was unable to accept the invitation to submit a Social Credit plan to the government. The matter had been taken completely out of his hands by the Social Credit conventions, "which desired his time and presence in the advancement of and studying of Social Credit throughout the province." "I must," he informed the premier, "bow to the mandate of the people."[25]

In making public his letter declining the government's invitation, Aberhart announced that he had received thousands of letters, telegrams, and telephone calls urging him not to accept it. Practically every constituency convention and group meeting had sent in resolutions to the same effect. His decision to accede to the request of the majority of his followers was received enthusiastically all over Alberta. "His refusal to go before the legislature," said one of his followers, "will remove any idea of so-called dictatorship of Mr. Aberhart over his Social Credit groups, when it shows quite clearly that he is only too willing to follow the demands and wishes of the people."

The same day that Aberhart finally rejected the premier's invitation saw also the completion of the hearings of Dean Weir and Professor Elliott before the Agricultural Committee. The evidence presented at these hearings, although somewhat technical, was published immediately

[24]A.S.C.C., April 12, 1935.
[25]Calgary Herald, April 12, 1935.

and distributed widely in the form of a pamphlet entitled, *The Constitutionality and Economic Aspects of Social Credit*.

This pamphlet falls into two parts: first, the evidence of Dean Weir on the constitutionality of Social Credit and second, the evidence of Professor Elliott on the economic aspects of Social Credit. Weir's testimony, after a brief introductory statement, was presented entirely in the form of answers to questions (by leading U.F.A. members of the legislature) based on Aberhart's statements as published in the *Social Credit Chronicle* and in leaflets for the use of study groups. Elliott, however, read a fairly lengthy paper in which he examined, cautiously but critically, the probable economic effects of Aberhart's proposals regarding basic dividends and the just price. This critical analysis was followed by Elliott's answers to questions regarding Aberhart's monetary theories in general.

In presenting his case, Dean Weir stressed sections 91 and 92 of the B.N.A. Act, and chapters 24 (section 138) and 43 (section 24) of the Bank of Canada Act, 1934. From these documents he built up an irrefutable case that the Dominion of Canada has exclusive jurisdiction over the issue of paper money. Alberta would be unable, he insisted, to issue any Social Credit substitute for such money. This view was developed in considerable detail and amply illustrated by reference to Supreme Court and Privy Council decisions. At the conclusion of Weir's testimony the Agricultural Committee invited Mrs. W. W. Rogers or any others interested in Social Credit to question him. U.F.A. leaders considered it significant that no Social Crediters took advantage of this opportunity.

In his testimony, Elliott emphasized that Alberta was not a self-contained province economically. It followed that Aberhart's proposals regarding basic dividends, in the form of non-negotiable certificates ordering the transfer of credits, would be ultimately unworkable in practice. Further, the introduction of such a fundamental monetary change would be accompanied by so much doubt, fear, and uncertainty as to nullify any slight immediate advantage that might accrue from such a move. A similar situation would accompany an effort to introduce and maintain a just price as outlined by Aberhart. If Aberhart's monetary theories were implemented, the people of Alberta would eventually be left without any acceptable circulating medium of currency. Only taxation or borrowing on unprecedented scales could prevent this outcome, and such procedures would merely result in a fantastic system of book-keeping. Aberhart's proposals were incapable, Elliott concluded, of providing any real solution for Alberta's economic problems.

Nothing could have been more acceptable to the U.F.A. leaders than the testimony of Weir and Elliott. In the struggle for power, the pamphlet containing this testimony played a leading role. It quickly became part of the equipment of every U.F.A. speaker, and was constantly quoted during the election campaign when the non-negotiable certificates became the subject of bitter controversy. In reporting the hearings the newspapers played up Weir's argument that Alberta was constitutionally unable to issue a Social Credit substitute for money. Addressing a meeting in Edmonton on the Agricultural Committee's findings, ex-Premier Brownlee challenged Aberhart to demonstrate the legality of the Social Credit proposals.

Aberhart took up the challenge immediately at the largest Social Credit mass meeting held in Calgary up to that time:

As to whether or not the Province had the right to issue non-negotiable certificates Mr. Aberhart stated that anyone who understood Social Credit knows that Dean Weir was wrong when he suggested that under Social Credit, scrip would be used. Social Credit does not use scrip. It was really remarkable even under the use of scrip how such towns as Raymond and Consort had progressed. Does Dean Weir mean to say that the province cannot do as much as these small towns. It is very puzzling to hear these learned gentlemen declare how little the Province can do theoretically, but when they look about them the Province is doing the very thing that they are not allowed to do.

"From legal advice I have received, I am informed that the Province could do anything it wished to do, providing it was done circumspectly," said Mr. Aberhart.

"Surely," continued the speaker, "No government under the British flag would have the power to enforce starvation and economic slavery upon any body of people. There must be equity in legal jurisprudence as well as technical interpretation. There is no British constitution that would prevent any province taking wise steps to feed and clothe the people within its own bounds."[26]

At the conclusion of his address, Aberhart received tremendous applause from the audience, which consisted mainly of railroad men and their wives.

Social Credit speakers throughout the province now knew how to deal with the Weir-Elliott evidence, and hundreds of them likewise received tremendous applause from hundreds of audiences. To Aberhart's followers the judicious report on Social Credit by "the Deans and Professors of the University of Alberta" soon became the subject of a stock joke. "I believe," said one Social Crediter, "some of those same men advise the planting of trees in the desert country of southern Al-

[26]*A.S.C.C.*, April 26, 1935.

berta, where the sage brush has ceased to grow, and the jack rabbit has to pack a lunch to cross some of that territory. Well, maybe the trees will grow; but, still Social Credit won't work, according to their judgment."

The leader of the Conservative party did not share the people's hostility to the dean and the professor. In a fighting speech at Edmonton, following the conclusion of the Agricultural Committee's hearings, Duggan made an uncompromising assault on the Aberhart plan, and the Douglas plan as well. Asserting that the two theories were diametrically opposed, he described them both "as perils which threaten ruin to the Province." He called for war against "the menace of Social Credit as a provincial scheme within a plan, theories, wishes, ideals, yes; but no plan." Comparing statements of Douglas and Aberhart before the Agricultural Committee in 1934, Duggan charged that Aberhart had instructed his followers to "decide against his acceptance of the invitation to come to Edmonton." In a later speech, the Conservative leader said that a Social Credit government would ruin the whole credit structure of Alberta, and he foresaw a drop in Alberta bond prices if Aberhart were elected.[27] Social Credit was subsequently described as "lunacy" by Major-General Griesbach in an address before the Edmonton Conservative Association.[28]

Unlike the Conservatives, the Liberals attacked neither Douglas nor Aberhart. Nor did they over-estimate the intelligence of the people, for they realized the political implications of a situation in which the people were laughing at the dean and the professor and giving enthusiastic ovations to the prophet. Liberal speakers announced that they were as strongly in favour of the payment of provincial or national dividends as were Social Credit supporters themselves. Liberals would not criticize Social Credit, at least until the plan for Social Credit became known. "We as Liberals should be ready to accept any ideas to see if they might be practicably applied for the betterment of the people's condition," declared the federal candidate for Calgary West. Liberalism stood strongly for pensions for the blind, those unable to earn enough to support their children, the disabled, and the underprivileged. "This is the system of Social Credit," the candidate declared, "that will come under a Liberal government."

Speaking at a mass meeting in Olds, following the Liberal nominating convention, Howson insisted that his party was the only political organization in Alberta that had definitely made known its stand on Social Credit. Outlining the existing monetary system, and the sweeping

[27]*Calgary Herald*, May 1, 1935.
[28]*Ibid.*, May 9, 1935.

reforms proposed by his party, he presented the monetary reform plank in the Liberal platform as the answer to Social Crediters. The Aberhart movement was a natural consequence of the existing monetary policy. The Liberals had no quarrel with Social Credit, but they feared too drastic steps: the people should keep their feet on the ground. In conclusion, Howson pledged himself, when returned to power, to employ three of the most expert Social Credit authorities to investigate all proposed schemes of Social Credit and submit the findings to the legislature. Almost to the end, the Liberals directed their attack on the U.F.A. and adopted a conciliatory attitude towards the Social Credit movement.

During the period when Aberhart was dealing with the personal and political problems involved in his invitation to Edmonton, his political opponents began systematically to maintain that Douglas could not, and did not, approve either of Aberhart's interpretation of Social Credit or of the Alberta movement's transition to political action. On the eve of the southern convention, the *Calgary Herald* initiated the new propaganda by publishing a letter sent to its editor from Douglas's London Secretariat. In view of the conflicting attitudes of various bodies throughout the world which were claiming to represent the principles of Douglas Social Credit, the Secretariat had found it necessary to make clear its general attitude towards both technique and policy. The Secretariat emphasized that

it would not support any proposal, scheme or plan which is in its opinion technically unsound, or which would limit the economic freedom of the individual by imposing moral conditions on his receipt of a national dividend. . . . it does not support the putting forward of detailed proposals by any group or party for election purposes, but is prepared in the person of its chairman, Major Douglas, to advise any government which has a mandate to deal with the existing financial system. Only one proposal, and that of an interim nature, has up till now carried the authority of Major Douglas and the Secretariat. This proposal was specifically designed and put forward in relation to the situation which existed in New Zealand in 1933.

The Secretariat believes that the function of democracy is to demand results, not to indicate methods.

Any person, group or party not in agreement with the principles expressed [above] may, of course, be doing invaluable work in attacking the credit monopoly, but cannot properly claim the title "Douglas Social Credit," or the authority of Major Douglas and the Secretariat.[29]

This announcement from London made no impact whatever upon the delegates to the Calgary convention. But, in their efforts to discredit Aberhart, U.F.A. and Conservative speakers circulated it widely.

[29]*Ibid.*, April 3, 1935.

Aware of his strength with the people, Aberhart realized that he must, nevertheless, strive to avoid an open break with Douglas prior to the election. Douglas, on his part, seems to have been equally anxious to maintain at least the appearance of concord with his prophet. Delicate situations, tending to impair this joint strategy, were not infrequently created by the people themselves. Wildly enthusiastic over Aberhart, they now showed a tendency to look upon Douglas as a government hireling. During this period many Social Crediters seem to have concluded that Douglas had created something too big for him to handle. Thus a mass meeting in Camrose passed unanimously a resolution "urging that Major C. H. Douglas be not brought to Alberta in the capacity of financial adviser to the provincial government until after the election." Then Premier Aberhart would be able to put him wise, not only to public affairs in Alberta but to "real Social Credit as well."[30]

During the spring of 1935 the people's loyalty and devotion to Aberhart were constantly being reaffirmed by resolutions passed at meetings of Social Credit study groups and nominating conventions throughout Alberta. At a conference of the groups in the High River-Okotoks constituency, for example, the delegates and visitors stated that they had no confidence whatever in the capacities or intentions of the U.F.A., even under Major Douglas's guidance, to implement the principles of Social Credit. Douglas's services, they insisted, should not be sought until after the forthcoming election. The delegates unanimously and enthusiastically affirmed their absolute confidence in Aberhart and his principles of Social Credit.

Shortly afterwards, the delegates to a nominating convention at Staveley insisted that the actions of the U.F.A. government had proved conclusively that it was opposed to Social Credit as advocated by Aberhart. Emphasizing, once again, their absolute confidence in their leader, the delegates informed Aberhart that they were now firmly convinced that they could trust no other leader or party to solve Alberta's problems. Bitter hostility to the U.F.A. and uncritical devotion to Aberhart had now become general attitudes among Social Crediters.

Many Social Crediters became convinced that the U.F.A. had invited Douglas to Alberta as bait in a last desperate effort to catch support in a dying cause. This view was elaborated in an editorial in the *Social Credit Chronicle* on March 29:

Surely every thinking man and woman in Alberta today must know that the "Bait" of bringing Major Douglas to Alberta to outline a social credit plan for the province of Alberta is only a blind for the present provincial govern-

[30]*A.S.C.C.*, March 29, 1935.

ment to try and retain their office. They know as everybody else knows, social credit is the most popular form of economics ever offered to Alberta, they know that it is being favored by more than seventy-five per cent of the people, they also know that social credit candidates in the next provincial election are the menace to their return to power. Hence in spite of ridiculing social credit, claiming that it cannot be worked, stating that Aberhart is only a dreamer, telling the people they are foolish to listen to it, they suddenly without any warning decide to spend thousands to secure Major Douglas to come over here and bring in a plan for social credit. Is it feasible or reasonable? Never mind how sincere they claim to be, doesn't it sound, putting it in plain language, "FISHY?"

Social Crediters, the editorial concluded, would not be taken in by the government's sudden anxiety to secure Douglas as its economic adviser. The whole affair was just a big political bluff. The people of Alberta would not allow themselves to be side-tracked by political promises and intrigues of the U.F.A. government. The people would support only Aberhart, for they knew that he, alone, had a straightforward solution to the paradox of "poverty in the midst of plenty."

In an attempt to counteract the uncritical enthusiasm of Social Crediters for their leader, the U.F.A. challenged Aberhart to produce a detailed plan for the solution of Alberta's economic problems. Aberhart, they argued, had not produced such a plan, because he really had no plan. Had he not admitted in Edmonton at the convention of the Northern Social Credit League that he had no plan? Douglas, government leaders insisted, was being brought to Alberta in the expectation that he would be able to formulate a plan.[31]

To the U.F.A. criticism that he had no plan, Aberhart replied that he had never asked that his name be tagged to a Social Credit plan. It was true that he had put forward no plan. *But neither had Mr. Douglas.* Stating that he was in perfect accord with the Douglas Social Credit system, Aberhart insisted that, when Douglas came to Alberta to prepare a Social Credit plan, he would be the first to say, "we will be glad to help you."

In their unceasing effort to discredit Aberhart, his opponents now shifted their tactics: they charged him with mixing up religion and politics as a substitute for an authentic Social Credit plan. The leaders in this attack were ex-Premier Brownlee and the *Calgary Herald.* Brownlee asserted that it was a tragedy for any man to go before the people of Alberta with hopes that could not be fulfilled. Aberhart, he said, had worked the people up to such a religious frenzy that they were refusing to listen to reason or common sense.

[31]*Calgary Herald*, April 20, 1935.

Brownlee's attack made no impact upon the mass following of the Social Credit movement. "Does he wish to infer," asked the editor of the *Social Credit Chronicle*, "that Mr. Aberhart has the power to work over seventy-five per cent of the population of Alberta into a religious frenzy, and hold them as it were in a hypnotic spell?" Everyone knew, the editor continued, that Aberhart's religious principles were "true and worthwhile." Further, unlike many others, Aberhart lived up to his religious principles. In promoting Social Credit, he had no other interest at heart than the welfare of mankind. Surely his actions were in full accord with the highest principles of religion!

If these people who are so apt to criticize [the editor concluded], produce a plan that is better than Social Credit and will work more scientifically and feasibly why the people would be only too pleased to listen, but to openly attack a plan like Social Credit, and have nothing whatever to offer in its place is simply a "Dog in the Manger" attitude, such as the big financial houses have been using for the past generations.

We appeal to the people of this province to stand firm in their belief in Social Credit, we know it is the most feasible proposal that has yet been offered to deliver us out of our present chaos, and we also know that Mr. Aberhart assures us of his own true belief in the proposals, and with that assurance let us be willing to give it a trial, we cannot be any worse than we are at the present time, and when Social Credit promises us hope for the betterment of conditions, let us have the faith to support it.[32]

But the *Calgary Herald* refused to accept such exhortations. Day after day it accused Aberhart of using religious fanaticism as a cloak for his inability to produce a genuine Social Credit plan for Alberta. Lashed beyond endurance, he finally struck back. On April 29, three days after Douglas sailed for Canada, Aberhart urged his followers to boycott the *Herald*: "Some of the citizens of this province," he exclaimed, "cannot distinguish falsity from the truth. I am cancelling my subscription to-morrow. What about yours?"[33]

The controversy between Aberhart and the *Calgary Herald* was at its height when Douglas reached Canada, early in May. At that time Aberhart was also in the midst of his long radio duel with Norman Priestley, vice-president of the U.F.A. The Liberals and Conservatives were issuing statements on Social Credit almost daily, the former conciliatory, the latter in bitter opposition. Amidst such an atmosphere, the U.F.A. and the metropolitan newspapers utilized every opportunity to alienate Douglas from Aberhart personally, to convince the people that Aberhart did not really understand Social Credit, and to elicit from

[32]*A.S.C.C.*, May 17, 1935.
[33]*Calgary Herald*, April 29, 1935.

Douglas a repudiation of Aberhart's leadership of the Social Credit movement in Alberta.

Douglas's journey across Canada to Edmonton had something of the air of a royal progress. Besieged by journalists at the larger centres, he did not hesitate to talk freely about Social Credit. His every utterance was dramatized and carefully analysed for clues concerning his attitudes to Aberhart and the Alberta movement. Nearly everything Douglas said in these interviews was interpreted by the enemies of the Social Credit movement in Alberta as hostile to Aberhart.

In the face of incessant efforts on the part of his opponents to separate him from Douglas, Aberhart insisted repeatedly that the two of them differed only on non-essential points. The hostile press, of course, tried to use everything that either of them said concerning the other to provoke a quarrel between them. Their most effective weapon became Aberhart's doctrine of basic dividends. The newspapers quoted him as saying he was at variance with Douglas on the question of dividends, and added that he himself favoured a dividend of twenty to twenty-five dollars a month. Then, in an interview at Winnipeg, Douglas was quoted as "seeing difficulty in Aberhart's twenty-five dollar dividend plan and as being opposed to Social Credit on a party basis."[34]

The relationship between the two men became more and more difficult to define. When Douglas arrived in Edmonton, on May 13, the journalists tried in vain to draw him out on the Aberhart plan. He remained silent. Ten days later Aberhart announced his willingness to take advice from Douglas on a Social Credit plan for Alberta.[35] The two did not meet until after Douglas had submitted his interim report to the government. Then Aberhart announced that he was confident his plan for Alberta would be favoured by Douglas. But a week later Douglas publicly repudiated Aberhart's Yellow Pamphlet, *The Douglas System of Economics*, published over two years previously.[36] The press was gleeful, for a split seemed inevitable. June the eighth was a field-day for the journalists. On the morning of that day Aberhart denied publicly that there was any split betwen Douglas and himself. In the afternoon Douglas, in a special report to the government, rapped Aberhart's taxation plans. In the evening, at a great mass meeting, Aberhart claimed that his Social Credit proposals and Douglas's proposals were identical; if they were not he (Aberhart) would be willing to make changes where necessary. Then Douglas criticized one of Aberhart's speeches. Aberhart

34*Ibid.*, May 11, 1935.
35*Ibid.*, May 23, 1935.
36*Ibid.*, June 3, 1935.

retaliated by criticizing Douglas's criticism of his speech. Douglas, he said, must have taken the speech he criticized "out of thin air." Contrary to what U.F.A. leaders had poured into Douglas's ears, Aberhart insisted that he "really and truly" did understand the principles of Social Credit.[37]

The newspapers' relentless criticisms of Aberhart, coupled with an insistent demand for a detailed Social Credit plan for Alberta, placed Douglas in an extremely awkward position during his three weeks' visit to Edmonton. As the paid economic adviser of the government, he was wined and dined and taken to the best golf-club by U.F.A. Cabinet ministers, who made no effort to conceal their contempt for Aberhart. At the same time, he appreciated the psychological significance of Aberhart's mass movement for the future of Social Credit. Contrary to the impression given to the public by the newspapers, Douglas seems to have been reluctant to appear even mildly critical of Aberhart. On June 2, in a last-minute attempt to counteract the newspapers' distortion of his statements concerning Aberhart's version of Social Credit, Douglas sent a personal letter to Aberhart:

In view of certain mischievous comments in the public press suggesting the existence of wholly non-existent friction in regard to our personal relations, I think it is desirable to assure you that no statement in regard to matters in Alberta which is not a written statement signed by me, has any authority from me, and to suggest that even in regard to such written statements or reports, if you consider them important, that you should assure yourself that they are complete and are not detached from matter that modify their meaning.

This letter, which was published on June 8 in the *Social Credit Chronicle*, cleared the air as far as Aberhart's followers were concerned. In their struggle for power Social Crediters constantly used this letter as a conclusive demonstration of Douglas's favourable attitude to Aberhart's programme for Alberta.

Whatever may have been the government's motives in inviting him to Edmonton, Douglas envisaged his own role as quite other than that of lending support to those who sought, by involving him in controversy with Aberhart, to denigrate the Social Credit movement. His duty, as he himself saw it, was to formulate a preliminary Social Credit plan for Alberta, and to this task he studiously addressed himself.

After ten days' study of the Alberta situation, Douglas submitted his eagerly awaited report to the government on May 23. The complete text of this report was not released to the public by Premier Reid until June 5.

[37]See *Calgary Herald*, Calgary *Albertan*, *Edmonton Bulletin*, *Edmonton Journal*, June 4–10, 1935.

It was subsequently published and widely circulated by the government in pamphlet form under the title, *First Interim Report on the Possibilities of the Application of Social Credit Principles to the Province of Alberta, by Major C. H. Douglas.* Included in this pamphlet was certain correspondence which followed the Report, between Reid and Douglas, and between the Honourable J. F. Lymburn, Attorney General, and Douglas.

Douglas introduces his Report with a lengthy preamble in which he comments, in a general way, upon the nature of the Alberta community, the essential wealth of such a community, the barter system as an earlier circulating medium, the modern cheque as a "credit instrument," and the art of banking. He concludes that the economic difficulties of Alberta require a departure from methods which, while moderately effective in the past, are no longer applicable to present conditions:

Any attempt to deal with the situation, which does not recognize its fundamental cause, must discredit the Administration and eventually result either in an abolition of organized forms of government in favour of a pure financial hegemony, or in a continuous disintegration of social morale, possibly ending in something approaching anarchy. Both Europe and America, under the Bank of England and the Federal Reserve System respectively, have been subjected to almost a complete financial hegemony for the past fifteen years, with the results which are evident.

If this aspect of the matter were that alone requiring consideration, it does not appear probable that any government could hesitate in immediately instituting modifications designed to rectify the situation. Unfortunately, however, this monopoly of the creation of effective demand, which has been allowed to pass for the most part into the hands of the banking system, from its very nature constitutes a formidable power, having objectives of its own not those of the general population, and it is therefore entirely proper that the consequences of challenging its interests should be examined. (P. 4.)

In the second section of the Report, "The Nature of the Preliminary Enquiry," Douglas begins by emphasizing the distinction between any particular plan for the utilization of the public credit, once control of it has been acquired, and the strategy for acquiring the power to deal with public credit. He must, he insists, confine himself in his preliminary report "to possible methods and strategy in regard to the preliminary objective, that of obtaining access to the public credit." No effective strategy could expect the whole-hearted co-operation of bankers and financiers who already possess the powers and privileges that accompany a monopoly of credit. "Every step in this direction," he writes (p. 5), "will be opposed by, e.g., the Bank of Canada, acting for the International Bankers." Taking the law as it stands, what rights does the province of Alberta possess as against the claim of the banking system to legal control of public credit?

In answering this question, Douglas admits that the power of printing paper money, or that which passes as money, belongs to the Dominion, which has delegated it to the Bank of Canada.[38] But such an admission does not dispose of the whole question, for banks issue cheques which pass as money, although they are not Dominion or Bank of Canada documents. Then, too, matters of property and civil rights are the exclusive domain of the provincial government. Surely, Douglas insists, an individual has the civil right "to write an order upon himself, calling for the delivery of a portion of his property." Furthermore, a province has the right to raise loans upon "the sole credit of the Province." If the provinces have no power to issue credit instruments, Douglas argues that the phrase "the sole credit of the Province" can have no financial meaning, although it may have a realistic meaning:

It would therefore seem that there is room for considerable action on the part of the Province without placing the Province in danger of the invocation of legal sanctions against it, by the banking system, acting on the premise that it has sustained a tort. The second obvious sanction (and one not contained in the legal system) to be considered is the effect which might be produced by a refusal of financial facilities from the existing financial system, together with an attack of a psychological nature upon the action of the Province. (Pp. 5–6.)

If credit instruments can be issued under the sanction of the legally constituted authority of the province, there would be no difficulty in obtaining their universal acceptance within the range of provincial jurisdiction. Douglas admits that a problem might arise in connection with payments for imports from outside the credit area. But this difficulty could be overcome by the accumulation of a considerable amount of "foreign currency" or credit. Action against the existing monopoly of credit is possible, therefore, within the constitutional powers of a province.

Financial interests would, of course, resist bitterly any attempt to break their monopoly of credit. But these interests, Douglas suggests, are not wholly in control of sanctions. In Alberta, where the people had become "money conscious," vindictive action by financial authorities

[38]As Douglas's understanding of the delegation of note issue to the Bank of Canada was confused, his statement on this point is misleading. The Bank of Canada legislation of 1934 required the chartered banks to *reduce* their issue by a certain percentage each year for a certain number of years. Then, finally, the balance was cut off. The right to issue notes was not, therefore, finally taken from the *chartered banks* until January 1, 1945.

could be counteracted by the use of the press and radio. Other sanctions (which would better be merely suggested than actually used) exist in psychological threats like repudiation of Alberta's external debt or secession.

The Report concludes that Alberta is confronted with the following alternatives: first, the continuance of orthodox financial policies, and second, the adoption of Douglas's Social Credit proposals. Past experience has demonstrated that the first policy cannot solve Alberta's problems. But, Douglas concludes, the second policy would, within a very short time, minimize Alberta's unemployment problem, raise its standard of living, and make possible a systematic development of its resources on a scale otherwise unattainable. The second policy would, of course, involve temporary difficulties with regard to imports, political conflict with the Dominion government, and considerable misrepresentation of the province's aims and policies.

In urging the Alberta government to implement his Social Credit proposals, Douglas concludes his Report as follows:

In general, and without at the moment going into too much detail, the preliminary steps to be taken in this direction are, in my opinion:

(1) The systematic provision of a News circulation system under the unchallengeable control of the Province, particularly in regard to radio facilities of sufficient power to cover a wide geographical area.

(2) The organization of some Credit Institution, either under the Dominion Bank Act or otherwise, which will give access to the creation of effective demand through the credit system, on principles already well recognized and established.

(3) Systematic organization directed to the accumulation of what, for the purposes of this report, may be termed "foreign exchange", i.e., effective demand not subject to attack as being recognizable as having been created within the Province. (Pp. 7–8.)

In a letter conveying his Interim Report to Premier Reid, Douglas emphasized his belief that no mere redistribution of purchasing power already available in Alberta could attain the results demanded by the general situation and by public opinion, nor could the required credit be obtained from ordinary sources. "Before I can proceed very much further," he wrote to Reid, "I must have some decision as to the general policy which is to be pursued, and I am aware myself that you will require a mandate for such a decision." Such a mandate, he recommended to Reid, should be asked for objectives rather than for mechanisms. The three objectives listed at the conclusion of his Interim Report, Douglas added, should be supplemented by a statement of four fundamental, ultimate objectives: (a) a drastic reduction of taxation, particularly upon real property; (b) a maintenance dividend as of right, possibly small at first, and graded so as to be at a maximum after middle age; (c) measures designed to produce a low price level within the province, with adequate remuneration to the producer and trader; and (d) development of internal resources based rather upon physical capacity than upon financial considerations. As such objectives could be achieved only by the control of local credit, Douglas pointed out that the problem was at least as much political as technical. Therefore, he concluded, a coalition government should be formed as soon as possible, and a Department of Public Relations should be set up both to keep the people informed and to discourage "by suitable methods loose accusations of defective administration." At the close of his letter, Douglas complained that he could do little more in Alberta until the government informed him specifically regarding its future policy: he proposed, therefore, to return to England where, with the information concerning Alberta already in his possession, he could continue his work for several months.

The leaders of the U.F.A. were, of course, keenly disappointed with Douglas's report. Contrary to their hopes and expectations when the father of Social Credit was invited by the government to act as its economic adviser, Douglas had failed to deliver the goods. Nowhere in his report had he declared that the Aberhart scheme could not be put into effect in Alberta as a unit: in fact, he had not even mentioned Aberhart's name once. The report could certainly not be used to end Aberhart's campaign to implement Social Credit at the provincial level.

But in spite of their chagrin, government leaders continued to treat Douglas with the utmost courtesy. Reid wrote to Douglas on June 1, reminding him that whereas the people had expected an outline of a Social Credit plan applicable to Alberta, he had replied that no such plan could be formulated "without much further study of statistical data with respect to production, imports, and other economic factors," and this study could not be undertaken until the power to deal with the public credit had been secured. "Undoubtedly questions will raise themselves in our minds," Reid concluded, "as a result of our continued consideration of these matters, and I will be writing you from time to time as there is occasion to do so." On this urbane note the U.F.A. leaders generally rested their case with the public as far as Douglas personally was concerned.

Although the canny Douglas had been fully aware of what he had been expected to do, in view of the political situation in Alberta, he was impressed by the government's reception of his report. Writing of this experience two years later, he stated:

While the receipt of the First Interim Report by Mr. Reid (the Premier) must have been a blow to any hope he may have entertained that the menace to the Farmers' Government would be disposed of by means of my appointment, it was received both by him and by the Members of the Cabinet, with the utmost courtesy.[39]

Douglas appears to have been impressed not only by the good manners of the U.F.A. leaders but also by their intelligence. It is reported that on more than one social occasion he confided to them: "I have all the damn fools on my side and all the clever men against me." The Cabinet ministers were not prepared to return the compliment: privately, they now agreed among themselves that Douglas was extremely fuzzy-minded —a conclusion they had more or less reached during his appearances before the Agricultural Committee a year previously.

The restrained public attitude of U.F.A. leaders to Douglas's Report was not exhibited by the newspapers and the spokesmen of other parties. Headlines like "Report by Douglas disappoints and puzzles City M.L.A.'s," "Is Called Conglomeration of Words," and "Douglas Plan Clashes with Federal Right" were spread over the front pages of daily newspapers as soon as the Report was made public. A Conservative M.L.A. declared, "If a plan can only be presented in words which cannot be understood, it has no place in a world where clear thinking is required." A prominent Liberal M.L.A. added: "It is hardly understandable, and I can get very little out of it; however, it is just what I expected." In a radio address D. M. Duggan, the Conservative leader and the Report's severest critic, said he was lost among "a conglomeration of words costing a dollar each."[40] In an all-out attack, he angrily insisted that Douglas had underestimated the intelligence of the Alberta people. Other speakers emphasized the glaring discrepancies between Douglas's vague Report and the scholarly Weir–Elliott testimony that had preceded it a few weeks earlier. Newspapers and political speakers who attacked the Report were in substantial agreement that Douglas had not formulated, and never would be able to formulate, a Social Credit plan for Alberta. At long last, in their opinion, he had been fully exposed as an intellectual faker.

While Liberals and Conservatives denounced Douglas's Report, and

[39]C. H. Douglas, *The Alberta Experiment* (London: Eyre and Spottiswoode, 1937), chapter 1.
[40]*Calgary Herald*, June 7, 1935.

the U.F.A. remained silent, Social Crediters were jubilant. The Report was published in full in the June 14 issue of the *Social Credit Chronicle* and given lengthy analytical reviews in the issues of June 28 and July 5. In discussing the Report at meetings, Social Credit speakers pointed out that the government had fully anticipated that Douglas would repudiate Aberhart's proposals as being inapplicable to Alberta. The Report, they insisted, showed clearly that their leader's proposals could be implemented at the provincial level. There could no longer be any question, therefore, regarding Douglas's favourable attitude to Aberhart's proposals. Throughout Alberta, Social Crediters used the Report with unrestrained enthusiasm as a new and dynamic support for their cause.

In a last desperate effort to discredit Aberhart, the Attorney General, J. F. Lymburn, submitted to Douglas excerpts from a broadcast given by Aberhart on May 28 in which he had explained the operation of the "Just Price," with the request that Douglas, as economic adviser to the government, should comment on the explanation. But Douglas would not be trapped. In reply to Lymburn he stated, in part:

It appears to me to be quite reasonable to assume that a popular leader, as distinct from a scientific expositant, is chiefly concerned with presenting an understandable picture rather than with great accuracy in detail.

As a matter of opinion, I think Mr. Aberhart has made the common tactical mistake of elaborating his detail to a general audience to too great an extent, but if this detail is to be taken seriously I think that Mr. Aberhart should as a matter of courtesy be asked whether such details are, or are not, a matter of principle with him. . . . Generally speaking, it would appear upon the face of it that Mr. Aberhart has not grasped that Social Credit involves the *creation* of additional purchasing power, either by the reduction of prices below cost, for the purpose of enabling the consumer to obtain more goods for a given amount of money in his possession, while the financial deficit thus caused is made up to the producer in fresh credit, or by issuing additional sufficient purchasing power which is not passed through the costing system, and therefore does not increase prices, in the form of a National Dividend, or more probably by both of these methods together.

But as I have previously said, these ideas are not easy to put over to large masses of people, and unless Mr. Aberhart were to persist in actually attempting to attain an increase of purchasing power by the processes he discussed I should not myself be inclined to take a political speech containing them with too much seriousness.

By publishing the Lymburn-Douglas correspondence as an addendum to the Interim Report, the government ensured both its wide circulation and the critical attention of the press.

Once again, Social Crediters turned a U.F.A. effort to discredit Aberhart to the advantage of their own cause. They declared that frustrated government leaders, to conceal their bitter disappointment over the Interim Report, had been forced to resort to publishing Douglas's private correspondence, which had obviously never been intended for the public prints. Further, they insisted that a careful reading of Douglas's letter indicated that he was not really against Aberhart or the adoption of Social Credit in Alberta. Douglas's criticism, Social Crediters added, had been based on a broadcast he did not even hear, indeed, merely on a newspaper report of a broadcast. Hence it was not at all a direct criticism of the broadcast, but an indirect criticism of a report of the broadcast. It was, therefore, not so much a case of Aberhart's failure to understand Douglas as of Douglas's failure to understand Aberhart. Had not Aberhart, they asked, won about 90 per cent of the voters of Alberta to the cause of Social Credit? After he had won the election by "a large and enthusiastic majority," he would, in all probability, employ Douglas to draft the actual Social Credit plan.[41]

During the difficult weeks of Douglas's residence in Edmonton, Aberhart, as we have seen, attempted to be irenic and conciliatory in the face of repeated efforts of opponents of Social Credit to stir up trouble between the two men. But he refused to accept passively Douglas's criticism of his exposition of Social Credit in the Lymburn correspondence. In a sharp radio reply to Douglas, delivered shortly after the latter had sailed for England, he insisted that U.F.A. leaders had misinformed their economic adviser. He rejected outright Douglas's charge that he had gone into too much detail in expounding Social Credit. "I am convinced," he declared, "that we could never have had the astounding results we have had if we continually spoke in generalities and did not bring the subject matter down to the detail of everyday life."

Social Crediters were now convinced that they had nothing to fear from Douglas. The newspapers and the U.F.A. had failed utterly in their efforts to break the people's faith in Aberhart. It had become clear that even if the attempt of the newspapers to alienate Aberhart and Douglas had succeeded, the people would not have swerved from their unquestioning loyalty to their leader. From the beginning, they viewed the duel that the press whipped up between the two men as just so much more anti-Social Credit propaganda. Instead of impairing Aberhart's leadership, such propaganda confirmed his hold over the masses. Impatient for an election, many people considered that Douglas's visit was a last desperate strategy of the U.F.A. to postpone the judgment day. Others saw in the renewed attempt to discredit Aberhart merely a repetition of the New Age Club controversy of the previous spring. However they

[41]*A.S.C.C.*, June 14, 1935.

might interpret the objective situation, Social Crediters were infuriated that the newspapers and the government should, once again, have tried to compromise the one man who could save Alberta. Their bitter resentment gave a new impetus to their cause.

Events in Alberta during the winter and spring of 1935 suggest that the conventional strategy and tactics of political parties are impotent in the face of a revolt of the masses. No matter how deeply the Social Credit movement might become involved in the web of politics, the rebellious masses had become convinced that it was not, and would never be, just another political party. Old-line politicians and partisan newspapers had tried desperately to make a political issue out of Social Credit. They had failed hopelessly. They must fail hopelessly because the Social Credit movement was *not* a political party. Though it might contest an election, it was still *not* a political party. What, then, was it? As the spring of 1935 passed into summer, Aberhart's mass following became aware of the answer. The Social Credit movement was, under God, a crusade beyond politics.

CHAPTER SEVEN

The Secondary Leaders

WE HAVE EMPHASIZED the position of Aberhart as undisputed leader of the Social Credit movement. That movement was, in essence, a following. But, in spite of Aberhart's ascendancy, the movement's entrance into politics necessitated the development of an *élite* to meet the requirements of constituency representation in the Alberta legislature. The political *élite* comprised the sixty-three candidates who were finally selected by Aberhart, in consultation with his advisory committee, to contest the sixty-three seats in the fifty-three constituencies, Calgary and Edmonton having multi-member representation, each with six seats.

As we have seen, these candidates were chosen from approximately 250 men and women who had been nominated at constituency conventions held in March and April of 1935. This larger group, in turn, comprised the survivors of balloting at the conventions: the top four names in each constituency were laid before Aberhart and the advisory committee. As seven or more names had been placed before each convention, the sixty-three candidates emerged as a result of an elaborate and long-drawn-out process of election and selection from a group ultimately consisting of over 450 individuals.

In a broadcast the day following the public announcement of the Social Credit candidates, Aberhart was greatly concerned to emphasize the representative character of the advisory committee's final choices. He insisted also that when the advisory committee examined the 250 constituency nominees, it had "sought the co-operative spirit of each of them." Invariably one question had been asked: "In case you do not receive the nomination or the decision to be the candidate for the constituency, will you continue to support with your very best effort the Social Credit principles as you have already done?" Without exception the nominees agreed and acquiesced in the committee's desire for co-operation. It was evident, Aberhart continued, that all the nominees could not become candidates. Some nominees and their friends were bound to be disappointed. But the advisory committee had taken great pains: they had "weighed the matter in every constituency using their very best judgment." It had not been an easy task, for they had found that in every instance at least two or three and sometimes four were equally qualified to represent the constituency. The fact that they chose one nominee rather than another implied no dishonour or discredit to those who had been unsuccessful. Enemies of the movement, Aberhart concluded, would be quick to take advantage of any dissatisfaction that might arise as a result of the committee's decisions. The Social Credit crusade was more important than its electoral candidates; those who thought otherwise were hindering progress. To refuse to vote Social Credit merely because a certain candidate had not been chosen was to exalt the individual at the expense of the welfare of the people. He appealed, in conclusion, to the unsuccessful nominees:

I therefore beseech you to face this question bravely. We are going over the trenches now. If you falter, we will fail, and remember the enemy will take advantage of your faltering. Please do not let anyone fill your soul with their abominable pride which suggests to you that Social Credit cannot carry without you, or some other one as a candidate. If you do, you may reveal to your fellows at once that after all it was not the welfare of the people at large that you were anxious about but that you had hoped for personal self-advantagement and therefore were not really qualified to be a candidate.[1]

Such an appeal revealed Aberhart's fear that the unsuccessful nominees might become rallying centres for dissatisfied followers. It also revealed something of the ordeal through which the sixty-three candidates had passed on their way to secondary leadership in the movement. As it turned out, Aberhart had no reason to be apprehensive as far as the unsuccessful nominees were concerned. If they felt critical towards the advisory committee or its selections, they never revealed their discontent. Without exception, they continued to work energetically for the movement. A number of them became federal candidates in 1935 or provincial candidates in subsequent elections.

There is considerable evidence that the candidates chosen were men and women thoroughly representative of most levels of Albertan society. It is doubtful, in fact, whether Aberhart and the advisory committee could have made more capable selections from the names sent forward by the constituency conventions. At the same time it must be emphasized that those finally chosen had convinced Aberhart of their absolute loyalty to his person, and that they had emerged as a result of a rigorous screening process perhaps unparalleled in democratic politics. Above the candidates hovered the requirements prescribed for them by Aberhart.

[1] U.F.A. File of Aberhart broadcasts, July 23, 1935.

Those requirements included acceptance of his, rather than Douglas's, interpretation of Social Credit. For most of the candidates this was no hardship. Very few of them had actually read Douglas's writings, and probably not more than three were open to suggestions that Aberhart's interpretation of Social Credit doctrine left something to be desired. They had all heard Aberhart speak many times, and had also read eagerly his expositions of Social Credit contained in the leaflets and pamphlets distributed from the headquarters of the movement at the Bible Institute. Immediately following its publication, early in July, 1935, Aberhart's Blue Manual became the doctrinal guide-book for all save one or two of the candidates. However passionately they might expound Social Credit, they always thought of that ideology in terms of the forms developed by Aberhart within the Alberta context. They never ran the risk of becoming technical critics of something they had failed to understand.

The general character of the candidates was determined by another requirement. At the southern and northern conventions Aberhart had instructed the delegates to advise the nominating conventions of the dangers of destruction of the movement from within by the infiltrating tactics of the opposition. He had suggested that no one who had been an official of, or strongly connected with, any other political party should be considered as a potential candidate of the Social Credit party. When the list of candidates was published, the newspapers commented that they were persons largely unknown to the public. The journalists failed to realize, however, that each candidate had become well known within the movement in his own constituency, and that a number who had been engaged in extensive speaking tours for nearly two years were widely known throughout the province.

Owing to the provincial reputations of a considerable number of the electoral candidates, it is more appropriate to designate the whole group as "secondary leaders" rather than "local leaders." The latter term has a grass-roots connotation, implying restricted leadership, at the most within a constituency. With the exception of candidates in remote areas like the Peace River and northeastern Alberta, no one functioned as a purely local leader. Candidates like Manning, Ansley, Anderson, Unwin, Mrs. Rogers, or Mrs. Gostick travelled the province more extensively than is the custom of most provincial Cabinet ministers. It was, in fact, the exception rather than the rule for a candidate to operate only in his own constituency.

No matter how widely he might range, however, each candidate had to follow the custom of other political parties and assume full charge, under

Aberhart's supervision, of the conduct of the election campaign in his own constituency. No sooner had Aberhart released the names of those selected by the advisory committee than he instructed constituency executives to co-operate with accredited candidates in planning the campaign, in arranging for speakers, in appointing scrutineers, as well as in all other matters concerning the election. But here, again, final direction came from headquarters at the Bible Institute. "We expect," announced Aberhart in a broadcast, "in the course of a few days to send to each of the candidates full instructions as to the points of importance that must be attended to as the days go by. . . . I trust that the candidates will attend to the matters referred to in the wire received from us. . . . We want everything to be in good order and in full accord with the duties of candidates. We shall be communicating from time to time with each of you."[2] For the activities of the candidates, as well as in all other matters concerning the Social Credit movement, the Bible Institute was the nerve-centre.

Although overshadowed by Aberhart, the candidates nevertheless made impressive contributions to the movement. As we have intimated above, a considerable number of them functioned in two capacities: first, as speakers throughout the province on behalf of the movement as a whole; and second, as local leaders of their party within the more restricted areas of the provincial constituencies.

Of the candidates who helped to build up the movement as a whole Manning was, of course, the most continuously active and the best known. He became Aberhart's closest friend and confidant in the movement, and this intimacy gave him a unique position. He accompanied Aberhart on the summer tours of 1933 and 1934, and was with him also during most of the election campaign in 1935. The pair were together on the road most weeks of the Christmas and Easter vacations. In addition, for several years they constantly made sorties out from Calgary to the towns and villages of southern Alberta.

Apart from his public appearances with Aberhart, Manning, as secretary of the Bible Institute, supervised much routine activity. He assisted in the preparation of radio scripts, and was heard frequently on the air, either as a member of a cast of characters (as in the "Man from Mars" series of broadcasts) or as a foil for Aberhart in a twosome, but until the summer of 1935 he rarely appeared alone on the air. In the thick of the struggle for power, however, Manning found himself entrusted with the conduct of the election campaign for some ten days, while his leader took a vacation.

2*Ibid.*

Manning was undoubtedly the candidate most closely associated with Aberhart. But there were others, like Fred Anderson or Mrs. Gostick, who enjoyed Aberhart's friendship and confidence in eminent degree. Although they never undertook prolonged speaking tours, such leaders frequently held meetings in the towns and villages of southern Alberta, sometimes accompanied by Aberhart or Manning or both, sometimes alone.

Next to Manning, Anderson seems to have enjoyed Aberhart's special confidence. His education at an English public school, coupled with his Anglicanism, had prestige value for the movement, and Aberhart was quick to exploit such sources of appeal to the socially *élite* of Calgary. In the spring of 1934, following Aberhart's controversy with the New Age Club, Anderson became a member of the inner group that controlled the movement through the Central Council. Thereafter, he came rapidly to the front. He became especially competent in the preparation and delivery of radio scripts; he was probably the most polished script writer the movement produced. That Aberhart relied heavily on Anderson's advice may be seen from his membership on the advisory committee. But, in spite of Aberhart's backing, Anderson's name was not among those sent up to the advisory committee by the Calgary Constituency Convention, although he had been nominated. It is said that his failure in the balloting was due solely to the strict attitude of the members of the Bible Institute concerning alcoholic beverages. Nevertheless, Anderson's importance to the movement was such that the advisory committee (with himself as a member) selected him anyway as one of the six candidates for the city of Calgary. Although Anderson's selection aroused relentless criticism, Aberhart defended him vigorously and he was elected.

Among the most conspicuous of the candidates were two women, one of whom was Mrs. Gostick. Possessed of boundless enthusiasm and energy, she was tireless as a speechmaker for the movement in southern Alberta. By 1935 there must have been few populated areas south of Red Deer that had not heard her colourful and forceful addresses on Social Credit. Next to Aberhart and Mrs. Rogers, she was perhaps the greatest single factor in rallying women generally to the movement. She was invaluable also as an organizer and member of committees at general conventions. Her uninhibited references to opponents of Social Credit made her a storm centre. She was perhaps second only to Aberhart himself in drawing down the wrath of the U.F.A. and the press in their condemnation of the wilder extravagances of the movement.

In the development of the movement as a whole the candidates functioned in several capacities. But their most impressive contributions, as far as the people were concerned, were made through their speaking tours. Most of these tours were anchored to the Bible Institute, in the sense that the participants reported back to Aberhart at frequent intervals. Some of them, however, seem to have been undertaken without Aberhart's explicit sanction: in such instances the participants were not under a pressing obligation either to inform headquarters of their activities or to conform to Aberhart's detailed instructions regarding the contents of speeches.

Whether superintended by the Institute or not, these tours differed from the briefer trips of such candidates as Anderson and Mrs. Gostick. Travelling great distances over long periods of time, speakers on such tours naturally became detached, in greater or less degree, from the routine preoccupations of the Institute. A number of them have testified to the feeling of exhilaration, to the sense of being something more than a mere disciple of Aberhart, that they experienced while on prolonged tours. There was thus built up in these individuals a certain independence and self-reliance that gave additional strength to the movement in rural Alberta.

Of the numerous speaking tours undertaken by secondary leaders, the most spectacular were those conducted, first, by Mrs. W. W. Rogers and, second, by R. E. Ansley. These tours were remarkable for the ground covered, the time spent, the number of meetings held, and the enthusiastic crowds addressed. With the exception of Aberhart and Manning it is probable that no other candidate made more effective appeals to more people than Mrs. Rogers. It is impossible to understand fully either the function of the candidates in the Social Credit movement or the texture of that movement without a careful consideration of her contribution.

Mrs. Edith Blanche (Cox) Rogers was born on a farm at Eastville, Upper Stewiacke, Nova Scotia, of Conservative and Presbyterian parentage. After attending high and Normal schools, she came to Alberta in 1912, at the age of eighteen, to teach public school. Intelligent and ambitious, she soon became dissatisfied with the isolation and loneliness inseparable from teaching on the prairies. She took a business course and entered the service of the Bank of Montreal at Edgerton, serving as paying teller. After some years she was transferred to Killam. Here, in 1923, she married W. W. Rogers, the principal of the local high school.

During the boom years the Rogers moved to Calgary where, in 1929, Mr. Rogers became a personal associate of William Aberhart. In 1930, Mrs. Rogers served as a member of the campaign committee of the national leader of the Conservative party, R. B. Bennett, in Calgary

West. But after Bennett's election to the prime ministership she seems not to have participated further in the activities of the Conservative party.

Like most people in Calgary in the early 1930's, Mr. and Mrs. Rogers listened occasionally to Aberhart's Sunday afternoon broadcasts from the Bible Institute. Although they knew Aberhart well, and liked him personally, neither of them was attracted by his religious doctrines: for several years they considered his broadcasts merely as "programmes" among others. But when they tuned into the Bible Institute programmes in the autumn of 1932, they realized that a new doctrine—Social Credit —had gradually been introduced into the script. They were receptive to the new emphasis, for they were both distressed by the suffering they saw all around them. Both felt that something was seriously wrong with an economic system when hunger and privation could descend so suddenly on thousands, in a province as rich in natural resources as Alberta. Poverty in the midst of plenty, they agreed with Aberhart, was criminal, a disgrace to the system which permitted it.

Late in November, 1932, Mrs. Rogers became enthused with Aberhart's suggestion that Social Credit offered a possible solution of Alberta's economic distress. She obtained Douglas's books from the Calgary Public Library and read them eagerly. Convinced that Social Credit was the remedy for the terrible economic conditions in Alberta, she telephoned Aberhart, and arranged an interview with him at his office in the Crescent Heights High School, shortly before Christmas. During their first discussion of Social Credit, she urged him to hold public meetings at the Bible Institute on week-nights for the exposition of Social Credit theory, independently of pre-millennial fundamentalism. She sensed that Aberhart was reluctant to do this. At that time he seemed apprehensive concerning his position as school principal and anxious not to offend the financial interests in Calgary by a downright onslaught on the monetary system. However, in response to Mrs. Rogers' strong urgings, he agreed to consider her proposal during the Christmas vacation. Early in January, 1933, as we have seen, he announced during a Sunday afternoon broadcast that a meeting for the purpose of discussing Social Credit would be held in the basement of the Bible Institute the following Thursday night.

Mrs. Rogers was one of the few women who attended that fateful first meeting: she was therefore one of the thirty charter members of the Social Credit movement: during the following years her life was destined to be devoted to that movement, with an abandon that can fairly be called reckless. She saw the original study group grow from a mere handful to the tumultuous mass meetings that shook the political structure of Alberta. She became one of the principal builders of the early movement throughout the province.

During the period when the original study group in the Bible Institute was growing to the size of a large public meeting, Mrs. Rogers organized a small group of ten people, most of whom had, like herself, worked in banks. This group, which met on the North Hill of Calgary, in the home of a wealthy plumbing contractor, specialized in the study of the banking system. All the participants felt that they had benefited so greatly from these discussions that the formation of similar groups outside the Bible Institute should be attempted. As the size of Aberhart's Thursday night meetings offered less and less opportunity for discussion, Mrs. Rogers strongly advocated the adoption of a study group system of instruction in Social Credit throughout the city of Calgary. Aberhart entirely agreed with her plan, for group study was his idea of how teaching should be carried on. During his Sunday broadcasts he had frequently urged his listeners to "get around the dining-room table and talk over what's wrong with the system." Many small informal house meetings had already been taking place. Under Mrs. Rogers' efficient guidance, and with the aid of newspaper advertisements directing those interested in the New Economics to interview her, the study group system now became a recognized adjunct of Thursday night meetings at the Bible Institute. Eventually some sixty study groups were organized in Calgary: a great many of these were initiated by the sheer hard work of Mrs. Rogers.

Late in the autumn of 1933, when the organization of study groups was well under way, the Central Council appointed Mrs. Rogers as "women's organizer." The remarkable flare-up of interest in Social Credit on the part of women's organizations which occurred early in 1934 was largely due to her tactics during that period. She advertised that four meetings for women only would be held in the basement of the Bible Institute. These meetings combined musical programmes with speeches on Social Credit by Manning, Gilbert McGregor, and Mrs. Rogers herself. Women from all over the city, who had not hitherto been interested, crowded into the basement. The inter-denominational character of these meetings was stressed; and a number of Roman Catholics were first contacted during these months. At each meeting, Mrs. Rogers invited the women to give their names and addresses and to state what they were prepared to do for Social Credit, such as opening their homes for group meetings, speaking, and distributing literature—among her recruits she claims Mrs. Edith Gostick, who had taken lessons in elocution and who soon became one of the movement's ablest speakers.

These four rallies were followed by an enthusiastic mass meeting in the auditorium of the Bible Institute, to which invitations were sent to every women's organization in Calgary. Then Mrs. Rogers decided to make a special appeal to the working class women of the city, and a series of mass meetings was held in the Labor Temple. She spoke at all of these meetings, and many who attended them have reported that she frequently "stole the show" from Aberhart or Manning. But her confidence in Aberhart was unbounded, and she did everything possible to build him up in the eyes of her own enthusiastic audiences. In fact, "Building the Leader" was, at that time, one of her principal themes.

Few women in Calgary had not heard of Social Credit by the time Douglas arrived in Alberta in the spring of 1934. Owing to her position in the movement, Mrs. Rogers was one of those chosen to accompany Aberhart to Edmonton to meet Douglas as well as to arrange luncheons and teas for Mrs. Douglas. Well aware of the various efforts that were being made by the Calgary *élite* to alienate Douglas and Aberhart, Mrs. Rogers "stage managed" Aberhart's appearances so effectively that his enemies largely failed in their petty tricks.

It is interesting to note that she became convinced, as a result of Douglas's visit, that Aberhart, and Aberhart alone, must be the leader of the Social Credit movement in Alberta. Henceforth, she advised all Social Credit speakers to play down Douglas and play up Aberhart. This, of course, brought her into conflict with McGregor and the leaders of the New Age Club; but, on behalf of Aberhart, she was prepared to fight them to the finish. During the period of McGregor's presidency of the movement, she constantly insisted that Aberhart must return as leader, and she organized several delegations to press him to do so. It is said that whenever Aberhart hesitated in adopting new tactics, Mrs. Rogers would invariably urge him to take the boldest course possible. "She pushed him on and on," a number of Social Crediters have stated, "until she finally pushed him into the premiership."

Early in May, 1934, Calgary seemed thoroughly organized for Social Credit and Aberhart was preparing to return to the leadership of the movement. But Mrs. Rogers was not satisfied. She remembered her school-teaching days, the lonely prairie homesteads, the discouraged hamlets, the isolated ranches, hard hit now by falling prices and shrinking world markets for everything they produced. It was to these, she now felt, that the new gospel of Social Credit must be carried. Her husband

and their friend Joseph Henry Unwin, another ardent Social Credit organizer and speaker, agreed that a speaking tour of rural towns and villages was essential to the future of the movement.

When Mrs. Rogers discussed the proposed tour with Aberhart, she found him far from enthusiastic. "You aren't going to take this to people's back doors, are you?" he remonstrated. He insisted that such a tour would involve financial risks, and that the Central Council could assume no financial responsibility whatever should they go ahead with their plan. He even refused to loan Unwin $40 with which to buy an old Model-T Ford for the tour. But the Rogers bought the car and, on May 9, the trio set out for Granum.

For Mrs. Rogers it was the beginning of a venture that caught the imagination of Alberta—during the next sixteen months scarcely a day passed without a speech from her somewhere in the province. In her stupendous activities on the road, she had the absolute support of her husband, who acted as chauffeur and business manager; and of Unwin who assisted, until the end of December, 1934, with the speaking at the meetings.

Fortunately for our knowledge of the rise of the Social Credit movement, Mrs. Rogers kept a diary of her speaking engagements. The number of points at which meetings were held is almost incredible; there is, however, ample supporting evidence for the diary from the rural newspapers of the period, as well as from the accounts of persons who followed her around from place to place in various areas.[3] Statistics for the eight months Mr. and Mrs. Rogers and Mr. Unwin worked together are as follows: in May, as the tour was just getting started, the trio managed to speak at only 11 places. But in June they visited 24 points; in July, 18; in August, 27; in September, 20; in October, 30; in November, 35; and in December, 25. During the autumn they frequently spoke at two places daily, holding afternoon and evening meetings. The diary indicates that a number of places were visited twice, owing to improved contacts after the first meeting, as well as to pressing invitations for a second meeting.

Aberhart, although unwilling to guarantee financial support for the tour, gave the trio a list of his contacts in places they expected to visit; he also assisted them considerably by announcing their itinerary during the Sunday afternoon broadcasts as well as by urging his listeners to attend their meetings. Mrs. Rogers found that Aberhart's contacts were

[3]A rural weekly, the *Stettler Independent*, for example, in its issue of September 20, 1934, lists the Rogers–Unwin speaking engagements in that area for a two-week period, a listing that corresponds exactly with Mrs. Rogers' diary.

something of a handicap: they tended to be restricted to the lower strata of the population, socially and educationally. At her first meeting in a place she sometimes observed that the bulk of the audience consisted of people of the type who believe in tea-cup reading and fortune-telling.[4] Such people, as local sponsors of her meetings, tended to put off those of the better class: to attract the latter it was often necessary to hold a second meeting at a later date.

It is difficult to appreciate the ingenuity that Mrs. Rogers and her associates displayed in penetrating the Alberta community. It was not easy for them, even with Aberhart's radio support, to drive into a town, make contacts, hire a hall, and put up the notices advertising a meeting. During "their first time around" (as they called it), Mrs. Rogers and Unwin sometimes addressed small gatherings; but on their second appearance the meeting would invariably be packed, with crowds standing outside on the street.

In the course of a few months it was widely recognized in Social Credit circles that the Rogers' tour was one of the most successful techniques of promotion and organization that the movement had produced. But Aberhart did not relent in his determination that speakers on the road must finance themselves. Although he appealed every Sunday for donations from his listeners, many of whom had been brought into the movement through the activities of Mrs. Rogers and Unwin, the latter never received a cent from the funds of the Central Council or the Bible Institute. While on tour, speakers lived off the land. Social Credit enthusiasts in whatever centre they were visiting would usually provide them with meals and lodging and fill their gasoline tank before they moved on to the next town. But for other personal needs, as well as for the cost of renting halls and advertising, the Rogers team was dependent upon collections—the nickels and dimes—always taken up at their meetings. The average collection was four dollars; a bumper meeting would occasionally bring in as much as ten dollars. Collections at meetings might have been larger had not many people supposed that the tour was being financed by the Bible Institute. The Rogers team knew that if they found themselves stranded financially they could count on assistance from one influential study group in Calgary, and the expense of overhauling their car was actually met on one occasion by this group. The

[4]It must be emphasized that this is the interpretation of an intelligent woman whose husband had been a high school principal, and who had always moved in the better middle-class social circles. Mrs. Rogers' somewhat superior attitude to Aberhart's religious followers in the small towns and villages of southern and central Alberta was not shared by other secondary leaders who met them while on speaking tours.

self-financing of the speaking tours must be accounted one of the impressive aspects of the Social Credit movement.

Equally impressive is the geographical area covered by the Rogers' tour. By June, 1935, Mr. and Mrs. Rogers had visited every district except the Peace River and Athabaska. From May to December, 1934, they travelled mainly south of a line drawn from Olds to Wainwright, an area readily accessible to, and greatly influenced by, Aberhart's religious broadcasts. Early in January, 1935, Mr. and Mrs. Rogers headed into the constituencies north of Red Deer, leaving Unwin to consolidate the work in the south. They continued relentlessly throughout that severe winter to carry the message of Social Credit northward, eventually reaching Barrhead, Vermilion, and Lloydminster. The records indicate that in the month of February, they visited thirty towns and villages, with time out for a conference (to which all speakers had been summoned by Aberhart) at the Bible Institute on the eighteenth of the month.

In spite of the bitter cold, these northern meetings were overcrowded even with loudspeakers for an overflow audience in the basement of the meeting place. At many of her meetings Mrs. Rogers could hardly force her way through the audience to the platform. Crowds were frequently turned away and insistent demands for a return visit were often heard. After the U.F.A. convention had rejected Aberhart's appeal to it, Mrs. Rogers noticed that more and more U.F.A. members were responding enthusiastically to her speeches. Following her meeting at Leduc, early in March, the local M.L.A. (a government supporter) remarked to her: "If you have many more meetings like that, the U.F.A. is finished." She was often heckled by U.F.A. officials (who marvelled at the crowds she drew) but always knew she could count on the response of the people. As the winter wore on, her mass appeal began to disturb local Liberal leaders also, and they in turn attempted to talk her down, especially in the towns on the railway lines radiating from Edmonton. But they fared no better with her audiences than did U.F.A. officials.

The popular support which Mrs. Rogers aroused for Social Credit in northern Alberta had an important influence on the course of the movement in Edmonton. Aberhart himself had been discouraged by the small meeting he had drawn in the capital city during the Christmas holidays of 1934. At a conference in the Bible Institute, he announced that he had lost fifty dollars on this meeting. "It is," he declared, "a hard nut to crack, and I'm not going up there again." Then he ordered Mrs. Rogers to go into Edmonton and organize it, but offered no financial support. Early in 1935, she and her husband met in Edmonton Dr. William S. Hall, an enthusiastic Social Crediter and an ardent follower of the Oxford Group. With some financial assistance from Dr. Hall, a successful dentist, Mr. and Mrs. Rogers opened an office in Edmonton, which served henceforth as the headquarters of the movement in northern Alberta.

In between her sorties into the northern rural areas, Mrs. Rogers began to hold meetings in Edmonton. Word of her prowess as a speaker had spread to the capital by numerous newspaper reports, as well as by word of mouth. In a short time, she was attracting such enthusiastic audiences in smaller halls and churches that Dr. Hall arranged a mass meeting for her in McDougall United Church, whose minister was sympathetic to the cause of Social Credit. This meeting was packed, with crowds standing on the streets for blocks, struggling to get in. The response of the people resulted in a second meeting in that church a week later, equally crowded and enthusiastic, at which she repeated her previous lecture. The Social Credit movement was now well under way in Edmonton.

By Easter, 1935, Mrs. Rogers had set up seventy-two study groups in Edmonton, and these were organized into a Central Council similar to that in Calgary. Aberhart was invited to speak in Edmonton during the Easter vacation. Under Mrs. Rogers' guidance, the meeting was well advertised and organized. This time the response was different: it is said that Aberhart was frightened as he faced the 9,000 people in the arena. But he was equal to the occasion, and he made a tremendous appeal to the audience.

Mrs. Rogers' boundless zeal for the movement and for building its leader received its reward: at the nominating conventions in the spring of 1935 she was named for no less than six constituencies. After careful consideration it was decided that she should uphold the honour of Alberta's women by running against ex-Premier Brownlee in the Ponoka constituency. She had, in fact, begun to cultivate this particular constituency at least three months before the election, in between appearances at nominating conventions as the key orator and the continuation of her speaking tour generally.

By the time the election was announced, Mrs. Rogers had organized a Social Credit study group in every schoolhouse in the large Ponoka constituency. During the campaign, she held meetings in practically every schoolhouse and hall, with packed audiences every afternoon and night; many people followed her around from meeting to meeting, hanging on her words. In Ponoka the Liberals virtually abandoned their campaign, and Brownlee has attested to the difficulty of holding meetings in fanatical Social Credit areas. When the votes were counted, Mrs. Rogers had won one of the most overwhelming victories for Social Credit in the province.

The spectacular character of Mrs. Rogers' contribution to the movement should not obscure the general significance of speaking tours undertaken by other candidates. As the movement increased in momentum, the people of central and southern Alberta formed the impression that "the roads were full of Social Credit speakers": Aberhart seemed to have at his disposal an endless supply of speakers in the cause of an irresistible movement. In every place these speakers visited they organized study groups, left literature, and established contact with the headquarters of the movement in the Bible Institute. In whatever town they were, the candidates also emphasized the desirability of having the great Aberhart himself—to whom they all seemed to exhibit absolute loyalty—speak there in the future. They insisted that they were merely fore-runners, their speeches merely a glimpse of what their leader could provide for his people. By continually building up Aberhart they did much to pave the way for his later triumphant appearances.

In addition, the tours of secondary leaders developed and maintained person-to-person relationships within the movement during periods, like the autumn and winter of 1934–5, when Aberhart was so occupied with school duties that he could not himself visit them. By stressing their role as surrogates, they linked the movement more effectively to Aberhart's person. They also contributed to group solidarity within the movement through the assembling of its devotees at mass meetings, at which they always tried to develop a feeling of primitive comradeship among all true believers in Social Credit. The personal relationships that were established between grass-roots officials of study groups and candidates during their tours helped to make possible the rapid transition to political action during the winter of 1935. Without such tours, it would have been much more difficult to institutionalize the Social Credit movement.

Through their tours the candidates contributed not only to the rapid organization of the movement but also to a considerable and much needed increase in its newspaper publicity. The rural weeklies, if not the metropolitan dailies, invariably carried lengthy reports of their meetings. The *Stettler Independent*, for example, in its issue of September 20, 1934, devoted nearly half of its front page to a report of Mrs. Rogers' meeting in that town five days previously. The occasion was described in glowing terms and the speeches of Mrs. Rogers and Unwin were outlined so fully that the material could readily be used by study groups in that area. Such extensive publicity, continuing for some fifteen months, was an invaluable asset to the movement in rural Alberta.

If the lengthy reports in rural newspapers of the speeches of candidates on tour helped to spread Social Credit doctrine, they also indicate that most of these speakers had absorbed Aberhart's interpretation of Douglas's theories. With not more than three exceptions, the most notable of whom was R. E. Ansley, they permitted themselves no deviation from Aberhart's teachings: they realized to the full that he would not have it otherwise. Unlike most of the candidates, Ansley had made a careful study of Douglas's writings and felt independent enough to offer his own interpretation. There is documentary evidence to show that Aberhart was greatly disturbed by what he considered to be Ansley's heresies; and attempts were made (without any great success) to correct this particular speaker's "misinterpretation" of Social Credit.

That the speaking tours had caught the imagination of the populace may be illustrated, finally, by the desire of many constituencies to have those engaged on them, like Mrs. Rogers, Ansley, or Unwin, as their candidates. A number of these speakers were actually nominated in several constituencies; and the advisory committee then had to decide which constituency would be most suitable for each of them. As a result of the people's enthusiasm for this or that touring speaker, a number eventually found themselves contesting constituencies far removed from their home base: Mrs. Rogers was selected for Ponoka; Unwin for Edson; and Ansley for Leduc. The touring speakers had done their work well: in spite of U.F.A. and Liberal charges that Aberhart was forcing urban outsiders upon rural constituencies, they all won their seats easily. If the response of the people enabled Aberhart to reward appropriately some of his most ardent workers, it also provided certain rural constituencies with Social Credit leadership of a higher calibre than they might, at that time, have been able to recruit within their borders.

We have hitherto considered the Social Credit candidates in terms of certain general categories: the methods by which they were selected; their relationships to Aberhart and his interpretation of Social Credit; and their contributions to the movement at large through writing, broadcasting, and speaking tours. It is necessary also to study them in terms of certain individual characteristics and their positions and activities in their local communities. They may best be envisaged by means of profiles. This approach not only illuminates the nature of secondary leadership but also provides multiple perspectives of the movement throughout the province. The profiles we have chosen to illustrate certain qualitative characteristics of the candidates take us into the depths of the Alberta community. Through them we are able to appreciate more fully not only the nature of the secondary leadership of the movement but also the significance, for various geographical regions and ethnic and occupational groups, of the theories of Social Credit, Aberhart's leadership, and the strategy and tactics of the movement.

Owing to limitations of space, it would not be feasible, even were it possible, to present meaningful profiles of all sixty-three candidates. Several factors have influenced the choice of the ten whose profiles are presented below. In making the selection, occupational status and geographical distribution have been carefully considered. At the time the field-work for this study was carried out, a number of the candidates were no longer available for personal interviews: several had died and others had moved away from Alberta. Of those who were available, no one who was approached was unwilling to be interviewed at some length. But several, although sympathetic to the research and willing to provide ample information concerning their careers and attitudes, were reluctant, for personal reasons, to have their profiles published even anonymously (they felt that in a group of sixty-three they could be too readily identified). On the other hand, most of those interviewed were quite agreeable to the publication of their profiles under their own names: these include members of the principal occupational groups represented and they are widely distributed geographically.

Occupationally, the candidates represented twenty-eight different economic interests. But two-thirds of them were drawn from five groups: small-town merchants, school-teachers, farmers, preachers, and agents or salesmen. In accordance with this distribution, the ten profiles include two small-town merchants, one school-teacher, two farmers, one preacher, one insurance agent, one lawyer, one chiropractor, and one service station operator and cartage contractor. As fifty-six of the candidates were elected, and only seven defeated, we have included in the profiles nine who were elected and one (M. W. Robertson) who was defeated.

The inclusion of only one teacher and one preacher in the profiles may be justified on the ground that the careers of another teacher (Mrs. Edith Rogers) and another preacher (E. C. Manning) have been considered elsewhere. It should also be noted that a third farmer among the secondary leaders, Norman Bloomfield James, has published his autobiography, in which he gives a full account of his participation in the Social Credit movement.[5] In effect, then, there are actually available studies of thirteen, or slightly over 20 per cent, of the candidates.

Geographically, the areas represented in the profiles range through southern, central, and northeastern Alberta. It was possible to obtain, but not to publish, a profile from the Peace River country, and this region had to be omitted. Farming and mining areas, villages, towns, smaller cities, and the capital city are represented; since a detailed account has already been given above of the rise of the movement in Calgary, that city has been deliberately omitted. (Numerous references have already been made to three of its six candidates, viz., Manning, Anderson, and Mrs. Gostick.) The course of the movement in Mormon, French-Canadian, and Ukrainian communities is depicted. Because of the existence of James's autobiography, which describes the movement in the drought-stricken area of east-central Alberta, as well as of Dr. Burnet's special study of the Hanna district, it was not thought advisable to include a profile from this geographical region.[6] It may fairly be claimed, then, that the profiles constitute a genuine cross-section of the secondary leadership of the movement. No claim is made, however, that any specific candidate selected for a profile is "typical."

During the interviews, attempts were made to secure from each candidate information for his profile on the following twelve points: birthplace; date of birth; ethnic origin; education and early interests; occupational and economic interests; community interests, including offices or positions held in organizations; religious affiliation; earlier political affiliation; the circumstances under which he first heard of Social Credit; why he became a Social Crediter; his attitude to Aberhart; and his activities on behalf of the Social Credit movement prior to August 22, 1935. The ten profiles are presented in alphabetical order, under the name of each candidate; his name is followed by his occupation in 1935 (as he identified it himself), and the constituency he contested.

FLOYD MILTON BAKER: HARDWARE, IMPLEMENT, AND OIL BUSINESS: CLOVER BAR

Born at Stevensville, Ontario, December 1, 1891, of English ancestry (U.E.L. stock), he was educated at the public and high schools there. In 1907 he came to Alberta.

Settling in Edmonton, he learned the hardware business, and then operated as a hardware merchant there, at Spruce Grove, and, from 1927, at Fort Saskatchewan. By 1933 he had also become interested in

[5]N. B. James, The Autobiography of a Nobody (Toronto: J. M. Dent, 1947).
[6]Jean Burnet, Next-Year Country (Toronto: University of Toronto Press, 1951).

the implement and oil business. In Fort Saskatchewan he was considered efficient and successful. In addition to merchandising hardware, he knew also how to work on building materials with his hands: he was exceptionally skilful in fitting tin and other metals in the construction of a house.

He was keenly interested in Sunday School and Young People's work, and in musical organizations. For twenty-five years he had been a member of the Independent Order of Oddfellows, and in this fraternity he was elected a District Deputy Grand Master for a term. In religion, he was originally a Methodist, and later an enthusiastic and hard-working member of the United Church of Canada. In 1935, he had served as a superintendent of its Sunday School at Fort Saskatchewan for eight years. Until the rise of the Social Credit movement, he took no interest in politics and had no political affiliation.

He first heard of Social Credit in the autumn of 1932 through Aberhart's Sunday afternoon broadcasts to which he had been listening since 1927. For several years a group of his friends had been accustomed to gather at his home on Sunday afternoons for the specific purpose of listening to Aberhart. During the years 1933 and 1934 he followed by radio the development of the Social Credit movement. He wrote to the Bible Institute for leaflets and pamphlets on Social Credit, and watched with great interest Aberhart's efforts to induce the U.F.A. government to take up the new economics.

He became a follower because Aberhart's broadcasts convinced him that Social Credit was the only possible approach to the problems of the depression, the only solution to the misery and suffering produced through a shortage of purchasing power in the hands of consumers. He had long felt that the old-line parties had nothing to offer beyond the alternative of a high tariff or a low tariff; more recently he had become disgusted with the apathy of the U.F.A. government in the face of the terrible economic conditions that had developed.

For Aberhart, Baker had unqualified admiration. As we have seen, he had been for years a devotee of the Sunday afternoon broadcasts from the Bible Institute. "Aberhart," he said, "believed in the Bible from cover to cover." When Aberhart took up Social Credit, he appealed more than ever to Baker, who was especially impressed by his analysis of and remedy for the persistent cycle of booms and depressions. "Aberhart," said Baker, "was the only man we had ever heard who had real solutions for all the problems of the depression. He talked like a man who had a vision—but he was also the greatest leader and organizer this country has ever seen."

The first public meeting in Fort Saskatchewan on behalf of Social Credit was organized by Baker's friend, Walter F. Kuhl (elected as the federal member for Jasper-Edson in 1935), a school-teacher whom he had known while in the hardware business at Spruce Grove. When the Liberal mayor of the town and several other prominent citizens refused to act as chairman of this meeting, Kuhl drafted the reluctant Baker who finally consented, protesting, however, that he didn't really know enough about Social Credit. When a study group was organized at the close of this large and enthusiastic meeting, the crowd demanded Baker as its president. He accepted and thereafter his life was spent in tireless service for the Social Credit movement.

It was not easy to become a Social Credit leader in Fort Saskatchewan in 1934. At first, Baker and his wife were criticized, ridiculed, and even ostracized by their business and professional friends. "People left us in the cold," he said. "It was the worst razzing we ever got in our lives." When his wife suggested they might have to leave town, he said to her: "No, Social Credit is right, it's Christian. I'm going to stay with it."

With inflexible determination, he set to work to build up the study group in Fort Saskatchewan. At first, owing to the ridicule of the business men, only the poor people of the town joined the movement. The group met for a time in people's houses; then the town undertaker was converted and let them use one of his large rooms. Discussions were based on Aberhart's leaflets and pamphlets and Douglas's books, and on articles in the *Social Credit Chronicle*. This literature was in such constant demand that a library was formed. As the group grew its membership became more representative, but the business men of the town steadfastly refused to have anything to do with it.

Once the Social Credit movement was established in Fort Saskatchewan, groups were gradually formed in adjoining rural areas. By the spring of 1935, there was a group attached to practically every schoolhouse in the constituency, the zone organization was well developed, and the constituency ready for its nominating convention.

Owing to his energetic devotion to the movement, Baker was nominated for the Clover Bar constituency. Although he was easily one of the most remarkable organizers and group leaders the movement produced, he was, at that time, extremely diffident as a speaker at a public meeting. So he and his friend Kuhl campaigned together, striking out from Baker's house every morning. In the beginning, he could not speak publicly for more than five minutes, but under Kuhl's encouragement and training he gradually became one of the more effective speakers in the movement. The pair worked together day and night for months.

"Neither of us," said Baker, "was interested in politics. We were not politicians. We were crusaders in a people's movement. The election campaign was a people's campaign. We were unbeatable."

SAMUEL WESLEY CALVERT: FARMER: VICTORIA

Born at Caledon, Peel County, Ontario, September 16, 1867, of English-Irish parentage, he attended public school at Dunchurch (near Parry Sound), where he lived from 1872 to 1897. His father was a blacksmith and wagon maker, also doing a little farming on the side. In 1892 the family moved to Alberta, but he did not join them until five years later, remaining at Dunchurch to operate the blacksmith shop and wagon business.

Between 1897 and 1900 he lived at Fort Saskatchewan, where he built and operated the second hotel in the town. During the next five years, he built and rented hotels in three other Alberta villages, including Chipman. In 1905, he finally settled down just outside Chipman on land he had bought earlier. He remembered vividly the day, October 5, 1905, that the first train steamed through that village at 6.00 P.M.: it was the coming of the railroad that led him to remain there. Eventually, he acquired two-and-a-half sections of land.

From 1900 to 1905 he was official overseer under the North-West Territories for most of what became the Victoria constituency on the formation of the province. In this capacity he organized in 1902 the two townships 55-17—55-18, west of the fourth meridian, and helped to organize a third. He was largely instrumental in setting up the first councils of these municipalities, and was subsequently Reeve of Chipman (which had a population of 500 in 1935) for two years. He was also active in promoting farmers' organizations: he helped to organize the Alberta Co-operative Elevators (later taken over by the United Grain Growers), the Alberta Wheat Pool, and the U.F.A. in his district. He was president of his local of the first for twenty years, of the second for twelve years, and of the third for eight years. Keenly interested in fraternal organizations, he was a member of the Masonic (raised to the Blue Lodge in 1901, to the Royal Arch in 1912), Forester, and Orange Orders, being a past master of both Masonic and Orange Lodges. In religion, he was originally a Methodist, and entered the United Church of Canada on its formation. Politically, he had once been a strong Conservative, campaigning for the federal party on several occasions. But when the U.F.A. went into politics, he gave his support to them, having concluded that "the Conservatives could never get anywhere in Alberta." His strong support of the entrance of the farmers into politics led to his being offered the nomination for his constituency but he declined the honour on the ground that he was not well enough educated.

He first heard of Social Credit in the autumn of 1932 from Aberhart's Sunday afternoon broadcasts, to which he had been listening ever since their inception. In the spring of 1934, he listened to the hearings of the Agricultural Committee of the legislature when Aberhart and Douglas appeared before it. Later, he journeyed to Calgary to meet Aberhart and hear him in person at the Bible Institute; and he attended Aberhart's first meeting in Edmonton shortly before Christmas, 1934. Following the U.F.A. convention in 1935, Mrs. Rogers (whom he considered "a wonderful speaker") held a meeting at Chipman. That night he finally decided to join the Social Credit movement, and the next day resigned as president of his U.F.A. local.

Calvert became a Social Crediter first, because of dissatisfaction over the inability of the U.F.A. government to deal with the problems of the depression. In 1931 he produced 20,000 bushels of oats that took six months to sell (there was still a surplus from the 1929 crop) and the best price he received was eight cents a bushel. He was forced in 1934 to turn over one section of his land to a mortgage company. The embittered farmers felt that such things ought not to be; there must be something seriously wrong with a financial system that forced farmers to sacrifice the land that had taken so many years of hard work to acquire. "That's what drove us," he said, "to Social Credit."

He became a Social Crediter second, because of the promise of the basic dividend. With nine living children, the basic dividend would yield an income of $3,300 annually to him and his family. Apart from his own situation, he felt that "the basic dividend would be like manna from Heaven to a starving and debt-ridden population."

He became a Social Crediter third, because Aberhart's broadcasts convinced him that it was the only Christian movement since Christ. "He drove the money-changers out of the Temple," said Calvert, "and so will Social Credit."

As we have seen, Calvert had been listening to Aberhart's religious broadcasts for over seven years before the Social Credit movement emerged. An old-time Methodist, he liked Aberhart's insistence on a literal interpretation of the Bible and the way he "brought out facts from the Bible, helping us to understand what was happening today through Bible prophecy." When Aberhart began to discuss the price of grain in 1933, Calvert called him "the fighting preacher." He now realized that Aberhart was not only a great Bible evangelist but also "a fighter for the rights of the poor man, the wage-earner, the middle class,

and especially the hard-pressed farmers." When Calvert finally decided
to break with the U.F.A., he did so partly because he had concluded it
was time for a change, and only Aberhart could lead the crusade that
would bring about that change. "I felt," he said, "that if we only gave
Aberhart a chance he would do wonderful things for the people."

As a strong U.F.A. man and president of his local, Calvert's first
activity on behalf of Social Credit consisted in heading a delegation from
his constituency, in the spring of 1934, to try to persuade the government
to accept the proposals of Douglas and Aberhart, take them both in as
advisers, and amalgamate the U.F.A. and the Social Credit movement.
When this idea was rejected, he continued to agitate for a union of the
two forces until the U.F.A. convention of January, 1935. By this time
he was becoming disturbed by the affiliation of the U.F.A. with the
C.C.F. movement: he feared socialism, under which, as he put it, "the
government takes hold of everything, and you become its servant—the
government controls all you do and have, as in Russia." He was also
greatly disturbed by the scandals involving two Cabinet ministers, and
the continual gossip concerning a third. The rejection of Aberhart's
proposals by the U.F.A. convention left Calvert ripe for Mrs. Rogers'
stirring appeal at her meeting in Chipman shortly afterwards.

The defection of the respected president of the Chipman U.F.A. local
to the Social Credit movement had a shattering effect on the U.F.A.
organization throughout the Victoria constituency. Following Calvert's
lead, the members, if not the officials, of most of the constituency's
U.F.A. locals joined the Social Credit movement. In organizing study
groups throughout the constituency, Calvert merely travelled around
and invited members of the U.F.A. locals to join Social Credit groups.
The officials of the locals remained, for the most part, loyal to the
government, but by election time there must have been a fair number of
these who were giving only lip-service to the U.F.A. cause: in a number
of rural polls the government candidate received only one vote.

Calvert was one of the few candidates who did not speak outside his
own constituency. He had, once again, feared that his lack of education
would handicap his candidature, but he had accepted the nomination
because of his deep convictions concerning Social Credit and Aberhart's
leadership and because of the people's enthusiastic insistence. In conducting his election campaign he appealed to the religious feelings of the
large Ukrainian population of his constituency (who were mainly of the
Greek Orthodox and Greek Catholic faiths) by stressing the essentially
Christian character of the Social Credit crusade. "I simply told them,"
he said, "that Social Credit was a movement put on earth for the sake

of Christianity—and that Social Credit would save the world from the depression." At Calvert's home poll, the U.F.A. candidate obtained only one vote. "Winning that election," Calvert concluded, "was easy—the people were red-hot for Social Credit."

ALBERT EDWARD FEE: HARDWARE DEALER AND UNDERTAKER: SEDGEWICK

Born on a farm near Chesley, Bruce County, Ontario, on May 3, 1880, of Irish parentage, he was educated there at Public School No. 10, Brant Township. After completing Grade VIII, he took a business course, but remained with his father on the farm until his twenty-sixth year.

In 1906 he went to Edmonton and worked for a year with a firm of wholesale hardware merchants and then for three years with a retail firm. When he felt he had learned the business he moved, in 1910, to the village of Killam. During the next twenty-five years he built up a prosperous hardware business in this trading village. A few years after settling there, he also became the undertaker for the Killam area, and bought the local theatre and a garage, both of which he rented. In 1935, he was considered one of the most affluent citizens in his constituency, and was highly regarded for his efficiency and integrity.

Before his sons grew up, he had to manage two rapidly growing enterprises, yet he found time to serve for many years on the village school board, the village council, and the Board of Trade. He was also active in fraternities, as a member of the Elks and the Oddfellows. In religion, he was an active Presbyterian, holding various offices in his local church. Before joining the Social Credit movement, he had never engaged in political activity. His father was a Conservative, but after coming west he voted Liberal and then U.F.A., without any strong convictions.

He first heard of Social Credit through his customers, who had been listening to Aberhart's radio addresses. Nevertheless he did not listen to Aberhart until after he began the study of Social Credit for himself, nor did he attend two meetings that Aberhart and Manning held in Killam. Only when the theories of Social Credit were already receiving considerable public attention, did he finally attend a meeting, at which the speakers were a farmer from a neighbouring village and a school-teacher. Neither of their speeches on Social Credit made sense to him, nor did their answers to the minor questions that were asked. "I wondered," he said, "if everybody was dumb, or if everybody understood it." He decided to put questions to the speakers, and quickly found they were unable to answer them. Yet there was so much discussion of Social Credit going on among the people he concluded there must be something to it after all. He, his son, and an engineer then decided to try and figure out for themselves how the banking and monetary systems were actually functioning in the Killam area.

Their constituency, Sedgewick, was considered one of the best sections of the province. It was almost entirely English-speaking, having been settled mainly by people of Anglo-Saxon origin from Ontario and the British Isles or of Scandinavian and German origin from the western United States. There had only been one total crop failure since it was opened up for farming. But the depression impoverished the farmers and the merchants were unable to sell their goods. After giving considerable thought to the "vicious circle" created by the depression, Fee concluded that the banking and monetary systems were indeed responsible for the economic plight of the people of Killam and the surrounding rural areas. Douglas and Aberhart were entirely right. He became a Social Crediter.

A shrewd business man, well established and secure in his own church, Fee does not seem to have been interested in the religious doctrines proclaimed from the Bible Institute, although he respected Aberhart's capacities as a Bible teacher. He respected Aberhart also "for his compassionate interest in the happiness, welfare, and future of his pupils," as well as for his efficient management of the Crescent Heights High School. But what most attracted him was Aberhart's tireless effort to present the theories of Social Credit in a form that appealed to the people. This, Fee felt, Douglas could not do.

Aberhart's approach to Social Credit [he said] was from an entirely different angle from that of Douglas. He accepted Douglas's findings without question and put them down as facts. However, his sales technique was unique. While Douglas used the slide rule and the tangent, Aberhart used the Golden Rule and the pulpit. Douglas had to prove his points, but seldom does one look for proof from the pulpit. You either take what you get on faith or you do not take it at all. The result was that Aberhart sold to the people of Alberta from the pulpit what Douglas was unable to sell in any part of the world from his drafting board.

Fee believed, also, that Aberhart was "an organizer of the first order," as well as a "master-hand" on the radio, without an equal in Canada. Great as was his admiration for Aberhart, however, the hard-headed Fee felt that while he was very convincing when dealing with "the causes, the abuses and the principles or lack of principles which led up to the depression, the solution of the problem was very elusive and indefinite."

Once Fee had concluded that the banking and monetary systems were responsible for the evils of the depression, he decided to dramatize the situation in his own theatre in Killam. With the aid of several of his business and professional friends, one of whom was experienced in the production of amateur theatricals, a play was designed and written. This play was then produced at a public meeting, held under the chairmanship of J. H. Caldwell, a leading local farmer and Social Credit enthusiast. So many people had to be turned away that in response to insistent demands the play was produced a second time, again before an overcrowded audience.

Much of the material in the play was impromptu, and the actors included study group members, business men, and local farmers, with Fee himself playing the role of bank manager. But, in spite of its amateur character, the dramatization of the functioning of the banking and monetary systems was carried out so skilfully and realistically that it caught the imagination of people not only in the Sedgewick constituency but in adjoining constituencies as well, and remained a subject of discussion for years afterwards. Among those present at the first performance was one of the most noted exponents of Social Credit in Alberta, R. Earl Ansley. At the close of the play, when called on to comment on it, he assured the audience that he had never thought the principles of Social Credit could be presented in as clear a form as they had been that night. During one of his subsequent addresses over an Edmonton radio station, Ansley told his listeners that if he had failed to make clear the theories of Social Credit those interested should see the play that had been staged at Killam. Letters by the hundreds immediately began pouring in to the secretary of the Social Credit study group for information concerning the play. One of the candidates in Edmonton, Dr. W. S. Hall, offered to defray all costs if the cast would repeat the play in the Empire Theatre there.

The play he had inspired largely determined the nature of Fee's participation in the Social Credit movement. Everywhere he spoke, whether before small study groups or large public meetings, he took with him copies of transfer vouchers, dividend vouchers, ledgers and passbooks, farmers' contracts, stage money, and charts that had been distributed to the audiences when the play was originally produced in Killam. With these stage properties as visual aids, he gave the interpretation of Social Credit which had been presented in the play. Hundreds turned out to his meetings and no halls could contain the crowds who wished to hear him: loud speakers had to be installed to accommodate the overflow which in many cases was larger than the audience inside. Even when he held open-air meetings, loud speakers were required to reach those on the fringe of the crowd.

At the nominating convention in his constituency, Fee's name headed the list. At first he refused to accept the nomination: he had enough to occupy him in his various business concerns. Only after three delegations had pleaded with him was he finally persuaded to allow his name to stand. An indication of the respect he commanded is that during the election campaign he and the other two convention nominees always held joint meetings, even after the advisory committee had selected him as the official candidate. He built the movement so thoroughly in the Sedgewick constituency that over twenty years later it was still regarded as one of the strongest Social Credit districts in Alberta.

HERBERT INGREY: SERVICE STATION OPERATOR AND CARTAGE CON-
TRACTOR: DRUMHELLER

Born at Leyton, Essex, England, December 9, 1886, of English parentage, he attended a municipal school there, leaving at the age of thirteen with an X-7 or Labour certificate (said to be the equivalent of Grade IX in Alberta). His father apprenticed him to a lawyer, for whom he worked for six months. After working for the East India Rubber Company for another six months, he joined the British Navy, where he remained for one-and-a-half years.

Soon after leaving the Navy, he arrived in Toronto, in March, 1903, with $2.50 in his pocket. Everywhere a job was open, he found signs posted, "No Englishman need apply." Through an immigration employment agency, he finally became a farmhand in Perth County (Ontario) at $10 a month and board. Subsequently, he worked in a brickyard for three months at $30 a month. Then he went to Battleford, Saskatchewan, on a homeseekers' excursion. Instead of taking up a homestead, he drifted about for several years, working in railroad camps, returning to Eastern Canada and going back to Saskatchewan again, working as a labourer on the construction of the Massey-Harris building in Saskatoon, harvesting, and various other odd jobs. During this period he experienced privation from long journeys in settlers' effects cars or from the bitter cold.

In 1908, he finally took up a homestead at Asquith, Saskatchewan. Here he prospered greatly for several years, eventually acquiring two-and-a-half sections of land, making a visit to England, and shipping 16,000 bushels of wheat in 1916. But then years of drought overtook him, and he fell heavily into debt. Refusing to work for mortgage companies, he gave up his land in 1923 and went to Drumheller, Alberta. Here he worked for six years as an operator of electric cutting machines in a mine. In 1929, he acquired a service station and a cartage and transfer business, and this was still his occupation when he was elected in 1935 as the Social Credit member of the legislature for Drumheller.

While farming at Asquith he was a member of the Saskatchewan Grain Growers' Association and the Co-operative Elevator Company (which sold out later to the Saskatchewan Wheat Pool). He was president of his local in the former for one year, but held no office in the latter: in both organizations he did more than his share of battling for the rights of wheat farmers. He was a member of the Knights of Pythias, whose philosophy and ritual he admired, and he went through the chairs in this fraternity. Later he joined the Buffaloes, but was not impressed. In religion, he was a member of the Church of England. Before taking up Social Credit, he had no political affiliation and, in fact, he had never voted before 1935 because he could see nothing to vote for.

He first heard of Social Credit through the publicity attending Aberhart's and Douglas's appearances in the spring of 1934 before the Agricultural Committee of the legislature. The emphasis of the U.F.A. government on the constitutional aspects of Social Credit infuriated Ingrey, as did also their efforts (as he thought) to embarrass and belittle Aberhart during the hearings at Edmonton. When the hearings were over and Douglas had left, he began to listen to Aberhart's week-night broadcasts. Then touring speakers held meetings in Drumheller: the Rev. William Morrison (a United Church minister, who was elected in 1935 for Okotoks–High River) and Eric J. Poole (a building contractor who became the Social Credit Member of Parliament for Red Deer in the federal election of 1935) were followed by the Rogers–Unwin team.

He became a Social Crediter because Aberhart's broadcasts and the speeches of touring candidates in Drumheller, especially Mrs. Rogers, convinced him that Social Credit could solve the problems of the depression. Socialism, which he had considered, repelled him when he heard it presented before a meeting of miners by two speakers from New Zealand. The apathy of the U.F.A. to Aberhart's cause convinced him that they were not interested in the welfare of the masses but only in political power. The Liberals and Conservatives were merely old-line parties, tools of Eastern interests. Social Credit alone made clear not only why there was a depression but also how the depression could be overcome.

To Aberhart's religious broadcasts Ingrey, a devout Anglican, was completely indifferent: he considered that people were over-influenced by his powerful voice. For Aberhart as leader of the Social Credit movement, on the other hand, he had boundless admiration. He felt that

Aberhart, unlike the leaders of mere party machines, was sincerely concerned with and determined to put an end to the economic distress of the people. So great was Aberhart's appeal to the people that when he was broadcasting from the Bible Institute, it was impossible, Ingrey said, for him to hold a meeting. Aberhart was envisaged as the leader of a crusade: only he could stir up the people to realize the possibilities of the philosophy of Social Credit: only he, with his wonderful capacity as an organizer, could overthrow the party machines. "All this," Ingrey concluded, "reverts back to the old tribal fact that we've always got to have a leader."

Immediately following the meeting at which Ingrey became a convert to Social Credit, Mrs. Rogers organized a study group and he was elected its vice-president. Shortly afterwards the president and the secretary-treasurer left the area so it fell to him to carry on the organization of the movement in Drumheller. This he did with the greatest energy and enthusiasm. Realizing that the coal-miners were dissatisfied with a system that gave them employment only three-and-a-half months annually, he circulated hundreds of Aberhart's white leaflets among them. Then he called a public meeting and for the first time in his life appeared on a platform as a speaker, expounding Aberhart's first leaflet on Social Credit. This first meeting was so successful that henceforth he held meetings almost daily until the election. He himself was surprised at the energy that he was able to muster for the cause: "once I had got going," he said, "nothing could stop me." Largely owing to his activity the whole of the Drumheller valley was recruited for the movement.

Mine operators and bank managers, to whom the Social Credit proposals seemed very radical indeed, attempted for several months to heckle Ingrey at public meetings and to ridicule Aberhart and the movement. He always answered their technical criticisms of his speeches by appealing to the human factor: "Humanity," he insisted again and again, "is the only asset in the world." Efforts to ridicule Aberhart and the movement proved a boomerang: the people of Drumheller bitterly resented being treated like fools, and were more strongly confirmed than ever in their allegiance to Aberhart and his cause. Operators and managers then attacked Ingrey as an uneducated rabble-rouser. He stated that, as a last resort, mine operators warned the people that if they attended Social Credit meetings or voted Social Credit they would be fired; but such threats merely resulted in larger meetings wherever he spoke.

His outstanding success with the people was due, in part, to the fact that for the first time in his life he was able to attack bitterly, with the support of a surging social movement, the economic system from which he himself had suffered in his earlier life. It was also due to his ability to use illustrations from the people's everyday experience as aids in the exposition of Social Credit. When he spoke in the rural areas of his constituency, which had previously been visited by several teams of touring candidates, the farmers felt, for the first time, that they really understood the theories of Social Credit. On one occasion, in the severe winter of 1935, two horses were needed to pull Ingrey's car through the snow, yet the schoolhouse in which he spoke was packed. Although he was the marvel of other speakers, owing to his capacity to inflame audiences, he understood, in part, one of the most important psychological aspects of the movement: "To me," he said, "it was a fanatical religious emotionalism that got the people, really!"

While his impassioned speeches disturbed the banking and mining interests, they offered no consolation to the Communists, who had been cultivating that particular mining region for years and who ran a candidate against him in the election. Sometimes as many as 60 per cent of his audiences would be Communists before he began his speech; in such districts he obtained 90 per cent of the votes in the election. One of his tactics in dealing with Communists illustrates the confused political situation in Alberta at that time. He took around with him to meetings an old Scottish socialist, who had been a student of Keir Hardie: the socialist discussed the old system, and Ingrey described the new age that would be brought in through Social Credit.

Ingrey held many stormy meetings, but his stormiest was held in Drumheller on the eve of the election, with 1,200 people attending. The Communists were determined to break it up and shouted question after question at him while he was speaking. Finally, the Communist leader threw the meeting into an uproar by challenging him to debate then and there the merits of Social Credit versus Communism. The roaring Communists had quieted down while their leader was speaking; without a moment's hesitation Ingrey accepted the challenge on one condition— that he take the side of Communism and that the Communist leader take the side of Social Credit! The Communist, who was entirely ignorant of Social Credit, refused the offer. Ingrey then launched a biting attack on Communism; the crowd swung over almost immediately to his side; and the Communist leader walked out of the meeting crestfallen and defeated. The Communist movement in the Drumheller area, which had been steadily rising up to 1934, has never recovered from the impact of Ingrey's rally of the people to Social Credit.

SOLON EARL LOW: TEACHER: WARNER

Born at Cardston, Alberta, on January 8, 1900, of Scottish-English ancestry, he was educated at the public and high schools there and the Normal School at Calgary. Later he continued his studies by correspondence and by attending summer sessions at the University of Alberta and the University of Southern California. His parents had come from Utah in the 1890's and settled on a ranch near Whiskey Gap in the Milk River Ridge, just on the border between Alberta and Montana. "Whiskey Gap," a pass through the Continental divide, was so named because it was used by American rum-runners who did an illicit business among the Indians and white settlers south of Macleod. On this rough and tough frontier, he spent his boyhood: he heard many tales about the exploits of the famous outlaw, Tracy, in that area; the scarlet-coated Royal North-West Mounted Police, in search of the good dinner his mother always provided, were frequent visitors to the ranch. In his youth he was keenly interested in basketball, boxing, and wrestling. One of his assets was a good left hook; indeed, the ability to defend himself from physical violence helped him more than once while campaigning for Social Credit: on one occasion he had to fight his way out of a threatening circle of miners who had gathered to break up his meeting.

His father's death when he was eighteen made it necessary for Low to make his own way. He began buying grain for the Home Grain Company when he was nineteen, and subsequently managed elevators and flour and coal businesses for this company in the towns of Big Valley and Rowley. Eventually, however, he was able to fulfil his ambition to become a teacher. Following Normal School, he served as principal of the Arrowwood Consolidated School, south of Gleichen, for three years. On obtaining a First Class teaching certificate, he was successively assistant principal of the public school (1926-7) and a member of the staff of the high school (1927-34) at Raymond. In 1934 he became principal of the new high school at Stirling.

Always keenly interested in community affairs, he was secretary of the Board of Trade in the town of Arrowwood and president of the Board of Trade in Stirling. Wherever he taught, he enthusiastically promoted baseball and basketball: he recognized in basketball especially a type of recreational activity through which boys and girls could be helped to become good citizens. This absorbing interest led him to become a coach in basketball, and his high school teams in Raymond won five consecutive provincial championships. In religion he was a devoted and active member of the Church of Jesus Christ of Latter Day Saints, commonly called Mormons; at the time he became a Social Crediter he had taught

Sunday School in this church for fifteen years. His earlier political affiliation was not specified, but he was considered a Liberal.

While studying at the University of Southern California in 1931, Low became interested in a particular phase of economics: the possibility of establishing a relationship between the appearances of major depressions in North America and the increase in the productive capacity of the United States and Canada as a consequence of technological advances. In doing research on this problem, he discovered that the frequency of major depressions during the previous hundred years was almost in exact inverse ratio to the increase in productive capacity of the economies. He concluded that as the ability to produce goods and services increased, the time between major depressions decreased. He became absorbed in finding out why.

About that time he read a series of articles that was appearing in several Western newspapers, written by C. V. Kerslake of Owen Sound, Ontario. In these articles, which summarized Douglas's economic theories, Low discovered suggestions concerning the reason for the relationships he had discovered between the frequency of depressions and the increase in productive capacity. As a result, he became keenly interested in Social Credit, and particularly in Douglas's explanation of the deficiency of purchasing power. In 1933, he began listening to Aberhart's broadcasts in which the writings of Douglas, Colbourne, and Hattersly were discussed. He obtained and read eagerly all the literature concerning Social Credit he could find.

He became a Social Crediter because he felt certain that he had discovered one of the most important reasons for the occurrence of business cycles, and that Social Credit could provide a corrective technique. He was also intrigued by the democratic challenge that he found in Social Credit: for many years he had believed that democracy was being perverted by political party machines. Social Credit offered an opportunity for men of goodwill and conviction to revitalize democracy and make it yield the results the people wanted from the management of their affairs.

During the years 1933 and 1934 he listened frequently to Aberhart's radio addresses and was greatly impressed by his marvellous voice and masterful discussion of Social Credit. Picturing Aberhart as a great reformer and potential leader, he went, whenever possible, to hear him speak in the Bible Institute. "Aberhart was," Low has said, "a huge man, strong and full of vibrant vitality. He spoke with such deep conviction and seemed to have such abiding faith that I looked upon him as one who doubtless would be able to successfully lead us in the effort to bring order out of chaos and abolish poverty in the midst of plenty. His dogged determination and his rugged individualism made people either love or hate him—there was no in-between."

In 1933, while still at Raymond, Low did considerable lecturing on Social Credit throughout southern Alberta. After moving to Stirling, he continued to work actively in the organization and instruction of study groups in several southern constituencies. Aberhart's programme of local organization in terms of study groups appealed to him greatly: he recognized in it the pattern of organization as taught to Moses by Jethro the Midianite. He set to work to test the programme, and found that it worked exceptionally well. Few constituencies in Alberta were better organized than those immediately north of the American border.

In the autumn of 1934, he was invited to attend, as a delegate, the Liberal nominating convention at Warner. At this convention he drafted and proposed a resolution calling for the Liberal party organization in the Warner constituency to adopt and promote the Social Credit proposals. After some discussion, the resolution was voted down. Low walked out of the convention and never attended another Liberal party meeting. In the election, he defeated the Liberal who was nominated at that convention by a vote of over three to one. Under Low's dynamic leadership the Mormon population of Alberta went almost *en masse* into the Social Credit movement.

DUNCAN BRUCE MACMILLAN: FARMER: LACOMBE

Born at Norland, Victoria County, Ontario, on August 27, 1887, of Scottish ancestry, he was educated at public schools in Ontario and Alberta. His family, who were farmers, settled in the Lacombe district in 1901.

In 1912, he acquired his own farm at Tees, and after the First World War became the elevator agent there also. With the exception of four years in the Canadian Expeditionary Force from 1915 to 1919, he had lived on a farm all his life.

A member of the U.F.A., he was secretary of his local for several terms. Later, he served as a member of the school board of his district for six years. In religion, he was a member of the United Church of Canada. Until the First World War he was a Conservative in politics; on returning from the war he supported the U.F.A. until the emergence of the Social Credit movement.

His war experience stimulated him to such an extent that after returning to his farm from overseas he began to read economics—all the "isms." None of the "isms" he encountered in his reading seemed to resolve his puzzlement about an economic system that led to wars. His farming and elevator interests then became so absorbing that he had little time for much else than his church and his district school board. Then came the depression. As a grain-buyer for the elevator at Tees, he constantly encountered the resentment of his fellow farmers over the ridiculously low prices of grain. He recognized the justice of their complaints, but what could he do about them? "I bought grain," he said, "not only below the cost of production but below the cost of threshing— Yet there was always a market even at that low price." He returned to the reading of economics, but once again the various theories made no sense.

He first heard of Social Credit when Ansley began lecturing on it in the Lacombe area, but he did not attend any of these meetings. Later, in the summer of 1934, Aberhart (to whose radio addresses he had never listened) spoke at Alix and MacMillan attended the meeting. Aberhart's exposition of Social Credit that night was a turning-point in MacMillan's life. He was convinced that Aberhart and Douglas had the answers to the economic problems of the depression. At Aberhart's suggestion, he read Douglas's *Monopoly of Credit*. This book confirmed his conversion to the Social Credit cause.

He became a Social Crediter from an intellectual conviction that Douglas's theories not only explained but also provided a remedy for the depression. These theories seemed particularly relevant to the problems which confronted him as a farmer in the Lacombe constituency. First, the outstanding feature of Social Credit was the emphasis on the *just price* (MacMillan explained that just price and parity price meant the same thing). Second, Social Credit offered a revision of the whole system of bank credit: under the old system, banks make production loans, but it is within the power of the local bank manager to distribute that credit as he sees fit; under the Social Credit system, if a farmer was worthy of credit, he would get credit, and such loans would bear interest at the cost of book-keeping only. Third, Social Credit offered the basic dividend. Under the present monetary system, production is financed to the point of over-production, but the financing of consumption is ignored; the basic dividend would put purchasing power into the hands of consumers. "It's immaterial," he said, "how much you sell your production for. It's the purchasing power you get that is important." Fourth, under Social Credit, taxes, if any, would be based on production: if a farmer were hailed out, he would have no taxes to pay. Fifth, Social Credit stressed, what everybody knows really, that goods are paid for with goods and not money. Production, not gold, is the real source of credit. Sixth, Social Credit offered "Freedom with Security." The concept of the cultural heritage puts the collective credit of the community behind the individual, but at the same time the individual does not become a victim of the slave state of socialism and communism.

MacMillan had clearly thought about Social Credit, and he had also thought about religion. He was not attracted to the religious doctrines of the Bible Institute, although he respected Aberhart for his sincerity and strong convictions about religion. But he felt that no one in Alberta could expound Social Credit with the clarity and authority of Aberhart. The only man capable of leading the Social Credit movement to political power was likewise Aberhart. To his leader, MacMillan gave unquestioning loyalty.

As soon as he joined the movement, MacMillan began to organize study groups in the Lacombe constituency. He also continued the study of Social Credit and discussed it constantly with farmers as he went around buying grain. A farmer in each rural community would be urged to organize a group composed of neighbours. Before the end of 1934 there was a network of such groups meeting in schools and farm-houses in the Lacombe constituency. MacMillan was himself surprised at the great uprising of the people that occurred in the autumn of 1934. He considered that by election time 80 per cent of the membership of the U.F.A. had joined the Social Credit movement.

While he worked hard among farmers, he was equally concerned to develop the movement in small towns and villages. Having been a U.F.A. man, he was aware of the antagonisms which had developed between town and country since 1921. In appealing to the people in towns and villages, he maintained that the Social Credit movement would reduce the existing tension between them and the farmers: the movement was the realization of a party of all the people, not the party of one class only, like the U.F.A. Following his lead, other candidates played up the unifying character of the new movement.

Unlike many of the movement's speakers, MacMillan always attempted to present the theories of Social Credit clearly and systematically. He never harangued his audiences or made emotional appeals. His success as a speaker was largely due to his clever use of charts to explain and illustrate the Social Credit theories. The idea of using charts was derived, of course, from Aberhart. But MacMillan made considerable improvements in his effort to reduce the theories to pictorial or visual form. The chart he used to expound Douglas's A plus B Theorem is a remarkable document of the movement; almost as remarkable are the charts and diagrams he devised to illustrate other aspects of Social

Credit theory. These charts and diagrams, done in black on large pieces of white cardboard, were taken all over the Lacombe constituency and into adjoining rural constituencies as well. They became one of the most discussed features of the movement in the rural areas between Calgary and Edmonton.

JOSEPH LUCIEN PAUL MAYNARD: BARRISTER: BEAVER RIVER

Born at Montreal, on February 17, 1908, of French-Canadian parentage, he was educated at the Edmonton Jesuit College, Laval University (B.A., 1928), and the University of Alberta (LL.B., 1931).

At the time the Social Credit movement emerged, he was in his middle twenties, busily engaged in building up a law practice in the village of St. Paul, northeast of Edmonton.

Owing to his youth he had not yet had time to serve on the committees of community organizations. He was, however, already secretary-treasurer of the St. Paul School District. In religion, he was an ardent Roman Catholic. His political affiliation before taking up Social Credit was not stated: he seems not to have been identified in his community with the traditional parties.

That he first heard of Social Credit while attending a school trustees' convention in Edmonton in February, 1935, suggests that the movement had not, before the late winter of 1934–5, penetrated the northeastern French-Canadian settlements. At this convention he met a considerable number of delegates from southern Alberta who questioned him, as a university-trained man, concerning his attitude to Social Credit. The enthusiasm of these questioners aroused his interest to such an extent that, on returning to St. Paul, he read the report of the Agricultural Committee of the legislature and Douglas's book, *Social Credit*. He still did not realize what an extensive movement had developed in Alberta.

He became a Social Crediter from intellectual conviction. He saw a close relationship between Douglas's theories and the teachings of the Roman Catholic Church: it seemed to him that Social Credit was implicit in certain Papal Encyclicals—notably *Rerum Novarum* and *Quadragesimo Anno*. The two approaches to social and political theory were in substantial agreement on such problems as the relationship of the individual to the state, the responsibilities of capital and labour, and the role of the state with regard to monopolies. Part of one of the Encyclicals even deals with the nature of credit in a manner that seems compatible with Douglas's approach. Maynard observed, of course, that some priests opposed Social Credit while others favoured it. Hence he did not claim that his personal convictions concerning the relevance of Social Credit to the economic problems of Alberta necessarily represented the views of his Church.

As a loyal Roman Catholic he was not, of course, more than mildly interested in Aberhart's religious doctrines. But while developing the Social Credit movement in the Beaver River and St. Paul areas in the spring and summer of 1935, Maynard became a whole-hearted admirer of the leadership of Aberhart. For northern candidates, personal contacts with Aberhart were infrequent until after the election: the bond of friendship betwen the chief and his lieutenants could never become as strong in the north as in the south. To Maynard, the strength of Aberhart's appeal was almost entirely intellectual: the Social Credit movement of that period seemed to him to be a rally of all the people, a real Union of the Electors.

Shortly after becoming a Social Crediter, Maynard began to work vigorously for the movement. His fluency in two languages was a decided asset in northeastern Alberta: at his first meeting, at Lafond, in April, 1935, he spoke entirely in French; at his second meeting, in an English district, entirely in English; later, he sometimes used both languages at the same meeting. From April to election day he was largely instrumental in organizing the two constituencies of Beaver River and St. Paul, both of which had a considerable French-Canadian population. Everywhere he spoke, study groups were organized. Each group was well supplied with Aberhart's leaflets and pamphlets, procured from the Bible Institute, and also with copies of the *Social Credit Chronicle*. Once he had organized a study group, he saw to it that the group met regularly for the discussion of the various aspects of the monetary system and the Social Credit proposals for its reform. In his areas, the groups always ended their evening meetings with a small supper followed by a dance. Many of his public meetings took a largely recreational form: there would be a baseball tournament in the afternoon, a picnic supper, a talk on Social Credit, and a dance at the close.

As a result of Maynard's efforts, the two constituencies where he developed the movement, after having oscillated between the Liberals and U.F.A. in previous elections, became and remained devoted to the Social Credit cause for the next twenty years. Part of the strength of his appeal to French-Canadians lay unquestionably in the new strategy he contributed to the movement: his constant emphasis on the close relationship between the social and political philosophy of certain Papal Encyclicals and the theories of Social Credit.

MARK WILLIAM ROBERTSON: INSURANCE AGENT: EDMONTON

Born on a farm at Hall's Mills, Lanark County, Ontario, on October 5, 1887, of Scottish-Irish ancestry, he attended public school there and completed Grade VIII. He educated himself further by taking courses from a correspondence school in Western Canada. On leaving public school he worked on farms in Ontario for several years.

In 1907 he went to Alberta and worked for ten years in the coal mines at Cardiff as a steam and electrical engineer. From 1917 to 1929, he was a trainman on the Canadian National Railway. In the autumn of 1929, he resigned from the railway and set up in Edmonton as an insurance agent. Before long the depression began to be felt in the city and the insurance business turned out to be much more difficult than he had supposed. Then in 1932 he fell ill and had to spend a long term in hospital. During this period, he lost his home and was forced to take cash value for his personal insurance policies. "For three years," he said, "I was unable to work or earn a dollar."

During his twelve years with the railway, he represented the trainmen for seven years as a negotiator-member of their general committee. For a term he was president of the Edmonton branch of the Native Sons of Canada. Keenly interested in fraternal organizations, he went through the chairs of the Masonic Lodge, and rose to Noble Grand of the Oddfellows' Lodge. In religion, he was a Fundamentalist Baptist. Before joining the Social Credit movement, he was an active Conservative, having been an Alberta delegate to that party's national convention in Winnipeg in 1927.

He had listened occasionally to Aberhart's religious broadcasts prior to 1932, but about that time ceased to do so owing to poor reception of the Calgary station. He first heard of Social Credit from a friend, a mining engineer, with whom he discussed it thoroughly. Then he read the newspaper accounts of the appearances of Aberhart and Douglas before the Agricultural Committee of the legislature, heard the broadcast of Douglas's address to the legislature, and listened to the broadcast of Douglas's mass meeting in Calgary in April, 1934. When the report of the hearings of the Agricultural Committee was printed, he read it again and again until he "found out exactly what it meant." Shortly afterwards he heard a federal Cabinet minister, the Honourable C. H. Cahan, state in a radio speech "that the reason the depression had deepened was because the banks had withdrawn $900,000,000 worth of credit." "I asked myself," said Robertson, "whose credit?" A little later he heard Cahan's leader, Prime Minister R. B. Bennett, say in a broadcast from Toronto: "Hardship has passed me by." "In five words," said Robertson, "Bennett indicated why he had failed to relieve the distress of the Canadian people. Bennett was a reformer at heart, but too wealthy to reform the monetary system, the root of all our troubles." Late in 1934, Robertson heard Aberhart speak in Edmonton at McDougall United Church, and again in March, 1935. After hearing Aberhart's speech at the latter meeting he decided to join the Social Credit movement, which was rising rapidly in Edmonton at that time. It was the contrast between the approaches of Cahan and Bennett on the one hand and Douglas and Aberhart on the other that finally drove Robertson from the Conservatives to the Social Crediters.

He became a Social Crediter, then, because of the inability of both the provincial and the federal governments to deal with the problems of the depression. "The bottom had fallen out of everything in Edmonton," said Robertson. Struggling in the depression-ridden city, he saw in Social Credit "the people's only hope of dragging themselves out of the morass of debt they had incurred."

He was greatly impressed not only by the Social Credit theories but also by the leader of the movement. He admired Aberhart's dynamic personality and warm humanity, but above all, his genius as a speaker. "Aberhart," he said, "was able to tell us about Social Credit in a language that everybody could understand. He seemed, while speaking from a platform, to be talking to the humblest woman in her kitchen or to a man digging a ditch. He was talking to you personally. He had a mastery of language that few men possess: he had a gift of placing the exact word in the proper place. He was in the top class as a speaker." Roberston was always thrilled by Aberhart's downright attacks on the monetary system. "The people who supported the system Aberhart condemned," he said, "never forgave him for his condemnation of that system. He made enemies and friends. You had to be either for or against him; he never pulled a punch, and never asked for quarter or gave it. I was absolutely for him. I would put Aberhart right at the top of Canadian leaders."

No sooner had Aberhart converted him, than Robertson joined the central group in Edmonton and set to work to master Social Credit doctrine. The devotees in that group had a sense of urgency: as the development and organization of the movement in northern Alberta lagged far behind the south, they had to work day and night to prepare for the general northern convention, the constituency nominating conventions, and finally, the election campaign itself. Robertson threw himself with zest into the feverish activity that now characterized the northern movement until election day.

While he served on the Central Executive in Edmonton and did a certain amount of organizational work, he was engaged mainly in public speaking. His itinerary, which was arranged by the Central Executive, included groups in Edmonton but was mainly a tour of towns and villages north of the city. He was astonished at the crowds that came to his northern rural meetings: frequently he had to speak outdoors from a truck as all the people who wanted to hear him could not be jammed into the building. "In Edmonton," he said, "the campaign was terrific. No matter where we went, our meetings were always crowded out, while the opposition parties would have an audience of only four or five. At one meeting, the opposition didn't have any audience at all. The candidate played the piano and a reporter sang a solo. It was absolutely the greatest election ever held in Alberta."

He attributed the remarkable interest of the people in Social Credit meetings to the fact that Social Crediters talked a language they could understand. "When the Liberals and Conservatives," he said, "talked to the people about millions of debt, they didn't understand it. But when we talked to people about the basic dividend of twenty-five dollars a month, they understood: it meant food, clothing, a trip to the dentist— things they understood. We said that if we were able to issue our own credit the basic dividend would be paid to them." He never mentioned the other parties in his speeches but concentrated on exposing the evils of the economic system and showing what Social Credit could do for the people. "The other parties," he said, "held out no hope to the people. The whole Social Credit campaign in Edmonton and northern Alberta was a campaign of hope."

JOHN LYLE ROBINSON: CHIROPRACTOR: MEDICINE HAT

Born at Belfast, Ireland, August 28, 1890, of Irish parentage, he was educated at the Torhea National School and the Larne Grammar School (1904–11); at the latter he served as science demonstrator for eighteen months in 1910–11. From 1910 to 1912, he attended the Marlborough Street Training College for Teachers in Dublin.

After teaching for a year at the Bushmill School for Boys in County Antrim, he migrated in 1913 to Alberta, where he was granted a certificate to teach in the provincial schools. He taught successively at Arbordale (north of Lacombe), Monitor, and Sunset Hill. While teaching at the last in 1916, he took up a homestead and continued farming and teaching there until 1929. Becoming afflicted with sciatica, he decided to attend the Palmer School of Chiropractic at Davenport, Iowa, where he took the three-year course in two years and graduated with high honours and the degree of Doctor of Chiropractic. He returned to Alberta, passed the provincial examination for chiropractors, and soon built up a substantial practice at Medicine Hat.

While farming at Sunset Hill, he was secretary-treasurer of the U.F.A. local. He also joined the Orange and Masonic Orders, rising to the thirty-second degree in the latter. In religion he was a Presbyterian. Before taking up Social Credit, he was a strong U.F.A. party man and on one occasion he was approached by the U.F.A. organization to stand as their candidate in his constituency; this honour he declined. His U.F.A. affiliation grew steadily weaker during the early 1930's when he was establishing himself as a chiropractor at Medicine Hat.

He occasionally listened to Aberhart's religious broadcasts, which he found very interesting. But he was not attracted to Social Credit until the early fall of 1934, and then not through listening to Aberhart's broadcasts but owing to his friendship with a university-educated farmer, Arthur H. Mitchell (who became the Social Credit Member of Parliament for Medicine Hat in the federal election of 1935). Mitchell persuaded him to read Douglas's books and to join a Social Credit study group in the city known as the "Business Men's Group." Through his membership in this group, which contained a number of able business and professional men, Robinson became a Social Crediter.

Owing to recurrent droughts in southern Alberta, Medicine Hat had been particularly hard hit by the depression. In that city unemployment was widespread and many were on relief; most of the farmers in the surrounding drought areas were in difficult circumstances financially. When economic conditions seemed at their worst, Robinson was deeply shocked by the charges of personal misconduct brought against two members of the U.F.A. government. The continuing inability of that government, which he had hitherto supported, to solve the problems of drought and depression, convinced him in the late fall of 1934 that new ideas and new leadership were needed.

He became a Social Crediter not because he understood the doctrines but because of Aberhart's leadership of the movement. "I don't understand and never have understood economics," he declared during an interview. He took up Social Credit, therefore, because he sensed a sincerity in Aberhart that seemed lacking in the U.F.A. leaders. "The time was ripe for a change," he stated, "and I became convinced that Aberhart could provide the dynamic leadership necessary to bring about that change."

In accordance with his image of himself as a strictly realistic and practical man, Robinson's contribution to the Social Credit movement was largely concerned with organization: during the election campaign of 1935 his constituency was one of the best organized in the province. He confined his activities to the Medicine Hat constituency, and in all his speeches he emphasized the remarkable personality and leadership of Aberhart and the practical desirability of a change of government. He gloried in the claim that in his speeches he never promised anything to anybody. "The basic dividend may have figured in the over-all campaign in Alberta," he said, "but in Medicine Hat I relied on Aberhart's leadership of the movement and my strong organization to carry me through." To him the Social Credit movement meant, "not the acceptance of a fancy monetary theory but a new approach to the purely administrative processes of government." This implied "good, clean government in every department," and this, he became convinced, was what Aberhart and the new movement would achieve. "Without Aberhart's leadership and the movement's organization," he concluded, "I wouldn't have even been elected in 1935. As it turned out, I received a vote double that of my Liberal and Conservative opponents combined."

THE REVEREND ROY CHARLES TAYLOR: CLERGYMAN: PINCHER CREEK

Born at Sunnyside, Alberta, December 11, 1889, of Scottish ancestry, he was educated there, at Wesley (now United) College, Winnipeg (junior matriculation), at Alberta College North (senior matriculation), at the University of Alberta (B.A., 1921), and at St. Stephen's Theological College (B.D., 1931). He was ordained to the Methodist ministry at Edmonton in 1919, and entered the United Church of Canada on its formation in 1925.

He served in the ranks with the Canadian army overseas from 1915 to 1919, rising to the rank of sergeant. As a clergyman, he was stationed successively on the Hobbema Indian Reservation, in the Crow's Nest Pass, and at Lethbridge. In 1932 he transferred to the village of Coleman, in the Pincher Creek constituency, and it was in southwestern Alberta that he helped to develop the Social Credit movement.

His ministerial duties brought him into relationships with most of the organizations in the communities where he lived. A member of the Oddfellows, the Knights of Pythias, and the Lions International, he was in considerable demand as a speaker at meetings of fraternal organizations and service clubs. While a student at the University of Alberta, he became interested in a public forum, which met in a theatre, where social and political theories and problems were constantly discussed. On one occasion, he addressed this forum on "Socialism—Good, Bad, and Indifferent." During his arts course at the university, he imbibed the version of Hegelian idealism then emphasized in its philosophy department; and while at theological college, he was indoctrinated with the social gospel approach characteristic of Methodism in the decades before Church Union. A Liberal during his earlier student days, he became impressed by the agrarian social philosophy of Henry Wise Wood and quietly voted for the U.F.A. from 1921 to 1930.

He first heard of Social Credit in the summer of 1934 through one of his friends, a high school principal, who had already been explaining the doctrine at meetings in southwestern Alberta. During the following autumn this principal loaned Taylor several of Douglas's books, took him along on speaking tours, and discussed Social Credit doctrine vigorously and incessantly with him as they drove around the country. Then Taylor, already saturated with the principal's conversation, began to listen to the "Man from Mars" radio series. Aberhart's arguments in these broadcasts finally persuaded him that Social Credit was the solution to the problems created by the depression in Alberta.

He joined the movement because the doctrines of Social Credit seemed to constitute a logical development or synthesis of ideas he had been struggling to incorporate into his sermons for some years previously. He had been influenced while at university by utilitarianism, and was strongly attracted to the ethical ideal of the greatest happiness of the greatest number. In sermons he had advocated equality of opportunity rather than equal distribution of wealth. He also believed in state medicine for many years before becoming a Social Crediter. Then, too, as a result of university courses in political economy, he had come to question some of the orthodox assumptions of economics, such as the feasibility of unlimited free enterprise. In the summer and autumn of 1934, he was profoundly disturbed intellectually and emotionally by the seeming inability of the U.F.A. government to come to grips with the problems of the people. In this disturbed condition, he was introduced by a friend into the new religious-economic movement. Social Credit now appeared as the real answer to the problems of the depression, problems which other social philosophies he had considered could not even interpret clearly, much less solve. The philosophy of Social Credit seemed to absorb into one great whole all the partial theories he had entertained previously:

it offered synthesis, clarity, and hope for the future. There was, however, one phase of the doctrine that Taylor did not accept: owing to his training in economics and political science at the University of Alberta, he never believed in the possibility, at the provincial level, of a basic dividend or, as he called it, "fountain-pen money."

He first heard of Aberhart in 1930, while ministering to the First United Church at Lethbridge. Fundamentalists in this congregation began praising the Sunday afternoon broadcasts from the Bible Institute. Taylor, a religious liberal, was not impressed by Aberhart's reputation at that time: he noticed that the latter's devotees were people of the emotional type, "given to being carried away by utterly fantastic interpretations of Bible prophecy." But as his interest in the Social Credit movement developed he became an admirer of Aberhart as an organizer and orator, a Moses leading the people out of bondage, the liberator of the masses. As a university man, he thought that Aberhart's utterances on economics sometimes had a certain evasiveness, but he never questioned his utter sincerity. Taylor felt that, unless the man had really believed in what he was advocating, he could not have appealed so effectively to the masses "as a sort of demi-god."

Although he became interested in Social Credit as a solution of the problems of the depression during the summer of 1934, Taylor did not formally join the movement until the following spring; for many months he considered that he ought not to alienate those members of his congregation who had diverse political opinions. But he felt that he could legitimately contribute to the movement as an educational enterprise, and he continued to accompany his friend, the high school principal, on speaking tours. They travelled southern Alberta as far east as Lethbridge, holding meetings in towns, villages, and hamlets on the way. In his speeches, Taylor stressed the moral and religious aspects of Social Credit, which he tried to relate to utilitarian ethics and the social gospel. The candidates numbered six clergymen among their ranks, including four from the United Church of Canada. Of these four, Taylor was the most dynamic and effective in inducing members of that church to rally to the Social Credit movement, and this was his distinctive contribution.

During the autumn and winter of 1934-5, he worked tirelessly in addressing meetings, organizing study groups, and distributing literature, without political ambitions or thoughts of personal reward for his effective contribution to the movement. He was very surprised, therefore, when a delegation of leading Social Crediters in the Pincher Creek constituency insisted that he must be their candidate in the forthcoming election. After deliberating for six weeks he reluctantly consented to allow his name to go before the constituency nominating convention and formally joined the movement. The demand that he be the official candidate was so insistent and widespread among the people that he was subsequently selected by the advisory committee without being asked to appear before it. That such a distinction was shared by no other candidate not on the advisory committee suggests that Aberhart fully appreciated Taylor's appeal to the membership of the United Church of Canada as an impassioned advocate of Social Credit.

During the election campaign his interpretation of Social Credit in religious-economic terms as the heir of the social gospel tradition invariably drew overflow audiences, while the attendance at the meetings of his opponents was negligible, and even sometimes non-existent. "Our meetings," he said, "stirred people to the depths—they figured that everyone associated with the Social Credit movement was basically a Christian."

CHAPTER EIGHT

The Response of the People: I

ANALYSIS of the strategy and tactics of the Social Credit movement, its transition to political action, and its involvement in politics, makes it clear that the dynamics of that upsurge cannot be understood without constant reference to the response of the people. In attempting to explain the overwhelming rally of the people to the movement certain commentators have resorted to such stereotypes as "debt," "greed," "religious fanaticism," "political illiteracy." Such interpretations are much too restricted, for the situations to which they refer were equally available to the three existing political parties for exploitation. Moreover, none of these interpretations has been based upon a systematic investigation of the attitudes of the people of Alberta.

Further, the revolt during the years 1933 to 1935 cannot be understood merely by a study of documents such as newspaper and magazine articles, as a rule extremely hostile to Social Credit. Even a study of the political propaganda with which all the parties and various groups with vested interests deluged the province before and during the election campaign of 1935 provides only a partial explanation. Underlying the remarkable Social Credit victory in that election was a mass movement which had emerged as a result of the response of the people to the three-fold challenge of the philosophy of Social Credit, the leadership of Aberhart, and the strategy and tactics developed during a process of dynamic interaction between the leader and the led. For an understanding of the deeper layers of the Social Credit movement it is necessary, therefore, to investigate systematically the response of people who were involved in that movement. We have, accordingly, undertaken a qualitative analysis of this response to the three principal social stimuli with which the people were confronted in their relationships to the movement. This analysis is based on intensive personal interviews with individuals who joined the movement before the election of 1935.

As thousands of people were involved in the movement, each of whom was unique, the interviews were necessarily selective. But care was taken to interview as representative a sample as possible in terms of age, educational, and income levels, as well as occupational, religious, and geographical distribution. The interviews usually lasted from two-and-a-half to three hours, and were sometimes extended to a second session. They were conducted in such a way that the subject would be influenced as little as possible by the form of a question. At the beginning of the interview each subject was encouraged to give something of his background, and thence drawn into general discussion of his personal relationship to the movement and why he became a Social Crediter. Then the interview was gradually tightened and focused around the appeal of Social Credit, the leadership of Aberhart, and the strategy and tactics of the movement. In practically every instance, the subject was so receptive to the idea of "a history of the Social Credit movement" that it was possible to record the interview in writing while it was actually taking place; and only those interviews that were recorded on the spot have been used.

The investigation of the response of the people to the philosophy of Social Credit must begin with a consideration of the extent to which the U.F.A. had prepared Alberta for Douglas's economic, ethical, and political theories. As we have seen in chapter VI, many of the U.F.A. leaders had periodically attacked the banking and financial systems as they functioned in Western Canada. Such attacks were frequently expressed in motions and sent forward to the government from the annual conventions, with recommendations for remedial legislative action. Between 1924 and 1932, at nearly every convention, the farmers debated the possibility of reforming the monetary system in terms of Douglas's proposals.[1] The minutes of the conventions indicate that such debates were usually precipitated by George Bevington, leading monetary reformer and perennial nominee for the presidency of the U.F.A. Bevington always withdrew from the contest, but not before his nomination for the presidency had enabled him and his highly vocal followers to embroil the convention in another well-publicized discussion of monetary reform as the only realistic solution to the farmers' financial problems.

Wood, in his seventieth year, finally retired from the presidency of the U.F.A. in 1931, in favour of Robert Gardiner, a socialist. During that same convention, Bevington's followers attempted unsuccessfully to put through a motion to meet the expenses involved in his educational work throughout the province on behalf of monetary reform. At the next convention, held at Edmonton in January, 1932, some six months before Aberhart became a convert to Social Credit, the monetary reformers took full advantage of the increasing pressures of the depression, as well as of Gardiner's inexperience in office and lack of the prestige that had

[1]See *Minutes*, Annual Conventions, United Farmers of Alberta, 1924–32.

been enjoyed by the venerable and revered Wood, to make a more determined stand than ever before. The convention was in an almost constant uproar, and no less than five pages of its minutes were required to record the motions, amendments, amendments to amendments and counter motions that the monetary reformers and their opponents introduced. When the monetary reformers were finally voted down the weary delegates felt that all the issues had been so thoroughly argued they could never be revived again.

The bitter debates over monetary reform which had rocked the 1932 convention were reported by both the metropolitan daily newspapers and the rural weeklies as evidence of serious dissension and weakening within the U.F.A. ranks. Additional evidence of that dissension was apparent when the delegates reported to their locals the convention's decision against monetary reform. Never before had the U.F.A. been so torn with conflict over monetary reform as during the early months of 1932. The interminable debates at the annual conventions and within the locals developed in the farmers a readiness to respond to the doctrines of Social Credit which Aberhart began to propound from the Bible Institute during the later months of that very year.

Ideas of monetary reform had, in fact, permeated the U.F.A. to such an extent that even a number of its leaders who had concluded that socialism was the ultimate solution were prepared to accept Social Credit as an interim programme: the attainment of Douglas's limited objectives was a necessary step to the distant goal, one phase of the strategy that must be adopted in the general attack on capitalism. On the other hand, the entanglement of the U.F.A. with the socialistic C.C.F. incurred the displeasure of the extreme monetary reformers among its membership. This faction bitterly resented Gardiner's attempt at the convention in 1933 to align the U.F.A. as the Alberta arm of the new C.C.F. movement. When Aberhart and Manning began their first summer tour, the political situation in rural Alberta could scarcely have been more propitious. The controversy within the U.F.A. itself concerning the best method of dealing with the depression had already initiated the political disintegration of that once powerful movement. One of its warring factions, the socialists, would attempt a merger with the C.C.F.; the other, the monetary reformers, seemingly crushed forever at the 1932 convention, would find an unexpected and powerful ally in the rising Social Credit movement.

The response of many farmers in Alberta to the doctrines propounded by Aberhart was due, therefore, in some measure, to the fact that he was merely pouring old wine into new bottles. It is unlikely that the infiltration of rural Alberta by the Social Credit movement would have occurred so rapidly or so completely had the way not been paved by the monetary reformers of the U.F.A. Continuities here, as elsewhere, are important in the understanding of social phenomena. The following excerpt from an interview with a farmer in central Alberta is typical:

For years I had studied and discussed in my U.F.A. local the various schemes of monetary reform. Long before Mr. Aberhart took it up, I knew all about Social Credit. I had been an enthusiastic member of the U.F.A. for many years, but during the depression it became apparent to even the most rabid supporter of the movement that it was in process of disintegration. Then the C.C.F. was formed. Farmers are not socialistically inclined and Alberta farmers in particular do not have any liking for collectivism in any form. Then I began to listen to William Aberhart on my radio. He talked a language I understood, for I knew all about the Social Credit theories. But he was different about Social Credit than our old U.F.A. leaders. I came to feel that Mr. Aberhart would actually do something about Social Credit, not just talk about it. So I became a follower of his and organized for him in my district. I took most of the members away from our U.F.A. local and organized them into a Social Credit study group. We got some of our earliest pamphlets on Social Credit from the U.F.A. office in Calgary.

This account directs attention not only to the continuity of the Social Credit movement with one phase of the U.F.A. movement but also to the positive aspect of Aberhart's programme: he induced in the people the feeling that something could actually be done about Social Credit. It would no longer be interminably debated as at the U.F.A. conventions. At long last the people would get action.

Even socialist supporters of the C.C.F. within the membership of the U.F.A. became involved in Social Credit ideas, as is illustrated by a letter which vice-president Priestley received two weeks after the 1935 convention. Signed by all the officers and directors of a U.F.A. local in south-central Alberta, three of whom had been delegates to the convention, the letter opened with a bitter insistence that, although the leaders of the U.F.A. had attempted to give the public a contrary impression, support for a provincial Social Credit programme was actually very widespread among the farmers of southern Alberta.

They [the delegates] were determined to have some social credit system for the distribution of goods and services, put in operation, in the province of Alberta. . . . If you think the delegates voted down the Aberhart plan of social credit, because they had made up their minds that it could not be done, I believe you are badly mistaken. I think they were just as determined that it must be done, as when they went there.

We had three delegates there, two at U.F.A. and one U.F.W.A. We all voted for the Aberhart plan but were perfectly willing to accept a better plan, if one could be found, by the U.F.A. convention.

We also all supported the resolution brought in by William Irvine, believing the executive board had got together and had come to believe, that something had to be done, and that there was sentiment enough in the province, to back up the government in doing it.

If this was not the sentiment of the larger percentage of delegates as we talked with them in lobbies, hotels and restaurants, then we are no judge of people. . . .

If our central executive and the provincial government . . . do not bring Major Douglas here and give authority to go just as far as he can toward putting in operation his system of social credit in the province of Alberta, they are no longer going to keep the confidence of a large part of the U.F.A., and the fault will be with the leaders, not the people, W. Aberhart, or any one else outside of our organization.

We are 100% U.F.A. here and intend to be. We do not think social credit is the final solution, we know it is not. We have supported our federal members 100% and intend to do so. We believe our organization as a social and economic organization is the best we have ever known. We have not been led into organizing a social credit group, nor do we intend to, but you must realize Alberta has sent enough men to Ottawa for twelve years, who have believed and preached and worked for our cause, that if the rest of the provinces had done the same, we would have had a C.C.F. government to give us national finance and credit, so there would be no need for provincial action along this line. But if we insist on sticking to that line of action, we believe we are going to lose our support in Alberta before we get enough in the other provinces to make up their minds to act. For this reason we are determined to use every means in our power, to see that some government in Alberta, undertakes to do this thing, and shows the public it can be done. Where enough people believe in it, and will support it, we are still hoping our leaders and provincial government, will get our view point and act accordingly, while they have the chance and power. Before it is too late.

If *action* is delayed until after election, *promises* will not be much good *at* election. If the thing is done, or well started before election, a new party will have very little chance at election.

I hope you will realize this is written in a kindly spirit, but with a purpose that will not be changed by anything but action. We know full well the difficulties in the way, but are fully convinced there must be a way around or over, the difficulties.

If the monetary reformers within the U.F.A. movement helped to prepare the farmers of Alberta for the Social Credit movement, it is clear that the ethical and political theories of the U.F.A. movement also had something in common with the philosophy of Social Credit. As a farmers' movement, the U.F.A. had always emphasized the rights of the individual against state control. Running through the speeches and reports of their abler leaders was a strain of Benthamite rationalism and individualism which is similar to Douglas's insistence on the absolute necessity of personal freedom and individual enterprise. At the same time, the U.F.A. leaders had been much concerned with the problem of economic security. The interviews indicate that the Social Credit slogan, "Freedom with Security," offered the best of both worlds to farmers confronted with the depression on the one hand and the threat of socialism to individualism (as they supposed) on the other. To some farmers, the moral ideas of Social Credit seemed, therefore, to be more closely akin to the orthodox ethics of the U.F.A. than to the collectivistic ethics of socialism to which many of the leaders of the older movement had become converts. The alliance of the U.F.A. with socialism appeared, to such people, as a repudiation of the rugged individualism which had always characterized the farmers of Alberta.

The interviews indicate that in a significant sense the Social Credit movement was also the heir of the political theory and practice of the U.F.A. Prior to 1935 the political history of Alberta falls into three phases: first, the period of territorial government, in which a non-partisan system prevailed; second, the period of Liberal rule from 1905 to 1921, in which the two-party system functioned fully only after 1910; third, the period of the U.F.A. revolt against the party system which began in 1921. The operation of democracy in Alberta in terms of the two-party system had therefore been tenuous and uncertain. The traditional national parties had been under criticism even before the province entered Confederation; and after 1905 there is a continuous tradition of great dissatisfaction with the conventional party system. The persistent unrest was inspired by the growing belief that existing political parties, dominated by Eastern financial interests or the money power, were oblivious to the class interests of farmers.

Into this situation there entered after 1915 the social and political philosophy of Henry Wise Wood (1860–1941). Migrating to Alberta from his native Missouri in 1905, Wood had soon become the dominant agrarian leader of the province, holding the presidencies of the three great farmers' organizations: of the U.F.A. from 1916 to 1931, of the Canadian Council of Agriculture from 1917 to 1923, and of the Alberta Wheat Pool from 1923 to 1937. During his long reign as "uncrowned king of Alberta," Wood persistently applied his philosophy of social co-operation and group action to the resolution of the two major crises with which the farm movement was confronted—the agrarian revolt in politics and the wheat marketing problem.

Three major influences had contributed to the development of Wood's social and political philosophy. During his earlier life in Missouri he was actively associated with the Disciples of Christ, from whose teaching and organization he derived a strong belief in the social message of Christianity and an invaluable experience in the practice of democracy. His observation of the political aspects of the Alliance and Populist movements deeply affected his attitude to agrarian political action. To these environmental influences was added deep and wide reading in the literature of economic and social reform.

Among the writers whom Wood read avidly were the novelist Frank Norris, and such philosophers as Karl Marx, J. S. Mill, and Herbert Spencer. Although deeply concerned with the class interests of farmers, he rejected Marx's interpretation of history in terms of a perpetual class war as alien to the religious and democratic traditions in which he had been bred. But his study of Mill and Spencer made him keenly aware of the difficulty of preserving democracy in a society which interpreted progress in terms of a struggle for existence in which only the fittest survived. How could the individual be protected against the forces of organized plutocracy that developed within a competitive, industrial society? Wood became convinced that if democracy were to survive, "humanity" must replace "money" as the motivating force in human behaviour. This was also one of Aberhart's most characteristic doctrines; he had derived it from his reading of Douglas's works; and it was reiterated endlessly by Social Credit speakers to rural audiences well prepared for it by Wood's speeches over a period of fifteen years.

The problems created by the rise of industrialism in an individualistic and competitive society could be resolved, Wood finally concluded, only by the co-operation of organized economic groups. The commercial and financial classes had, in fact, already organized to advance their own interests and, in so doing, had not hesitated to exploit the unorganized classes. The chief victims of commercial and capitalistic exploitation were the farmers. Only if the farmers were likewise organized as an economic group or class could they hope to bargain effectively for their rights and secure social justice. What was impossible of achievement for individuals could be realized through group co-operation and group action. "Democracy may be simply defined," Wood wrote in 1919, "as the people in action."[2]

The application of Wood's philosophy to politics had far-reaching results in Alberta and the larger West. His theory of group action determined the underlying principles of agrarian political participation in Alberta. Under his paternal guidance, the U.F.A. entered politics not as a political party but as an organized class, and this was a turning-point

[2]Wood's presidential addresses to the annual conventions of the U.F.A., 1917–31, which are on file at the Head Office of the United Farmers of Alberta Co-operative in Calgary, contain statements of his social and political philosophy.

in the political history of Alberta. The victory of the U.F.A. in 1921 transformed the conditions of politics in Alberta. By shattering the traditional party system, the farmers helped to prepare the way for the acceptance fourteen years later of Aberhart's interpretation of the Social Credit crusade as non-political. Further, Wood's theory of group action was a fore-runner of Douglas's interpretation of democracy as the realization of the general will, which Aberhart took up and used with great effect during the struggle for power in 1935.

It must be noted, however, that there was a significant difference in the range of appeal of the two movements. The leaders of the U.F.A. directed their appeal almost exclusively to farmers, that is, to one class only within the Alberta community. The leaders of the Social Credit movement, on the other hand, directed their appeal to townsmen as well as farmers, and were thereby enabled to claim, in contrast to the class-conscious U.F.A., that the new movement was a true people's party, a rally of the whole community.

But even here the U.F.A. had, in a certain sense, again prepared the way. By 1931 the organized farmers had finally concluded that they could never attain federal power on the basis of an appeal to the electorate solely in terms of their own class. This conclusion was the basis of their decision at the 1932 convention to broaden the scope of their movement by an alliance with labour. From the ensuing conference of U.F.A. and labour leaders at Calgary the following summer emerged the new C.C.F. movement, deliberately designed to be more comprehensive in its appeal than the old U.F.A. Unfortunately for the political future of the U.F.A., the socialistic programme of the C.C.F. frightened the farmers of Alberta. Suffering from disillusionment over the failure of their government to solve their problems, grown sceptical of the possibilities of further political action solely in terms of their own class, and in despair owing to the increasing severity of the depression, they were not yet ready for socialism. They responded instead to the rising Social Credit movement which bore no taint of failure, which took them out of their political exclusiveness, and which promised a simple solution of their economic problems in terms of monetary reform without the dangers of socialism. The interviews suggest that between 1932 and 1935 almost every move made by the U.F.A. government to overcome the limitations of its earlier theory and practice not only accelerated its own decay but also directed the response of the people towards the challenging philosophy of Social Credit, with which its own characteristic doctrines had such a remarkable affinity.

It is important, then, to recognize that the response of the people to the philosophy of Social Credit was determined, in part, by the heritage of the U.F.A. theory and practice. But an emphasis on the preparatory work of the U.F.A. movement should not obscure the significance of the response of the people to Douglas's theories as they were presented by Aberhart within the context of the Social Credit movement. The people themselves felt that they were involved in a glorious new movement, not merely in a continuation or rebirth of the decaying U.F.A. movement. The Social Credit movement must be interpreted, therefore, as an autonomous social movement in its own right. Such an interpretation is not incompatible with the view that the economic, ethical, and political theories of the U.F.A. had induced in the people of Alberta a readiness to respond to the more tightly articulated philosophy of Social Credit. Gathering into itself much that had gone before, the Social Credit movement not only transformed the old norms but also established new ones.

While Aberhart unquestionably emphasized the negative or critical side of Social Credit theory in his stiffening of the traditional U.F.A. attacks on the financial and political systems, the interviews leave no doubt that it was essentially his popularization of the positive or constructive side of the philosophy which aroused the greatest enthusiasm among tens of thousands of people. But the popular impression that the expectation of *basic dividends* was the most attractive of the three aspects of the Social Credit programme is not borne out by the interviews. On the contrary, there is overwhelming evidence that Aberhart's emphasis on monetary reform exerted at least as powerful an appeal as his promises concerning basic dividends and the just price. Despite the preparatory work of the U.F.A., most people in Alberta were still confused regarding the nature and function of the monetary system. "The monetary system," said a prominent farm leader, "is like an unbreakable glass wall of unlimited height and depth. You can see through it, but you can't dig under it or climb over it. You can never get to the other side." Aberhart, with his arithmetical mind, reduced the abstract logico-mathematical economics of Social Credit to the simplest of formulae. His famous expositions of the "A plus B Theorem" and the "Bloodstream of the state" led multitudes of people to believe that, at long last, they really understood the nature of the monetary system. These people responded to the Social Credit "illumination" by volunteering to teach others, either by means of discussions or through the numerous study groups that seemed to spring up spontaneously everywhere.

To his positive exposition of monetary reform, Aberhart linked the charge that the depression, although an inevitable and recurrent feature of an unreformed monetary system, had been accentuated in Alberta by the machinations of bankers and financiers, the "Fifty Big Shots," who controlled financial credit. Amidst the confused and desperate circumstances of those years it was easy for Social Crediters to incorporate the appeal of the C.C.F. attack on the capitalistic system into Douglas's explanation of the causes of the depression. To thousands of people that explanation seemed to make meaningful the grievous shortage of purchasing power from which they were suffering, the paradox of "poverty in the midst of plenty." During the rise of the Social Credit movement, and especially during its struggle for power, the A plus B Theorem became part of the language of nearly every Albertan, regardless of party allegiance.

An unyielding insistence that the monetary system was uniquely responsible for the depression attracted a wide variety of people to the Social Credit movement. In small towns and villages teachers, merchants, ministers, druggists, farmers, railroad workers, and doctors frequently assembled in the same study group. "At our house in the village of ————," a teacher has reported, " we had a study group in which we read Douglas's books. People from every walk of life came and we would talk Social Credit until all hours of the night with anyone who would listen." For the members of such groups, monetary reform, and the slogans that went with it, carried a multivalent appeal. To some, talk about monetary reform was nothing more than highly charged emotive utterance; to a few it appeared as a rigorous analysis of social causation. Most of the interviews indicate, however, that a Social Crediter's response to the philosophy of monetary reform was directly related to the economic frustration he and his relatives experienced during the depression period.

Economic frustration was unquestionably the determining factor in the impressive rally of school-teachers to the cause of Social Credit, especially in the rural communities. An excerpt from an interview with a rural teacher, whose father was a farmer, illustrates both the impact of the depression upon members of the teaching profession and their response to a promised solution in terms of monetary reform:

In my younger days crops were good, prices of farm produce reasonably satisfactory, and an air of prosperity and general well-being pervaded the whole province. My father bought a new car, a new tractor, a new grain separator, a new washing machine and a new radio on the installment plan. No one seemed in the least bit worried about the future.

Then came the terrible stock market crash in 1929 and with it a fall in grain prices, which in succeeding years fell to unprecedently low levels. Unfortunately for the farmers, while the prices of farm produce grew steadily less, the freight rates and prices of farm machinery, gas and oil, and other farm necessities remained comparatively high. To add to my father's worries, a series of drought years set in when crops were exceedingly poor, often only averaging eight or ten bushels to the acre. The drought was accompanied by a swarm of grasshoppers which ate the scanty crops we succeeded in producing.

Within a year or so of the stock market crash other effects of the depression began to be felt in our district. Prices of all commodities began to fall, wage cuts became common and fear of unemployment began to affect all of us. Unemployed workers, seeking employment in the cities and in the grain fields, began to drift from one district to another, and transients who "rode the rods" became a familiar sight. Soon the cities were forced to set aside large sums for relief. I remember my mother estimating that during one of the worst years of the depression we must have produced meals for at least a hundred men during the year.

About 1931 the Bank of ———— closed its branch. The train service from ———— east to ———— was reduced to running three times a week instead of daily. Everybody began to feel uneasy about his job.

Teachers' salaries were drastically reduced. My salary was cut from $1,050.00 to $400.00 over a period of years. The number of unemployed teachers rose and salaries even in the most prosperous areas were not more than $600.00 or $700.00. Unemployment among teachers became so acute that all sorts of methods were adopted to solve the problem. . . .

It became common to find people returning furniture, radios and other articles bought on the installment plan. In 1932 or 1933 farm foreclosures or crop seizures became quite frequent.

Into this condition of poverty and uncertainty moved Mr. Aberhart with his Social Credit ideas. I had never understood the money system. Mr. Aberhart made clear to me the money system and the causes of the depression. I became convinced that Social Credit was the only remedy to end the depression. I began to explain it to my friends and it was not long before everybody in our district was talking it up. Social Credit groups for a systematic study of the theory were organized all over. Social Credit became the chief topic of conversation and everywhere you would hear Social Credit supporters enthusiastically expounding the theories of Major Douglas. Catchwords and phrases such as "control of credit," "monetization of natural resources," "basic dividends," "just price," and "cultural heritage" became part of the everyday vocabulary of Social Crediters. Wherever you went you found Social Credit was the main topic of conversation.

Drastic salary cuts, widespread unemployment among their membership, and the inability of even their brightest pupils to secure jobs on leaving school were vital factors in the response of large numbers of the teaching profession to the appeal of monetary reform. Their prestige in rural areas reinforced attitudes favourable to monetary reform which already existed in the farming communities of Alberta.

In considering the farmers' readiness to respond to the appeal of monetary reform, it is important to realize that the depression had merely accentuated, rather than originated, attitudes of hostility to financial and banking interests in Eastern Canada. Even well-to-do farmers who constitute the backbone of Alberta's rural communities have frequently expressed the view that such hostile attitudes were due, ultimately, to the "hard-boiled" approach of banks and loan companies to payments of interest and principal on farm mortgages and notes for farm equipment. Some consideration of the situation that had developed in Alberta not only explains the response of the people to the Social Credit movement but also illuminates at least one factor involved in the shortage of money or purchasing power from which most frontier rural economies chronically suffer.

The development of Alberta during its pioneer stage was dependent upon the capacity of its provincial and municipal governments and its individual citizens to borrow money. The difficulties experienced by governmental bodies in meeting their obligations constitute an interesting chapter in the history of public finance, but we are concerned here with the financial problems faced by farmers. To purchase, prepare, and equip a farm required a considerable outlay of money and labour. For a decade after the First World War the farmers of Alberta experienced little difficulty in borrowing money, usually on little or no collateral, from the banks and loan companies. Owing to uncertainty of repayment, however, interest rates were high, running on mortgages from 8 to 12 per cent.

Until 1927 there had been, on the whole, a fifteen-year period of good crops and fair prices: the selling price of wheat, for example, had ranged from $1.25 to $1.75 a bushel. But the same period had seen a change from horse power to machine power. The mechanization of farms involved a heavy investment. Implement companies, competing with one another and anxious to sell machinery, readily accepted long-term notes, with little or no collateral, from the over-optimistic farmers. Here, again, interest rates were high. The companies turned in the notes to local branch banks for collection: interviews with farmers often include jocular references to the stacks upon stacks of notes for farm equipment that reposed in bank vaults. During the good years, payments of interest were usually kept up, and a reduction of principal might even be made. It is said, however, that as long as interest payments were regularly met, farm machinery companies usually did not press for payments on principal.

Even in the good years preceding 1929 and, in fact, as far back as the late 1890's, the payment of exorbitantly high interest rates had constituted a heavy drain on the financial resources of Alberta's frontier rural economy. The constant outflow to Montreal or Toronto of payments on interest and principal had gradually become too heavy a burden for many farmers to bear, even in good times. Certainly, it was an important factor in the origin and maintenance of the chronic shortage of purchasing power in the province. Monetary reform had been discussed, as we have seen, for at least three decades before 1929, as a possible remedy for a situation in which the farmers were being "bled white" (as they put it) by absentee bankers and financiers.

Attitudes of frustration changed to attitudes of despair as the depression worsened and prices of agricultural products fell to unprecedented low levels. With the financial position of the farmers steadily deteriorating, their creditors began to press, ever more relentlessly, for the repayment of debts. In interviews with farmers from widely separated regions of Alberta, the story is always the same: the banks and mortgage and machinery companies closed in on the hard-driven farmers.

The situation in the Lloydminster area, for example, had already become so acute by 1932 that the twelfth annual convention of the Alexandra U.F.A. and U.F.W.A. constituency association, held at Kitscoty on July 18, was devoted almost entirely to a discussion of how farmers could escape from "the control of financial rackateers." The mimeographed minutes record that the local M.L.A., P. J. Enzenauer, said in part:

Today ruthless foreclosure is occurring in Alberta. This method of liquidating debts benefits only 5 per cent of the people, whereas extension of credit—inflation—would materially benefit 95 per cent of our population.

Ruin faces farmers under the present financial rule. The current cost of operating farms should be given priority over the rights of mortgages and would enable farming to continue. The tendency to over-produce under such a system would be checked by the curtailment of loans . . . ways and means of overcoming the existing spectacle of famine in the midst of plenty must be found at once if a general collapse is to be avoided.

Delivered some two weeks before Scarborough persuaded Aberhart to read a book on Social Credit, Enzenauer's speech led to a series of resolutions being forwarded to the annual U.F.A. convention of 1933, strongly urging the need of provincial legislation to protect the debt-ridden farmers of Alberta against their insistent creditors.

Within the limits of what it deemed its proper constitutional powers, the conservative Brownlee government attempted to deal with the problem of farm debt adjustment. But in its efforts to alleviate the situation it received no co-operation whatever from the banks and loan companies. The head of a large Eastern trust company, for example, told a committee of the Alberta legislature that "farmers must pay their debts at the interest contracted for." This uncompromising attitude, which was headlined in the press, fanned afresh the intense feeling over debt legislation which already existed in Alberta. A prominent farmer in the Peace River area has declared, in an interview, that "the relentless attitude of Eastern financial interests towards debt legislation and reduction in interest rates was responsible for creating in rural Alberta a state of mind that accepted Social Credit as the only solution for the financial problems of farmers."

A farmer in the Lloydminster area has given a vivid description of the extent to which he was hounded by his creditors:

Ninety-five per cent of the farm homes in my district were loaded down to an impossible position with debts to the banks and mortgage and machine companies and even to the storekeepers in local villages. . . . The bank manager threatened to sue me for debt. He sent me a notice through a lawyer. I had borrowed money from him, at 8 per cent interest, compounded every three months. I had been paying off the debt, had reduced it by several hundred dollars. . . . The farmers' problem was that creditors would still go on threatening them, no matter how hard they worked to pay off their debts. . . . We began to feel that the situation was hopeless. Year after year we farmed, and each year thought we'd have enough to provide for our wife and family and it didn't come to pass. . . . Every week when I went to the post office, I got a bunch of dunners (bills). I took these home in my wagon six miles unopened and gave them to my wife to open. She opened them because she had more pluck than I had. I didn't have the courage to open them. I said to my wife, "Open these and see what they are going to do next." But these creditors didn't threaten me as much as they did my sick illiterate neighbour who had five children and was depending for groceries on the sale of eggs at four cents a dozen. That wife carried 24 dozen eggs six miles, for which she received 96 cents in trade to buy groceries for a family of seven. Is it any wonder her husband was a Social Crediter?

The unremitting efforts of creditors to exact payment of debts from Alberta's farmers led to many harrowing scenes throughout the province. A bailiff in northeastern Alberta has described two scenes that fell under his jurisdiction:

The winter of 1932 was grim and tough. Eggs were five cents a dozen; hogs two cents a pound; cattle around five or six cents a pound. There was great pressure put on by creditors to collect debts for land and machinery. The situation grew desperate in 1933. Evictions for non-payment of debts began to take place. I had to go out north of ———— to give a family the bad news that they were to be evicted immediately. On this farm a man and his wife, three or four children, and a bed-ridden mother-in-law lived in an old shack. I had to tell that middle-aged man and his fragile wife, "My instructions are to put you on the road allowance at once." Another time I had to seize all a man's furniture. This man lived in a poor shack on a farm with his wife and children. He owed money for the furniture which he had in his possession. I was ordered to take his furniture away from him. The furniture was removed.

With the development of the Social Credit movement, the frustration and despair in rural Alberta were transformed by the shining vision of monetary reform as the solution for all their misfortunes. A farmer who lived some fifty miles north of Edmonton has recorded how it caught the imagination of the hard-pressed.

Although we had sweat blood to build up productive farms we were broke. We could not buy clothes and we could not even pay our taxes although our granaries were full of grain, and the mortgage interest was piling up. And then Aberhart came.

His sonorous voice rolled out from the radio each Sunday and it contained a message of hope, and what was more to the point, some sensible economics.

The farmers who had a small radio would invite their friends and neighbours on a Sunday afternoon and the whole group would gather round and drink in his words like thirsty souls. The paradox of "poverty in the midst of plenty" was unfolded to them and tears would come into the eyes of some as they realized that here was a man who understood that they were not dishonest because they were not paying their debts or their taxes; but the plentiful fruit of the Earth which was God's gift to man—and which they had helped to produce so abundantly—had been prostituted by the money-changers into an undesirable thing, which they called over-production. The demands of the MONEY DEBT, which could only be paid in money, not in produce, pauperized them so that although the evidence of their industry was proved by the stooks in the grain fields and the cattle in the yard, they were in danger of losing all that they had striven so hard to obtain, and even their homes, because of the operation of the money system. Aberhart explained that there was an insufficiency of purchasing power in the hands of the people and a certain Major Douglas had analysed the situation and found there was a flaw in the existing method of accounting and that the real wealth of the country was not truly reflected by its financial counterpart. And we KNEW he spoke the truth. Thirty years of our bitter experience tested and buttressed every word and argument he used and we knew he was right and so we became Social Crediters.

Interviews with farmers from diverse and widely separated regions indicate the powerful appeal of Aberhart's doctrine of monetary reform throughout rural Alberta. The excerpts quoted below were recorded in interviews with farmers from various areas.

The arid Magrath area in southern Alberta
Conditions were very terrible at Magrath during the early thirties. Wheat was 19 cents a bushel; the best pigs sold at two dollars each, not two dollars a hundred but *each*. A number of farmers shipped cattle to market, and were billed back for excess freight—the cattle didn't pay the cost of freight

charges. Hundreds of people in our area were on relief. Mortgages and interest piled up to excessive rates. I had a quarter section with 100 acres irrigated. Irrigation taxes on my 100 acres piled up to $9,000. What was the use of paying any kind of taxes when you had $9,000 against a quarter section? Practically every farmer fell heavily into debt and was also heavily mortgaged. The scene was set for Aberhart's doctrine of monetary reform in our district. People were willing to take a chance on Social Credit. Can you blame them?

The fertile Leduc area

Almost every farmer in our district was licked by 1935 and ready to lay his problem on the shoulder of anybody who would accept it. . . . We had lost our equity and everything we had built up. This was true whether you were a good farmer or a bad farmer. The farming communities in our constituency were down, down, down! The financial position of farmers was desperate in 1935. . . . Monetary reform offered the only hope of solution.

The Olds area in west central Alberta

I became a Social Crediter because Mr. Aberhart convinced me that the root of our troubles was the faulty money system we had, and that Social Credit was the only organization that would actually endeavour to overthrow this monetary system. . . . In 1935 we had an abundance of everything, but no money. Social Credit was a means of distributing the production of the country among the people. . . . It was absolutely the depression that made Social Credit actually have the landslide that it did owing to the fact that people got down to thinking about where the trouble lay.

The ranching area east of Calgary

During the depression I lost over $30,000 in livestock, horses, etc. The loan companies cleaned up on all their clients and I, like many ranchers, lost a great deal. . . . Bankers were robbing the people through interest charges. Ranchers could not pay their debts because of the tremendous interest, and they lost their land. Aberhart saw that monetary reform would work and that it was feasible. . . . I am a Social Crediter because I am sure we are right. . . . If the interest is taken off the medium of exchange, there will be less poor and less rich people. There won't be the incentive to pile up money.

The Westaskiwin constituency

We were at the very bottom of the depression in our district and all of us farmers were looking for a way out. Then I heard of monetary reform through Mr. Aberhart. He simplified the idea of monetary reform so that we could understand it. Now, here, I said to myself, is the solution! I got a lot of pamphlets from the Bible Institute by mail and read up on Social Credit in the mornings before getting up at 6 o'clock to work on my farm. After careful study, I got the picture. I was so filled with the vision of what monetary reform could do for us that I began telling all my neighbours about it.

The Camrose constituency

We were all poverty-stricken by the depression in our district, even though we had good land and most of us had worked hard. We didn't have to wear gunny sacking for clothing and eat gophers as they did down in the dried-out Youngstown area. But I had neighbours who were living on skimmed milk and potatoes. The telephones were taken from one farm home after another, until we were finally the only farm with a telephone. . . . The poverty was incredible. Then along came Aberhart. I am a university educated man, and I saw at once that he was right as to why the financial system wasn't working. I realized that monetary reform was the only solution to the problem of creating the purchasing power we needed.

Nearly all the interviews with farmers who became Social Crediters indicate some awareness of the prior existence of monetary reform ideas within the U.F.A. movement, but Aberhart's exposition of monetary reform carried a conviction that had hitherto been lacking. An excerpt from an interview with a farmer in the drought-stricken Hanna area expresses an attitude that what was widespread:

Instead of saying, like the old U.F.A. men, "We shall try to get monetary reform for you," Aberhart said to us, "We most assuredly will get monetary reform for you. We won't bother with Ottawa about monetary reform. We're going to establish our own bank and our own monetary system in Alberta."

Compared to Aberhart, Bevington and the other U.F.A. monetary reformers were children. Aberhart's appeal to the desperate farmers of Alberta represented the final flowering of the idea of monetary reform in that province.

The cause of Social Credit flourished in rural Alberta but it was also a small-town movement. The response of the people in small towns and villages was partly due to the opportunity the new movement gave them of re-entering the great game of politics from which they had been well-nigh excluded since 1921 by the class-conscious U.F.A. on the one hand and the weaknesses of the Liberal and Conservative parties on the other. But in the interviews with small-town and village business men there is a fuller explanation of the phenomenal rally of the people of these centres to the Social Credit movement. In Alberta the small towns and villages function as distributing and servicing centres for the rural areas surrounding them. The near-collapse of Alberta's agrarian economy as a result of the depression precipitated a corresponding crisis in the towns and villages. The prosperity of the business men in these centres was indissolubly linked with the prosperity of the farmers they served.

The merchants were especially hard hit by the depression. Not wishing to alienate old customers, they permitted credit buying to such an extent that they were no longer able to meet their commercial drafts from wholesalers. Here, again, the local branch banks came in for considerable criticism, as it was their function to make collections on wholesalers' commercial drafts for their main city offices. The local merchants felt that they were caught in a gigantic squeeze between the farmers and the wholesalers, with the banks applying ever-increasing pressure. The situation gradually worsened to the point where the merchants could neither extend any further credit nor sell their goods without doing so. Heavily in debt, and with an abundance of goods which their impoverished customers needed piled up on their shelves, the merchants were naturally looking for a solution of their problems.

Interviews with business men in widely separated towns of Alberta offer convincing evidence of their response to the appeal of monetary reform. It is significant that eleven of the sixty-three secondary leaders belonged to this class: profiles of two of these, F. M. Baker and A. E. Fee (who lived in Fort Saskatchewan and Killam respectively), are presented in chapter VII. Excerpts are given below from interviews.

A dry-goods merchant in Brooks

I was dealing with the big wholesalers and the bankers on the one hand and these poor farmers on the other hand. The farmers around Brooks began to get more and more hard up; and then the merchants, too, for they had extended credit and couldn't get at it. One of the hardest working farmers in the district had borrowed $1,300 from the bank, and he had got hailed out and couldn't pay. Then he had to borrow more. The next year he owed the bank about $2,400. The bank manager went out to his farm and asked for a bill of sale and promised to "take care" of him. He believed the banker. But the banker then *cleaned that farmer out completely*! I saw that farmer standing up against the corner of my store with the tears running down his cheeks! When the depression got worse the wholesalers and bankers put the squeeze on the merchants. This practical experience I had dealing with the wholesalers and bankers on one side of the counter and with the poor farmers on the other side prepared my mind for Social Credit. When Aberhart started talking monetary reform over the air, I got interested. . . . I got some of Douglas's books and read up on them. . . . I decided to fight hard for Social Credit.

A general merchant in Carstairs

When we were going through the depression, I couldn't understand why I had an abundance of goods on my shelves and the farmers couldn't buy them, even though they were having good crops. . . . One of the large wholesalers of Edmonton came to me in 1933 and begged me to take $8,000 more of stock. I already had $20,000 of stock in my store and couldn't sell the better quality stuff. This big wholesaler told me I could pay for the

$8,000 additional stock whenever I wished. This started me really thinking about economics more than anything else. I didn't know that every dollar wasn't backed by gold or that the banks had the right to create credit. I first heard of Social Credit at Mr. Aberhart's and Mr. Manning's meeting at Carstairs in the spring of 1934. Aberhart's exposition of monetary reform cleared up the thing that had bothered me—the lack of purchasing power in spite of all the goods we had on hand. Aberhart convinced me that we had the right in the province to handle the issue of our own credit by balancing production and consumption. So I became a Social Crediter and helped organize the movement in our district.

A druggist in Coronation

Coronation was in the drought area, known as a Special Area. The municipalities went broke and the provincial government took them over and depopulated the area. Depopulation was going on in 1934–5. In our town we had organized a men's forum which was associated with the United Church. . . . Here we had lectures and discussions, among others several attempted explanations of the gold standard. This got the Coronation people interested in economics, and then Aberhart came along with his ideas about monetary reform and we were all stimulated to join the Social Credit movement. . . . I got converted from the bank-lending-depositors' money theory over to the creation-of-credit theory of Douglas. Four or five of us business men in Coronation joined with others in neighbouring towns to trade information and we held meetings which were attended by large crowds. These people were very poor but very hospitable. It was the greatest experience of my life to associate with these people.

A men's clothing and shoe merchant in Edson

We were experiencing depression conditions in our town. Our first Social Credit study group was organized by a Douglasite, Sydney Cliffe, editor of the town's newspaper. But the first introduction to Social Credit that really impressed me were the news reports of Douglas's emphasis on the need for monetary reform when he appeared before the Agricultural Committee of the legislature in the spring of 1934. I supported the Social Credit movement because I felt we needed a different monetary system than what we had. Another man in Edson who owned a store said to me at that time: "If the bankers are against Social Credit, I'm for it."

A keeper of a general store in Dapp

In my general store business I came into daily contact with the people and saw their condition—their need—their want. In order to serve these people a storekeeper had a constant struggle himself to keep from going under. Seeing farmers come in there and trying to make things go on 19 cent wheat made me realize the whole system needed changing. I began to attend Social Credit meetings and gradually got an idea of the thing that would change the system. I saw Aberhart for the first time at an open-air meeting of 2,000 people. He convinced me that monetary reform was the answer. So I got into the Social Credit movement and started to help organize study groups in the Pembina constituency.

Monetary reform as the answer to depression conditions also appealed to small business men in the metropolitan centres as is attested by excerpts from interviews.

A bookseller in Calgary

The financial system here in Calgary wasn't doing the job and I came to see how it was operating on bank credit. They really could create credit. I remember asking how the Bank of Montreal could pay the overhead on its building here. They don't do it by just loaning out the depositors' money. I used to read accounts of the Revision of the Bank Act. The majority of bankers didn't know how their own system worked. They didn't know the control they have through issuing of credit. I went to hear Douglas speak at the Armouries in the spring of 1934. He said that 50 or 100 years from now people would speak of this time of the depression as a time of scarcity—when all it was due to was a lack of tickets. I thought there was something to Social Credit after hearing Douglas. So I took up monetary reform and got behind Aberhart's movement.

A grocer in Edmonton

Conditions were really tough in Edmonton. People were acutely dissatisfied owing to unemployment and no money. If you have an adequate supply of goods in your store, and the people have no money, where are you? I got into the Social Credit movement because I was heartily in favour of monetary reform.

If the Social Credit movement was a rural and small town movement, it was equally a lower middle and working class movement. Unlike the farmers and merchants, the members of this third group depended for economic survival upon the ability of its members to sell services and labour, rather than products and goods, to other members of the community. This group also differed from the farmers in that its members had no clearly articulated consciousness of class. The interests of farmers and small-town business men actually seemed to be much more cohesive than the interests of farmers and workers. Compared to the organized farmers, organized labour had played a relatively small role in the economic, social, and political life of Alberta. The U.F.A. had, it is true, sometimes entered into a limited and temporary electoral co-operation with organized labour; but it had always emphatically repudiated any identification of class interests.

A recognition of the mutual interests of farmers and workers finally came in 1932–3 with the foundation of the C.C.F. movement. But the scandals caused the puritanical lower middle and working classes to turn away in disgust from the U.F.A.–C.C.F. alliance in Alberta. As a result, the working classes failed to develop a sense of identity that participation in a socialist movement might have given them: the interviews indicate that their class interests remained indistinguishable from those of the lower middle classes.

The members of this third group, with the exception of several thousand hired men on farms, lived mainly in the cities, small towns, and villages. Most of them, if not unemployed, were at least suffering from drastic wage-cuts. Certainly, thousands were on relief. Even those individuals who were not themselves suffering too drastically from the depression had numerous friends and relatives in dire straits. In search of a vital centre, this amorphous third group responded to the appeal of Social Credit, but whereas interviews with farmers and small-town business men indicate a not inconsiderable unanimity of response to Aberhart's programme of monetary reform, the attitudes of the members of this group were more varied. Many were more impressed by the leader and the strategy and tactics of the movement than by its philosophy; and a large proportion of those who took its philosophy seriously interpreted monetary reform exclusively in terms of basic dividends. But Aberhart's general programme of monetary reform was not without a specific appeal to the lower middle and working classes, as is indicated by excerpts quoted below from interviews.

A railway shipping clerk

I first heard about Social Credit in 1933, but didn't do anything about it until Major Douglas spoke at the Calgary Armouries in April, 1934. . . . I tried to go to that meeting, but couldn't get anywhere near it owing to the crowds. But I read Douglas's speech in the paper and then started going to the meetings in the Bible Institute. . . . Aberhart convinced me that the Social Credit movement was definitely a movement of the common man. I wasn't out of work myself during the depression, but a lot of my friends and relatives had been unemployed for four or five years, and a lot of others were working only part-time. Most of them started going to the Institute meetings. Aberhart didn't say that all the leaders of finance were crooks, but he did say that if we were to survive we had to wrest some of their power from them by monetary reform. . . . He was prepared to battle these financial moguls. I became deeply conscious of the need for some basic change in our economic life. . . . I sincerely believed that the Social Credit party would do its best to endeavour to give us that change.

A married nurse

I am a Roman Catholic so I was not interested in Mr. Aberhart's religious beliefs. . . . The Bible text that impresses me is, "I will give you the earth and the fruits thereof." The earth is for the use of the people. The one idea should be to *produce* with the greatest amount of efficiency and ease. Production is to give the people what they want. As a nurse, I have always been worried about the economic system. In childbirth, for example, all women go through exactly the same experience, whether they are rich or poor. But the *care* a woman commands in childbirth depends upon her economic status. The rich woman commands attention, and the doctors flutter around her. But the poor woman is put into a different type of bed and ward. I have observed, too, that the poor woman often has a mental anguish about the economic future of her child. . . . From my experience as a nurse, I had felt the urge to help people get financial security. This urge boiled up in me during the depression. We had big production here without the possibility of consumption owing to no buying power. . . . A big production under a wrong system gets you nowhere. Consumption is necessary for production. As the depression went on, the machines became idle, and the men became hungry. They were not turning the raw goods into finished products because the people had no money to buy goods. The wheels couldn't turn, the merchants began to close their doors, no orders came to the factories, the workmen were laid off and then put on relief which came out of the taxpayers. I knew people who had to sell their bonds and live in dives and halls! I realized we were under a financial system which is entirely wrong. This system is man-made. My first contact with Social Credit was listening to Mr. Aberhart on the radio. I was ready for something that would explain the depression. I realized that Social Credit was what I was looking for. I became convinced that monetary reform was the answer. It explained my past experiences. I had been a Social Crediter a long time without knowing it! As soon as I made up my mind that monetary reform was the answer I read and read and read about Social Credit until 2 o'clock in the morning until my head would fairly burst. But it was easier for me than for a labourer I knew who didn't have even an average education. That man read a book on Social Credit slowly and painfully word by word—he could hardly understand some of the words. . . . My understanding of debt-free credit was the great turning-point of my life. I started to work hard for the Social Credit movement. Not any opposing political party, but the whole existing monetary system was our opponent. We Social Crediters are the only ones who have asked for debt-free money. That's the only way we can fulfil the text, "I will give you the earth and fruits thereof."

A department store salesman

I lost my job after two years of depression. Listening to Aberhart explain the depression on the radio convinced me that the Eastern financial interests had put on the depression. I've been robbed myself by capitalistic interests very badly. We people in the West were pretty well disgusted with the Eastern financial interests. We felt the East had been milking us long enough. They had kept manufacturing down East. I joined the Social Credit movement as a protest against the rule of the big money interests which have their tentacles everywhere. I believed that monetary reform would put an end to their rule in Alberta.

A chef

I had been a student of Mr. Aberhart's at Crescent Heights High School. My friends and I were all hard hit by the depression, so we were attracted to his meetings at the Bible Institute. His discussions of Social Credit made us see that all the suffering caused by the depression was completely unnecessary. If we could just change the money system we wouldn't have those terrible conditions any more.

A lower middle-class housewife

The depression made me feel we were going to rack and ruin, and my husband and I were feeling very low in spirits. All our savings had gone— we had to take them to protect our home. We were down to our last dollar. I knew there must be something wrong with the set-up, but I couldn't figure it out. Then some friends took me to the Bible Institute. Mr. Aberhart told us that night that the depression was all due to the money system. To illustrate his talk he put on this old, old coat, and then put a patch on it. The other material of the coat was so rotten it couldn't hold the patch. The money system, he explained, had to be completely changed. I saw now why there was lots of goods and yet people couldn't provide for their families. That night I decided to get into the Social Credit movement, and I did, and worked frantically for it.

A machinist

I wasn't unemployed but some of my relatives were and I was trying to figure out why we had to have a depression. The C.C.F. was started and I was a supporter at first and began to read up on socialism. But I rebelled against socialism because I wanted to save individual rights and liberties. . . . I was a strong member of the United Church and didn't approve of Mr. Aberhart's religious views. But my brother-in-law, who had helped to build the Bible Institute, persuaded me to listen to Mr. Aberhart's broadcasts on Social Credit. I threw away my religious prejudices, and began going to the Bible Institute to hear him. We were handed a series of coloured leaflets in which Mr. Aberhart had boiled down Douglas's books on Social Credit. I studied these and became convinced that monetary reform was the right philosophy. Once I came to this conclusion I was a Social Crediter for life.

A working man in a large repair plant

I came to Alberta from Scotland in 1910. I had seen this West growing up from barren spaces. . . . We have a pretty fair country here, but the depression hit us so hard we had no money to buy anything and people couldn't borrow the money to buy. I began to wonder what was the use of us working so hard trying to develop this country, if nobody could get the good of it. As I saw it we were not producing goods for the consumer, as he often had no money to buy them. I was employed myself and didn't owe anybody anything. I was living entirely within my means, which was damn poor living! I was supposed to be a first class worker, but here I was going out and buying the cheapest cuts of meat and we were living on stews. But what really burned me up was this—there were men knocking at our door, straggling over the country. One night three men straggled in from Toronto. They wanted the use of a bath rather than something to eat. Everybody except me was in bed, so I gave them the price of a meal and a bath. I said to my wife, "It could have been me or our boy!" Then we had the trek of unemployed workers to Regina—I'll never forget those poor unemployed people walking past our street down the hill at the beginning of that trek! Residents giving them coffee and sandwiches—it was really shocking. The conditions in ———— Park in our city were terrible—you wouldn't believe they could exist in a civilized country. That was at a time when the stores were full of goods and the merchants couldn't sell them. I'll never forget the 1934 Christmas—a lot of people had to tell their kids there'd be no Santa Claus that year. At Christmas time the stores were full of people looking at presents, to see if there was something a few paltry pennies could buy. . . . I first heard of Social Credit through one of Aberhart's broadcasts. Then he came to our plant and talked to us workers one noon hour. I could see from his talk that monetary reform would give us increased purchasing power and might be the solution. He said, "You don't create assets, but you create debts." I thought that Aberhart must have something on the ball, with so much goods in the world and no money to buy them. I have always been a strong man for organized labour, so when Aberhart got through talking, I asked him where trade unions would be if Social Credit came into Alberta. He said, "It won't make any difference—trade unions will be just as free under Social Credit as any form of government. If I don't stand for you boys, I can't for the life of me see who I stand for." So I went forward and talked to him after the meeting. He gave me to understand that in all matters of labour policy, the elected members for labour would always be consulted and he would welcome any people from the labour groups. So then our shops formed a Social Credit group, and eventually our whole plant was organized into the ———— group for Social Credit. We had hundreds of members. Our group raised more money for the movement than any other—gangs of us workers would assemble to raise money to pay for Aberhart's Social Credit broadcasts.

Unlike the school-teachers, the members of the much more prosperous legal, medical, and engineering professions were, with few exceptions, antagonistic to Social Credit. There was, however, considerable support for the movement from the more evangelical clergy, if not from the Anglicans and Roman Catholics. With the exception of the United Church of Canada, much of this support was based on religious rather than philosophical considerations: Baptists, Presbyterians, and especially the numerous sectarian groups were attracted by Aberhart's fundamentalist approach to Christianity.

Many clergy of the United Church responded to the secular appeal of monetary reform rather than to the Bible prophecy and pre-millennial fundamentalism with which Aberhart's expositions of Social Credit were interlaced. The first two meetings Aberhart addressed on behalf of Social Credit in Edmonton, for example, were held in one of the most historic and largest churches in the city, under the chairmanship of its minister, a leader in the United Church of Canada. Excluding Manning, five of the secondary leaders were clergy, and of these one was a Lutheran while four were United Church.

The interviews indicate that the depression, coupled with the infiltration of the neo-orthodox theology of Barth and Brunner, had caused the United Church clergymen in Alberta to reconsider the interpretation of Christianity as a social gospel which had been dominant in liberal Protestantism for some thirty years. Their attitude to socialism was, not unnaturally, profoundly influenced by the scandals which for them became indissolubly linked (at that time) with the U.F.A.–C.C.F. affiliation. Concluding, under the stress of the depression, that the social gospel approach was lacking in social realism they turned to Social Credit. In monetary reform, they found an explanation of, as well as a solution to, the economic problems created by the depression. Many study groups both in small towns and in rural communities were encouraged by interested United Church clergy and laymen.

Although the response of the people was remarkable, it is said that Aberhart was greatly distressed at his inability to rally the substantial professional and middle classes to the movement. He accepted, of course, as a foregone conclusion, the bitter opposition of financiers, bankers, and big business men in the metropolitan centres and larger towns. But, as interviews with two such men reveal, Social Credit was not without an appeal to the wealthy. In a period when the capitalistic system had obviously broken down, Social Credit (in striking contrast to socialism and communism) promised to "make capitalism work." Both of these men, who were animated by humanitarian ideals, repudiated absolutely Aberhart's teaching regarding basic dividends and strongly urged him privately to abandon this aspect of Social Credit doctrine. Yet they were absolutely convinced that monetary reform, along Social Credit lines, was necessary to prevent the overthrow of the capitalistic system by socialists and communists. As they interpreted it, the Social Credit movement was a revolt of Tory radicals. Being members of the social *élite*, they could not afford to be seen in public with Aberhart, although they dined with him privately. It was a great source of satisfaction to him to know that he had recruited at least two men of rank and wealth to the movement. If they could not publicly avow their allegiance to Social Credit, their financial contributions to the cause were not inconsiderable.

The excerpts from interviews quoted above indicate that the Social Credit movement made its way, in part at least, by the appeal of monetary reform. The more prosperous farmers and small-town business men who became Social Crediters almost invariably deny that they were at all influenced by the prospect of basic dividends. They add that they certainly never expected to receive them. They frequently go out of their way to explain that Aberhart used the "suggestion" of $25 monthly merely as a figure of speech, for the purpose of "illustrating" what *might* be achieved under a proper monetary system. But, after making this apology, they usually admit that the poorer farmers and small-town business men, as well as the lower middle and working classes, were completely taken in by the promise of $25 monthly, and really believed that Aberhart would secure it for them. Indeed, these men often concede that even they themselves eventually decided that certainly nothing could be lost by supporting a leader who promised monthly dividends, if only as a figure of speech, and something might actually be gained. But the dividends, they emphatically conclude, were not a primary consideration in their support of the movement. On the other hand, the U.F.A. leaders, the more prosperous members of the middle and professional classes, and practically all journalists usually declare that the promise of basic dividends was the sole basis for the mass support of the movement.

There is abundant evidence in many of the interviews to confirm the popular conception that the materialistic appeal of a basic dividend did rally thousands to the movement. And most of those who admit unreservedly that they really believed a Social Credit government would give them $25 monthly do belong to the poorer and less educated classes of the metropolitan, small town, and rural communities. Certainly, there can be no question that large numbers of the poorer members of foreign-language groups like the Ukrainians, Scandinavians, and Germans responded enthusiastically to the idea of a basic dividend. Many of the older generation of these and smaller ethnic groups could scarcely speak English and the $25 monthly was probably all that thousands of them heard or understood of Social Credit.

The response of many people to the appeal of basic dividends was due entirely to their desperate economic need—they were like drowning men grasping at straws. As one impoverished small-town clerk has put it, "Everyone was to be made financially secure. Standards of living were to be raised and interest rates lowered. No one would need to worry any more about unemployment, mortgages, or crop failures." To all such economically dispossessed people, the principle of a basic dividend seemed to offer a financial paradise. They made no attempt to justify the payment of basic dividends beyond stating firmly and somewhat irascibly that they needed adequate food, clothing, and shelter.

In addition to the satisfaction of the primary needs of the economically dispossessed, the basic dividend held an attraction for thousands of the lower middle and working classes who saw in it a chance of raising their status through the satisfaction of certain secondary or derived needs. The $25 monthly would provide them with better medical and dental care, more educational facilities, greater opportunities for recreation and travel. Many stories circulate in Alberta concerning people who were planning trips to England or elsewhere as soon as they began to receive the basic dividend.

Those who saw in the basic dividends a chance for the greater satisfaction of secondary needs generally justified their attitude in terms of oft-repeated slogans like "the People's Right" and "Cultural Heritage." For them, the basic dividends were an essential component of the total philosophy of Social Credit, becoming fully intelligible only if considered in the larger context. Others held that the principle of monetary reform was utterly meaningless without the $25 monthly: the basic dividend was the tangible embodiment, the incarnation, of monetary reform.

Of the large section of the Alberta public which came to believe each adult was entitled to a basic dividend, only the more reflective people raised the embarrassing question of the ultimate source of the $25 monthly. Whenever this question was raised, Aberhart always gave assurance that the dividend could easily be met out of an "unearned increment levy," an idea which had been taken over from Social Credit theory, and which was not to be confused, he insisted, with any increase in taxation.

Varying attitudes to the promise of basic dividends are illustrated by excerpts quoted below from interviews.

The wife of a farmer in the Calgary area

We were all going through grinding poverty in our district. We sold 200 lb pigs at $3 each; some farmers had to kill their pigs rather than finish feeding them. We sold oats at 8 cents a bushel, after paying 5 cents a bushel to have them threshed. Wheat was around 25 cents a bushel, eggs 5 cents a dozen, cream 12 cents a pound. We were Social Crediters because we thought that Aberhart would change the whole system. The least of our thoughts about Social Credit was the $25. That $25 wasn't a factor in our support of Social Credit. We wanted to change the whole system that could produce such terrible poverty.

A farmer in the Edmonton area

I supported Social Credit because I was interested in getting more money, more purchasing power. That $25 a month appealed to me more than anything else. That was the big appeal, $25 a month, for all of us hard-up farmers. There wasn't one of us farmers that wasn't after that $25. . . . We had got nothing from the U.F.A. We talked up Social Credit constantly among ourselves. "By golly," I said to my neighbours, "we're going to get $25 a month from this new system that honest Abe's going to introduce. Then we'll be able to buy things." I counted on that $25 because I figured with our wonderful wealth there was no reason why the $25 couldn't be paid.

A farmer in central Alberta

You can strip down the appeal of Social Credit to the $25 a month. All of us farmers were in desperate straits. Here was William Aberhart promising $25 a month, and he was a minister of the gospel. I asked him about that $25 after one of his meetings, and he told me I must have faith.

A farmer in southern Alberta

I supported Social Credit because I wanted to get the $25 monthly. There can be no question that in our part of the province the promise of $25 a month was largely responsible for the success of the Social Credit party.

A farmer in southeastern Alberta

In our community there were a lot of ex-coal miners from England and the Glasgow district. We had come out to Canada looking for $10 bills, but had found farming a pretty tough job. I guess you could call us poor whites. We all fell for the $25 a month. That $25 dividend swung the election. No matter how much people denied it later, that's what they really wanted out of Social Credit.

A small-town businessman

The $25 was the main reason why I joined the movement. I thought there was a possibility we might get it by squeezing the ill-gotten gains of the plutocrats and looters.

A working man in Calgary

Try to picture us working men trying to figure a way out of the depression and you'll see why we wanted that $25. I believed we would get it and I talked it up with the other workers in our plant. They would say: "Where's the money coming from?" This was asked not only by opponents but also by supporters of Social Credit. My answer was: "You tell me where it's gone and I'll go and get it!" Why can't we get $25 a month? We were all poorly paid, semi-employed, unemployed. Everybody competing for a job, and this made for little returns for the day's work.

A Ukrainian school-teacher northeast of Edmonton

My father was the first Social Crediter in our community. He listened to Mr. Aberhart on the radio—whenever Aberhart was broadcasting he would even leave guests in the house and go and listen on the radio. The dividends appealed to my father and he talked them up all the time with the other Ukrainian farmers. There is no doubt that the dividend was the main thing for Ukrainians getting behind Social Credit.

A school-teacher in the Vegreville area

I lived in a wheat-growing community. People were groping for something better than the U.F.A.—the Brownlee scandal was given wide publicity. The dividend carried a great appeal. I used to hear people say: "When we get the dividend we're not going to milk any more cows." A bachelor said: "I'm going to live in the city and sell my farm. If I don't get a job I can live on the dividend." A lot of people thought it might not hurt to try out the chance of getting the dividend. At many polls on election day Ukrainians and Poles would ask, when handed a ballot, "Vich vun twenty-five dollar man?"

A farmer in the Lloydminster area

In the summer of 1935, a high-powered car drove into my farmyard, apparently looking for the farm owner. One of the well-dressed occupants came across to me—I was sitting on the binder—and asked if he could speak to the hired man. I directed him to Tom who was stooking at the time. After half-an-hour's conversation with the visitor, the hired man came to me to ask if $50 of his wages could be advanced. I said, "Tom, you know our agreement—I'm to pay you after we've threshed. But what do you want it for?" Tom said, "I want to make a down payment on a correspondence course—$50 now and $200 during the winter." "Now, Tom," I said, "when you get back on your homestead this winter where will you find the other $200?" "You know very well," Tom said, "where I'm going to get it—only you don't believe it. I'm going to get $25 a month from Mr. Aberhart." "All right, Tom," I said, "You've earned the $50. I'll get it for you somehow." I did, though it brought my bank account down to $20. I was just living from hand to mouth myself.

The third aspect of the philosophy of Social Credit, the just price, had, like monetary reform, long been the subject of agitation among the farmers of Alberta. Here, too, the ideas of Henry Wise Wood had exerted a powerful influence. Closely connected with the whole course of the Wheat Pool movement from the early attempts in 1920 and 1921 to the great international movement of 1927 and 1928, Wood had continuously supported the contract pool as the method most likely to solve the farmers' wheat marketing problems. For a few years the Alberta Wheat Pool, which had been established after the remarkable oratorical campaign of Aaron Sapiro in 1923, seemed to be the type of marketing organization that would best meet the needs of Alberta's farmers.[3] The U.F.A. leaders felt that they could solve all the farmers' economic problems by co-operation and co-operatives.

But the Alberta Wheat Pool, in common with other Canadian pools, found itself in serious financial difficulties at the very beginning of the depression owing to its large overpayment on the 1929 crop. During the next few years of turmoil and confusion, agricultural prices reached their lowest level on record and many farmers concluded that the co-operative method had failed. At this point the Winnipeg Grain Exchange took advantage of the complicated situation by a renewed attack on the

[3]For illuminating studies of the economic problems of prairie farmers see: G. E. Britnell, *The Wheat Economy* (Toronto: University of Toronto Press, 1938); Vernon C. Fowke, *The National Policy and the Wheat Economy* (Toronto: University of Toronto Press, 1957), especially chapters x–xiv.

whole pool idea, hoping thereby to discredit the farmers' marketing organization.

This attack failed, but it encouraged the monetary reformers within the U.F.A. to proclaim that the farmers' marketing problems were due to the nature of the financial system and could not, therefore, be solved by contract pools alone. Their view began to receive more and more support by 1932 when No. 1 northern wheat sank to a price of 18 cents per bushel. Late that year the farmers of Alberta heard Aberhart expounding in Sunday radio broadcasts from the Bible Institute the principle of the just price.

The just price was interpreted by Aberhart to mean what farm organizations in Alberta had previously called, more simply, a parity price. The prices farmers receive for the produce they sell should be on a par with the prices of goods they have to buy. This was a somewhat different version from the technical definition of Douglas, but it was a version to which the farmers of Alberta could respond, more especially in view of the preparatory work of the U.F.A. monetary reformers. Convinced that the whole economy of a country could be changed merely by changing its monetary policy, the long-time advocates of parity prices within the U.F.A. identified their cause with the principle of a just price and rallied to the Social Credit movement. The rationalistic leaders of the U.F.A. were astonished at the uncritical mingling of political and economic concepts which became the characteristic attitude of thousands of farmers both within and without the U.F.A. movement during the years 1934 and 1935: years of educational effort on the part of the U.F.A. now seemed to have been spent in vain.

No matter how strongly U.F.A. leaders might criticize it, the principle of the just price had a special appeal to every farmer in Alberta who had been forced to sell his grain or livestock at the incredibly low figures prevailing in the early 1930's. The interviews indicate that most rural teachers and small-town business men were also aware of the farmers' marketing predicament and were influenced, although to a somewhat lesser degree than the farmers themselves, by Aberhart's exposition of the just price. But the lower middle and working classes in the metropolitan centres were much more keenly interested in basic dividends than in the just price: hardly any of the representatives of these groups who were interviewed made any mention of the just price as a factor in their support of the Social Credit movement.

The interviews indicate also that even among farmers the principle of the just price tended to blend into, or to become identified with, the more comprehensive idea of monetary reform. After rattling off a list of depression prices for farm produce which seemed indelibly burned into their memories, farmers would usually insist that they were not after hand-outs like basic dividends or special favours like the just price. Then they would launch into a torrential diatribe against the existing financial system as the cause of the depression. Finally, they would expound and defend Aberhart's doctrine of monetary reform as the cure-all for the depression. For many the fixed idea seems to have been: "Seek ye first monetary reform, and basic dividends and a just price shall be added unto you."

But the just price was not without its own specific appeal, as is indicated by excerpts quoted below from interviews.

A farmer in northeastern Alberta

I supported Mr. Aberhart because I was convinced he would guarantee us a just price. The U.F.A. people had been in for fourteen years and we were all starving. I never expected to get $25 a month. But Mr. Aberhart promised us a just price. I sold a bull in 1935 for five dollars. I voted for Social Credit because I wanted a just price for the next bull I sold.

A farmer in northern Alberta

As the depression years hit us we found that good crops only meant more work and not necessarily prosperity. Prosperity, we found, was dependent on "price." By bitter experience we learned that even if we raised No. 2 wheat, top steers, special grade cream and prize-winning hogs and sheep, we were always hard up if the price was low. It did not matter if our hens laid 150 eggs or even 200 eggs per year when the price was 5 cents per dozen, even when the fact that they were a good grade of eggs did not bring in sufficient to even pay for putting straw into the hen-house. . . . The mortgage interest began to go unpaid and we tried to make our underwear and overalls last for four years instead of two. In our U.F.A. local we discussed the merits of the gold standard, co-operative activities, etc., and one man from the south of the line roused our enthusiasm by quoting William Jennings Bryan, "Shall humanity be crucified on a Cross of Gold?" . . . Then Aberhart came. . . . He spoke of a just price and adequate purchasing power, and these words stuck in our minds. When hauling wheat in bitter 40-below weather and running beside the sleigh to restore circulation in feet and hands, the idea of a just price would conjure up visions which revived the hope which increasing debt and the fear of losing our homes and farms had well-nigh killed. Here was something that farmers could grasp, and so Aberhart's gospel grew and multiplied in our district. We realized that with the just price in operation we would receive a new lease of life.

A small-town businessman in central Alberta

I joined the Social Credit movement because Aberhart made me see why the farmers in our district couldn't pay their debts at my store and why they had no money to buy goods from me. Since available credit was not sufficient to move available goods, the common sense thing to do was to increase available credit to the point where it would do the job of distributing the goods. To do this, Aberhart introduced what he called the just price. This is the basic thing in Social Credit for me. Of course, I realize that to find the necessary money to effect this price stabilization objective, we'll have to change the monetary system. Aberhart sold me the idea that we'll have to do this if we're ever going to get the just price.

If this analysis of the response of the people to the philosophy of Social Credit indicates that each of its elements carried a specific appeal, it must be emphasized that the interviews are replete with admissions of a lack of understanding of the technical mechanisms or procedures that would be involved in carrying out monetary reform or in the provision of basic dividends and the just price. All such matters, people constantly insisted, could safely be left to Aberhart and the experts he would call in to implement his Social Credit programme. There was, therefore, widespread approval of Aberhart's teaching that the people must demand what they wanted, clearly and urgently. "What we wanted," interviewees said repeatedly, "were *results*." Experiencing the frustrations of the depression, they were especially heartened by Aberhart's assurance that their distresses and worries could really be overcome. "I realized," said one lower middle class housewife, "that Aberhart had the secret when he told us to stick together and vote for the results we wanted, rather than try to work out a whole programme by ourselves."

Although they accepted Aberhart's teaching that the essential function of the politician was to bring mass desire to bear on the experts, many farmers and representatives of the lower middle and working classes were extremely suspicious of socialism. Influenced by the propaganda of the period, many people confused socialism with communism. But others who were able to distinguish between these two philosophies feared that socialism would lead inevitably to a loss of personal liberty. All such people distrusted profoundly the U.F.A.–C.C.F. alliance as a threat to individualism. The very same people who emphasized the realization of mass desire as the ultimate aim of democracy responded to Social Credit with a firm conviction that it alone could provide both individual freedom and economic security. At the same time, a number of socialists and even communists responded to Aberhart's relentless criticism of the monetary system with an equally firm conviction that Social Credit was a truly radical movement.

These considerations make it clear that the philosophy of Social Credit aroused a response from practically every section of society. In its pattern of thought could be found some element or elements which, granted the social, economic, and political background of Alberta in the early 1930's, would carry some appeal to educated and uneducated, rich and poor, eager and apathetic. No aspect of the response of the people of Alberta to Social Credit is more impressive than this: once a person got this Protean philosophy into his head it was almost impossible to dislodge it. In a very real sense Social Credit became a social norm, and over the years Alberta has remained a citadel from which evangelists of the great idea have constantly emerged upon a reluctant world.

CHAPTER NINE

➤➤➤➤》《《《《

The Response of the People: II

DOUGLAS'S DOCTRINES of monetary reform, basic dividends, and the just price, as re-interpreted by Aberhart, played an important role in the rise of the Social Credit movement. Of equal, if not more, significance in the determination of the response of the people were the leadership of Aberhart and the strategy and tactics of the movement.

In considering the movement as a whole, its leadership and strategy and tactics could be studied as interwoven themes. Certainly, Aberhart combined in himself the dual functions of prophet and executive-planner-organizer of the movement. The response of the people to the strategy and tactics he gradually developed between the years 1932–5 derived ultimately from their response to his personal leadership. It is, therefore, difficult to investigate the people's response to one of those aspects of the movement in isolation from the other. If it is recognized, however, that the two aspects may properly be differentiated for purposes of emphasis, then an analysis of each may profitably be undertaken.

As we have emphasized, the philosophy of Social Credit had a not inconsiderable history of advocacy by U.F.A. men and others in Alberta before Aberhart took it up. But, previous to Aberhart's decision to take the Social Credit movement into politics, Alberta had never seen his like as a political leader. He was, indeed, a unique phenomenon, not only in the political experience of Alberta but in that of Canada at large.

The response of the people to Aberhart's leadership was stimulated primarily by that factor which made him unique in the history of Canadian politics, namely, his earlier and continuing career as the founder of a religious movement.[1] But the people of Alberta were also profoundly impressed by certain traits of leadership he possessed in addition to his religious influence. His presence and his voice, for example, contributed to inspire in his followers a fanatical and mysterious zeal: they felt that he spoke as one having authority. Aware of

[1]For a sociological discussion of the relationship between Aberhart as a religious and a political leader see S. D. Clark, "The Religious Sect in Canadian Politics," *American Journal of Sociology*, vol. 51, no. 3 (November, 1945), pp. 207–16.

his capacity to hypnotize people by these qualities he used them throughout his political career. His resolute and inflexible will combined with his doctrines and his strong personal attraction to give him a power over his followers which verged on dictatorship. He was infinitely resourceful, and once his mind was made up no obstacles could turn him aside from his self-appointed task.

He was fully cognizant also of the emotional attitudes which had developed among the people of Alberta during the early years of the great depression. There can be no doubt that he appealed directly to these emotions, for he realized clearly that an emotional attitude when once aroused tends to radiate over all concurrent conscious processes.

If it would be unfair to deny that he sought to educate the people as well, it must be emphasized that he had an uncanny knowledge of the art of making up people's minds for them. He led people to believe that he alone could think constructively; that he had the finer feelings; that his was the responsibility of decision and others had only the right and obligation of acceptance. But, through it all, he gave the impression of utter sincerity and that sincerity seemed to enter the very souls of his followers.

Impressive as were these extra-religious traits of Aberhart's leadership, it is doubtful if the Social Credit movement would have evolved as it did had the people not previously developed a perception of its leader as a Man of God. Under his leadership the Social Credit movement glided almost imperceptibly from a religious to an educational to a social to a political movement, but throughout that evolution the people's perception of Aberhart as a Man of God was never dimmed and was one of the principal factors in inspiring them with loyalty and devotion to the Social Credit movement. In its extreme form, this perception was accompanied by a belief that Aberhart had been divinely chosen and prepared for his mission in Alberta, as is illustrated by an excerpt from an interview with a lower middle-class housewife in Calgary:

The secret of Mr. Aberhart's appeal to us was his whole-heartedness and sincerity for religion. He loved us common people because of his religion. We felt he was a born leader, with something great to do in the world. It seemed to us as if God had picked Mr. Aberhart and then prepared an audience for him in Alberta first as a religious leader and then as leader of the Social Credit movement. The life of Mr. Aberhart in Alberta was a fulfillment of a Divine Plan.

It is, perhaps, not surprising that the attributing to Aberhart the "special grace" of a "man of destiny" recurs in interviews with the most ardent of his religious followers. For nearly a quarter of a century he had been widely known and enthusiastically accepted in certain quarters as "the greatest student of Bible prophecy in the world." Under these circumstances, some of his followers naturally found it easy, by a certain shift in the apocalyptic emphasis, to endow their leader with Messianic qualities. Believing that he had an historic mission in the world, such people referred to him as "Our Great Prophet," "Our Beloved Leader," "That Man of God," "The Last Hope of Mankind," "That Heaven-Sent Saviour." If such attitudes represent the response of religious extremists to Aberhart's leadership, it must not be forgotten that this group included some of the most vocal proponents of the Social Credit movement.

The response of the majority of Aberhart's followers to his role as a religious leader was, of course, usually much more restrained. But it was not, on that account, necessarily less influential in the promotion of the Social Credit movement. Then, too, there was always the tendency, under the stimulation of great mass meetings, for more or less normal people to behave like the most fanatical of Aberhart's followers. Even when seemingly dormant, religious feelings contained explosive possibilities, especially after the development of bitter opposition to the Social Credit movement. Excerpts from interviews quoted below illustrate attitudes to Aberhart's religious leadership; these are typical of those from a much wider range of classes and occupations.

A lower middle-class clerk in Calgary

You can't understand the Social Credit movement unless you keep in mind that Aberhart was a great religious teacher. He lectured on the Bible in the Calgary theatres and the Bible Institute over twenty years before he entered the Social Credit field. I heard him numerous times lecturing on Bible prophecy. Whether his listeners always agreed with him or not, he was recognized as one of the greatest Bible students of our time. . . . At Social Credit meetings Aberhart would sometimes read a letter he had received on a religious question—having nothing to do with Social Credit actually. It was wonderful to see the mental gymnastics he displayed in answering such questions. On numerous occasions I have heard him quote numerous and lengthy texts of Scripture from memory. I got into the Social Credit movement because I felt that Aberhart was a God-fearing man who really did know the Bible. Aberhart's religious appeal was the strongest I've ever felt. Some think he only appealed to fanatics. That's not true. I'm not a fanatic. He appealed to a lot of religious people, whether Baptist, or Anglican, or United Church, because of his knowledge of the Bible. He preached conversion, but was always strong for practical Christianity. He used to say at Social Credit meetings, "I may preach, brother, but if I don't feed you, you are going to be awfully weak!" He gave himself wholly to religion without the least thought of his personal comfort. For years on end, after school was over at 4 o'clock, he went down to the Bible Institute and taught for hours until 11 o'clock at night without any supper. Do you wonder that I was ready to work for Social Credit when I knew that such a religious man as Mr. Aberhart was behind it?

A public school teacher in Central Alberta

I had listened to Mr. Aberhart for years before I became interested in Social Credit. His religion seemed to me to be sincere, unlike that of the regular churches. When people are doing something which they believe to be right, they have a powerful source of strength and driving power. Religion is the most compelling force in my life; if its aid can be secured in your life you will exert an influence far beyond any other source. That is why I believed in Social Credit as soon as he took it up. Mr. Aberhart showed me that Social Credit and the Christian religion are the same thing. Whenever he could he would use texts from the Bible to support his Social Credit ideas. I realized that if the Bible is true, Social Credit would be a sure cure for all the sufferings of Alberta. I believe that if we are to fulfil God's purpose for man, we must all take up Social Credit.

A small-town merchant in central Alberta

In our town we all knew about Mr. Aberhart's religious reputation. In fact, many people throughout our entire district would scarcely ever miss one of Mr. Aberhart's religious broadcasts. Our United Church minister told me it was hard to hold services in country points around our town because a lot of their members preferred to listen to Aberhart. Many farm children belonged to his Radio Sunday School. Everybody knew Aberhart's and Manning's voices and even members of the United Church, like myself, got interested in Bible prophecy to some extent. The depression came and hit everybody hard in our town. Aberhart began introducing the Social Credit material of Douglas into his Sunday broadcasts. Gradually he disclosed to the public the mechanisms of banking and finance. He was really conducting an adult educational campaign in economics. A lot of United Church people who were only mildly interested in Bible Prophecy, like myself, felt that here was a truly moral man who could really come to grips with the depression and solve it. Don't forget that we had been soured on the U.F.A. by the scandals, and we felt the Liberals were just tools of Eastern financial interests.

A small-town real estate and insurance broker north of Calgary

I first heard of Mr. Aberhart through his preaching the gospel. I liked him tremendously as a preacher. Most people in our town heard of him in this manner and he came to have a very large radio congregation. When he brought Social Credit as a solution for the terrible depression into his religious broadcasts he had a very receptive audience ready to hand. He arranged to address a Social Credit rally in our town in the summer of 1933 and because of his popularity as a radio preacher he attracted about 2,500 people into our arena. He showed us how Social Credit was a natural result of the Bible and Christianity. A lot of us were convinced that this God-inspired man had a plan which would, without any possibility of failure, solve the problems of the common man forever.

A farmer in the Edmonton area

I was an old U.F.A. man and had worked for our local for years. But our government in Edmonton refused to do anything about the depression. Then two or three Cabinet ministers got involved in scandals. I am religious, but not a fanatic, like a lot of Aberhart's followers. All the same I was religious enough to be sickened by those scandals. Then along came Aberhart and his standing as a religious teacher attracted me to Social Credit, so I left the U.F.A. for good. I didn't understand Social Credit theories very well but I felt that Aberhart was a God-fearing man who we could all trust. If he said Social Credit would work, then I figured it would work. I was more and more impressed with Mr. Aberhart's grasp of conditions us farmers were facing. I also felt he was a very sincere man who would do what he said. I've only got worked up over religion once in my life. One night I went to a Social Credit meeting in a town near us where Mr. Aberhart was speaking. A U.F.A. man began to throw questions at him and made a disturbance. I got real mad at this U.F.A. man for doing that, and I couldn't hold myself in. So I jumped up and led the meeting in prayer. I said, "Let us pray for Mr. Aberhart. Let us pray for his soul." As we prayed aloud, the U.F.A. man got frightened and shut up. There were, all down on our knees praying for Mr. Aberhart. We were a bunch of hard-working slaves—over-worked, over-tired, eyelids half closed from exhaustion and misery, children lying all about, under and over the benches. When we finished praying, tears were rolling down practically everybody's cheeks. Later on, I was surprised myself that I had led that meeting in prayer for Mr. Aberhart.

A farmer in northwestern Alberta

I listened to Mr. Aberhart's religious broadcasts from 1925 on. I heard the third broadcast he ever gave and I liked his Biblical instruction because it was based on Bible prophecy. The clarity with which he explained Bible situations always appealed to me. He got that clarity by linking the Bible situation with some incident in our daily lives. He was very good at that. I went down to the Bible Institute in 1928 to be baptized by Mr. Aberhart, because all my life I had been seeking religious satisfaction and he finally gave it to me. I had attended quite regularly practically all the churches, and never seemed to get satisfaction until Mr. Aberhart clarified the main points in religion for me. He really got down to fundamentals. . . . Then the depression struck Alberta in 1930–1. Us farmers, being the producers of real wealth, were the first to feel the pinch and we felt it the hardest as the years went by. When we were all feeling down and out, Mr. Aberhart began to show the link between the economic injustices of today and the economic injustices of Christ's time. He linked these two up and showed how Christ had cleared the money-changers out of the Temple. Then he showed us how the money-changers of today had everything cornered. When he introduced his economic theories into his broadcasts, I felt he had reached the fundamental cause of the depression. He showed us why Christianity wasn't working and why democracy wasn't working. . . . This tie-up between religion and economics made me realize that Social Credit was the answer to all our problems. Once I realized this, I went out and talked up Social Credit and organized groups among farmers all through our district.

The interviews indicate that it would be difficult to exaggerate the psychological significance of the response of the people to William Aberhart himself during the rise of the Social Credit movement. They indicate also that the most recurrent factor in the people's enthusiasm for him was his long-standing reputation as a religious leader. Once he began to introduce Social Credit into his radio addresses, the enthusiasm of thousands of his followers for his prophetic and fundamentalist doctrines was gradually transformed into eager support for the social and economic theories he was now promoting.

If the rapid rise of the Social Credit movement was due, in part, to the alliance of Aberhart's Social Credit programme with his religious appeal, it must be emphasized that his constant invocation of Divine guidance for the success of that programme eventually had an influence far beyond his own religious following. Many adherents of the numerous sectarian groups in Alberta rallied to his support.[2] But it must also be recognized that his unusual mixture of religion and politics likewise attracted to Social Credit a considerable number of the members of established institutional churches. Baptists and Lutherans had long been impressed by Aberhart's old-time gospel and his stalwart defence of fundamentalism against modernism. Members of the United Church, although not often partial to his specific religious doctrines, were usually convinced that he was, at the very least, a "good man," in a world where personal immorality had become prevalent in high political places.

Scarcely less influential than religion in arousing the enthusiasm of the masses was Aberhart's programme of social action. Owing to the economic distress created by the depression, thousands of people in Alberta were experiencing ego-displacement to a greater or less degree. They were not merely oppressed by serious financial difficulties; they were also suffering from feelings, often deep-seated, of guilt or of personal inadequacy for being unemployed or on relief. The meaning of their world, as far as that world was constituted by their economic and social environment, had often well-nigh vanished: to a greater or lesser degree large numbers of people stood in need of psychological guidance or counselling, if not of actual therapeutic treatment.

Confronted with such persons, a clinical psychologist or psychiatrist of the individualist school of that period might well have advised them to "adjust" to their environment. The psychological shrewdness of

[2]Sociological analyses of the development and function of sectarian movements in Canada in general and in Alberta in particular are provided by S. D. Clark, *Church and Sect in Canada* (Toronto: University of Toronto Press, 1948); and by W. E. Mann, *Sect, Cult, and Church in Alberta* (Toronto: University of Toronto Press, 1955).

Aberhart consists in that he helped these people to regain their self-respect and in some measure to re-integrate their personalities by providing them with a philosophy which, in explaining the break-down of the economic system, liberated them from their feelings of guilt and personal inadequacy.

At the same time, and this aspect is of major importance in understanding the mass support of the movement, Aberhart offered the people a programme of social action. They could adjust to their environment by transforming that environment. Social Credit, a *subjective* system of ideas, could become, through human effort, the *objective* economic and social reality. In the interviews this theme recurs:

Mr. Aberhart led me to see that I need not suffer hopelessly any longer from the depression or the money barons. I could, by supporting Social Credit, end all this misery and change the terrible system that had brought us such poverty. I need not be out of work and heavily in debt. Mr. Aberhart gave me a new feeling about myself and a new respect for myself. He made me realize that if we all stood together for Social Credit we could build a new world under his leadership.

The microcosm could become the macrocosm. Participation in the Social Credit movement offered the individual a dynamic purpose in life, and the person of Aberhart became the living symbol of the purpose. The movement provided the possibility of social sanitation on a wide scale. During the years 1933–5 thousands of people who had been frustrated by the depression achieved a renewed self-confidence, greater in many instances than they had ever previously experienced.

This ego-enhancement was made possible largely because Aberhart brought to the promotion of Social Credit ideas the same techniques he had previously used so successfully in his religious work. Realizing that most of his followers needed a reorientation of their lives, Aberhart always challenged those who accepted Social Credit to carry the idea to others. During the summer of 1933, for example, when the movement was barely under way, he put his leading converts of the previous winter to a severe test by leaving them in charge of the large study group at the Bible Institute while he went on an extended lecture tour, at the conclusion of which he took a vacation. The successful completion of such assignments nearly always transformed those entrusted with them into unshakeable devotees of Aberhart and dynamic proponents of Social Credit.

A considerable number of converts to Social Credit had been unemployed, in whole or in part, for months or even years. The possibilities of action that Aberhart opened up relieved them from the aimlessness into which they had drifted and gave new force to their lives. No approach of Aberhart's was more characteristic than his continual call to these people to save themselves by working for Social Credit: "*I* can't change this economic system," he would declare, "but *you* can change it." He also displayed a calculated wisdom in demanding that the people themselves should pay *in full* the expenses of the movement. As the movement grew in volume no one was more surprised than Aberhart himself at the people's enthusiasm for Social Credit. Like many other leaders of social movements, he had begun without a clear realization of where he was ultimately going. The response of the people drew him on and on: at each critical stage in the development of the movement he managed somehow, despite the absence of well-defined goals, to adapt his leadership to the pressing demands of his followers.

There can be little doubt that Aberhart was sincere in his initial attitude that his campaign for Social Credit was entirely educational. He was the type of man who had always considered that he must work tirelessly for whatever he believed to be right. His ardent belief in the essential rightness of Social Credit drove him on relentlessly to convert others to the faith. To his enemies he appeared as a man of demoniacal compulsions; to many of his followers he gradually became a man with an historic mission. There could be no half-heartedness in the personal allegiance he demanded and received from thousands of people. As his greatest disciple and successor in the premiership of Alberta has simply and fervently put it: "You either believed he was right and followed him wherever he led, or you had nothing to do with him."

The multivalent appeal of Aberhart as a person and a leader is illustrated below by excerpts quoted from interviews.

A railway employee in southern Alberta

Mr. Aberhart won my complete loyalty because of his sympathy with the poor and unemployed. I've seen him cry. I've seen tears rolling down his cheeks when he was describing the suffering caused among the poor by the depression—through no fault of their own, as he made clear to us. He would dramatize the situation that had caused the depression. He seemed to feel the characters of the poor people he was talking about. He had a voice that made the pilot lights on your radio jump. You simply had to believe him. Sometimes when I heard him, I used to say to my wife: "This man seems to be in direct contact with the Supreme Being."

A manager of a laundry in Calgary

I was down and out during the depression. Mr. Aberhart explained why we had a depression and I got back my self-respect by working for Social Credit. I felt I could have gone anywhere and done anything for that man Aberhart. He would say to us: "You can overcome the depression. You can

do it. I can't give you $25 a month, but you can do it yourselves. . . . "
When you are trying to do something for the common good, it is wonderful
how the inspiration comes. There is no doubt that Mr. Aberhart was
inspired by some Higher Power to carry out the gruelling Social Credit work
he did. He had the mental strength that comes from long meditation on
things spiritual. I was willing to work long hours for him and Social
Credit because he gave a new inspiration to my life. I guess some of his
spiritual strength flowed into me by being in the same great cause with him.

A working man in Calgary

You ought to have heard Aberhart telling us working men about coupon
clippers, and the moneyed interests from the East taking all our money out
of Alberta. The condition we were all in during the depression made
Aberhart's explanation of how we got that way sound really wonderful
to us. He convinced me that if we got behind him we could really change
conditions for poor people. I was unemployed, and he made me feel I
could really be somebody again if I got behind him. He had a wonderful
brain and a wonderful knowledge of the whole depression situation. He
seemed to know about the problems of labour better than we did ourselves.
He really lived his religion—he was not one of those shyster fly-by-night
religionists like so many in the churches. He gave me back my self-respect,
because he was a real honest-to-God man himself.

A small-town business man in southeastern Alberta

You can't understand how we felt about Mr. Aberhart unless you realize
that he could arouse great and loyal support and also great hatred and
bitterness. You either gave him your all-out support or you hated him
with a mighty hatred. I was absolutely for Mr. Aberhart. In fact you could
say that I loved Aberhart. My view is that it's a long time since people
have seen a situation in which men "loved" a man. But there were an enormous number of men who did love this man Aberhart. He was capable of
inspiring great love and at the same time great hatred. What inspired the
great love I had for Aberhart? The forcefulness of Aberhart inspired this
love. He was a great orator and a great personality. But, above all, he had an
absolutely great love for the sufferings of the common people. This is
what drew me to him.

A farmer in central Alberta

What I admired about Mr. Aberhart was his ability as a speaker. We've
had two really great orators in Canada—R. B. Bennett and William Aberhart. For me, Aberhart was a greater speaker on the platform than Bennett.
He was really more forceful and eloquent than Bennett. Aberhart would
really stir me up when I heard him speak. Some farmers said he was
emotional as the devil. Maybe he was. But I got behind him because I
knew he really understood how farmers were feeling about the depression.
He took up our problems and made them his own problems. That's why I
worked for him. In Aberhart, prairie farmers found a real leader at last.
Wouldn't any real leader have to be emotional when we were faced with
depression conditions? Aberhart's speeches stirred us all up, and gave us
new hope for the future.

A clerk in a metropolitan department store

I had lost my job as the result of the depression and was down and out, feeling pretty sorry for myself. I used to feel so tired out that I would fall asleep over the newspaper after supper. Then I heard Mr. Aberhart expound Social Credit at the Bible Institute. He made me see why we had a depression. He told us we could end it if we all pulled together. So I decided to take up Social Credit and work for Mr. Aberhart. An amazing change took place. After Social Credit came into my life, I had plenty of pep and energy. It was amazing. I went out speaking at nights in villages and small towns around Calgary. Sometimes we didn't get back home until two or three o'clock in the morning. But, in spite of the late hours, I never felt tired any more. It was because I had something to work for.

A farmer in southern Alberta

I was one of Mr. Aberhart's greatest supporters and I would have done practically anything for him. But I wasn't alone in this feeling about him. Many times I have seen Mr. Aberhart walk into a crowded meeting. He would be detained at the back of the hall by people who wished to get near him. His progress would be impeded right up the aisle. Each one wanted to get the best view of him that could be obtained. The applause would be deafening. It was impressive to see that big man with the mischievous grin on his face climbing up on the platform. We felt he was the law— he was the only man who could give us a decent hope in the future—who could free us from the money barons of Eastern Canada. Who wouldn't gather around a man like that? Who wouldn't love him?

A business man in a town in the Peace River area

I first heard about Social Credit from speakers whom Mr. Aberhart had sent into the Peace River country. As conditions were very bad in the Peace, I began to wonder if Social Credit was the remedy. To me, the man in charge counts about 75 per cent, so I decided to go down to Calgary and meet the man in charge of the Social Credit idea. It was quite a long trip, but I made it. Mr. Aberhart gave me a wonderful welcome in his office at the Bible Institute and explained his whole outlook to me. He never made me feel that he was in a hurry, or that I was an outsider. I couldn't have received more attention than he gave me. Before I left I concluded that here was a really big man who was absolutely devoted to the cause of the common people. As a result of my impression of Mr. Aberhart, the man, I became a Social Crediter for life. I worked my head off for Mr. Aberhart in the Peace River country. I thought it was the least I could do, considering what he was doing for the suffering people of this province. Aberhart was the most wonderful man I've ever met. No one would dare to say one word against him in this town in my presence. Here was a man who really cared about people, and the people sensed it and followed him like I did.

An elementary school teacher in Edmonton

When all is said and done I think what really attracted me to Aberhart was his showmanship. Brownlee and Reid were cold and distant, especially Brownlee. I didn't trust the Liberal leader—all he wanted was to be premier, and he wasn't really interested in us. Aberhart didn't really want anything for himself, so he could afford to be human and give his audience a good time. I was 22 years old at the time and liked lots of fun at political meetings. Aberhart's meetings were always a good show. He sure was a wonderful showman. You couldn't beat his sense of humour, either. He always captured the crowd. He would sometimes do this by telling a humorous story on himself. I'll never forget the fun we had at a meeting in the thick of the election. Aberhart was lighting into the financiers and bankers like anything and the crowd was warming up. Then he pulled out a letter from his pocket. He waved this letter, as he stood there—a big man physically—on the platform and said: "Listen, folks, the Bible Institute just got this letter from one of our opposition—a big banker who lives in Eastern Canada. This banker expresses deep sympathy for me in this letter. Let me read you what he says. He writes, 'I understand that Mr. Aberhart has lost his equilibrium completely, that he's left Mrs. Aberhart, and is living in a shack up in the mountains.' " Well, you should have heard the audience roar with laughter when Mr. Aberhart finished reading that banker's letter. He held that crowd in the hollow of his hand the rest of the meeting. You've got to be a good showman to be a popular leader, and Aberhart was the best showman we've ever had in Alberta.

A farmer in a drought-stricken area

Mr. Aberhart had the faculty of tapping us farmers right on the heart. He was quite a chap to tell human interest stories, which always had a meaning and were linked up with Social Credit in some way. He certainly was down on the banks and the mortgage companies. Once I heard him say to an audience of farmers: "You know Jones—he's well fixed. I've investigated and found he has a mortgage on his farm, on his machinery, and on his car. So he's well fixed. Boy! I'll say Jones is well fixed! Now the Opposition tells you that if I give you $25 a month for food, clothing and shelter, it will ruin you. Now, you may believe that it will ruin Jones, but you don't believe it will ruin you, do you?"

The quality of Aberhart's leadership became especially apparent in the spring of 1934 when he relinquished control of the movement for a few months. As we have seen in chapter III, it was the response of the people that persuaded him to return as their leader. Thereafter, his renunciation and enforced return invested him with a halo in the eyes of his followers. Having created the impression of indispensability, he was now able to make ever-increasing demands on them for the support and promotion of the movement. The greater his demands, the more the people responded. Finally, their response led to the decision to force legislative action by transforming the social movement into a political party to contest the provincial election of 1935.

Amidst all the dramatization of his leadership, however, Aberhart was clever enough to realize that propaganda is feeble and ineffectual without techniques of organization and promotion. The response of the people to the strategy and tactics of the Social Credit movement was facilitated, like their response to its philosophy and its leadership, by certain factors that had been in operation prior to the rise of the movement. As educator and religious leader, Aberhart had been developing techniques of instruction, organization, and promotion for over twenty years before he took up Social Credit. During this period he had tried and tested many methods. The strategy and tactics of the Social Credit movement were built, to a marked degree, upon those methods that had already proved successful in Alberta. Here, again, it must be emphasized that the new movement profited by the preparatory work of the U.F.A.

Owing to the cautious manner in which Aberhart introduced Social Credit ideas into his religious broadcasts, the new movement was well under way before most of his listeners realized what was happening. The interviews indicate that many of his religious followers considered that Social Credit was a development of the pre-millennial fundamentalism which they had long associated with him. At the very least, they thought of Social Credit as applied Christianity. Their inability to distinguish clearly between the two approaches is not at all surprising, since in the same broadcast Aberhart presented the two sets of ideas as interwoven themes.

Some fifteen months elapsed before there was a general realization that a new movement, distinguishable in several important respects from the old religious movement, was already well in progress. In its first phase, the Social Credit movement may be described, therefore, as a period of unconscious patterning of the ideas and responses of those who were involved in it. During this formative period, the strategy and tactics of the movement were such that its following had already become deeply committed to it before its ideology became the subject of public criticism. The interviews make it clear that the major factor in this process of unconscious patterning was Aberhart's use, on behalf of Social Credit, of all the highly successful techniques of radio broadcasting he had learned during the seven years prior to 1932.

With the exception of Aberhart's Sunday afternoon broadcasts, no aspect of the movement's early programme elicited a greater response from the people than his techniques of systematic instruction and group organization. Here, too, as has been pointed out in chapter III, there are striking parallels between the strategy and tactics developed at the Bible Institute in the pursuit of Aberhart's earlier religious aims on the one hand and his later Social Credit aims on the other. In responding to Aberhart's challenge to form new groups, many local leaders often endured great hardships. Most of them gave their time and energy to the organization and promotion of group activities without any thought of recompense. In one interview, for example, an unemployed accountant who was a very influential group leader has recorded that in the coldest time of the winter of 1934, without sufficient money to buy himself a street-car ticket, he would tramp miles through the snow-filled streets of Calgary to keep his teaching appointment with a Social Credit study group.

The texture of the movement in Calgary during this early period may be illustrated by an excerpt from an interview with a middle-class housewife:

I attended Mr. Aberhart's religious meetings for many years before he went in for Social Credit. . . . I remember him selling bricks to build the Prophetic Bible Institute. . . . One Sunday afternoon in the fall of 1932 he began talking about Social Credit. . . . Several weeks later he said: "Let's have a show of hands of those who think there's something in Social Credit, and we'll hold a meeting downstairs after this service." Well, at that meeting, one of the deacons was asked by William Aberhart to take the names. . . . I was standing close to this deacon, and he said to me, "Let's put your name down first." So I was the first person enrolled. The following week Mr. Aberhart called a meeting of the 30 of us. Then he started in and gave us lectures for a few months on Social Credit. We met every week in the Bible Institute. I sure was hit with the Social Credit bug. Aberhart boiled the books on it down so anybody could understand it. It was like going to school again and we always enjoyed the way Mr. Aberhart taught us. He was a wonderful teacher. We all had to study his leaflets. I've never seen people study the way he made us.

Then one night he said: "We'd better organize and get out and tell everybody in Calgary about Social Credit. Who will help?" Then he asked each one of us separately what part of Calgary they lived in. I was near the Victoria School District. I wanted it and I got it. Each person in that first group had to get out and organize a group. I thought the world of Aberhart—he really was a wonderful man. So I started in and organized the first group in my district. I called it Victoria Group no. 1. I organized twelve Victoria groups, all in my district.

To organize these groups, I went around to all the people I knew—I got their names and their husband's names and their addresses and then kept in touch with them by telephone. It was wonderful the way the people crowded into my groups. Such crowds came that the houses where we had started out couldn't hold them.

So I went over to the Labor Temple where ——— was in charge, preaching Socialism and Communism to the poor working men. I found out I could hold meetings there, so for over three years all my groups met as a large group in this Labor Temple. The time we were taking the straw vote I had over 8,000 names signed up in that district. I took those people right away from Socialism and Communism and sold them on Social Credit.

I used to ask Mr. Aberhart to announce our group meetings over his radio. I got the speakers for all my groups myself. My husband and I had a big rooming house at the time, and I neglected it for Social Credit.

I used a front room of our rooming house as an office and had it filled with Social Credit literature which I sold all over our district. In 1933 and 1934 my groups had a big part in the Calgary Stampede. Each of my groups had its name on a car and the applause was terrific as all my groups drove by. Prime Minister Bennett led the parade and he could hardly believe his eyes when all our Social Credit cars rolled by, each representing a group.

During the time all these groups were operating Mr. Aberhart would put on a public meeting every week at the Institute, and all the groups in Calgary came to the Institute. You see, nearly everybody who studied in Mr. Aberhart's group felt they should get out and organize groups. So Calgary was full of Social Credit groups in a year or so. We really took over the city with our groups! I don't think we missed any street or block in the whole city. It was a perfect organization. We were everywhere. Everybody wanted to get into a group and find out what it was all about.

Numerous other interviews confirm the view that it is impossible to understand the character of the Social Credit movement during its early years unless one realizes clearly that it evoked a surging response from ordinary people.

In the organization and promotion of the Social Credit movement, Aberhart used the facilities and resources not only of the Bible Institute but also of the U.F.A. For nearly a quarter of a century, large numbers of U.F.A. locals had been carrying on the study and discussion of farmers' problems. Within a few months after he began to introduce Social Credit into his religious broadcasts, Aberhart was receiving numerous invitations to lecture before these locals.

Always receptive to new ideas, the members of these democratically constituted locals were naturally eager to meet Aberhart personally and hear him discuss Social Credit. As many U.F.A. community halls were free of rent for community gatherings sponsored by U.F.A. locals, Aberhart's expenses for these meetings were usually limited to his transportation costs. Although he had no rental charges, he always asked and received permission to take up a collection to cover the cost of gasoline for the trip. When such collections were high, the board of directors of a U.F.A. local would sometimes invite Aberhart to make a contribution for the use of the hall. But, much to the annoyance of local U.F.A. officials, Aberhart never did. "He always," one of them has said, "put the entire collection in his pocket and took it home. Who got what was left over after gasoline expenses, we never knew. Aberhart never once ran a meeting for farmers without begging for money to finance his movement."

The interviews indicate, however, that most rank and file members, as distinguished from officials, of U.F.A. locals were not at all disturbed by Aberhart's financial techniques. "I think our officials," a number of farmers, who became Social Crediters, have reiterated, "were quite petty about Aberhart's taking up collections at these meetings. The presidents of our locals were so worried to death about such technical trivialities that they had no time to realize what a wonderful message Aberhart was bringing to us downtrodden farmers. That's why we changed our U.F.A. locals into Social Credit groups. Can you blame us? I could never understand why our officials made such a fuss about Aberhart getting those collections at our locals. What difference did a few nickels and dimes make when we had a big man like Aberhart offering us Social Credit?"

The technique used by Aberhart in presenting the philosophy of Social Credit to U.F.A. locals is revealed by an excerpt from an interview with a farmer northeast of Calgary:

Aberhart's meeting at ——— under the auspices of our U.F.A. local was the largest ever held there. He had a chart of the bloodstream of the state which he used in explaining his theories. He appealed to us because he attacked the banks and mortgage companies really fierce. You should have heard the crowd applaud this part. He appealed to us still more when he described the conditions farmers were facing. You must remember he was speaking to an audience entirely composed of farmers. He could certainly dramatize the hard times farmers were having. At this jam-packed meeting he said, "Let's knock on the door of an imaginary farm home. A poor dispossessed farmer's wife comes to the door. Let's ask her some questions. 'How long have you lived here?' 'Twenty-five years.' 'Have you a car?' 'Oh, my, no. We ride in a wagon.' 'You have an electric refrigerator?' 'Oh, no, not even an ice-box.' 'Would you like a car and a refrigerator?' 'I certainly would!' 'Have you been to Calgary lately?' 'Not for a year.' 'Would you like to go?' 'I certainly would and so would my children!' 'Would you be interested in a plan that would give you a car, a refrigerator, and trips to the big city? Social Credit, without any cost to you individually, will give you all these.'" Aberhart could certainly talk the language of farmers. That was the amazing thing about him. Here he was, a big high school teacher—he had a B.A. from a university too. Yet he knew how we were feeling about the things we were deprived of by the depression. He convinced me that night that we had a God-given right to a far better life than we were getting. He agreed with us that we should have the things we needed. He said Social Credit would give us these things. It was just as easy as turning on a light switch—no trouble at all to get Social Credit for the whole province. At the end of his address, he said, "Now you folks get behind Social Credit and you'll never need to worry again about where the money's coming from. You continue to listen to our broadcasts from Calgary. You support us and we'll work for you day and night." Aberhart emphasized constantly in this address that Social Credit could give all of these services to us farmers *without cost* to the individual. It could be done simply by the issuing of debt-free money. Hearing Aberhart was the greatest experience I ever had at our old U.F.A. local. That night I became a lifelong Social Crediter.

At a meeting of another U.F.A. local, the vice-president of the U.F.A. himself tried to give a critical analysis of an address made by Aberhart to that same local the previous month. Priestley characterized certain of Aberhart's statements as ridiculous, and emphasized the utter impossibility of fulfilling his promises concerning what Social Credit would do for farmers. The audience grew more and more restive. Finally, a farmer's wife became hysterical and began to cry and scream. "Don't talk that way to us," she shouted at Priestley. "This is the first time since I've been in Alberta that I've had hopes of getting some of the things I've wanted and I don't want to lose the chance of getting them." During interviews, U.F.A. officials almost invariably reported that "Aberhart's addresses to our locals worked the people up to such a pitch that nobody could reason with them."

The interviews also indicate that nothing surprised, exasperated, and saddened local U.F.A. officials more than the increasing defection of members of the locals to Social Credit study groups. It is reported that in some locals Aberhart's tactics resulted in the entire membership, apart from the officials, going over *en masse* to the Social Credit movement. Although they might lose almost their entire following, the U.F.A. officials usually remained loyal to their own organization. It was reported in some interviews, however, that in a number of instances most or even all of the officials of U.F.A. locals rejoined their followers by rushing into the Social Credit movement with them, thus leaving the U.F.A. without even a skeleton organization in their communities.

In this "functional penetration" of the U.F.A. movement itself, Aberhart had three tactical advantages: he appeared before the farm people as a "Man of God," in marked contrast to the popular impression of certain of their own leaders; they were convinced that he had no personal political ambitions, but was working "absolutely disinterestedly" (as many of them have put it) for the welfare of his fellow men; and they were in a state of readiness to respond to his claim that a philosophy with which many of them had long been more or less familiar could be applied to Alberta immediately, if only the U.F.A. government would get busy and do it.

But the most important factor of all in Aberhart's success with U.F.A. locals was his over-all strategy in maintaining constantly that the Social

Credit movement was educational and not in the least sense political. Here, again, the process of unconscious patterning of the response of the people was much in evidence. Aberhart's method ensured that attitudes favourable to Social Credit were well established in many communities in rural Alberta before systematic criticism of that philosophy as a political programme had developed. When that criticism was finally launched in full force by the U.F.A. leaders during the winter of 1935, it was then much too late to turn back the surging response of the people in rural Alberta to the Social Credit movement.

Under the stimulus of Aberhart's developing organization, many people in rural areas not only joined Social Credit groups but also actually turned violently against the U.F.A. movement itself. The Social Credit movement thus split the farmers into two bitterly opposing factions. As the division engendered in rural districts was a phase of the division of the Alberta community in general, it will be considered later in this chapter. It must be emphasized here, however, that the extreme bitterness that developed throughout the province during the years 1934–5 heightened the appeal of Social Credit meetings. The interviews indicate that a considerable number of people were attracted to these meetings, and more especially Aberhart's, in the expectation of seeing "fireworks." In addition to providing dramatic effects, the tension that had developed in local communities gave the crowds of country people who assembled to hear Aberhart or his speakers the feeling that "something was imminent," that a new world was in the making.

In the promotion of the Social Credit movement beyond the bounds of Calgary, Aberhart's religious following played a role somewhat similar to that of U.F.A. locals in rural areas. A nucleus of disciples, in whom attitudes favourable to Social Credit had been built up through the Sunday afternoon broadcasts, existed in nearly every small town in southern Alberta and in many small towns in the area bounded by lines drawn from Red Deer to Edmonton to Lloydminster to Wainwright. The initial promotion of the Social Credit movement in these small towns (and also, of course, in the rural areas) was based on radio broadcasts. The use of radio was followed up, as we have seen in chapter III, by the speaking tours of Aberhart and Manning during the summers of 1933 and 1934. The organization and consolidation of the movement beyond Calgary was due, therefore, not only to radio broadcasts but also to a considerable number of personal appearances of Aberhart and speakers trained by him. In fact, the effective organization of the movement in any centre, whether rural or urban, seemed to require the personal presence of either Aberhart or one of his secondary or local leaders.

The penetration and organization of small towns and villages for the movement required, of course, much more strenuous activity than the conquest of Calgary. This activity actually commenced as early as the spring of 1933, when the Bible Institute began to receive requests from members of Aberhart's radio audience beyond Calgary for addresses on Social Credit to be given in their local centres. It is said that Aberhart realized almost immediately that a corps of trained speakers would be required if such invitations were to be accepted. In the autumn of 1933 he put the problem to the members of the first study group and called for volunteers. An unemployed clerk has described Aberhart's challenge:

I'll never forget that night. I had lost my job, and had no backlog of savings. I was penniless, unemployed, a charge on the public purse. I was placed alone on Centre Street to sweep the crossings. This was called relief work— 40 hours work per month gave $52.40 relief per month. A wage indeed! More than $1 an hour but only for 40 hours per month. It was most humiliating when my friends walked by and saw me reduced to that level—sweeping street crossings! Can you wonder that I was attracted to the study of Social Credit under conditions like that? I well remember that Friday evening at the Bible Institute when Aberhart called for speakers. He told us his correspondence indicated people in the country were clamouring for speakers. So after the meeting would those remain who could devote time to the work. He said it would be hard and tedious. And there would be a fight. Then he fired this question at us and I thought he was looking right through me: "Do you want to fight for yourself or do you want others to fight for you?" Well, I jumped up and volunteered to go out speaking wherever he might send me.

Over two dozen volunteered immediately and these were then given special training in public speaking in what came to be called "Aberhart's School for Speakers." One of the first volunteers, a cashier in a department store, has described the procedure of training speakers:

After I had volunteered to go speaking on Social Credit outside Calgary, Mr. Aberhart asked me to read a great many books and pamphlets on Social Credit. Then he gave us lessons on public speaking, how to control breathing, how to use your voice and hands and so on and so forth. Next, we were told how to prepare addresses. He didn't want us to write out our addresses in full—just wanted us to work up outlines. This was so we could "talk it up" and not just read it to our audience. After all these lessons in public speaking we had to give twenty-minute trial talks to groups, with Mr. Aberhart in the audience. He would call on one speaker after another to do this. Then he would decide whether we were prepared enough to go speaking out of town. Well, I passed this test and away I went. I don't think that anything but Social Credit would have taken me to the public platform!

As the movement developed, more and more speakers were required, but there was never a shortage of enthusiastic volunteers.

These speakers, who may be called local leaders (as distinguished from the secondary leaders whose activities on behalf of the movement are discussed in chapter VII), helped to give to Social Credit the quality of "a people's movement." Receiving no financial support from the funds of the Institute, they were dependent for their expenses on collections, consisting mainly of nickels and dimes, taken at their meetings. Such collections were, in fact, the sole means of support of a number of these local leaders.

If a local leader was employed, his contribution as a speaker usually consisted in making nightly sorties into the towns and villages of southern Alberta. Excerpts from interviews with two such promoters of Social Credit indicate the character of their achievement on behalf of the movement.

A housewife who was employed in a commercial firm

I would leave my job at 6.30 P.M., jump into a car, drive out to the country town, speak at the meeting, and not have my supper until the meeting was over. I went to places like Blackie, Lethbridge, Macleod. I would speak for one hour and forty minutes and then have a question period after that. U.F.A. people would come to my meetings with long strings of questions. The proudest moment of my life was after my meeting in the Majestic Theatre in Lethbridge. I was really pepped up when I overheard a couple of men saying: "If Mr. Aberhart has half a dozen students of Social Credit like that, the U.F.A. is doomed!" I was speaking pretty steadily all through 1934 and 1935. Sometimes I was out speaking five nights a week. I usually averaged two or three nights a week. I would usually get back home between 2 and 6 o'clock in the morning. To show you how eager the people were for these meetings—on one occasion my car broke down and I didn't get to the meeting until 10 o'clock at night. But the crowd was still waiting when I finally got there.

A railway employee

I went out speaking at meetings of country groups and in villages and towns. It was quite a gruelling experience but when you are trying to do something for the common good it's wonderful how the strength and inspiration come to you. I went into the German districts quite a lot. Someone had to go in there so I volunteered. Wherever I went into these German districts they looked after me marvellously well. My audiences would be composed of the old generation and the new. If you are going to make an impression on the Germans you've got to talk to them in such a way so that what you say will be discussed in their house afterwards. I had a German driver, ———, take me to the German districts. On the way there, he would give me the German for a certain sentence that I would give him in English. Then he would give me the German words. I would take each word and transform it into phonetics and write down these phonetics. Then I would speak these phonetic sentences—sometimes I'd do whole paragraphs—at my German meetings. I got so I could handle the situation so well that German women would come up to me after and say, "You are a German." I told Mr. Aberhart I wanted these older Germans to go home and be able to say they'd heard a little bit at least about Social Credit in something that sounded like German. Then we got a pamphlet, "What Will Social Credit Do For You?" translated into German, and this was sold at meetings.[3] It was wonderful to see those Germans devouring it! You know we won over those German districts almost solidly to Social Credit.

At my meetings, we took up collections to pay expenses, and I got anything that was left over for car expenses and so forth. At some meetings the collection would be $6 to $7, at others it might be $60 to $70. After a meeting, the local committee would sometimes come to me and say: "We are very sorry but after the rent for the hall has been paid, and other incidental expenses, there is only $6 or $7 left over." I never felt depressed about this. "Isn't it splendid," I would say, "that we have covered all the local expenses and still have some left over for car expenses." The people were wonderfully kind to me. Very often, in a town or village, when you got back to your car after the meeting, you would find your gas tank filled, your battery fixed up, your radiator warmed, and your tires pumped up. I well remember a woman in black came up to me one night after a meeting with a parcel. She said she hadn't anything to put in the collection plate, but would I put the parcel in my car and take it home. Well, it was a small chicken, all plucked, trussed up, and ready for the oven!

Local leaders, some of whom were unemployed, not only made one-night sorties into the towns and villages of southern Alberta but also went on extended speaking tours. In this latter respect their contribution to the development and organization of the movement was not unlike that of certain secondary leaders whose tours are discussed in chapter VII. But the speaking tours we are concerned with here were undertaken by individuals who were not candidates in the election of 1935. Such individuals may, therefore, be differentiated from the political *élite* of the movement. The character of local leaders' speaking tours and the backgrounds of local leaders who undertook them are illustrated by excerpts quoted below from interviews.

A clerical jack-of-all-trades

I had been a bank clerk, but I gave that up to sell insurance. That folded when the depression started biting. Then one job after another I tried would fold up. I was a clerk on the Calgary Stock Exchange. Then I had several jobs as a book-keeper, but lost them all. In the late fall of 1932 I heard Aberhart say on the radio that he was going to have a class to study Social Credit. It was cold at nights but the Bible Institute was always well heated. Aberhart turned out to be a wonderful teacher, so I stayed with him all

[3]This pamphlet, which was actually entitled, "What Would Social Credit Do For Us?" is summarized in chapter x, pp. 298–9.

through the terrible winter of 1933. I had been slung from one job to another and from pillar to post. Social Credit clicked with me. I never thought of it as being political at all. Our poverty was so terrific and it seemed the only solution. . . . Then Aberhart called for volunteers to organize groups all over Calgary. I got right into this work for him, as I realized he couldn't carry the whole burden of putting over Social Credit. . . . Well, we got Calgary pretty well organized for Social Credit. Then Aberhart called on us again for volunteer speakers to go out into the country. I remember him saying the need for Social Credit was terrific all over Alberta. I had got a job with a gasoline filling station. It folded. Then I got a job for three weeks in a department store at Christmas time selling electrical trains for kids. With Aberhart calling for speakers to go outside Calgary, I decided to quit this job and go on a speaking tour for Social Credit. I had been through Aberhart's School for Speakers and was acceptable to him. I left my wife and kid to scramble with her father and started out on a shoe-string, without even a car. The people at my meetings drove me to the next one. Maybe it was a silly thing to do. But I was desperate and knew something had to be done. You'd hardly believe the ground I covered. Why in one week I held meetings at High River, Blackie, Retlow, Travers, Tern, Maryland, Cronsfield, and Yankee Valley—all in one week, mind you. All this was done without a dime from Aberhart. I took up collections at these meetings and paid for the hall. The co-operation of the people was such as you never saw before. People would drive you ten miles, put you up overnight, feed you. Everything was whole-hearted, everything went. Farmers who drove me around would milk their cows at two o'clock in the morning. After these meetings I was often ready to drop from weariness. I used to grab the collection and put it in a bag—I was too tired to count it. But, somehow, I kept going. The terrific drive I had was a natural thing. I'm Irish, impulsive, impressionistic. Poverty makes me ill. The work had to be done for Aberhart and I did it. I just knew it was right to do that work. I hadn't been able to make a living under the system. Something got me, when I decided to tear full belt into Social Credit.

After getting the south pretty well lined-up, I tore up to Edmonton. There, I helped organize study groups in different sections of the city. People fed me and put me up at nights. In March, I took to the country towns again. I was dead broke, and didn't have a dime ahead. I didn't know where the next meal was coming from—or the next bed. But a school-teacher friend gave me a $5 bill and I tore out on the road. I lit into the Ukrainian districts east of Edmonton. I went down the line to seven places in seven days. Then I headed further east and didn't stop until I hit the Saskatchewan border. I had big meetings and terrific applause at Marwayne, Streamstown, and Lloydminster. Everybody responded like a house on fire. In the hotel at Mernym they wouldn't give me my bill. The manager, a Ukrainian, said: "You're doing everything you can to better this country. I won't take your money." I don't think I was ever happier in my life than when I was on those tours for Social Credit.

A chicken rancher in central Alberta

I had a chicken ranch, but in the depths of the depression we all got hopelessly behind in debts and taxes. Then along came Social Credit. . . . I

began to organize groups among the farmers in our constituency. Then I
started to hold meetings in towns and villages. I held 35 meetings in the
Red Deer constituency. I really organized the district from Red Deer to
Rocky Mountain House. I got so keen on Social Credit that I quit our
chicken ranch. Then I hit the road again and toured the Camrose and
Stettler constituencies. Aberhart told us he needed speakers north of Edmonton, so I headed north and held meetings in lots of places from St. Albert
and Westlock right up to Athabaska. Then came requests for speakers in the
Peace River. So I headed up there. My speaking tour in the Peace River
country lasted five months. I held from one to five meetings a day. Sometimes
I spent as much as eight hours a day on the platform. We would start out at
10 o'clock in the morning and go miles between meetings in the Peace River
and Grouard constituencies. Once we started for a meeting and were held up
by a bad snow-storm at Falher. So we sent out some half-dozen men on
saddle horses. The men had signs on their backs in French, to advertise the
meeting. They did it so successfully that we had several hundred people at
our meeting in that French town of Falher.

On these speaking tours in the Peace River I just slept in the daytime while
we were going 70 or 80 miles between meetings. When we got to the next
place the people driving me around would wake me up. I organized dozens
and dozens of study groups and distributed Social Credit pamphlets all
through the Peace River country. We had 10,000 copies of the Dean of
Canterbury's pamphlet and sold them all over the place. To raise money, in
addition to collections and the sale of this pamphlet, I sold pennants for use
on the backs of automobiles—"Boost for Social Credit," and so on. These
pennants were in different colours and I had a variety of slogans. They were
painted for me by a painter in Bashaw. I had him make thousands and they
were all distributed. Some people wouldn't put a dime in the collection plate
but would pay you 25 cents for a flag that cost you eight cents.

I travelled thousands of miles on my speaking tours. I tried to cover every
possible point in the Peace River country, and I had that whole country
talking Social Credit. It was no problem to get a crowd. We even attended
dances and talked to people during the intermissions for supper. You couldn't
keep people away from these meetings. At a little dump of a schoolhouse
you'd have a jam-packed audience. Once we didn't arrive for the meeting
until 12 midnight, but the crowd was still there. There's never been anything
like it. The people were simply mad for Social Credit.

The phenomenal response of the people in small towns and villages
to the Social Credit movement was due, in some degree, to the political situation that had existed in Alberta for the previous twelve years.
Although Aberhart's strategy and tactics split the rural communities, the
movement offered the people of the towns and villages a new opportunity
of re-entering the political life of Alberta, from which they had felt
themselves excluded ever since 1921. For example, most of the members
of the Social Credit study group that was formed in 1933 at Fort Saskatchewan (then a town of about 900) had previously taken little part

in politics because they were thoroughly disillusioned with the old-line parties and felt they were not wanted by the U.F.A.

In contrast to the U.F.A., the Social Credit movement welcomed all classes of people, regardless of their occupational status. If the movement had certain small-town aspects, it was partly because so many people who had long felt themselves submerged politically responded enthusiastically to the chance that Social Credit meetings and study groups provided for discussion and action. The advent of Social Credit thus restored a measure of the unity between town and country that had been disrupted by the rise of the earlier U.F.A. movement.[4]

It was a cardinal principle with Aberhart that the response of the people at meetings addressed by himself or his speakers must always lead to the organization of the Social Credit movement in centres being visited for the first time. Further, any organization that already existed as a result of a previous visit must be consolidated and expanded on subsequent visits. Speakers were therefore instructed to take immediate advantage of the enthusiasm they had engendered by organizing, or re-organizing, study groups at the conclusion of their meetings. The organization of such groups involved, of course, the election of officers, consisting of at least a president, vice-president, secretary, treasurer, and, usually, several committee members. But Aberhart insisted that definite arrangements must also be made to hold regular meetings and to secure from either the speaker or the Bible Institute sufficient Social Credit literature for study and discussion.

The response of the people in small towns and villages to this technique was usually so enthusiastic that a study group organized by a visiting speaker would lead to the organization of additional study groups by members who had been trained in the initial group. These small-town groups would then overflow into the surrounding rural areas. Groups organized in such adjacent farming communities would then lead to the organization of more rural groups detached altogether from a town or village base. These strictly rural groups would then multiply until they came into contact with other rural groups that had fanned out from other towns and villages. By the spring of 1935 the existence of a vast network of study groups in southern and central Alberta made it possible

[4]For a discussion of certain aspects of the social background of the Social Credit movement in Alberta see Jean Burnet, "Town-Country Relations and the Problem of Rural Leadership," *Canadian Journal of Economics and Political Science*, vol. 13, no. 3 (August, 1947), pp. 395–409. In her *Next-Year Country* (Toronto: University of Toronto Press, 1951), a sociological analysis of rural social organization in Alberta, Professor Burnet considers the problem of town–country relations in chapters IV–VII.

to transform the Social Credit movement into perhaps the most disciplined and powerful political machine Canada has ever known.

The response of the people to the organization and promotion of the Social Credit movement outside Calgary is illustrated by excerpts quoted below from interviews.

A business man in Vulcan

Mr. Aberhart made a speaking tour of Alberta in the summer of 1933 and came to Vulcan. He already had quite a religious following in our town. At his first meeting he had about 500 people. When he came the second time, in 1934, he had 2,500 and we had to hold this meeting in the skating rink. What made the difference was the terrific organizing job we did in Vulcan and the country around in between Aberhart's visits.

At his first meeting there was terrific enthusiasm. People asked Aberhart what *he* was going to do about it. He said, "It's what *you* are going to do that matters. Organize! Organize! Organize!" Well, he made us get busy and we organized our first group at Vulcan after his meeting that night. I was the first president. Within a week we had that group really working hard. It seemed no time at all before we had the whole town organized. Then we helped the farmers outside our town organize groups. Soon we had groups of farmers organized around places a short distance out of Vulcan, like Red Cross, Berrywater, and Highland. I used to go out nights and speak to a lot of these groups. These groups would be composed of forty to fifty farmers. Those farmers were always eager to have a speaker come out from Vulcan to help them get going as a study group. Then we moved into other districts like Champion and Carmingay and organized groups there. This gave us a kind of district organization long before political action was considered. When we did decide to go into politics, everything was ready. I was really surprised the way leaders sprang up all over the countryside to take offices in these groups. You must remember that these leaders of groups in our district had not been through a course of training under Aberhart at his Bible Institute. They just jumped into the movement and organized groups as a result of all the popular excitement that was going on.

A merchant at Brooks

Once I became a Social Crediter, Aberhart made me realize I'd have to get busy and work for the movement. So I became an organizer. . . . I had never been on a public platform before in my life. People in places around Brooks urged me to come out and speak. . . . I remember my first meeting at Makepiece. Just a rural district, but here were 220 people packed into one little schoolhouse—sitting on planks right up to my table. You could hear a pin drop. If R. B. Bennett himself had been there he couldn't have got a better reception than I got. The tenseness and eagerness of that audience made me realize that there was something more radically wrong with the system than I had thought. People had no money to buy gasoline for their cars—they had to use wagons to get to my meetings. I realized it was time somebody was trying to do something for these people when they would drive a wagon nine miles to hear me. The enthusiasm and tenseness of the people drove me on to become a leader and I worked hard to organize groups.

A farmer in the Carstairs area

I was won over to Social Credit when I heard Mr. Aberhart and Mr. Manning at their meeting at Carstairs in the spring of 1934. Aberhart said we'd never get anywhere if we didn't organize. I began by organizing a study group in the farming district where I live. After I got this group going well I started out to organize others. I would hold meetings in country school-houses. You've no idea how the people took hold of Social Credit. Aberhart and Manning, of course, would pack any hall. What surprised me, though, was the reception I got. Here I was, just an ordinary farmer, not really knowing very much about Social Credit, yet I would pack halls in villages and country schoolhouses. I had a packed meeting one night at a little country schoolhouse that lasted till three or four o'clock in the morning. We were talking about how we could get more groups organized. I think I'm safe in saying that there wasn't a hamlet or a schoolhouse in that whole district that didn't have a Social Credit study group. All this required considerable lecturing and travelling around.

A Ukrainian school-teacher

Aberhart sent speakers on Social Credit to Vegreville and other towns in the Ukrainian country. My father was a farmer and had been listening to Aberhart on the air. Aberhart had won him over to Social Credit. My father insisted on my going with him to a meeting in the village near our farm to hear one of Aberhart's speakers. The hall was packed. You could hardly have crammed in another person. This speaker was very emotional and he worked up us younger Ukrainians like anything. I hadn't thought much of Social Credit till then, even though my father had taken it up. But this fellow made me realize there was a great deal more to it than I'd thought. Well, this speaker said we Ukrainians would have to follow the rest of Alberta and get organized. He wouldn't let us leave that meeting until we formed a group and elected officers. So I decided to get into it. You know at that time very few Ukrainian farmers had radios or even newspapers. To get groups started, personal contacts were necessary. So that fall of 1934 I really got busy and went around at nights and week-ends forming study groups among our Ukrainian people. The U.F.A. had been pretty strong there. But wherever we got Social Credit groups really going the Ukrainians left the U.F.A.

By the summer of 1935 it seemed to an observer of the Alberta scene that every Social Crediter he met was an organizer. The enthusiasm of the people in town and country alike was, of course, continually whipped up by Aberhart's capacity to use the blunders and weaknesses of his opponents to further the development of the Social Credit organization. His control of the radio facilities of the Bible Institute enabled him to appeal immediately to almost the whole province, once any issue had arisen. At each critical stage in the development either of the movement or of the attacks of the opposition, he used the device of taking the people into his confidence, of asking them for their help and advice as to what he should do next. From the thousands of letters that poured in, he and his advisers were able to develop the organization in such a way that it was scarcely ever out of touch with the people. As a result, the people came to feel that they themselves were the founders of the organization. With each new step that he took, Aberhart was always able stoutly to maintain that the people were forcing him on.

During the winter of 1934 the strategy and tactics of the Social Credit movement became front-page news in the daily papers. Henceforth, the philosophy, leadership, and organizational activities of the movement were almost constantly before the public eye. For nearly two years, as has been described in earlier chapters, Alberta was kept in a state of ballyhoo by a series of episodes generated by the Social Credit movement which followed one another in rapid succession: the signing of petitions, the repeated efforts to persuade Alberta's political leaders to take up Social Credit, the bitter controversy between Aberhart and the New Age Club, the resignation of Aberhart as leader, Douglas's famous speech in Calgary during his first visit in 1934, the return of Aberhart as leader, the foundation of the *Social Credit Chronicle*, the radio calls for "One Hundred Honest Men," the "Man from Mars" broadcasts, the straw vote, the strenuous speaking tours about the province, the incessant question as to Aberhart's final personal objectives, the decision to enter politics, Douglas's second visit. Finally, came the tumultuous election campaign of 1935. The response of the people to the events of the Social Credit movement was also stimulated, in part, by the disasters that befell the U.F.A. and the situations that developed as a result of the indecision of its leaders in the face of Aberhart's challenge.

With these dramatic episodes crowded into a period of less than two years, it is not surprising that scarcely anyone in the province remained unaffected by the Social Credit movement. Those who were opposed to it, of course, marshalled their energies to fight it, as we shall see in the next chapter. But their efforts seemed merely to increase the driving power of Aberhart's followers.

By the summer of 1935 the conflict between Social Crediters and their opponents had become so bitter that it split the Alberta community. The *Calgary Herald*, in common with many other newspapers, both daily and weekly, attributed the disruption of the province uniquely to the moves of the Social Credit leaders. It was alleged that the attempts of Social

Crediters to boycott merchants, as well as the *Herald*, for opposing the movement, signified an intolerance unparalleled in democratic societies.[5] Interviews with U.F.A. leaders are replete with bitter comments on the movement's division of rural communities into two hostile factions.

Confronted with such charges, Social Crediters hurled back accusations that it was their opponents, not they themselves, who were responsible for the split. Aberhart and his speakers constantly insisted that Social Credit speeches were distorted in news reports and subjected to merciless ridicule in editorial columns. They charged also that Eastern, and even English, financial interests were subsidizing an all-out effort to destroy the movement.[6] In a broadcast on June 24, 1935, Aberhart himself affirmed that several strong Social Crediters in Edmonton had been approached by representatives of old-line parties and offered one or two dollars with the request that they "vote for Social Credit." Care was taken to see that a third person was present at such transactions, by which opponents hoped to discredit Social Credit supporters before election day and so prevent them from voting. "It is no use working as hard as we are doing for people who will throw away their right to vote for one or two dollars. Have nothing to do with such tactics," he warned his supporters, as he told them of attempts that were being made "to sow discredit in Social Credit ranks by other methods."[7] The fight, he assured his followers, was "absolutely between finance and the common people as represented by Social Credit."

Numerous newspaper reports during the spring and summer of 1935 suggest that an atmosphere of fear and suspicion hung miasma-like over Alberta. Speakers opposed to Social Credit not infrequently declared that they were threatened with phyiscal violence and even, in some instances, with death. The following press report indicates the hazards of life in Alberta after the Social Credit movement became political:

Threatening letters have been received by Harry Humble, one revealing a plot to have him tarred and feathered, he told a radio audience Sunday afternoon, during an address on Aberhart Social Credit. "This of course," said the speaker, "is only an outward manifestation of the attempts being made in the movement to win converts by threats, bullying, and thuggery. Mr. Aberhart may be quite sincere in his proposals, but it is an unquestioned fact that he has secured as part of his following, a number of people who are prepared to suppress all opposition by violence. Cracking a few skulls, and stealing a man's character are mere trifles to such people when $25

⁵Calgary *Albertan*, April 15, July 26, 1935.
⁶*Ibid.*, July 26, 1935.
⁷*Ibid.*, June 24, 1935.

a month is at stake. I have made up my mind," Mr. Humble declared, "that at whatever cost to myself, I shall oppose those people who think they can suppress opposition to any movement by such tactics. I appeal to all fair-minded citizens not to have the issue befogged by such impressive measures."[8]

Some three months later, opponents of the Social Credit movement faced even greater hazards. A Conservative speaker, for example, delivered a radio address on July 24 in which he accused Aberhart of attacking the private character of his critics, of threatening to expose the private affairs of his opponents, of attempting to muzzle the press, and of generally maligning all who did not see eye to eye with him on Social Credit. "Aberhart," he declared, "used the pulpit to spread his incendiarism of hate, to set class against class, to foment the fires of revolution, to stir up the fountains of bigotry and intolerance amongst a suffering people and to crucify them upon his political ambitions."[9] This speaker subsequently claimed that within the twenty-four hours following his address he was threatened three times with shooting and physical violence. He also received numerous anonymous letters and telephone calls informing him that he could "expect plenty of trouble," and that "gangs would gang up on him and make him crawl and plug him full of holes."[10]

Other speakers who were also threatened with physical violence for their efforts expressed the fear that unless Aberhart was "put in his place" and his party defeated in the election, there was a possibility of religious persecution in Alberta under a Social Credit government.[11] Two weeks before the election an independent speaker at Drumheller asserted that the strategy and tactics of the Social Credit movement had split the Alberta community so critically that riots and bloodshed were imminent. Such catastrophies could only be avoided, he declared, by a crushing defeat of Aberhart's party.[12]

Local bankers disturbed the community further by freely predicting a large transfer of bank deposits from Alberta banks to branches outside the province if Social Credit won the election.[13] Such warnings were followed by announcements in metropolitan newspapers that the flight of the dollar from Alberta had already started: cases were cited of bank depositors who had already transferred their money to Winnipeg or

[8]Ibid., April 15, 1935.
[9]Calgary Herald, July 25, 1935.
[10]Ibid.
[11]Cf. Calgary Albertan, July 26, 1935.
[12]Ibid., August 8, 1935.
[13]Calgary Herald, August 7, 1935.

other cities.[14] The fears of the moneyed classes regarding their financial future were not assuaged by the sharp decline in prices of Alberta government and municipal bonds.[15]

Additional evidence regarding the attitudes that had developed within the Alberta community during the summer of 1935 is provided by a newspaper report of the refusal of a Social Credit farmer to allow a Liberal speaker to land his aircraft on the former's farm:

Challenged in landing in a field at Three Hills, Mayor G. G. McGeer, K.C., of Vancouver, flying to a Liberal meeting, was told he could not land there as it was a Social Credit field. Taxied to a stop in his plane in a pasture, the Vancouver Mayor was about to emerge from the plane when the challenge was made Saturday. "Is this McGeer's outfit?" the challenger asked, receiving an affirmative reply. "You can't land here," the Social Crediter said, "This is a Social Credit field." "Had I known that, I wouldn't have landed here in the first place," was Mayor McGeer's retort. Mayor McGeer instructed his pilot to fly to some other fields. . . . At his meeting he remarked that the City of Vancouver had shown William Aberhart every courtesy during his recent visit to that city, and he regretted the welcome in Alberta had not been mutual. Landing his plane elsewhere had been difficult, due to unsuitable ground.[16]

The interviews confirm and amplify newspaper reports on the splitting of the community by the Social Credit movement. Social Crediters insisted during interviews, however, that their speakers were also threatened with physical violence. They frequently complained bitterly that although the press magnified all such incidents involving their opponents it remained silent on the difficulties faced by Social Crediters in hostile communities. One prominent Social Credit speaker has related that on several occasions he was warned that he would be beaten up if he spoke in certain towns, but he always carried out his assignments in spite of such threats. On the occasion of this speaker's visit to Ponoka, however, the insinuations were so ominous that he took the precaution of providing himself in advance with a bodyguard of stalwart young Social Crediters. In its report of this meeting, the movement's official newspaper included the following statement: "There is no truth to the rumor that the speaker was accompanied by plainclothed policemen. A Social Credit speaker always has a bodyguard, it is true, but in every case this consists of at least seventy-five per cent of his audience wherever he goes."[17] Another eminent Social Credit speaker has related that on one occasion

[14]Cf. *Edmonton Journal*, August 16, 1935.
[15]*Ibid.*
[16]Calgary *Albertan*, August 19, 1935.
[17]*A.S.C.C.*, April 12, 1935.

he had to fight his way out of a threatening circle of miners who had gathered to break up his meeting.[18]

The interviews also indicate much more adequately than do press reports the extent to which the Social Credit movement split rural communities. Farmers in Alberta claim that, by reason of the daily requirements of living, they are much more involved in the community than urban people. On this account, as a farmer in the Lloydminster area has put it, "The actual division of the people in cities and small towns into two hostile camps was not felt nearly as acutely as in the farming districts." "In rural communities," he concluded, "the personal differences created by the Social Credit campaign were nothing short of tragic."

The publisher of a metropolitan newspaper has related that for years he had been on friendly terms with the farmers in an area where he went duck-hunting annually. But in the autumn of 1935, following his newspaper's strenuous campaign against Aberhart, not one of these farmers, who had all gone Social Credit, would speak to him!

The cleavage became so great in farming communities that the customary courtesies of rural folk were often suspended. "If you were a U.F.A. man," a farmer in southern Alberta has related, "and your car was broken down on the road, a Social Crediter who came along would not help you."

People who supported Social Credit would sit on one side in a rural church and those who remained loyal to the U.F.A. would sit on the other side. Supporters of the one cause would scarcely speak to supporters of the other as they stood around outside after church. A farmer in the Vermilion area has related: "Social Credit ideas and actions were so abhorrent to me that I couldn't sit in the same church as a prominent Social Crediter and remain in a Christian frame of mind. So I told our minister that I could no longer attend the services." It is said that in a church in east-central Alberta, the advent of Social Credit created such strong divisions of opinion that many people left the church and have never returned to it. "Social Crediters," said a farmer, a member of this church, "couldn't understand why everybody couldn't accept Social Credit. They were extremely intolerant of their opponents." Another farmer has related that in a village in central Alberta the Social Crediters wanted "to superimpose the religious theories of the Prophetic Bible Institute, as well as Social Credit, upon all the regular churches." "This," he said, "created quite a lot of hard feeling in our community."

Hostility between the two factions reached such a pitch that farmers who had been close friends since pioneer days now found that they

[18]See chapter VII, p. 210.

could no longer visit one another. Neighbours who had spent many happy evenings together exchanging gossip or listening to the radio might never actually quarrel, but henceforth a cold politeness existed between them. "A friendship between a U.F.A. man and a Social Crediter," said a farmer in the Edmonton area, "simply could not be continued."

It is related that in a certain rural community all the farmers, with one exception, joined the Social Credit movement. The exception, a long-time resident of the province, remained loyal to the U.F.A. These farmers had formerly all talked and laughed together, but the Social Crediters now refused even to speak to the loyal U.F.A. supporter. He felt so lonely and utterly out of things in his community, and the silent hostility of his neighbours was so unbearable, that he decided to leave Alberta.

In various rural communities throughout the province much bitterness was also occasioned over efforts made by Social Crediters, including many who had formerly been members of U.F.A. locals, to acquire U.F.A. property, the title to which was held by the locals. Struggles over the right to such properties naturally increased the division between the two factions and led to unprecedented quarrelling, and even to fighting in some instances, in the communities concerned. The U.F.A. leaders, who were convinced that farmers who became Social Crediters had not previously been aware of social and economic problems, naturally resisted to the utmost every attempt of their erstwhile followers to secure titles to U.F.A. property.

During interviews, U.F.A. leaders were usually prepared to admit that their movement had, to a certain extent, split town and country. But they also insisted that such a split already existed under the Liberal régime from 1905 to 1921, a period during which a government composed essentially of lawyers and business men from cities or towns had been oblivious to the class interests of farmers. "It is true," said one of the outstanding U.F.A. leaders, "that our movement did not succeed in perfecting democracy in Alberta. But, viewed in historical perspective, the Social Credit movement was the most divisive thing that ever came into this province. It split the Alberta community wide open."

During the summer of 1935, "the Alberta community shook and trembled," as a farm leader in central Alberta has put it, "under the terrible impact of Social Credit and anti–Social Credit propaganda." The unity of that community, if not permanently shattered, was so seriously impaired that over two decades later cleavages still existed, the heritage of the strategy and tactics of the Social Credit movement.

The massive strength of the Social Credit organization was not based, however, upon Aberhart's gift of dramatizing the movement nor upon the creation of long-enduring tensions within the Alberta community. Of much greater significance were the quiet daily activities of the groups. Participation in the life of the groups was the elementary source of the satisfaction that most people obtained from the movement. The effect of group activity upon the people seems to have been almost hypnotic: they forgot their sorrows, their resentments, their selfish interests; they experienced new hope, new concern for others, a release of life. To many, their work with the groups was the most wonderful and unforgettable period of their lives. On the purely organizational side, the groups provided the Social Credit movement with a nucleus of dynamic supporters in almost every city block or rural district. Indeed, in later years Aberhart often said that the groups won the election of 1935.

CHAPTER TEN

The Struggle for Power

To SOCIAL CREDITERS the provincial election of 1935 was a glorious episode in a glorious movement. To the leaders of the U.F.A. it was a demoralizing ordeal from which they were never fully to recover. To Liberals and Conservatives it was an exhibition of mass hysteria unparalleled in the history of democracy. The Social Crediters nominated 63 candidates, one for each seat in the legislature. The U.F.A. nominated 45, the Liberals 61, and the Conservatives 39. Other candidates included 12 nominees of the Alberta branch of the Canadian Labour party, 8 Independents, 9 Communists, and 1 Single Taxer. There was also 1 C.C.F. candidate, whose appearance indicated a certain dissension within the U.F.A. ranks: in affiliating with the C.C.F., the U.F.A. was supposed to retain its autonomy and identity in the provincial sphere. For all parties there was a total of 239 candidates, a larger number than in any previous election.

Whatever interpretation may be offered, the central figure in the events of that fateful campaign was William Aberhart. In his struggle for power he gave full value to the populace. His colourful techniques stirred the imagination of an electorate satiated with stereotyped politics. Even the journalists found it difficult to exaggerate the three-ring extravaganza he staged: religion, politics, and second-rate vaudeville with a dash of horse-racing.

The campaign opened on July 6 with what was extensively advertised as a "Big Northern Alberta Social Credit Picnic," held at the Exhibition Grounds in Edmonton. Scattered about the sawdust walk in front of the grandstand, which was crowded by mid-afternoon, were numerous housie-housie and ring-toss games, hot-dog stands, and soft-drink booths. Signs were displayed everywhere, urging all to boost Social Credit, and hundreds of attendants displayed Social Credit ribbons. Especially prominent were numerous prospective candidates, but some of Edmonton's leading citizens could also be seen wearing bands about their hats, reading "Alberta Needs Social Credit," or "Aberhart and Social Credit."

A programme of sports, platform attractions, children's races, and

THE STRUGGLE FOR POWER

carnival features filled the afternoon. Then the band struck up. To the strains of "Tell Me the Old, Old Story," Aberhart gave a spiritual invocation and was presented with an illuminated address of welcome. Groups of children from a dancing school provided an exhibition of minuets, waltzes, military dances, toe ballets in coloured costumes, tap dances, and acrobatic numbers. Then a none too good baritone wailed out "Old Man River."

Finally, the main act took place. This was a comedy horse-race between the four political parties contesting the election, in which Aberhart himself took over the loudspeakers. Flailing his arms, he related the progress of "Social Credit," the horse which started out badly but came in on the stretch to the delight of the spectators. The Liberal horse came second, and the Conservative placed third, but the U.F.A. horse was so far in the rear that it was marked "also ran." Then everybody sang "What a Friend We Have in Jesus."

The programme concluded with one of Aberhart's greatest oratorical efforts. With tears in his eyes, he described the pitiable conditions into which the depression had plunged hundreds of thousands of people in Alberta. He promised that a Social Credit government could end all this by giving every adult in the province a monthly dividend of $25. "You remain in the depression," he declared, "because of a shortage of purchasing power, imposed by the banking system. Social Credit offers you the remedy. If you have not suffered enough, it is your God-given right to suffer more. But if you wish to elect your own representatives to implement the remedy, this is your only way out." In closing, Aberhart graphically described the struggle of a deep-sea diver with a devil-fish, and compared this struggle to Alberta's terrific struggle with the money octopus. "We still have one hand free," he roared, "with which to strike—to mark our ballot on election day. Let us strike then with all our might at this hideous monster that is sucking the very life blood from our people!"[1]

Thunderous and prolonged applause from ten thousand picnickers assured him that the people were with him in the fight. Hundreds in the audience wept as the meeting closed with "O God Our Help in Ages Past."

As the election campaign developed, and mass meeting followed mass meeting, the wild enthusiasm for Social Credit and the fanatical belief in Aberhart as the saviour of Alberta reached unprecedented proportions. Unable to gain admission to the packed halls of towns and

[1]*Edmonton Journal*, July 8, 1935; *A.S.C.C.*, July 12, 1935.

villages, cheering crowds surged in the streets to catch a glimpse of Aberhart as he rode by. Through it all, Social Crediters continued to insist that their activities were purely religious and educational and not, in any sense, political.

The use of the Bible Institute as the headquarters of the Social Credit campaign gave a certain plausibility to their contention that they were participating in the election as a non-partisan crusade. Although it had been established for religious purposes, Aberhart used the Institute's facilities as freely during the struggle for power as if it had been a political club. From its pulpit he gave lengthy radio broadcasts, constantly urging the election of Social Credit candidates. Its halls and offices were used for training speakers as well as for preparing pamphlets, bulletins, and press releases. It was the mailing centre for sending out campaign literature, directions for organizing, and instructions to study groups. To it came requests for speakers and from it scores of speakers were sent out. To it the candidates reported their activities and from it received advice on strategy and tactics.

During the election campaign the Institute served as a rallying centre for study groups from far and near. Every Sunday afternoon it was host to groups whose members might have journeyed a hundred miles or more to attend its services. Through this device, devotees who had previously only heard Aberhart broadcasting from the Institute were given an opportunity of seeing him in person.

Visits of groups to the Sunday afternoon services were always accompanied by considerable publicity. An excursion to the Institute by groups from Ponoka illustrates the kind of ballyhoo that was promoted during the summer of 1935. To the people of Ponoka this expedition was the outstanding event of the election campaign.

About 9 A.M. on Sunday, July 7, some 300 persons boarded a special train at Ponoka. On the way to Calgary they were joined by over 700 others from such towns as Lacombe, Red Deer, Innisfail, and Olds. On reaching Calgary the pilgrims were given an enthusiastic reception as they marched from the railway station to the Bible Institute, headed by the Ponoka brass band, which was augmented by members of the Wetaskiwin band.

At the Institute they were welcomed effusively by Aberhart, who had provided a Welsh male choir in their honour. On such occasions, the members of visiting groups always sat together in one section of the auditorium. During the introductory part of the service, Aberhart would announce that members of such-and-such a group were present, and its members would then be asked to stand. Each group in turn would be vigorously applauded. On the afternoon of the visit of the Ponoka groups, Mrs. W. W. Rogers (who was subsequently named as their Social Credit candidate) was called to the platform and presented with a wrist watch, the gift of friends in her constituency, by the Reverend Mr. Cantlon. The visitors, electrified by Aberhart's address, returned that night to their home towns vowing that when the election was held "there would be nothing to it."[2]

In what kind of service did the groups from Ponoka and other provincial towns participate during such visits? Apart from the sense of urgency introduced by the election campaign, the pattern of Aberhart's Sunday afternoon meetings had become familiar to hundreds of thousands of radio listeners during the previous year. Those present at the Institute, however, as distinguished from the radio audience, were stimulated not only by Aberhart's voice, but also by his physical appearance and gestures, as well as by the behaviour of the crowd. To the casual listener, the programme of the service might seem chaotic. Actually it was formalized, and followed the same order week after week. Following the welcoming of visiting groups, Social Credit meetings for the coming week were announced, a task often taking fifteen minutes for even a partial list. Then the congregation sang a hymn, usually the Social Credit theme song. Several minutes were devoted to reading the names of groups and individuals whose contributions were making the broadcasts possible. A fervent plea for more and larger contributions was always entered. Aberhart then dealt with letters he had received during the week and replied to hostile criticism that had appeared in newspapers or on the radio. During this part of the service he was always the consummate actor. He never failed to appear deeply hurt or to express righteous indignation over the methods that were being used to discredit him and the movement. The more bitter or unjust the criticisms of his political opponents became, the more he welcomed them, for they provided him with new opportunities for stating his own position and for carrying the war into the enemy's camp. As he refuted the "false charges" of newspapers and radio broadcasters ("the tools of the money interests"), his audience never failed to enjoy, and applaud vigorously, his biting sarcasm. He was perhaps at his best when holding critics of the movement up to merciless ridicule.[3]

Apart from criticisms of his offer of a $25 dividend, the most relentless attacks on Aberhart were concerned with his mixture of politics and

[2]This expedition to the Bible Institute is described in the weekly *Ponoka Herald*, July 11, 1935.
[3]Cf. U.F.A. File of Aberhart broadcasts.

religion. His opponents in the election professed to be outraged at the sight of the Social Credit party, supposedly religious, using Sunday services, intermixed with prayers, songs, and political propaganda, trying to climb to power through religion. Social Crediters defended themselves by saying that it is right to do right on the Sabbath Day. But why could not this reason be applied to every political party, because all parties claimed that their object in winning, or in retaining, power was to bring health, happiness, and contentment to the people. A writer in the Calgary *Albertan,* a newspaper not unfavourable to the Social Credit cause, expresses the bitter attitudes of those who opposed the mixture of politics and religion at the Bible Institute:

One fears that history will repeat itself, as parties or individuals in the past who have tried to grasp power through religion have frequently betrayed both God and man. The Social Credit party has already betrayed God, by claiming what they advocated is the Divine Will, and insisting that their opponents are dominated by unworthy motives or are under the thumbs of heartless intriguers and Money Grabbers.

I ask when has any other aggregation seeking power offered such bribes as these.

1. Every bona fide citizen is offered $25.00 per month, if he helps to establish Social Credit, all as a gift.

2. He is further told that they could as easily pay $75 or $100.00 per month, were they not afraid to disrupt the present business operations.

3. He is guaranteed from $10.00 to $20.00 monthly for each of his children over 16 years of age.

4. He is told that he will be allowed loans free of interest for production purposes.

The citizens of this province are due to get a great awakening, and the sad part of it is that the jolt will come from the very people who claim to be leading them in the name of God.

When the awakening comes, as it will surely come, if the Social Crediters reach power, then religion and honor will receive a blow the like of which they have not had for many a day.

Imagine a political organization asking that the members reveal their intimate desires and requests from Almighty God, to the political headquarters for consideration and recommendation, and when such is done, to have instructions issued over the radio, to not be so humble in their requests nor so wavering in informing the Almighty what should be done in Alberta at the present time.

Language fails one in condemning such procedure.[4]

Far from denigrating the Social Credit movement, such outbursts provided Aberhart and his followers with more and better political propaganda. They were passionately convinced that it was a Christian's

[4]Calgary *Albertan,* July 15, 1935.

obligation to give the people moral direction in reforming the social and economic system. As they put it, "You cannot get to Heaven with a Bible in one hand and a foreclosure mortgage of your neighbour's house in the other." Unless the people turned to God, they argued, there could be no improvement in economic conditions. God, and God alone, they insisted, had the basic solution of the problem of "poverty in the midst of plenty." Until the people of Alberta elected a government that would forget the worship of Mammon, they would continue to suffer as they were doing. The sooner the people got down on their knees and asked for God's guidance, the sooner He would deliver them from misery and despair. The attitudes of thousands of Albertans to whom Aberhart appeared as a Man of God have been stated by one of his ardent disciples:

There are those who ridicule Mr. Aberhart on his fervent religious principles, but then there are others who not only know, but realize that it is those religious principles that make the man worthwhile. They know that his fight for Social Credit is backed by his faith in Almighty God and with such a backing he cannot fail. Let the scoffers rave on, let them ridicule, but let the majority pray for more men like Aberhart who can place God first in his every endeavour to help and save the people of the country from desolation, despair, and poverty.[5]

Criticism of the use of the Bible Institute as headquarters of the movement became especially intense during the month preceding the election. Late in July, a spokesman for the Conservatives stated, in a radio address, that unless Aberhart was put in his place and his party defeated in the coming election "there was a possibility of religious persecution in Alberta." The same speaker bitterly attacked the Social Credit leader for "hiding in the pulpit," and declared that any religious person who would use his pulpit to further his own political interests was guilty of blasphemy. He had, he said, "no use for anyone who posed as a 'Man of God' for political purposes, and who attacked the private character of opponents from the pulpit as did Mr. Aberhart."[6] A few days later, a Liberal speaker derided the Social Credit party as an "Aberhart Prize Prayer Political Party."

To such attacks, and they were many, Aberhart replied by making a passionate plea for more prayer, as is well illustrated from the report of his address at the Bible Institute on Sunday, July 21:

He felt probably there was no greater point of interest in connection with the common welfare of the people than to begin with prayer. The crisis was

[5]*A.S.C.C.*, July 12, 1935.
[6]Calgary *Albertan*, July 26, 1935.

fast approaching, he said, declaring that if the people of the Province are depending alone on the cause, or its leader, they were doomed to disappointment, and after the election it would be too late. I want the people to be ready to offer a prayer, he said. "O God help the common people to find a remedy, and not to be deluded," were the words he suggested as a prayer acceptable to the cause. "If the people refused to seek God's help," Mr. Aberhart said, "How else could they get the victory." The people who said, "it can't be done," might be right, if Social Crediters refused to ask God's aid. "Your strength is not in your leader," he said, "but in your God; one person had suggested the words, "If Social Credit is good for us, please give it to us," but the Social Credit leader was of the opinion that as a prayer it was too wavering. Mr. Aberhart made reference to a radio address given by a Conservative speaker from Calgary. The speaker he stated had said that he, Mr. Aberhart, had claimed to be a Moses, or a Daniel, and in doing so had jeered about it. "It is rather strange what some people will do for a little filthy lucre," he said, denying he had ever laid claim to being a Moses, a Daniel, or anyone else.[7]

Although the pulpit of the Bible Institute resounded with appeals for God's help, Social Crediters welcomed the support of such clergy as they could muster to their cause in institutional churches. Thus the sympathetic attitude to Social Credit of the Reverend G. Harrison Vilett, who had opened the historic McDougall United Church for Aberhart's earliest rallies in Edmonton was widely publicized. Constant use was made also of the name and prestige of Dr. Hewlett Johnson, Dean of Canterbury, at that time an ardent writer of Social Credit pamphlets which Albertans were urgently advised to read.

Aberhart's most effective answer to those who criticized his mixture of religion and politics lay in his insistent denial that the Social Credit movement had become a political party. Critics of the use of the Bible Institute as headquarters of the Social Credit party thus found themselves repudiated by the majority of the people, who accepted Aberhart's interpretation of the Social Credit movement as a religious and educational enterprise. Aberhart's denial carried conviction simply because the movement had become, by the summer of 1935, an overwhelming crusade against both the U.F.A. and the old-line parties of Alberta.

But while it was plausible for the leader of a social movement to deny that he had entered politics, no such strategy was possible for the leaders of these other parties. The three parties were forced, by virtue of their past traditions, to conduct their election campaigns along orthodox lines. Each of them announced a platform,[8] sponsored radio broadcasts, ad-

---

[7]*A.S.C.C.*, July 26, 1935.

[8]See Appendix II for an outline of the platforms and attitudes of the U.F.A., Liberal, and Conservative parties.

vertised extensively in the newspapers, and arranged political meetings throughout the province. None of them realized the true nature of the Social Credit movement, and all underestimated its political strength. As the election approached, however, the older parties were forced to take notice of the new party. With the exception of the Conservatives, they adopted the tactics of offering concessions to Douglas Social Credit. The U.F.A. and Conservatives launched violent personal attacks on Aberhart; but the Liberals, who wanted to make sure of garnering every vote possible, sought to drain off wavering Social Crediters by antagonizing him as little as possible.

Although Aberhart denied repeatedly that he was in politics, the decision of the Social Credit conventions to contest the election had been accompanied, as we have seen, by a platform dealing with the problems of Alberta in a general way. Social Crediters had been flooding the province with leaflets, broadcasts, and speeches for over two years. To the literature already in circulation was now added Aberhart's famous *Social Credit Manual*, popularly called the "Blue Manual," owing to the colour of its cover.[9]

The Blue Manual, some 60,000 copies of which were sold for twenty-five cents each at election meetings, was a booklet of sixty-four pages sub-titled "Social Credit as applied to the Province of Alberta." It made no mention of Douglas. Over half of its pages were completely filled with advertisements by various merchants in Calgary, Edmonton, Medicine Hat, and Lethbridge. The other half contained an outline of Aberhart's interpretation of Social Credit, followed by sixty "puzzling questions" and answers.

During the campaign, Aberhart found it easy to fend off constant criticisms of the material in the pamphlet by pointing to its opening sentence, "This is not a Detailed Plan for the Province of Alberta." Such a plan could only be prepared

when the operation of its establishment is about ready to begin and the facts and figures are all well-known. Our people must not be confused in this matter. A man may have in mind the general outline of the character of the house he intends to build. He may know the number of rooms that he intends to have and their relation and connection one with the other, but he does not ask the architect to draw the plan until he knows the size of the lot, the position in which the house will be placed, the materials available, and so forth. So it is with a detailed plan for Social Credit in the Province of Alberta. It is surely evident that the Plan for Scotland, for example, will not do for Alberta. The circumstances, the resources, and the people are so different.[10]

[9]See Appendix III for an outline of this Manual.
[10]*Social Credit Manual*, p. 1.

The sixty questions and answers which followed Aberhart's formal exposition of Social Credit doctrine (as he interpreted it) were mostly designed to enable him to relate his basic principles to the Alberta scene or to refute charges of his political opponents. One of these answers, especially, was aimed at his U.F.A. and Conservative critics who were insisting that an infinite time would be required to introduce Social Credit. To question 55, "How long would it take you to introduce Social Credit into the Province of Alberta?" Aberhart replied: "That is a difficult question to answer with precision. Much information will need to be gathered. Expert investigation will have to be made. I would judge that fifteen or eighteen months might be required."

Although the only new point presented in the Blue Manual was the fifteen to eighteen month time estimate, it did contain a much more systematic exposition of Aberhart's doctrines regarding the cultural heritage, basic dividends, non-negotiable certificates, and the unearned increment than he had hitherto attempted. During the campaign it became a constant reference for charges and counter-charges in radio broadcasts, speeches at mass-meetings, and newspaper comment. There must have been few adults in Alberta who did not read at least a part of it at some time or another during the election campaign. Its doctrines provided the basis for the speeches of Social Credit candidates. Their political enemies claimed that most of these candidates knew no Social Credit save the Blue Manual.

Such a claim was, of course, an exaggeration. In addition to the popular Blue Manual, Social Crediters circulated more widely during the election campaign the extensive series of coloured leaflets and white pamphlets that had been used in study groups during the previous two-and-a-half years.[11]

One new and effective white pamphlet, however, was added to the old list during the election campaign. Entitled "What Would Social Credit Do for Us?" this pamphlet opened with a cartoon, "No More Wolves at the Door." Here the father of a family of three was depicted smiling and holding a gun labelled "Douglas System." His wife and two older children were resplendent in new fur coats. In reply to his wife's query, "How do you like our new winter furs, Horace?" her husband replies "Fine an' dandy! And to think they came from the wolves that used to howl at our door. Thanks to the old Trusty." Then the son replies, "An' we're getting lots to eat. Ain't we Paw?"

[11]This material, including the controversial white pamphlet, *The B.N.A. Act and Social Credit*, has already been discussed in chapters III and IV in connection with the development of the movement's strategy and tactics.

Seven advantages of Social Credit were then outlined in glowing terms. It was maintained that Social Credit would (1) drive away the two vultures, FEAR and WORRY; (2) maintain individual enterprise and restore a high morale to Alberta's citizens; (3) immediately improve the standard of living and create a better class of citizenship; (4) solve the problem of mortgages and high interest charges, thus retaining many farms and homes for the present owners; (5) provide a better opportunity for the youth of the province; (6) protect the honest producer from loss by fall in prices or failure of crops; (7) replace the present medium of exchange with a sound economic system based on the issue of non-negotiable certificates. Among educated people this pamphlet, and more especially the cartoon with which it opened, provoked sarcasm or ridicule. But to thousands of Aberhart's mass following it was one more proof of his superior understanding of the needs of the people of Alberta. Translated into German, it found eager acceptance among a group whose members were already strongly predisposed to him.[12]

Social Credit pamphlets played an important role in the election of 1935. But of course they could not compare in popular appeal with radio broadcasts or mass meetings. To many Albertans, the most spectacular feature of the campaign was the long-drawn-out radio debate between Aberhart and Priestley, the vice-president of and principal broadcaster for the U.F.A. Begun in February, this duel was carried on relentlessly until the eve of the election. On various occasions another speaker might substitute for one of the major proponents of the Social Credit or U.F.A. causes, but the return of Aberhart or Priestley to the contest would always be eagerly awaited by the public.

In the popular imagination, Priestley was considered the principal bulwark of the farmers' government against the tumultuous social movement threatening to engulf it. The premier, as we have already intimated, was no match for the more colourful Aberhart; the ex-premier's reputation had been so shaken by the court action that the farmers were unable to reap the advantages of his brilliant talents. The Cabinet ministers, also suffering from the impact of the scandals, even though personally innocent, were being forced to fight for their political lives in their own constituencies. The president of the U.F.A., Robert Gardiner, was so heavily involved in the federal C.C.F. movement that he seems to have had neither the time nor the inclination to give much support to the faltering government of Alberta. It fell to the lot of Norman F. Priestley to lead the attack on the Social Credit movement.

Priestley was perhaps better equipped for this difficult task than any

[12]Cf. chapter IX, p. 277.

other major leader of the U.F.A. He had formerly been a clergyman of the United Church of Canada; his personal reputation and motives were beyond suspicion; he had long been admired as a man of the highest courage and integrity; he possessed great intellectual gifts. His training in the liberal theology encouraged by his church had long before made him fully aware of the nature of Aberhart's prophetic religion, though not of the deeper sources of its psychological appeal to the people of Alberta. Long experience in the U.F.A. Co-operative had given him a knowledge of economic realities which admirably supplemented his university training in the social sciences. He entered the radio duel with energy and zeal, for he had long been disturbed by the presence of Douglasites within the U.F.A. movement itself. Never attracted to Social Credit theory himself, he knew every twist and turn in Douglas's writings; but even such an extensive knowledge did not prevent him being caught off guard occasionally by the novelties of doctrine introduced by Aberhart. Priestley had realized, as early as the summer of 1934, the explosive possibilities of the rising Social Credit movement. His luminous mind now enabled him to see more clearly than any other of Aberhart's major opponents that the real challenger of the U.F.A. in the election was the Social Credit, rather than the Liberal, party.

The celebrated "Man from Mars" series of broadcasts had given place, early in February, to a new approach. Henceforth, instead of a cast of characters, Aberhart himself (with occasional substitutes such as Manning or Fred Anderson) was generally the only participant. This departure was necessary, he explained, owing to the need for dealing at length with specific points of doctrine and of refuting specific charges of opponents. In addition, the new scripts were certainly much easier to write, as well as to produce. It was also undeniable that Aberhart's radio appeal far exceeded that of any or all of his lieutenants. Ten years of religious broadcasting had made him familiar with every technique of radio propaganda.

Following their January convention, the officials at the U.F.A. headquarters in Calgary had begun systematically to monitor and record Aberhart's Sunday afternoon and mid-week broadcasts. The texts of these were transcribed and distributed in mimeographed form to all U.F.A. speakers and electoral candidates. It became Priestley's task, in weekly broadcasts, to analyse and refute Aberhart's radio expositions of Social Credit doctrine, as well as to present the positive case for the U.F.A. It was unfortunate for the farmers' cause that, from the beginning, Priestley found himself on the defensive. He was rarely able to seize the initiative from the more aggressive Aberhart. Perhaps it could not have been otherwise with the tide running so strongly in favour of the Social Credit movement.

For seven months Priestley argued brilliantly and tirelessly against what he, as well as the other U.F.A. leaders, considered an utterly irrational approach to economics, politics, and religion. But there can be little doubt that his clear and forceful broadcasts failed to appeal to the economically dispossessed people of Alberta. The vice-president of the U.F.A. was certainly out-debated on the air by Aberhart. Nevertheless, if he lost the great radio debate, and with it the fateful election of 1935, Priestley won the enduring respect and admiration of all who remained loyal to the political cause of the U.F.A. In fighting a mass movement, his principal weakness (if it may justly be called a weakness) was his reliance on rational arguments in the face of Aberhart's highly charged emotional appeals. The incisive logic of the great spokesman of the U.F.A. withered before the sarcasm and ridicule of the prophet of the new social movement. By the summer of 1935 it was evident that the U.F.A. leaders, Priestley included, were almost completely out of touch with the mass of the people. But no matter how hopeless the case for the government might become, Priestley's broadcasts never reflected the U.F.A.'s final mood of desperation. If he felt personally frustrated in the face of the people's response to Aberhart, he gave the U.F.A. cause heroic leadership to the bitter end. His own supporters were convinced that his conduct in a hostile world illustrated, in unusual degree, the ultimate U.F.A. belief in the dignity of reason and democracy. If he failed in the struggle with the Social Credit movement, they would always believe that no one else could have succeeded.

If Priestley was a hero in the eyes of the supporters of the U.F.A., he was the arch-villain in those of Social Crediters in their struggle for power. Throughout his long debate with Aberhart, he was faced with the ever-increasing hostility of the populace. Aberhart himself fanned this hostility by mocking attacks on Priestley, and suggested that if the people did not want to listen to U.F.A. radio speakers, they didn't have to—they could escape Priestley's nonsense by merely turning off the dial!

The hostility of the people to Priestley, as well as to the government cause generally, was manifested in hundreds of letters that poured into the U.F.A. headquarters from all over Alberta. Most of these were signed, but the more vindictive were frequently anonymous. The writers invariably emphasized that the day of the farmers' government was over; Priestley was therefore fighting for a cause that was hopelessly lost. The people of Alberta, the letters insisted over and over again, were now 90 to 95 per cent for Social Credit. Why didn't Priestley recognize this fact and get behind the Social Credit movement instead of knocking it every week on the radio? Almost all the letters were discourteous. The meanness and passion expressed in a number of them are unbelievable. Few of the writers were willing to attribute sincerity or good faith to Priestley (or indeed to anyone else) for criticizing Aberhart's Social Credit proposals, and many letters contained violent personal attacks on Priestley for daring to criticize a Man of God like Aberhart.[13] As the campaign drew to a close, Aberhart's supporters wrote and talked as if a war to the death existed between them and the vice-president of the U.F.A. Priestley himself was disturbed, not so much by the violent abuse heaped upon him by Social Crediters, but rather because so much of that abuse came from persons who had been lifelong supporters of the U.F.A. movement.

The U.F.A. maintained that Aberhart himself was largely responsible for the development of bitter hostility to their leaders during the campaign. He counter-attacked by complaining of the treatment he was receiving from his opponents; he talked vaguely and continually of "mud-slingers," "back-biters," and "slanderers." He played for sympathy by reading at nearly every broadcast a sheaf of letters from his supporters, who railed against the U.F.A. and expressed devotion to him. The U.F.A. replied that their speakers were confining themselves to a criticism of Aberhart's proposals, which was entirely legitimate, as he had entered politics. They had, they insisted, never indulged in personalities, nor had they ever attacked Aberhart personally, but a consideration of Aberhart's speeches and writings revealed that he was constantly making personal attacks on their leaders. A widely circulated pamphlet, issued by the Little Bow U.F.A. Constituency Association and entitled *Fallacies of Aberhart's Proposals*, contained a section on "slandering":

Let us now consider Mr. Aberhart's methods. Some of the names he has called the U.F.A. Government members directly or by implication, include the following: Grafters, crooks, scheming politicians, insincere office seekers. In the May 17 issue, Social Credit Chronicle, we find him calling them Hogs! He has also called them "henchmen of the financial interests," "Worshippers of the Golden Calf." He teaches his followers to believe that all who oppose Social Credit are in the pay of the financial interests.

On Sunday, March 24, he preached a sermon in which he attacked some unknown person whom he said was guilty of "fornication, graft and hypocrisy." It was obvious he was referring to Mr. Brownlee.

Mr. Aberhart said (May 3 Broadcast) "We're out to put Christianity into practice," and says that what he and his workers are doing is for love of their fellow men.

[13]These letters, which are on file at the head office of the U.F.A. Co-operative in Calgary, have been examined at some length.

YET he speaks of what is said in opposition to him as "the ravings of the henchmen of high finance." (May 10). In speaking of Mr. Brownlee, he says, "The only reason for his broadcasting activities at this time must be accepted as merely vote catching propaganda for the personal benefit of himself and his friends in office."

On May 12 he spoke of the "Splutterings, the ramblings, the prattlings and all the bologney of the men broadcasting nothing but destructive criticisms. I can take it all if you think I should do it. I can take no heed to it all for your sakes but I warn those fellows please don't stick your nose too close into my face. I declare most of you can't afford to have your past reputations dug up."

On April 9, Mr. Aberhart reached the climax of his vituperation when he said, "The principles of the old line politicians and their henchmen are like those of the man who betrayed the Christ."

Is it not possible for Mr. Aberhart to concede that men like Mr. Brownlee, members of the cabinet and private members of the U.F.A. may be quite sincere in their opposition? Does it HAVE TO FOLLOW that because they do not agree with Mr. Aberhart they are sold to the Evil one?

The integrity of their leaders had always been the source of one of the strongest appeals of the U.F.A. to the electorate. Aberhart's tactics aroused strong doubts in the minds of the people concerning that integrity. No one would listen to speakers who attempted to clear the reputations of government leaders: at mass meetings the people jeered at the U.F.A. and rallied to the Social Credit movement.

Apart from personal attacks on their leaders, nothing infuriated the U.F.A. speakers more than Aberhart's repeated allegations that they had hopelessly failed to understand Douglas's theories. Speaking of Brownlee, on April 28 Aberhart had said, ". . . judging by what has already been said by this broadcaster I question very much if he could tell if it was genuine Social Credit principles if he saw them."[14] The U.F.A. speakers retaliated by emphasizing fallacies in his interpretation of Social Credit. In support of their case, they referred to Douglas's aloofness to Aberhart during his two visits to Alberta, and quoted Douglas's letter to J. F. Lymburn, the Attorney General. Douglas, they insisted, had pointed out therein that Aberhart had mistakenly used such terms as "just price" and "unearned increment" as employed in orthodox Social Credit literature. Aberhart, and not themselves, they concluded, had failed to grasp some of the main principles of Social Credit. Aberhart replied that the Attorney General had suppressed part of Douglas's correspondence with the government. This accusation, which was prominently featured in the press, was hotly denied by Lymburn.

The U.F.A. then stressed the long acquaintance of their members, and

14U.F.A. File of Aberhart broadcasts, April 28, 1935.

especially their Members of Parliament, with Douglas's writings. Aberhart promptly denounced the U.F.A. Members of Parliament as socialists, and referred in scathing terms to the dissension within U.F.A. ranks owing to the farmers' affiliation with the federal C.C.F. party. This particular assault proved embarrassing to the U.F.A., as most of their Cabinet ministers were not favourably disposed to socialism. In reply, however, government speakers complained that Aberhart aroused sympathy by talking against the capitalistic system; yet his proposals did not even touch capitalism, for he insisted that they would not affect individual ownership or initiative, nor would they interfere with private business. It was grossly unfair for him, the U.F.A. protested, to use the terms, phraseology, and propaganda of the C.C.F. party in decrying capitalism and, at the same time, to belittle the work of the U.F.A. members at Ottawa and to hold both the C.C.F. and the U.F.A. up to ridicule in his radio addresses. But these arguments were no more effective than others advanced against Aberhart.

In their effort to expose the glaring inconsistencies in Aberhart's exposition of Social Credit, the U.F.A. published and distributed widely a systematic collection of statements he had made in recorded radio addresses, in articles published in the *Social Credit Chronicle*, and in the evidence given before the legislature in 1934 (referred to as the "Book of Evidence"). In compiling this material, U.F.A. workers and speakers tried to touch on the subjects that were being hotly debated during the election campaign, such as basic dividends, taxation, the nature of purchasing power, the just price, non-negotiable certificates, and Aberhart's relation to Douglas. The technique of discrediting Aberhart used by the U.F.A. may be best illustrated by reference to their treatment of the problem of the relation of basic dividends to taxation.

Aberhart and all his speakers, the U.F.A. pointed out, had insisted that basic dividends would simply come off the end of a fountain-pen, out of thin air, or that they were simply book-keeping entries in a ledger. Some of his speakers had also made statements that $100 monthly could be paid as easily as $25:

And yet in the *Alberta Social Credit Chronicle*, May 3 issue, with regard to basic dividends, he says, "The state could not simply make these monthly credit entries each giving the citizen a claim on goods and services without providing for the ultimate recovery of the same."

In the same issue of May 3, he says, "The unearned increment is a levy imposed over and above the cost of production. . . ." "The unearned increment would be paid to the state through the producers."

These statements are all very contradictory. If it comes out of thin air, why does it have to be recovered? If it comes off the end of a fountain pen, why does he say it will come out of something he calls a levy on imports (which is really a straight consumer's tax)? If it is only a bookkeeping entry, why does he say it will be paid to the state through the producers, and at once be re-distributed in the form of basic dividends?"

He has said many times that he would take a levy on the production of wheat up to at least five cents a bushel. That he would make a levy on goods imported into the province, and Major Douglas says that Mr. Aberhart's proposals entail levying a "processing tax."

April 9 Broadcast—

Question: "If the world price of wheat is $1.00 per bushel and the just price 60 cents, what will the farmer receive?

Mr. Aberhart: "The farmer will receive his 60 cents first of all and then he will receive an additional amount, BUT NOT ALL THE PROFIT.

June 4 Broadcast—

Mr. Aberhart said: "If wheat were $1.00 a bushel and the just price 60 cents, the difference of 40 cents would be spread between the farmer and the government."

Broadcast June 14, he repeats this statement and suggests 50 per cent of the difference to the government, but says that the state WOULD SELDOM REQUIRE MORE THAN TEN OR FIFTEEN CENTS per bushel.

Yet in spite of all this we find the following:

April 2 Broadcast—"No, the farmer is not taxed on his wheat."

April 9 Broadcast—"The truth of the matter is the farmer will not be taxed."

AGAIN—If it comes off the end of a fountain pen, why does it have to come out of the farmer's wheat? Or out of a consumer's tax which he calls an import levy?

All these statements cannot be true, for that is physically impossible. What does he mean, taxes or no taxes? WHAT IS IT? INK OR TAXES?

Where, the U.F.A. persisted, would Aberhart get the money to pay the basic dividends? In his broadcast on May 5 he had said:

The other day I heard $250,000 was sent into Alberta to see that Social Credit was not passed. Do you think any man would put $250,000 into Alberta unless he's going to get it back? Ah, they say Aberhart is going to tax you. And I tell you I'm not going to tax you. I don't believe in it. Taxes must be removed from the backs of the people—I say to you it's taken out of the price spreads—You're not taxed any more. . . ."

Which of all this maze of contradictions, the U.F.A. asked the people, was the truth? In his broadcast on June 4, Aberhart had said: "We pointed out that Social Credit was not a system of taxation in any form. In no case was the purchasing power of the consumer reduced in any way by its operation. . . . As a matter of fact they are not taxed at all."

Yet, in the May 3 issue of the *Social Credit Chronicle*, he had written: "We cannot give dividends without providing for ultimate recovery of the same. . . . The unearned increment would be paid to the state THROUGH THE PRODUCERS. . . . The unearned increment is a levy imposed over and above the cost of production." These statements, the U.F.A. pointed out, contained absolute contradictions. Which did Aberhart mean—taxes or no taxes?

The attempt of the U.F.A. to discredit Aberhart, by directing attention as in this sample to contradictory statements in his speeches and writings, failed hopelessly. He replied periodically to charges of inconsistency by attacking the newspapers for misquoting him. U.F.A. leaders then announced that they had not used quotations from newspaper reports, but had confined themselves to material from recorded broadcasts or published articles: they offered to provide the people with free transcripts of Aberhart's broadcasts and invited them to read the report of the 1934 legislative investigation as well as the *Social Credit Chronicle*. All such appeals fell on deaf ears, for Aberhart speedily explained on the air that the U.F.A. had quoted him out of context. In calling attention to his so-called inconsistencies, the U.F.A. speakers were, he insisted, merely pecking away at something they didn't understand.[15] He had accurately sized up the attitude of the people to the U.F.A.: his mass following would not be deflected from its goal—the election of a Social Credit government.

The rally of the people to Aberhart's cause was especially apparent in the attendance at Social Credit meetings compared to those held by the U.F.A. and the Liberals, as well as in the number of meetings each party was able to hold. Social Crediters spoke to hundreds, while opposition speakers attracted tens. When the U.F.A. or the Liberals announced a meeting, Social Crediters announced a dozen. Scores of Aberhart's speakers toured the province, speaking twice a day at one-afternoon and one-night stands, so that scarcely a single populated area remained unvisited. These speakers were all self-supporting: they proudly announced that their expenses were paid by the nickels and dimes contributed at their meetings. One of the most astonishing features of the campaign was the number of adherents to the Social Credit movement who became its active political supporters. Never before in Alberta, not even in 1921, had a political campaign aroused so much support, and all of it on a voluntary basis.

The decline in the popular appeal of the U.F.A., noticeable at all levels during the campaign, was nowhere more apparent than at their

[15]*Ibid.*, July–August, 1935.

nomination meetings. In 1921, for example, over eighty delegates had been present at the convention in the Vermilion constituency which nominated Reid; in 1935, despite the fact that he held the premiership, his nominating convention attracted only fourteen delegates. The U.F.A. organization had obviously broken down at the grass-roots level. This break-down may be attributed in part to the idealism (based on Henry Wise Wood's philosophy) of the U.F.A. with respect to patronage and campaign funds, but the collapse of the U.F.A. political machine was ultimately due to the shattering impact of the Social Credit movement.

With a fine naïveté, the U.F.A. blamed Aberhart for their inability to attract people to their meetings. They complained bitterly that even during the winter he had begun "by suggestion" to tell his followers not to attend U.F.A. meetings. He had ordered them not to hold debates with speakers opposed to Social Credit, and had even once threatened to discipline those groups which persisted in debating with members of the U.F.A. In his broadcast on June 9, Aberhart virtually denied these charges, with the exception of the order not to debate. He defended this order by stating that the U.F.A. could not get crowds together and were proposing debates in order to attract people to listen to anti-Aberhart propaganda.

The U.F.A. also accused Aberhart of arousing much unfair antagonism to their speakers by misrepresentation. On March 24 he had said: "I am told that a hundred or two hundred trained speakers are going to flood this country against Social Credit and against religion before the election." He had repeated this allegation on March 26, when he said he had heard that "they" were going to import 100 to 150 public speakers to combat Social Credit. Although Aberhart had not specifically said that the government was going to send out these speakers, he had left this idea with the public. Mrs. W. W. Rogers had also made the same type of statement in Edmonton, inferring that the government proposed to bring in hired speakers from both the East and the West. The U.F.A. indignantly denied that the government had any hired speakers. But Aberhart had succeeded in convincing the people that, whereas Social Credit speakers were acting without payment from the purest of motives, the U.F.A. and Liberal speakers were vile hirelings of the money barons.

While the U.F.A. and Liberal speakers experienced ever-increasing difficulties in attracting sizable audiences, it was quite otherwise with Aberhart and his corps of orators. For a high school principal, the election could not have been called at a more propitious time. Released from his professional duties at the end of June, Aberhart, accompanied by Manning, toured the province for the third summer in succession,

Wherever he appeared, the roads leading to that place would be jammed with traffic all headed for the meeting place. The large audiences that always assembled would await his arrival with spontaneous expectancy. His appearance on the platform would be greeted with waves of thunderous applause. Even in small or remote villages like Sylvan Lake or Marwayne there was no relaxation of the heightening tempo of his campaign. The people who flocked to his meetings, invariably overcrowded, wanted a good show and they always got it. The great spellbinder never failed to lift his audiences to a state of hysterical enthusiasm.

His rallies began impressively with the theme song, "O God Our Help in Ages Past." Then, after an introduction, usually by the local candidate, Aberhart would begin to speak. He caught the attention of his audience at once and held it for the next hour-and-a-half. To his mass following, he was describing, in the simple language of the schoolteacher, with elementary illustrations, how it should be possible for them to feed, clothe, and shelter themselves, at least with the bare necessities of life. After expounding the significant points of his religious-economic doctrine, he would launch his culminating appeal for action to end Alberta's needless state of poverty in an age of plenty. Hard-bitten farmers might burst into tears and women might swoon as Aberhart's eloquence soared to its climax, but his followers would always vehemently deny his opponents' oft-repeated charges that he aroused mob passion, that he descended to vituperation, that he appealed to religious or class prejudice.[16] He might lash the old-line parties with sarcasm for their ineptitude in the face of the depression, but Social Crediters would also deny that their leader was making disrespectful references to responsible individuals in public life. They would admit, however, that behind the calm, orderly exposition (as they saw it) of the high school master with an attentive class, there was a tremendous reserve of impassioned appeal. They maintained that he had made the true leader's conquest of himself in seldom allowing "the deeply burning fire of the crusader for social justice" to blaze up. "No one," a passionate admirer of his speeches has said, "with ears to hear could listen to this new Canadian statesman without being made aware of the latent dynamic urge within him—it was the urge of spiritual leadership."

Many journalists, on the other hand, formed quite a different im-

---

[16]The file of the *Alberta Social Credit Chronicle* for July–August, 1935, contains numerous accounts of Aberhart's mass meetings during the election campaign. Cf. also the *Calgary Herald*, *Edmonton Journal*, and *Edmonton Bulletin* during the same period.

pression of Aberhart's speeches during the struggle for power. They felt that, even when sitting down, he was the most impressive citizen they had seen on any platform. They admitted that, once he rose to speak, the audience was his until he chose to stop talking. But his strength, to them, lay simply in the fact that he was bringing good news: he told the people what they wanted to hear, that heaven and earth were to be had for the asking, and he did it like a prophet receiving a revelation from heaven. He was equipped for his role of the new Elijah by nature and experience: he had a loud voice, a noble brow, and a massive frame: he was a practised pedagogue and preacher. They felt, however, that he was "as sentimental as a Mammy song and as sincere as a boy asking for jam." They did not doubt that he really believed what he said, or that everything would be wonderful if he were right.

But, as they followed him around the province on his third summer tour, most newspapermen became convinced that on the intellectual side he was more hopeless than any other party leader they had ever heard. He was almost wholly emotional and hardly capable of reflective thought. Those who had read the Blue Manual were quite certain that he neither understood Douglas's theories nor had the foggiest idea of how he was going to work out his own brand of Social Credit. "The evidence for this opinion," one informed reporter has stated, "was Aberhart's string of fallacies and sophistries. His speech was especially rich in false analogies, the sure symptom of bad reasoning. He would tell a story or a parable, consider the point made, and move on to another. This, in fact, was his characteristic method of arguing, but his analogy was sour every time."

As the turbulent campaign drew to a close, journalists became especially irritated when Aberhart came to that part of his speech where he compared the bloodstream with the flow of credit. "People ask where the money is coming from to supply $120,000,000 worth of goods a year to the people of Alberta," Aberhart would boom. "That's a very important question. The heart pumps so many ounces of blood in a minute and so many gallons a month. Where is all the blood coming from?" This reasoning was a tremendous success with the audience, and journalists rarely got a hearing if they tried to point out the fallacy of the bloodstream analogy. Confronted with such criticism, Social Crediters would imitate the master and prove the theory once more by twirling their forearms around one another in concentric circles and describing the circulation of the blood.

More jocular devotees of Aberhart, when confronted by questioning reporters at political meetings, would use the story of the keg of beer and the ten-cent piece to illustrate the flow of credit through the blood-stream of the state:

Pat and Mike were rival saloon keepers in a dried out prairie town, now deserted. It was a hot day, and the two saloon keepers sat in their respective doorways waiting for custom that never came. Pat's stock-in-trade consisted of a keg of beer and a ten-cent piece. Mike's stock consisted of a keg of beer and a thirst.

Called Mike, "Say Pat, I'd like a drink this fine day."

"Why don't you help yourself?" replied Pat.

"It's my stock-in-trade and I can't afford to treat myself," Mike argued.

Whereupon Pat thought of a way out. He crossed over to Mike's saloon, thrust his dime on the counter, and called loudly for a glass of beer. Surprised, Mike filled the order.

Pat quaffed the glass, turned to Mike and remarked, "Now you cross over to my saloon and buy yourself a drink, me boy."

So, for the rest of that day Pat and Mike crossed and recrossed the road, buying first a drink here and a drink there until the kegs were exhausted.

At this point, the interpreter of Aberhart would laugh heartily and wait expectantly for the light to dawn on the newspaperman. "Don't you see the point? Ten cents can buy two kegs of beer. Now you know what money really is. This Mister Aberhart says that he can circulate ten million dollars every month by giving every man and woman $25 to spend on dividends just in the same way. Now THAT's Social Credit." While the reporter hesitated, the devotee would add: "If I only had time I'd like to tell you the one about the bad dollar cheque that did ten dollars' worth of business before the bank got hold of it—and every merchant made a profit. Yes, sir! This Social Credit's got everything beaten." If the reporter retorted that, while ten cents could buy up two kegs of beer in twenty-four hours, it could not refill the empty kegs, the Social Crediter would denounce him as an enemy of society in league with the Fifty Big Shots—his mind was dead.

Although they deprecated the intellectual level of Aberhart's speeches, most journalists were prepared to admit that he had grasped the humanitarian aspect of Douglas's philosophy, and that he presented that aspect clearly and forcefully. They agreed with him in his denunciation of the poverty and destitution that existed in Alberta that summer. But, on the technical or constructive side, they felt that a speech by Aberhart was "as helpful as a road map on a sinking ship." They concluded that he himself did not know where he was going. He had a vague acquaintance with Douglas's unsound proposal for economic reconstruction and, not really understanding it, had turned it into something different but equally ridiculous.

Secure in the ever-increasing adulation of the populace, Aberhart urged his followers to ignore the idle vapourings of journalists, "paid henchmen of the Money Power." Reporting on the progress of the campaign during his broadcast on Sunday, July 21, he stated that during the previous week he had addressed more than 15,000 people at mass meetings, all of whom would vote for Social Credit. He said 2,000 were present at a meeting in Sedgewick, 2,500 in Athabasca, 2,500 in Chipman, 2,000 at Olds, and 3,000 at Camrose. Then he declared that candidates of the other parties were dismayed by the people's indifference. At one Liberal meeting in the north there were only forty people present, twenty-five voters and fifteen speakers! At the U.F.A. convention in the same place, there were only twenty-two people present.

When we were north we heard a number of the old-line party candidates were giving up in disgust. One resigned and they put another one in his place. They can get no one to attend their meetings and their neighbors tell them that they can't get their support. No wonder they give up. A person would be foolish to do otherwise. These old-line party organizers should not ask their men to face such odds. There is no use a man running when 70 or 80 per cent of the voters in his constituency have pledged themselves to Social Credit. Where does he hope to get by it? The leader and his organizers should take the pains to find out how much support they have in the constituency. No use hoping for it. Why don't they find out—before they ask their candidates to face the music on election day. It's only inefficiency that asks a man to run against an overwhelming Social Credit vote. There is nothing to be gained but disappointment to the fellow that runs. I would not be surprised on election day to see many polls carried by acclamation. However, if they persist we shouldn't object—I am not arguing for the purpose of saving anything to us because it makes no difference. Think of the money we shall secure for government use, $100.00 for each candidate that loses his deposit.
One U.F.A. candidate not being able to get a hearing, sent word to a school-house telling them he would be glad to come if they wished it and they replied—"There's no use coming. We are all Social Credit here." (Laughter) I am glad I am not running for an office or I could never bear such indifferences. These men must know there is no hope. Then why do they go on?
I find the Conservatives are really ahead in that respect, for in many districts the Conservatives are not putting a candidate in. They know there is no use.[17]

As a guarantee of his assurance that the people were rallying as never before to his cause, Aberhart left on July 28 for Vancouver. He remained on holiday in British Columbia for well over a week, leaving the efficient Manning in command of the campaign in Alberta during his absence.

[17]U.F.A. File of Aberhart broadcasts, July 21, 1935.

This dramatic move, unparalleled in Canadian electioneering, left Aberhart's political opponents gasping. The Liberals were especially alarmed. Realizing, at long last, something of the real strength of the Social Credit movement, they now began to train their guns on it rather than concentrate their fire on the collapsing forces of the government.

To Aberhart's followers, his constant ridicule of other parties, coupled with a refusal to recognize good faith in critics of his doctrines, reflected a heady assurance that the Social Credit movement was identical with the Alberta community. But the U.F.A., as well as Liberals and Conservatives, gave such tactics quite a different interpretation. They argued that unwillingness to recognize opposition parties indicated that the Social Credit movement was, in essence, totalitarian. Aberhart's denial of a community of basic political values was nowhere more apparent, his opponents charged, then in his instructions to Social Credit speakers not to answer questions at political meetings.

Social Crediters' rejection of the time-honoured custom of a question period may be illustrated by a press report of one of their meetings in Calgary. When a Liberal lawyer, A. M. Sinclair, K.C., attempted to question J. W. Hugill, K.C., a Social Credit candidate for the city, permission was refused:

He was told by Chairman J. T. North that instructions had ruled out a question period. Mr. Sinclair asked for an opportunity to ask questions at some future meeting. Mr. Hugill and Mr. North said that William Aberhart would be consulted in the matter. . . . The chairman said it was not intended questions would be accepted from the audience during the present series of campaign meetings. Mr. North said policy as to questions was formulated because of the time factor involved in a full schedule of meetings.[18]

In an editorial entitled, "Tongue-tying the Orators," the Calgary *Albertan* commented acidly on this episode:

We imagine it must be rather irritating for a gentleman like Mr. J. W. Hugill, a practitioner at the bar and a King's Counsel withal, skilled and experienced in the art of debate, not to be free to make use of it; to have convictions, to have the courage to voice them and yet to be told he must not. Imagine not permitting a lawyer to argue! It is like taking a thirsty horse to water and refusing to let him drink.[19]

Such incidents, which were not infrequent, encouraged the accusation that Social Credit candidates were yes-men, completely under their leader's thumb. These candidates found it difficult to appreciate a

[18]*Calgary Herald*, August 11, 1935.
[19]Calgary *Albertan*, August 12, 1935.

waggish parody, entitled "Abe's Parrots," which the Liberals circulated with the hope of inducing the people to laugh with them rather than at them:

> Abie was a birdman
> Lived in our town
> Specialized in parrots
> Mostly golden brown.
>
> Yellow feathered fledglings
> Hopped from perch to perch
> Fluttered, muttered, spluttered
> Food and shelter search.
>
> Everyone was tongue-tied
> Abie saw to that
> Were not talking parrots
> Simply chit and chat?
>
> "Abie is our master
> Abie knows it all"
> This the yellow fledglings
> One and only call.[20]

In more serious vein, the newspapers complained that Social Credit speakers tiresomely repeated the same thing over and over again to each succeeding audience. Under these circumstances, what could a newspaper do more than to say that, in effect, "Mr. A. said last night the same as he said before." Surely, they argued, even the most brilliant speaker's inspiration must reach a saturation point. "Then the source of its replenishment," wrote one editor, "is in the questions raised by men and women who want to know." The man in the audience could give a speaker the chance to get back into the conspicuous news columns.

The newspapers' enthusiasm for controversial questions at Social Credit meetings was not shared by Aberhart's mass following, as is obvious from the report of a meeting at Vulcan:

O. L. McPherson, M.L.A., former minister of public works, was shouted down by a crowd that jammed William Aberhart's Little Bow riding rally.

Following Mr. Aberhart's address to the crowd of 2,000, the former government member pressed forward a series of questions but the crowd noisily interrupted.

Mr. McPherson stuck to his guns after the chairman had appealed to the crowd for order but finally it was ruled only one more question could be put by Mr. McPherson.

[20]*Ibid.*, August 17, 1935.

"Are you going to let this man cross-examine me?" asked Mr. Aberhart. No! No! scores shouted. The place was in an uproar and Mr. McPherson was forced to retire.[21]

Referring to the noisy demonstration that would not permit the continuance of the question period, the *Vulcan Advocate* commented: "The audience seemed to deny an individual the right for free speech, yelling and shouting unkind remarks in their apparent enthusiasm for Mr. Aberhart. What started out to be a well-conducted meeting ended in a wild demonstration that no Canadian should be proud of."[22] Speaking at Carmangay a few days later, McPherson himself declared that never in twenty-five years' experience with the U.F.A. had he seen such a mob spirit as had characterized the Aberhart meeting at Vulcan.[23] Social Crediters, on the other hand, maintained that the uproar at Vulcan indicated clearly that the people resented efforts of hostile questioners to disturb the aura cast over mass meetings by Aberhart's speeches. "Aberhart," said Tim Buck sadly at a speech in Calgary, "appeals to the emotions. It is not for nothing that Aberhart tells his followers not to go to meetings, other than Social Credit, and not to answer questions." But the audience jeered when the Communist leader concluded: "No matter what golden promises are made you cannot get them—Aberhart says he can give you something for nothing, and I say it cannot be done."[24]

Hysterical enthusiasm for Social Credit reached such a pitch during the last month of the campaign that Aberhart's opponents risked an uproar at their meetings if they ventured even the slightest criticism of his doctrines. Aware of the temper of the people, almost from the beginning the Liberals usually soft-pedalled their attitude to Social Credit in the hope of gaining a hearing for their own constructive proposals. But the relative calmness of their meetings, as compared to those of the U.F.A. and Conservatives, ended abruptly when the Liberals decided, early in August, to attack Aberhart's proposals. They ended, in fact, by holding one of the stormiest political meetings in Canadian history.

To strengthen their case against Aberhart, the Liberals had imported the leading monetary reform exponent of their party, the colourful Gerry McGeer, then Mayor of Vancouver. Speaking in support of the

[21]*Edmonton Journal*, July 6, 1935.
[22]*Vulcan Advocate*, July 11, 1935.
[23]*Edmonton Journal*, July 11, 1935.
[24]*Calgary Herald*, August 19, 1935.

Liberal candidate at Drumheller to an audience of 1,200 five days before the election McGeer

was unable to get to his subject due to the necessity of replying to an almost incessant barrage of heckling questions fired at him from the darker recesses of the huge building by an organized group of what he called "Aberhart hoodlums and Communists." For five minutes, as Mayor McGeer stood before the microphone which was to have carried his monetary reform message to the audience, cat-calls, boos, yells and questions made it impossible for the smiling first citizen of Vancouver to utter one word. His first words, an appeal to the sportsmanship of the crowd, was the signal for renewed yells and cries. . . . Time and again Gerry sought to get on the subject dearest to him—an attack on the financial interests—but on each occasion he was brought to a halt as the rowdies yelled, booed, stamped their feet, and threw out challenging queries, turning the arena into a pandemonium.[25]

After making numerous allusions to the interjections, McGeer became caustic when appeals by the chairman and the Liberal candidate had failed to quiet the uproar: "I never," he declared, during a brief lull, "saw a party with so many ne'er-do-wells and something for nothing gangs as the Aberhart movement, and decent people can look forward to a continuation of the conditions they see this evening if Aberhart attains power."[26] A few hours earlier, addressing a meeting of farmers at Kiever's Lake, McGeer had encountered similar rowdyism: a number of people had here too turned the meeting into pandemonium, shouting "liar" and booing, whenever he criticized Aberhart's proposals.[27] Before returning to the coast McGeer stated that he believed the obstructionists at the Drumheller and other meetings had brought many votes to the Liberals, "for right-minded people could not approve such tactics." The Communist candidate at Drumheller immediately dissociated both himself and his supporters from the tactics Social Crediters were using to break up Liberal meetings.

Throughout the campaign U.F.A. speakers, whenever they criticized Aberhart's theories, faced the same difficulties with audiences as the Liberals. The experience of ex-Premier Brownlee in his own constituency of Ponoka provides ample illustration of the hazards faced by U.F.A. speakers. The rural district of Waterglen, which had largely been settled by Welsh people, had gone almost 100 per cent for Aberhart, with one of the strongest Social Credit study groups in the province. When Brown-

[25]*Ibid.*
[26]*Ibid.*
[27]Calgary *Albertan*, August 19, 1935.

lee's campaign manager advertised a meeting at Waterglen, he was immediately informed by the local officials of the Social Credit League that the ex-premier should not be allowed to speak in Waterglen, as his previous addresses had indicated he had nothing to offer Alberta. The constituency executive was naturally disturbed to receive such a communication, and advised Brownlee to cancel the meeting. This he refused to do, taking the stand that as the U.F.A. had advertised the meeting he would not be intimidated, though he also knew full well that it would be futile to speak there.

The night of the meeting was the night of a devastating frost, a finishing touch to the government's hope of a last-minute rally of the farmers to its support. Brownlee himself has described his experience at Waterglen:

It was a large hall and it was packed. People had come from miles around, owing to the threats of Social Crediters to sabotage the meeting. During the first forty-five minutes of my address, I didn't touch on Social Credit and no one could have had a better hearing. Up to that point an outside observer who had not sensed the mind of the audience might have thought that all was well and that it was a successful meeting. After three-quarters of an hour I stated that, as their member in the legislature, they would expect me to discuss my attitude to Social Credit. So I began to tell them in all sincerity what I thought of Social Credit. A group of big fellows near the door then left the hall, slamming the door violently as they went out. Some of them then got into cars and started to blow horns. Others got logs and began pounding the walls and doors of the building from outside, while they hooted and yelled. Some of my supporters went outside and the rough stuff stopped. But the meeting inside was in a tumultuous uproar.

The ex-premier was by no means the only U.F.A. speaker who encountered similar demonstrations when Social Credit theories were criticized at rural meetings. It is not infrequently said in Alberta that Aberhart encouraged such tactics by suggesting to his supporters that eggs were cheap and could be used for purposes other than eating.

Even when their meetings were not broken up by downright rowdyism, U.F.A. speakers knew that they were constantly in danger of losing control of their audiences. An account of a meeting at a small centre in the drought area given by one of the most forceful of the U.F.A. speakers, illustrates something of the atmosphere that prevailed in rural Alberta in the summer of 1935:

The hardest meeting I had was at Veteran. I remember the night we arrived there, a dried-out, utterly depressed looking town. The Social Credit candidate had announced a meeting at a school some distance out, but he cancelled it and his supporters came to hear me. It was one of the tensest meetings you could imagine—two or three times it was near a riot. If I had shown the least sign of fear I would have been through. All in all, the campaign of 1935 was a tremendous ordeal.

By the beginning of August, mass hysteria had reached such a pitch that U.F.A. speakers found it almost impossible to carry on meetings in many country schools. Social Crediters would assemble outside schools and honk automobile horns, so that government supporters could not be heard. There were numerous reports of tires being deflated on the cars of U.F.A. speakers, of sand being poured into gasoline tanks, and of cars being pelted with overripe tomatoes or rotten eggs. Liberals were also sometimes molested. The car of the Liberal candidate for Olds, for example, was put out of commission and smeared with red paint while he was speaking at a rural point. As all the farmers in that district were Social Crediters, he was rescued from a night in a haystack by the Minister of Agriculture, who happened to pass by the stranded car. Alfred Speakman, Member of Parliament for Red Deer, reported in a letter to the Calgary *Albertan* that while speaking at a U.F.A. meeting in the village of Lousana, all four tires of his car, as well as the spare tire, were deflated. "In order," he concluded, "that there might be no misapprehension as to the perpetrators of this discourtesy, the sign manual of the Social Credit movement was scrawled upon my car."[28]

Even when U.F.A. meetings were not thrown into tumult by resentful supporters of Aberhart, government leaders felt that their speeches were falling on deaf ears. One Cabinet minister, who led the U.F.A. speaking campaign in southeastern Alberta, has described the situation he faced during the last few weeks of the campaign:

In my speeches I tried to discuss the significant achievements of the government. My audiences would listen to this part of my address. But just as soon as it became apparent that I was going to discuss Aberhart's theories in a critical way, down went the people's heads. The men would scowl fiercely at me. They didn't want to hear Aberhart criticized. If the Apostle Paul had been loose in Alberta for six months, he couldn't have stopped Social Credit. In my own community, I tried to appeal to the farmers in terms of our common life, our mutual experiences of joy and sorrow at weddings and funerals and so on. I assured them as a friend or neighbour that the Cabinet had examined Social Credit thoroughly, and reminded them that the British Labour Party had also looked into it thoroughly over twenty years previously. "Don't be misled," I pleaded with them, but it was like shooting peas at a warship.

[28]*Ibid.*, August 21, 1935. The sign manual of the Social Credit is a cross within a circle known as "the wheel and cross."

"We couldn't," another Cabinet minister has put it, "get inside the asbestos curtain that Aberhart had laid down on Alberta."

Unlike the Liberal leader, the premier had no illusions concerning the strength of the Social Credit movement. Early in his speaking tour, Reid realized that the government forces were fighting a hopeless battle at the level of the U.F.A. locals. The situation he faced at a meeting in Elnora is typical of what he encountered everywhere during the campaign. This rural area had been as hard hit by the depression as any other area in the province; it was naturally a hotbed of Social Crediters.

Our candidate [Reid has related] spoke first. The audience constantly inter-rupted him and jeered him. When I arose to speak, I got a certain amount of the carry-over. But after three minutes the audience settled down and listened to me for an hour. There, as at practically every place I spoke, old supporters came up to me and told me they were going to vote against me. In every case, the reason given for deserting the U.F.A. was financial distress.

Even at meetings where his speech seemed to have turned the tide in his government's favour, Reid was not deceived. He knew that, within twenty-four hours, the positive effects of the meeting would be diffused and the members of his audience would be back on the Social Credit bandwagon. Two weeks before the election the U.F.A. leaders finally realized that the people's minds were irrevocably closed to their appeals.

In the struggle against the Social Credit movement, the three parties were joined by the six daily newspapers of Alberta—two in each of the leading cities of Calgary and Edmonton, one in Lethbridge, and one in Medicine Hat. Although all claimed to be independent, the *Calgary Herald* and the *Edmonton Journal*, both members of the Southam chain, were traditionally Conservative; the *Edmonton Bulletin* and the two papers in the smaller cities were definitely Liberal; the Calgary *Albertan*, which had had a Liberal tradition, tempered by Labour sympathies, was probably best classified after 1928 as independent. In addition to the city dailies, there were a considerable number of weekly newspapers, published in such small towns as Vulcan, Hanna, or Grande Prairie. The rural papers, with few exceptions, had always sought to be non-committal on all problems except those of a purely local nature. By the summer of 1935 all the dailies, and most of the weeklies as well, were fighting the Social Credit movement, as the editor of the *Hanna Herald* put it, "tooth and nail."

Of all the newspapers, none surpassed the *Calgary Herald* in editorial denunciations of the Social Credit movement. Early in April, as a result of heavy bombardment from its readers, it began to publish each Saturday pages of "letters to the editor," for and against Social Credit, a policy that was continued until the election. As the campaign developed, readers could not help noticing that letters condemning Social Credit were of a fairly high standard, whereas those favouring it were so absurd as to suggest that they had been deliberately selected for publication, if not actually written, by the *Herald*'s staff. Lashed to fury, Aberhart subtly urged his followers, once again, to cancel their subscriptions to the *Herald*.[29] But, as this newspaper had a near monopoly of the daily field in Calgary and southern Alberta, the proposed boycott (Aberhart himself carefully avoided the use of that incriminating word) seems to have been taken seriously by only a few of its Social Credit readers.

Refusing to be intimidated, the *Herald* redoubled its editorial attacks on Aberhart and the Social Credit movement. Reporters of all the newspapers now tended to become antagonistic to the self-styled martyr: they seized every opportunity of stressing any of his statements that would make him appear in an unfavourable light. As we have seen, many journalists even argued strenuously against Aberhart's theories with whoever would listen to them at Social Credit meetings. But the mass of the people, whether in the city or the country, were ultimately influenced not by the writings of reporters or editors but by Aberhart's broadcasts and speeches. At many Social Credit meetings reporters were greeted with boos and jeers as they took their places at the press tables.

The publication of the Blue Manual was the signal for all the daily papers to step up the tempo of their assaults on the Social Credit movement. Aberhart's doctrines, as developed therein, now proved too much even for the Calgary *Albertan*, which henceforth gave the Liberals its whole-hearted support. From early July until the election most of the statements in the Blue Manual were the subject of incessant and adverse editorial comment. Day after day, week after week, editors exposed the weaknesses of Aberhart's campaign at the constitutional and economic levels. Over and over again, they pointed out that he contradicted himself repeatedly, in the Manual, in the white pamphlets, and in recorded broadcasts. They were especially infuriated by his refusal to tolerate legitimate criticism. "He has no reply to contrary opinions," wrote the editor of the *Calgary Herald* on July 31, "except to exhort his followers not to listen to any views except those delivered by loyal henchmen. . . . It is inconceivable that even the most devoted followers will not note these things and speculate upon them. . . . All other political

[29] U.F.A. File of Aberhart broadcasts.

leaders invite questions, and if they cannot answer them candidly admit the fact. Not so, Mr. Aberhart. His life has been spent in the classroom or the pulpit where questions of an embarrassing nature are not tolerated."

The editors of all the urban dailies, as well as those of most rural weeklies, agreed that Aberhart's instruction to his followers to refuse to listen to or read opposing arguments was unique in Canadian politics. "This intolerance," the *Calgary Herald* claimed two days before the election, "has been attended by the inevitable manifestations—the use of the boycott, efforts to break up meetings of opposing parties, slurs at the old parties, the development of credulity on a scale that is unbelievable in this era of a supposedly informed electorate."[30] In numerous editorials Aberhart was compared to Mussolini and Hitler, who had likewise attained their ends by the application of stiff censorship. Only views supporting their policies were permitted to be published in Italy and Germany: the public heard only one side of every issue. "The Aberhart party," wrote the editor of the *Calgary Herald*, "has adopted exactly the same policy and it is a policy that breeds fanaticism, intolerance and prejudice. . . . Members of the older parties can agree to disagree and still be gentlemen. They observe the courtesies of life. Not so, many of the fanatical adherents of the new political cause."[31] The people of Alberta could never honestly complain that they had not been adequately warned.

Neither Aberhart nor the Social Credit candidates felt strong enough to treat hostile newspapers with silent contempt. In addition to urging his followers to boycott the *Calgary Herald*, towards which he conceived a special enmity, Aberhart kept up a counter-attack at mass meetings and on the air. But if the newspapers expected a rational reply to their charges of inconsistency, contradiction, and intolerance in his campaign they must have been grievously disappointed. Aberhart answered the editors, whether in the pulpit of the Bible Institute or on the hustings, with fresh outpourings of sarcasm and ridicule. The newspapers, he repeated over and over again, were the kept darlings of the money barons: editors and reporters expressed, not their own views, but merely those of the "Fifty Big Shots." Whenever he lashed the capitalist press, his vast audiences would rock with laughter. In more serious vein, he would then urge the people, once again, not to poison their minds by listening in any way, shape, or form to newspaper propaganda opposing

[30]*Calgary Herald*, August 20, 1935.
[31]*Ibid.*

Social Credit. As the campaign drew to a close, the anti-Aberhart propaganda in the daily press assumed unprecedented proportions. To the
newspapers' final offensive, Aberhart replied, three days before the
election, by announcing that, if victorious, the Social Credit party
would enter the publishing field itself.[32]

In the long fight with the metropolitan newspapers, Aberhart had the
majority of the people on his side almost from the beginning. As the
struggle for power moved to its climax, there can be little doubt that the
criticism to which the press constantly subjected Aberhart assisted,
rather than hindered, the victory of the Social Credit movement. In later
years even the publisher of the newspaper most bitterly opposed to
Aberhart was prepared to admit that perhaps it had helped to elect him
by virtue of the very severity of its attacks on him. "We ought to have
realized at the time," this publisher reminisced, "that if you attack too
violently there is bound to be a reaction."

The intensity of the newspapers' campaign against Aberhart, coupled
with the publication of the Blue Manual, finally aroused certain influential business men in southern Alberta to the danger to their interests
(as they supposed) inherent in the Social Credit movement. Their intervention at the eleventh hour to avert an Aberhart victory was one of the
spectacular features of the election campaign.

The organization of the business community to fight Douglasism was
initiated early in July, by the Drumheller Board of Trade. Hoping to
secure the support of other Boards of Trade and Chambers of Commerce, its executive empowered Jesse Gouge, a prominent coal mine
owner and a Liberal, to form the Economic Safety League. Most of the
Boards of Trade were reluctant to intervene in the campaign, ostensibly
on the ground of their non-partisan tradition. It is said that the real
reason, however, was the fear that business men who joined the new
League would be boycotted.

Nevertheless, with the support of the Medicine Hat Board, the
Economic Safety League was formed, with the Honourable William
Egbert, a former lieutenant-governor, as president, and Gouge as Secretary. In a public manifesto these officers described the League as an
association of Alberta citizens, non-political and representative of all
social and business classes. It had been organized to give concrete
expression to the united opposition of its members to Aberhart's Social
Credit proposals. Members of the association must be agreed as to
the fallacy of Aberhart's doctrines, however much they might differ from

[32]*Calgary Herald*, August 19, 1935.

one another concerning the economic reconstruction of Alberta. "We consider Mr. Aberhart's presentation of his ideas," the manifesto announced, "both indefinite and contradictory":

We regard his Monthly Dividend promise of something for nothing an attempt to secure votes by a cruel and heartless deception, for this promise cannot be fulfilled.

We believe his proposed tax (or levy), if ever brought into force, would prove an utterly intolerable burden upon the farmer, who is, of all Alberta citizens, least able to bear the burden.

We are unable to see how it will be possible for the Aberhart "Just Price" to operate and any attempt to work it would require an enormously costly administration.

Mr. Aberhart's wage and income control proposals are a direct attack upon the freedom of the individual.

We resent most vigorously the use of the boycott by Aberhart Social Crediters at the instigation of Aberhart himself, as a weapon to silence all opposition.

All members have pledged themselves to work and vote against Social Credit in the forthcoming election, to avoid a major disaster to the Province.

Those in sympathy with its programme were invited to join the Economic Safety League. In view of the threat of boycott, prospective members were asked, when sending in their names to the secretary, to state whether they were willing to have their names made public. There was no membership fee, but contributions were invited.

As it turned out, the League's financial supporters and members were permanently kept secret, "through fear of retaliation." But it did raise sufficient funds to publish pamphlets, to advertise its objectives in the newspapers, and to broadcast once daily from July 24 to 31 and twice daily from August 1 to August 22. The League also issued several "stunt" publications, such as the blank-paged booklet entitled, "All about Social Credit," and the cardboard "Baloney Dollars," which were widely circulated. One week before the election it released a sixteen-page pamphlet, "The Amos and Andy of Social Credit," in which Manning, Aberhart, and the movement generally were lampooned mercilessly in dialogue and cartoon. The League claimed that it made no contributions to candidates or radio speakers opposing Social Credit, but it did pay for the services of Professor Henry F. Angus, head of the Department of Economics at the University of British Columbia, whom it imported as its consultant.

The principal propaganda piece of the League was a twenty-eight page pamphlet entitled *The Dangers of Douglasism*, of which over 20,000 copies were sold at ten cents each. Its subtitle was, "A One

Night Study of the Craze called 'National Dividends,' purporting to be written in language anyone could understand." Announced as not in the interest of any political party, the pamphlet called upon farmers, labourers, merchants, and all producers to "strike a blow for the defense of Alberta and its credit." Part of the introduction to the pamphlet illustrates the attitude of the sponsors of the Economic Safety League to the Social Credit movement and its leader:

For two years citizens of Alberta, who have a radio (and who hasn't), have been listening to a weekly broadcast of the strangest conglomeration of political economy, fantastic proposals for unemployment relief and government financing, punctuated at appropriate intervals by unctious [sic] quotations from the scriptures, and loud choral singing of evangelistic hymns. The thoughtful man soon discerned that this badly distorted imitation of a theoretical economic proposal, enunciated some fifteen years ago by Major C. H. Douglas, and referred to as the "Douglas System" was an Alberta manifestation of a chronic epidemic of untenable theories and quack remedies for economic ills, which epidemic exists all over the world.

The leaders of existing political parties in Alberta gave indirect and covert support to the movement, each imagining that to do so was weakening the opposition, confident that his own political party could not be seduced by vague, indefinite, unintelligible jargon, beginning with nothing and ending nowhere.

All have discovered now on the very threshold of an election, that they underrated the organizing ability of the political parson, who has appointed himself leader; and the tendency of the public, or that portion of it which accepts its political ideas ready made, to grab at anything in a depression, coupled with a liberal offer of "something for nothing," promised without conditions or obligations. A solemn promise to put a Christmas Tree in every month and make every postman a Santa Claus.

No proposal or scheme for getting money, seems absurd or ridiculous to the fellow who thinks he is going to get it.

Our business people and others not carried away by this fallacy are now realizing the magnitude of this danger. They recognize the small army of exhorters travelling about the country, holding meetings, as an "omnium-gatherum" of political odds and ends, business failures, social misfits and imitating parrots, reciting ready made speeches, which they do not understand, and realize what it would mean to turn Alberta over to this heterogenous aggregation of incompetents, led by a man with no business experience, with no knowledge of the law, and imbued with ideas of political economy, that were discredited and discarded, repeatedly, before he was born.

Of course scattered among the following are a few well meaning, good intentioned but misguided individuals, mostly young men, thoughtlessly following what they think is a beacon light of leadership, while trailing along blindly behind a fox fire or will-o-the-wisp headed toward the abysmal depths of a dismal swamp.

Following this introduction, twenty-two pages of the pamphlet were devoted to an amused analysis, from the point of view of orthodox economics, of the fallacies of Douglas's proposals, and the even greater weaknesses of Aberhart's version as sponsored by the S.F.N. (Something for Nothing) Party.[33]

As election day approached, the aggressive attitude of the Economic Safety League won it increasing financial support among the business men of Calgary and Edmonton. On August 6, the Edmonton Chamber of Commerce followed the lead of other business organizations in the province and issued a manifesto, throwing its whole-hearted support to the Economic Safety League. Less impassioned than its Calgary ally, the Edmonton Chamber of Commerce gave Aberhart full credit for his zeal, as well as for his exceptional organizing and oratorical abilities, and also acknowledged his high position as a religious leader. It did not impugn his motives and suggested that he and his followers give the same respect to it, or fair-minded people would conclude that Social Crediters could not meet the arguments which the Chamber of Commerce presented. In appealing for Aberhart's consideration of the fears of the organization, the manifesto assured him that criticism was being offered with all respect and not in a personally antagonistic spirit. "We both," it declared, "earnestly desire the same thing—the improvement of material conditions for ourselves and our fellow citizens. But conditions will not be improved but made much worse again by plunging into ways that seem new and glorious, but which lead nowhere and are full of pitfalls, being, for the most part, merely man's old errors with new names."

The Edmonton Chamber of Commerce, the manifesto insisted, could not remain silent when, to a distressed people, glowing promises were being made which far surpassed any government's power to fulfil. Aberhart's promises were impossible of realization because they were at variance with basic economic facts. The hope of creating something out of nothing, which was the essence of Aberhart's doctrine, rested on a fundamental fallacy concerning the nature of banking credit:

We have not met the banker who "with a fountain pen entry in a ledger" creates credit based on nothing. In our experience he wants security on suitable assets fully pledged to the Bank and kept intact. To all intents, it is the same as if we parted with ownership of the assets to the Bank—sold them to it, in fact, with the right to buy them back by paying off the loan. These Social Credit proposals are affecting the available credit. We know of many specific cases where they have done so.

[33]See Appendix IV for a summary of the case of the Economic Safety League against Social Credit.

After stating its opposition to Social Credit in general terms, the Edmonton Chamber of Commerce listed, with some comment in each case, eleven consuming fears of Aberhart's proposals:

We fear Mr. Aberhart's scheme for Alberta because it threatens the ultimate mortgaging or confiscation of all private property. . . . We fear Mr. Aberhart's plan as simply a huge debt-making scheme—a further mortgaging of our future. . . . Alternatively we fear Mr. Aberhart's plan as a colossal scheme of fresh taxation. . . . We fear Mr. Aberhart's plan of a crushing sales tax. . . . We fear Mr. Aberhart's attempt to fix Just Prices on thousands and thousands of articles and services, many changing almost daily. . . . We fear his attempt to pay "dividends" out of such intangible assets as "Cultural Heritage" and undeveloped natural resources. . . . We fear his issue of certificates—an irredeemable paper currency tending to all the evils of excessive inflation as in Germany. . . . We fear his seizure of all "good money" to be replaced by these depreciating certificates. . . . We fear his seizure of all good Dominion money received for "Exports" from the province. . . . We fear his attempt to put Alberta on a different monetary basis to the rest of Canada and indeed to all the rest of the world, still further hampering our export and other business. . . . Finally we fear the attempt to isolate Alberta for this experiment, creating frictions and difficulties with other provinces and the Dominion.

It was then pointed out what such apprehensions meant, in each case, to various sections of the community, including farmers, coal operators, merchants (especially in small towns and villages), employers, and to consumers generally. Those groups were already suffering greatly, the manifesto concluded, from the confusion and lack of confidence caused by Aberhart's proposals. This was the more deplorable because there had been signs of substantial improvement. But, if Aberhart were defeated, all would be well. "With these new-fangled notions disposed of, it is our confident belief that a real revival of business will be possible— the recovery building up on itself in much the same way as, but happily in a reverse direction, to the acceleration of the depression." The intervention of the Edmonton Chamber of Commerce in the election campaign was followed, within a day, by similar action, for identical reasons, by the Calgary Board of Trade.

The broadcasts sponsored by the Economic Safety League were initiated by its president. In the opinion of many opponents of Social Credit, the choice of a former lieutenant-governor for such an office was ill advised. Following Egbert's opening broadcast, various speakers, some unnamed, others well-known, gave radio addresses under the League's auspices. It was widely rumoured that most of these speeches were written by Professor Angus, who on occasion also appeared in person as a most effective broadcaster. In almost every broadcast the

League concentrated its attack on Aberhart's doctrines as outlined in the Blue Manual and repeated, somewhat dully and unimaginatively, the criticisms contained in its own pamphlet *The Dangers of Douglasism.*

The activities of the Economic Safety League provided the newspapers with new opportunities for attacking the Social Credit movement. During the four weeks between July 25 and August 22 the press gave elaborate coverage almost every day to the League's broadcasts. The campaign of the Social Crediters was correspondingly played down in news columns, and their doctrines and tactics subjected to even more relentless criticism than formerly in editorials. A close examination of the editorial pages of the six dailies reveals that not one editorial favourable to Aberhart was published during the last month of his struggle for power. Each increase in the tempo of the newspaper campaign against Aberhart was accompanied by more vigorous attacks on the Social Credit movement by the Economic Safety League.

To Social Crediters the League's propaganda also furnished new opportunities for vitriolic counter-propaganda. As Aberhart himself left for British Columbia shortly after the League's formation, the reply to its propaganda was left mainly to his lieutenants. The pattern of their counter-attack was established by the speech of one of the Social Credit candidates for Calgary (who was subsequently elected to the legislature) delivered only a few hours after the League's preliminary announcement of its objectives:

That the Economic Safety League . . . was being financed by interests in Great Britain, was charged by Mrs. F. Gostick . . . when she addressed a meeting in St. Michael's and All Angels' Church Wednesday evening. Mrs. Gostick declared it was known the money was coming from the Old Country, and added that the Social Credit party did not fear money but that Alberta would lead the world to a higher standard of living and a better social system.

Suggesting the name of the Economic Safety League should be changed, the speaker said she would give it another name with the same initials, E.S.L., proposing that it be called "The Elevated Society of Lunatics".[34]

In a broadcast from the Institute on Sunday, July 28, Manning (also a Calgary candidate) read numerous letters, all questioning the propriety of a former lieutenant-governor intervening in an election campaign. Aberhart's right-hand man assured his listeners that

the public as a rule will not stand to be harangued by public speakers as a bunch of ignorant, foolish people. Mob psychology would lead a crowd of citizens to resent most vigorously the loud declarations of that which they know is largely false and which is declared to besmirch the good name and

[34]Calgary *Albertan*, July 26, 1935.

reputation of any citizen who may differ with them. . . . A few wavering individuals may be upset by the fierceness of the onslaught but the best and most intelligent people will not be at all disturbed by it. They will refuse for the most part to listen to it. The thinking portion of our population does not pay much heed to anyone who speaks as if eighty per cent of our people were foolish. . . . The bombastic warnings of chaos and utter ruin offered to an intelligent majority of our thinking people with the suggestion that they place the old-line party politicians back in power is too obvious to be taken seriously. . . . All Social Crediters have been expecting these tactics; rumours have been abroad for weeks what was to be done to our leaders and all those who dared to resist political financial combinations which has been the basic cause of our difficulties. It is no wonder that the cool, deliberate way in which the people are dealing with these base degrading tactics has encouraged our leader. You may be sure that these bitter opponents must see some real truth and power in the Social Credit proposals or they would not be so violently concerned with the whole matter. These great leaders of old-line political thought with the aid of the unscrupulous financier do not present a case against Social Credit clearly enough to convince the general public without resorting to mud-slinging and sneering at religious faith, the integrity, and the sanity of the common people. One thing is plainly evident. They cannot convince the people that they are so free from self-seeking or self-aggrandizement as the man they are criticizing, Mr. Aberhart. At no time has he sought political honours or financial reward.[35]

Taking their cues from the Calgary candidates, Social Credit speakers throughout Alberta characterized the Economic Safety League as merely a last-ditch stand of the financial interests. Its president had earnestly assured the public that the League itself had no constructive programme to offer. It existed, then, only for the purpose of convincing the people that they were incompetent to choose the only leader who knew how to relieve their economic distress. Social Crediters stressed especially the cost of the League's propaganda.

There is one thing certain [a third Calgary candidate declared] the League must have money to burn. I wonder if all that money comes from Alberta. Isn't it wonderful to think that so many good, kind gentlemen in Alberta, and perhaps even in Montreal and New York are so fond of us and feel so sorry for our ignorance that they are willing to spend all this money just simply to help us out and to teach us what is good for us. Look at all they have done for us in the past and how happy and contented they have made us. . . . Cannot the financial interests realize that we, in this province, are at last awakened?[36]

Such speeches were naturally followed by wild rumours that large sums of money were pouring in from St. James and Bay streets or that Eastern business interests had contributed an amount that ranged from $50,000

[35]U.F.A. File of Aberhart broadcasts, July 28, 1935.
[36]A.S.C.C., August 2, 1935.

to $400,000 to destroy the Social Credit movement. Officials of the League denied that they had received donations from Eastern Canada; but their denials merely gave Aberhart's speakers further chances of making sarcastic references to the heavy expenditures obviously involved in the League's frequent radio broadcasts, daily newspaper advertising, widespread billboard displays, and numerous pamphlets.

On Aberhart's return from holidaying in British Columbia the people's hostility to the Economic Safety League was everywhere apparent. He realized that his lieutenants had effectively answered the League and that silence on his part was the best policy. But he claimed in a speech at Calgary on August 9 that traitors in the ranks of his opponents enabled him to know of the League's plans ahead of time:

Points of attack in the next two radio broadcasts of the Economic Safety League . . . were already known to him, the Social Credit leader asserted. He also announced, amid laughter, that a bank planned to sponsor a "big banquet" at 12.30 o'clock Monday noon in opposition to the Social Credit movement. "What some of these fellows in the Economic Safety League don't seem to realize," said Mr. Aberhart, "is that, in a camp of that kind, there are always traitors. If I don't bother to answer their attacks, you'll know that I at least knew their plans ahead of time."[37]

While Aberhart made only passing references to the League itself, he gave rough treatment to Professor Angus, its economic adviser. In speeches and broadcasts Aberhart suggested that Angus, having no standing in British Columbia, had been forced to come to Alberta to get a hearing. When the President of the University of British Columbia, Dr. L. S. Klinck, issued a statement to the Alberta press that Angus was well known and highly regarded, not only in British Columbia but throughout Canada also, Aberhart promptly asked why such a celebrated economist did not give his message of humanity to his own province. In the League's next broadcast Angus replied:

If, by my message to humanity, Mr. Aberhart means a scheme by which we can all get rich quickly and get something for nothing, then I have no message for humanity, but if he is generous enough to include among the messages, which are worth delivering, a word of warning to people who are in danger of doing something very foolish, and who are being asked to engage in a reckless expenditure, then I think I have a message. If I deliver this message in Alberta, and not in British Columbia, it is because I think it is needed in Alberta while it is not needed and I hope never will be needed in British Columbia.[38]

[37]Calgary *Albertan*, August 12, 1935.
[38]Private File, Broadcasts of Economic Safety League.

When introducing Angus to its radio audiences in future, the League found it advisable to announce that it still believed in his competence as an economist, nothwithstanding the opinions expressed by Aberhart and his speakers.

There are conflicting interpretations of the impact of the League's intervention in the struggle for power. Certainly, U.F.A. and Labour opponents of Aberhart were astonished to find themselves allied with their old enemy, Big Business. It is said that many people who had been looking upon Social Credit with amused condescension now flocked to Aberhart's side, having decided that there must be something to a philosophy which was being opposed so vigorously by financial interests. According to the other interpretation, the League should be given credit for reducing Aberhart's popular support. The first interpretation seems more plausible, for there can be little doubt that the cry of persecution raised by Social Crediters in answer to the League's attack rallied the people anew to Aberhart's cause. In the summer of 1935, nothing could penetrate the mass hysteria that had enveloped the province.

On August 19, in his farewell radio address for the Economic Safety League, Professor Angus made a last desperate effort to call the people back to political and economic realism. He began by protesting against the recklessness with which Social Crediters were prepared to disregard Alberta's legal obligations to the other provinces of Canada. The effects of Social Credit were as obvious as those of arsenic. Aberhart and his followers had not met criticisms of their doctrines by simple explanations and arguments but had resorted to angry protest. "To replace answers by abuse," he added, "is the behaviour characteristic of men who are beaten and who know that they are beaten." He recalled Aberhart's threats regarding tariff barriers, a separate monetary system, and even a separate Post Office department as evidences of disregard of constitutional rights within the Dominion. Turning to the economic phase of the Social Credit campaign, he declared, "It is mad to say 'Give Social Credit a trial' before you condemn it. The reason why it is mad is that the cost of trying out Social Credit would be high and the chance of success negligible." The first effect of paying people $10,000,000 every month would be an inflation, which could be avoided only if the credit were withdrawn from circulation by a tax or levy.

While Mr. Aberhart admits that the credit must be recovered, he uses language which leads ignorant people to believe that $120,000,000 a year can be paid in dividends for all time if $10,000,000 is recovered once. This suggestion is utterly absurd, and Social Crediters say little or nothing about it today, though they do not admit, as scientifically-minded men would, that they have made a silly mistake. Yet the Social Crediters did in a very indirect way admit this when they spoke of getting the full sum of $120,000,000 a year by a levy on price-spreads. In making this proposal they just imagine that the price-spreads exist on this scale; just as a child imagines Santa Claus with a sack of candy.[39]

In conclusion, Angus insisted that Social Crediters had not looked closely to see whether price spreads really existed, and if so, how big they were; or if they had, they had not thought it wise to publish their conclusions. They had talked a great deal about experts but they had not publicly asked a single recognized expert this simple question, "Can $120,000,000 be obtained by a levy on price spreads in Alberta?" nor the equally simple question, "Can any substantial sum be obtained?" Yet, if Aberhart's price spread tax failed, Alberta would be driven back to the alternative of disastrous price inflation. The basic dividends of $25 a month would then become worthless, unless their monthly rate were progressively increased. But such an increase would increase the gap between the payments and the receipts in taxes and would lead to a further depreciation at a faster and faster rate. Economically, "this would be the end of Social Credit."

In his final speeches, Aberhart was much more concerned with issuing elaborate instructions regarding techniques of marking ballots to ensure a Social Credit landslide than with ideology. But he reminded the people, once again, that great men in England, Australia, New Zealand, and Canada were favourable to Social Credit. "Do our opponents think," he asked, "that many of our people will relish the idea that the Very Reverend the Dean of Canterbury and the Marquis of Tavistock have taken up a foolish, fantastic theory which cannot be done and which would cause chaos and confusion if attempted? These men must surely presume that the voting public are still very gullible and ignorant." In another vein, he suggested: "Now you mustn't be too hard on Professor Angus. He just came from British Columbia, and he doesn't understand the situation."[40]

At his final rally, the night before the election, Reid talked to many farmers personally after the meeting had formally closed. He noticed a young man, of perhaps twenty-five, who had been born and educated in that rural community, walking outside the hall. Several groups of people were standing around arguing about Social Credit. As the young man paced up and down, alone, the premier of Alberta heard him say, to nobody in particular, "Well, I guess Social Credit's no darn good, but

[39]Ibid.
[40]U.F.A. File of Aberhart broadcasts, August 18, 1935.

who's there to vote for anyway—I guess I'll vote for Social Credit anyway." Such was the heritage of the once powerful U.F.A. at the close of the struggle for power.

Election day was bright and warm throughout Alberta. Advance polls in Calgary and Edmonton had indicated a heavy vote, but leaders of the old-line parties were astonished at the unprecedented turn out of voters. From the Cypress Hills to the Peace River, from Cardston to Lloyd-minster, people began lining up to vote as early as 6.00 A.M. In most centres the polls were congested all day. The organizers of each of the parties did their utmost to get out every potential voter. Thousands voted who had never done so previously. At the 1930 provincial election 182,219 people had voted; 301,752 voted in 1935, an increase of over 63 per cent.

Aberhart had instructed his followers to line up early on election day and settle the issue once for all. The U.F.A., Liberals, and Conservatives were amazed at the smooth functioning of the Social Credit machine: they discovered, too late, that their own organizations were infiltrated with Aberhart's supporters. Officials of the three old parties had counted on a certain number of workers at the polls: by noon they found that scores of their workers had either deserted or had not appeared at all. There were rumours that stenographers in Liberal headquarters in cities publicly boasted that they had voted for Social Credit candidates. Certainly, at one rural poll, the Liberal candidate discovered, after the ballots were counted, that even his paid workers had voted Social Credit for no other party had received any votes. It is said that enthusiasm for Aberhart ran so high that amateur Social Credit scrutineers were able, through ignorance, to break almost every rule in the Electoral Act concerning conduct at polling booths with only a few official protests. In the face of a Social Credit landslide, the officials of the other three parties realized that it was the better part of valour to ignore the breaking of rules, especially at rural polls.

Election night was the most memorable in Alberta politics. Of the 63 seats, the Social Crediters won 56, the Liberals 5, and the Conservatives 2. Not a single U.F.A. candidate was elected. Although Aberhart had publicly predicted an even greater landslide, Social Crediters were astonished at the magnitude of their victory, which actually far surpassed their most optimistic expectations. Supporters of other parties were dumbfounded, for none had envisaged a defeat so overwhelming.

Not the least amazed was the Liberal leader, who had confidently expected the return of his party to power after fourteen years in opposition. Emerging from a railway station where he had been visiting a friend passing through Edmonton on the transcontinental train, he saw the ruin of his political career as a newsboy sold him a paper headlining the landslide. It is said that his first impressions of the result were conveyed, in forceful language, only to the inner circle of the Liberal hierarchy. But, in later years, his admirers were fond of relating how philosophically he had taken defeat. As they tell the story, he left his political head-quarters early. Then, with a few close friends and refreshments appropriate to the occasion, he spent the evening reflecting, somewhat sadly, somewhat anxiously, on the past history and future fate of Alberta.

The Social Credit victory was received quite otherwise at Rochfort Bridge, in the bush country northwest of Edmonton. Here, a road gang of dispossessed and hard-bitten youths in their late teens listened to the returns over a battered old radio. The faces of these young men lit up with new hope. They felt, one of them has related, that they might have a future after all. As the sun set over the mountains, they gave cheer after cheer for "Mr. Aberhart, our Saviour." Later that night, still listening in the darkness, they were doubly assured as they heard the prophet's voice from the Bible Institute quoting, "Fear not, for I am with thee. . . ."

In Calgary, amidst the subdued splendour of the Ranchmen's Club, symbol of the aristocracy of the Old West, the members listened to the returns in silence. No words, several of them have related, sufficed to convey their astonishment and incredulity, even to one another. That night it seemed as if the heavens had fallen and the world lay in ruins. They had a momentary glimpse of a ray of hope, however, when they heard Aberhart say, shortly after midnight, from the Bible Institute, "Those of you who have investments or money or savings, Social Credit will not confiscate these. . . . Great care will be taken in carrying through this new Social Credit Order. You may rest assured that nothing rash will be done. . . ."

At the village of Chancellor, Social Crediters were frantic with joy. To celebrate the victory they piled up packing cases, boards, and poles in the main street and built a huge bonfire. They made a straw man, to represent the former member and defeated U.F.A. candidate for Bow Valley, Jonathan M. Wheatley. Around this effigy they wrapped the election posters of all the opposing parties, and heaved it into the flames with a pitchfork. This act, they explained, was not to be understood as an attack on Mr. Wheatley. They meant nothing personal: they were burning the monetary system.

In London, on hearing of the victory, John Hargrave's Green Shirts assembled in Threadneedle Street. To symbolize the coming collapse of the existing monetary system throughout the world they marched seven times around the Bank of England, while chanting praises to Aberhart's name.

To Douglas, Aberhart cabled: "Victorious. When can you come?" From London, Douglas cabled: "Congratulations. There will be others but only one first."

The Dean of Canterbury, the Very Reverend Dr. H. C. Hewlett Johnson, cabled: "Magnificent. Congratulations. Given best Social Credit skill to produce watertight scheme and pressing it forward courageously, Alberta will kindle a world-wide torch."

In Edmonton, the defeat of the U.F.A. government was conceded at 10.00 P.M. by the premier, who had been receiving the returns in the Legislative Buildings along with other members of his Cabinet. Pressed by a Social Credit journalist to comment on the annihilation of the U.F.A. as a political force in Alberta, Reid replied, "What can one say, the will of the people has spoken."

At Acadia Valley, a hamlet in the federal constituency represented by Robert Gardiner, president of the U.F.A., we are told that farmers' wives gossiped far into the night over the rural telephone lines. As they exchanged the latest election results and confided to one another their bright hopes for the future, they wept tears of joy.

In Calgary, at the crowded Bible Institute, enthusiasm was boundless. Announcements of the returns were interspersed with tumultuous applause. About 10.30 P.M. a messenger handed Aberhart a telegram from the Canadian Press conceding the election to the Social Credit party. As he finished reading it, the victorious leader turned pale and fell against the pulpit, realizing, as some of his admirers have put it, "the magnitude of the task to which Almighty God had called him." To help him bear that heavy burden, the audience arose and sang "O God Our Help in Ages Past."

Aberhart had, of course, experienced only a momentary weakening. Soon he was back again on the air praising the people for their intelligence, thanking his thousands of workers, emphasizing the inevitability of the victory, castigating his critics, explaining the nature of Social Credit, invoking Divine guidance, and predicting a glorious future for Alberta under a new government.

≫≫≫≪≪≪

Interpretations of the Movement

THE SOCIAL CREDIT UPSURGE in Alberta was essentially a people's movement which sought to reform, but not to revolutionize, the existing social
order by changing the pattern of certain institutions. We have seen that,
during the years it rose to political power, this movement passed through
the stages of social unrest, popular excitement, formalization, and insti-
tutionalization; and that it exhibited, in the course of its evolution, the
mechanisms of agitation, *esprit de corps*, morale, ideology, and operating
tactics. Considered as a phenomenon of mass psychology, the Social
Credit movement may best be interpreted in terms of a tripartite pattern
which involves its philosophy, its leadership, and its strategy and tactics.
There is no implication here that these three aspects are exhaustive, but
they do offer a convenient framework in terms of which the important
psychological factors may be grouped.

As we have seen, the philosophy of Social Credit includes both a
severe criticism of certain phases of the present capitalistic system and a
number of constructive proposals for its reform. The psychological
functions of this philosophy in the development of the Social Credit
movement in Alberta will be discussed here in terms of four principal
factors—the social context, the desire for meaning, the satisfaction of
needs, and the conditions of suggestibility.

On its negative or critical side, Social Credit appealed to Albertans for
two reasons: it exploited the preferred group tendencies connected with
economics and politics that had been developing in the province for over
a generation; and in "explaining" the causes of the depression it did not
run counter to, but rather accentuated, the extremely hostile attitudes
towards the existing economic system that had arisen in a period
characterized by "poverty in the midst of plenty."

Of these preferred group tendencies, the most significant was the
criticism of the capitalistic banking and financial system that had long
been encouraged by the U.F.A. Previous chapters have told how at its
annual conventions, especially during the decade preceding 1935, there
were bitter debates on resolutions attacking the system and calling loudly
for its reform, and indicated that there was scarcely a U.F.A. local that
did not have a member or members dedicated to the task of keeping up

an incessant criticism of the monetary system. When Major Douglas himself appeared before the Agricultural Committee of the Alberta legislature in the spring of 1934, the U.F.A. members applauded his devastating criticisms of the system, while at the same time they were highly dubious of his constructive proposals. On its critical side, the philosophy of Social Credit definitely fitted into old social norms; in this respect, Albertans were perhaps more suggestible to the appeal of Social Credit than the people of any other Canadian province.

During the depression, which, for a variety of reasons, was probably felt with greater severity in Alberta than in any other part of Canada, social unrest and widespread discontent developed on a hitherto unparalled scale, but the provincial government, grown conservative through long years in office, offered no solution of the people's economic problems. Further, as we have seen, the representatives of the Eastern financial interests who visited Alberta to discuss the payment of loans and mortgages were insistent that the obligations of the hard-pressed farmers must be met in full: the lowering of interest rates was unthinkable; there could certainly be no adjustment whatever of principal indebtedness. Confronted with the depression on these terms, it is not surprising that thousands of people had developed embittered and hostile attitudes towards both the government and the monetary and financial system. Social Credit was a philosophy made to order for distribution among people with such political and economic attitudes.

In recent years social psychologists have emphasized the importance of the "desire for meaning" in the individual's organization of his experience. The desire for meaning arises when primary, or even derived, needs are frustrated of realization, that is, in critical situations. These situations arise when an individual finds himself involved in a chaotic social environment which he cannot interpret and which he wants to interpret. In such circumstances people who have become accustomed to the established order of society are susceptible to social change. Under the impact of an appropriate philosophy, old values may be overthrown and new social norms may arise.

The feature of the depression which puzzled Albertans most was the discrepancy between the abundance of goods produced and offered for sale on the one hand and the shortage of purchasing power in the hands of the consumer on the other. According to the Social Credit analysis, this discrepancy was simply due to the fact that under the monetary and financial system the rate of flow of purchasing power to the masses was always less than the rate of flow of prices, that is, the purchasing power of consumers was always less than the cost of production. It was also argued that in Alberta the depression, although an inevitable and recurrent feature of an unreformed monetary system, had been accentuated by the machinations of bankers and financiers (the "Fifty Big Shots") who controlled financial credit. To thousands of people this "explanation" of the depression seemed to make meaningful the grievous shortage of purchasing power from which they were suffering, the paradox of "poverty in the midst of plenty." Social Credit interpreted the chaotic external environment in a form simple enough to be "understood," and during the rise of the movement the A plus B Theorem became part of the everyday vocabulary of nearly all adult Albertans.

As the depression increased in severity, Alberta passed into a phase approaching social disorganization: psychologically considered, conditions could scarcely have been more ideal for the setting up of new social norms. Social Credit thus satisfied the desire for meaning and intelligibility amidst a chaotic social environment. On its positive or constructive side, Social Credit advocated new norms, and the upsurge of the movement represented an active attempt to realize a new social order through a specific programme of monetary and financial reform. It was maintained that if the Social Credit proposals could only secure legislative approval, the horrors of the depression would automatically end and a new world would surely come into being. There are also indications that to many of Aberhart's personal religious following the philosophy took on the character of an eschatology, a prophetic vision of a divinely ordained future for the world.

The major factor in the psychological appeal of the philosophy of Social Credit was unquestionably the promise it held out for the satisfaction of the primary needs of food, clothing, and shelter. In a depressed and debt-ridden province where thousands of people were unemployed and living on relief, and where farmers were forced to sell their products at such incredibly low levels that they were often on the verge of starvation, the prospect of a basic dividend and a just price had an almost irresistible attraction.

In its offer of a basic dividend, generally understood to be $25 a month for each adult citizen, the Social Credit plan resembled to a certain extent the Townsend Plan which was attracting millions of adherents in the United States, especially in California, at the same time.[1] This "fountain-pen money" (as it was called in derision by the opponents of Social Credit) would provide every family with economic security and would banish forever the fear of poverty. Further, the basic

[1]Dr. Francis Everett Townsend, a physician, proposed a $200 monthly pension to American citizens 60 years of age and over who had not been convicted of a felony. Early in 1936 the Townsend movement claimed more than 3,500,000 paid members in the United States. This movement was responsible for the collapse of a rising Social Credit movement in California during the 1930's.

dividend was to be presented without any eleemosynary taint, for was it not the people's right, their cultural heritage? Like many another panacea in the long procession of schemes for the salvation of society, the promise of a basic dividend gave the leader of the Social Credit movement the chance to take his followers along a Glory Road.

The social context, the desire for meaning, and the prospect of satisfying their needs combined to produce in Albertans a psychological condition in which they were extremely open to the appeal of Social Credit. At the same time, most of them lacked sufficient knowledge of philosophy and the social sciences to enable them to assess its claim to be *the* authentic interpretation of their world. Unable to deal with Social Credit in any critical way, thousands of people accepted it because it brought order into their confused world. They were at once bewildered and had the will to believe. They were in a condition of readiness to respond, and the philosophy of Social Credit lent itself admirably to short-cut rationalizations in the form of slogans and symbols. For those who could not understand the philosophy as a whole, slogans like "Control of Credit," "Monetization of Natural Resources," "Basic Dividend," "Just Price," and "Cultural Heritage" became crowded with meaning. No small part of the appeal of Social Credit was simply due to the fact that it met so well the conditions of suggestibility which existed in Alberta at the time that Aberhart began his crusade in 1932.

An emphasis on the profound and multivalent appeal of the philosophy of Social Credit to the people of Alberta must not obscure the importance of the leadership of William Aberhart as a major factor in the rise of the Social Credit movement. This factor has been stressed throughout this study. Aberhart brought to the movement his great prestige as an educationist and religious leader: it is doubtful if the movement would have won political power in Alberta without his leadership. This does not imply that we should think of him as a sort of genius with a mystic power of prestige that compelled assent and loyalty for Aberhart, like the leader in any field of social life, was both cause and effect. He was the product of the life of his people, and his power lay in his offer to lead in a direction in which those people wished to go, to resolve a difficulty for which no other man had so good a solution.

In his leadership of a mass movement, Aberhart combined the functions of the prophet with the executive capacities of the great planner and organizer. As a prophetic leader, Aberhart may be interpreted in terms of his unification of Christianity and the philosophy of Social Credit, his resolution of his followers' problems of ego involvement, and his charismatic appeal.

Aberhart's leadership gave the Social Credit movement a threefold religious context: he used the excellent facilities of the Calgary Prophetic Bible Institute as the headquarters of the movement; he attracted into the movement most of his large personal religious following which had been built up over a period of some twenty years; and he identified unmistakably the philosophy of Social Credit with the variety of Bible prophecy and Christian fundamentalism he had long been advocating. Aberhart had no hesitation in presenting Social Credit to Albertans as a Divine Plan for the salvation of society, the parallel in the economic sphere of the Divine Plan for the salvation of the individual. While such an approach infuriated many institutional religious and political leaders, it had a powerful attraction for thousands of people who were undoubtedly led in this way to join the movement.

Aberhart's presentation of Social Credit as a Divine Plan enabled him to insist that ultimate victory was inevitable: the cosmic forces were all on his side. In building up this feeling of inevitability in his following, he swept into the movement many persons who might otherwise have hesitated, but who wished to be on the winning side. He was shrewd enough, however, not to rely entirely upon the Divine Plan for the cosmos: he also used extensively the secular appeal. The names of noblemen, dignitaries of the church and state, and "experts," mostly in *England*, who accepted the proposals of Social Credit were constantly invoked as an answer to the criticisms of orthodox economists in *Canada*. No name, apart from that of Major Douglas himself, was more useful in this connection than that of Dean Hewlett Johnson, of Canterbury Cathedral, who at the time was an ardent advocate of Social Credit. To Aberhart's earlier prestige as an educational and religious leader there was now added the halo that came from his advocacy of a philosophy which not only mirrored the Divine Design, but which had the support of many great and powerful authorities on earth as well.

As a result of the depression, such economic chaos had developed in Alberta that the majority of the people were experiencing at least the threat of economic insecurity, if they had not already become unemployed, been forced to the verge of starvation, or gone on relief: as has been said above, there was a widespread disturbance of cultural norms and frames of reference, and thousands of people felt that they had lost their status in society. This impairment of status was naturally accompanied by problems of ego involvement. In a society that had emphasized so strongly that individual effort was the key to success and respectability, many people now appeared as hopeless failures: they were obsessed with feelings of guilt for their inability to cope with the system. To these people, Aberhart's explanation of the "real" causes of the depression—and of their plight—brought a new outlook on life. In making clear to them that they were not personally responsible for their desperate situation, in naming the bankers and financiers as the "devils" who had ruined them, he lifted (as in the religious confessional or the psychiatric clinic) the heavy burden of the guilt of failure from their lives and started them on the road back from ego displacement to ego enhancement.

In a society in which the individual is also motivated by the desire to maintain or increase his own feelings of self-regard, Aberhart helped his followers to achieve ego enhancement by insisting on their direct participation in the activities of the Social Credit movement. Through incessant *personal* effort, a new orientation was given to their lives and, as we have seen, many of them exhibited surprising qualities of local leadership. In addition, the movement appealed to their feelings of self-regard in that it promised a restored, a redefined, or a greatly improved status for all of them when victory should be achieved. Aberhart's success as a leader was partly due to his ability to persuade so many people to work so vigorously for the "cause": these people, on the other hand, were willing to work so hard because they experienced thereby so much psychological healing of their disorganized lives. They escaped from the horrors of the depression by developing new ego involvements in the Social Credit movement.

Although Aberhart always paraded his Queen's University degree and his titles as Principal of Crescent Heights High School and Dean of the Prophetic Bible Institute, he was careful also to preserve membership character with his followers. To maintain a "folksy" appeal, he had an act, as we have seen, in which he would come on the platform in a tattered, patched up "coat of many colours" to illustrate the fallacious approaches of various well-known political leaders to the problems of the depression. His grammatical errors, although made unintentionally, served to increase this folksy appeal. He received rich and poor alike in his office at the Bible Institute, with the same unflagging interest in their problems. He appeared to his followers as a man who was absolutely devoted to their cause. It is not surprising that people identified themselves with a leader who possessed such characteristics. This identification included an acceptance of *his* objectives as *their* objectives, of *his* unusual mixture of religion and economics as *their* interpretation of the world. His followers were so convinced of his sincerity and conviction that they felt, in their turn, that he identified himself with them, and Aberhart naturally encouraged the development of this attitude.

Ego involvement in the movement became so acute for many people that they refused to discuss the validity of the Social Credit proposals with opponents or, finally, even to listen to the speeches of leaders of other political parties, whose meetings they boycotted. By the summer of 1935 a large number of Social Crediters had developed such intolerance that they viewed any attempt to analyse Social Credit theories critically as a personal attack on William Aberhart. As we have seen, the incisive, scientific analyses of Social Credit presented by the vice-president of the U.F.A., Norman F. Priestley, in a brilliant series of radio broadcasts, lashed them to fury: they retaliated, not by rational arguments but by writing abusive and even scurrilous letters to Priestley, questioning his right to criticize "that Man of God, William Aberhart." Nor would they listen to Professor Angus, spokesman for the Economic Safety League. Two weeks before the election, several of the U.F.A. leaders finally realized the nature of the social movement with which they were confronted. "A dead calm," one of the then Cabinet ministers has put it, "descended over our meetings. We moved like ghosts across Alberta, and everywhere the Social Crediters faced us in ice-cold silence. We carried out our assignments and kept up a bold front, but I knew we had hopelessly lost."

The social disintegration into which Alberta drifted as the depression wore on had produced a state of mind in which thousands of people were expressing a desire for a strong-willed, dauntless leader who would take them out of the wilderness: they realized, however dimly in many instances, that only collective action under a great leader could solve their problems. Aberhart's imposing physical presence, his performances as orator and organizer, his resolute and inflexible will, his infinite resourcefulness, his ability to hypnotize people by his voice, his contagious belief in himself—all these characteristics combined to produce in many people the attitude that "Here is the *Leader*." In the crises which occurred at various times it was always personal allegiance and absolute loyalty to William Aberhart that finally prevailed, and not any agreement on thought or action. Charismatic leadership gave singular unity and additional drive and momentum to a movement that already maintained, on the philosophical side, the inevitability of the realization of Social Credit in the world. To the assertion that Social Credit could not, under the B.N.A. Act, be applied in the province of Alberta, his followers had one simple, confident answer—"William Aberhart will find a way. If we all stand behind him we can build a new world under his leadership."

If Aberhart's character as the prophet of the Social Credit movement gave his leadership a Messianic quality, his ability as an organizer and planner was no less remarkable. Around his person the whole movement gravitated and, with the exception of the short period in the spring of 1934, he maintained undisputed control over its development. The strategy and tactics that gradually emerged in the course of this development may be considered in terms of six major factors: systematic instruction, a people's movement, the use of old norms, the media of propaganda, dramatization, and the groups.

Throughout our analysis of the rise of the Social Credit movement we have emphasized its continuity with a long-existing religious movement. But, as a movement in its own right, it was born in the basement of the Bible Institute the night its leader began systematic instruction in the literature of Social Credit. Those who received this instruction had an irresistible feeling that they had gone back to school to study the causes of the depression and its remedy under a master teacher. The experiment was so successful that its members enthusiastically invited others to take part. Systematic instruction was the dynamic underlying the organization of the groups. As the movement developed, hundreds of people had been so well trained in the philosophy of Social Credit that they could organize and conduct new study groups on their own initiative. Organization within organization gathered momentum and enabled Aberhart to extend the movement indefinitely.

The response of the people was, indeed, so enthusiastic that Aberhart was able, after a few months, to maintain truly that it was a "people's movement." He invariably said to his audiences, "It's *your* movement; *you* must carry it to others; I can't solve the problems of the depression but *you* can. Study! Study! Study! And then *you* carry the truths of Social Credit to others." Sometimes the appeal was grimmer, especially after the decision to take the movement into politics, as in the radio refrain, "If *you* have not suffered enough, it is *your* God-given right to suffer more; but if *you* wish to elect *your own* representatives to implement the Social remedy, this is *your* only way out." A person whose interest in Social Credit had been aroused was immediately put to work for the movement, in his family circle, among his relatives, in his neighbourhood district. These tactics account for both the tremendous drawing-power of Social Credit meetings and the remarkable coverage of Alberta that the movement achieved in a short time. People were attracted to a movement which gave so many signs of being aggressive and dynamic.

The structure of the Social Credit organization was given added strength because it paralleled so closely that of the U.F.A. which had been functioning in Alberta for nearly twenty-five years; earlier chapters have described this advantage in detail: Aberhart's study groups corresponded to the U.F.A. locals; his zones (usually containing ten or a dozen groups) were modelled on the U.F.A. districts; there was little difference in the constituency organizations of the two movements; and, finally, the Social Credit League was inspired by the U.F.A. provincial convention. For nearly two-and-a-half years, Aberhart, as well as other Social Credit leaders and speakers, had the use of both organizations: as we have seen, they engaged actively in functional penetration of the U.F.A. locals until the Social Credit movement was finally transformed into a political party in April, 1935, only five months before the election. The similarity in the organizational structure of the two movements and Aberhart's tactics of functional penetration made it easier for members of the U.F.A. to transfer their allegiance to the Social Credit movement; we have already learned how in some locals nearly the whole membership deserted their leaders and went over to Social Credit groups.

Apart from the remarkable personal activity of the people themselves, Social Credit ideas were promoted mainly through the use of the radio, the lengthy speaking tours of Aberhart and Manning in the summers of 1933 and 1934 (and later of numerous local and secondary leaders), the *Social Credit Chronicle*, and the large-scale distribution of literature. Paradoxically enough, newspapers hostile to the movement (and eventually there were scarcely any exceptions) helped to spread the philosophy. The very publicity they gave to the movement through the violence and bitterness of their personal attacks on Aberhart, and the ridicule they heaped on the Social Credit proposals boomeranged; they turned people to the movement who might otherwise merely have watched the great contest from the side-lines.

The most effective medium of propaganda was unquestionably Aberhart's use of the radio. As we have seen, he had already had nearly ten years of experience as a broadcaster; a representative of the British Broadcasting Corporation who visited Canada in the middle 1930's declared there was no device or technique of the radio speaker that Aberhart had not thoroughly mastered; a former Prime Minister of Canada concluded that "Aberhart had the greatest mass appeal of any leader in Canadian history." Whoever has observed in Alberta the far-flung loneliness of the country-side (as in the vista from the great hill east of Cochrane on the Banff road) can appreciate the psychological significance of the penetration of Aberhart's radio voice into thousands of isolated farm homes. He thundered his exposition of Social Credit in a voice which had many tones and ranged up and down the octaves, but perhaps his greatest attraction was his capacity to project his personality over the air. Through his radio addresses, Aberhart built up contacts in every region of Alberta except the Peace River and the far north, to which the Calgary radio station CFCN could scarcely penetrate at that time. Correspondence resulted from these contacts; radio instructions for the formation of groups were sent out and the movement was on its way even in the most isolated districts. It may be doubted if there could have been a Social Credit movement without Aberhart's use of the radio.

Aberhart brought to the promotion of Social Credit ideas all the techniques of dramatic appeal he had developed during twenty-five years as an expounder on Sunday afternoons of Bible prophecy and Christian fundamentalism: whether in religion or politics he could always be depended on to give the public a good show. We have noted in chapter ix how the response of the people was aroused and sustained through the wide publicity he was able to secure for the movement at each critical stage in its development: by the use of numerous devices such as petitions, appeals to the U.F.A. government, the straw vote, the radio calls for "One Hundred Honest Men," mass meetings, and great picnics and teas. He thus kept the movement rolling so effectively that people listened to the radio or read their papers eagerly for news of it and tried to anticipate what he would be up to next. Even the split in the movement which occurred in the spring of 1934 merely heightened the tension among the people and dramatized anew the movement.

Dramatic effects were perhaps nowhere so successful as in his radio plays in which a cast of characters representing various vested interests (the Banking system, the mortgage companies, industry, etc.) argued with Aberhart and Manning (always the heroes of the piece) the merits of Social Credit. The most spectacular of these was, of course, "the Man From Mars" series (described in chapter iv). The opponents of Social Credit were never able to put their case before the public with anything approaching Aberhart's effectiveness, and his use of dramatization must be considered an important psychological factor in the appeal of the movement.

The study groups were the genuine organizational foundation of the movement. When public enthusiasm for Social Credit was approaching the stage of mass hysteria in the summer of 1935 there were sixty-three groups in Calgary alone, and some 1,800 in the whole province. Membership in the groups ranged from 10 to 800; many of them had between 100 and 200. The groups were privileged to send delegates directly to the Central Council or later to the Social Credit League in proportion to their numbers; they also functioned as the principal medium through which funds were raised for the movement. Groups usually held weekly or fortnightly meetings, and for years the main item on the agenda was the study of Social Credit literature.

Other social movements have used the group form of organization, but a close examination of the Social Credit groups suggests that they probably played a much more important role in Alberta than in movements elsewhere. Considered psychologically, the groups had three important functions: they sustained the microcosm; they developed a remarkable type of primitive comradeship; and, as the movement changed into a political party, they maintained in the minds of their members the hope of the ultimate realization of Social Credit in the world.

Why did Social Credit, rather than some other philosophy, for example socialism, become so widely accepted among the people of Alberta as the hope of salvation? Would Aberhart have been equally successful as the leader of a socialistic movement? Only speculative answers can be given to such questions, but various considerations may be adduced. Let us explore the possibilities in terms of philosophy, leadership, and methods.

In this book, we have stressed repeatedly that Social Credit fitted in with the norms of a province where monetary reform as a solution of economic problems had long been advocated. As such, it exhibited a remarkable congruence with preferred group tendencies. Socialism, as contrasted with Social Credit, had no real roots in the Alberta community. The weakness of the appeal of socialism may be attested by the fact that its devotees among the U.F.A. Members of Parliament were themselves strongly attracted to monetary reform in general, and to Social Credit in particular, both as an explanation and as a solution of the problems created by the depression. The indecision that existed in the minds of leading Alberta founders of the C.C.F. concerning the competing claims of socialism and Social Credit confirms our view that the existing social norms were heavily weighted in favour of the latter.

Given more favourable circumstances than actually existed for its reception in the Alberta of the 1930's, it is conceivable that the philosophy of socialism could have been presented in such a way as to satisfy "the desire for meaning" of the better educated classes of the community. Socialism offers at least as plausible an explanation of the cause and cure of depressions as Social Credit. But the former represents a much more penetrating, as well as a much more comprehensive, critique of the capitalistic system than the latter. Then, too, the objectives of socialism seem to be much more remote and difficult of realization than those of Social Credit. As such, the latter offered the more immediate and, therefore, under depression conditions, the more attractive lure of the satisfaction of needs than the former. Social Credit was undoubtedly presented in such a grossly over-simplified form that even the most economically and politically illiterate person thought he understood it. It may be doubted whether even Aberhart could have presented socialism in such a way that it would have met the conditions of suggestibility that existed in Alberta during the 1930's. Nor should it be forgotten that Social Credit lends itself admirably to the kind of exposition of which Aberhart was capable, whereas socialism does not.

Socialism is not, in fact, the type of philosophy that would have appealed, in any significant sense, to a man of Aberhart's capacities and temperament. Whether considered in terms of nature or nurture, Aberhart was an arch-conservative in education, religion, and politics. The Social Credit movement has always been at great pains to appear as a *reform* rather than a revolutionary movement. As such, it has differentiated itself sharply from socialism (whether Fabian or Marxian) in several important respects. It seeks a limited objective, the transformation of the monetary and financial system of capitalism (it will make capitalism "work"), never the revolutionary reconstruction of society at large. It is strongly steeped in the current *mores* of capitalistic society. It attempts to establish a claim on existing institutions by emphasizing its respectability and its essentially Christian character. Finally, as a merging of social reformist and religious interests, Social Credit has constantly reaffirmed the ideal values of Christian capitalistic society. Aberhart would not, therefore, have been equally successful as the leader of a socialist movement for the reason that the philosophy of socialism was utterly foreign to his mind and personality. But it would probably be difficult to discover a leader whose intellectual and emotional capacities were more ideally suited for the acceptance and propagation of the philosophy of Social Credit.

In the light, then, of the conditions that existed in Alberta, as well as of Aberhart's actual capacities and personality, it was inevitable that a Social Credit rather than a socialist movement would prevail. This conclusion is confirmed by the historical fact that socialism was, in reality, an alternative to Social Credit in 1935. While it is true that socialism appeared as such an alternative only within the equivocal context of the U.F.A. movement, it was still an alternative. Surely the inability of socialist ideas to revitalize the decaying U.F.A. movement may be adduced in further support of our argument.

Indeed, for well over two decades following its disengagement from the U.F.A. in 1938, the C.C.F. was unable to make headway against the Social Credit movement. The perennial failure of the C.C.F. in the province of its birth to defeat the Social Credit party may be taken as a final justification of our view that not even Aberhart could have led a socialist movement to victory in 1935. But such a final justification requires a consideration of the bitter struggle between the Social Credit and socialist movements in Alberta in the years following the memorable election of 1935, a consideration that would take us far beyond the scope of the present book.

We have offered a pluralistic interpretation of the rise of the Social Credit movement. Given the social, economic, and political situation in Alberta, the principal psychological factors were the philosophy, the leader, and the strategy and tactics of that leader. Each of these major factors includes, as we have seen, a variety of subsidiary elements, so that as a phenomenon of mass psychology the movement appears as a complex pattern of events functioning in conjuncture within the wider social context. Finally, our functional and phenomenological analysis has never lost sight of the fact that the Social Credit movement was ultimately based on the experiences of people who had endured incredible frustration and suffering. Considered as a whole, the movement was *their* dynamic assessment of the possibilities of their world.

APPENDIXES

Appendix I

THE SOCIAL CREDIT PLATFORM, 1935

1. FINANCE AND THE DISTRIBUTION OF GOODS

(a) The Cessation of Borrowing from Outside Sources and the creation of our own Credit, thus gradually eliminating heavy interest charges and retaining our own purchasing power. (b) The Distribution of Purchasing Power to bona fide citizens by means of Basic Dividends sufficient to secure the bare necessities of food, clothing and shelter. This distribution is to be based upon active willingness on the part of the individuals to co-operate in the welfare of the people of the Province. (c) The establishment of a Just Price on all goods and services, and the regulation of the price spread on all goods sold or transferred within the bounds of the Province. This Just Price is to be just and fair: 1. To the producers and to the distributors. They should not be required to sell goods for less than the cost of production or of import. 2. To the consumers. They should not be exploited or unduly deprived of fair returns for their purchasing power. (d) The Establishment of an authority to deal with production loans.

2. THE PRESENT PROBLEM OF DEBT

(a) Private, or Mortgage and Tax Indebtedness. 1. The Distribution of Basic Dividends and the Establishment of a Just Price will at once begin to give our citizens the ability to cope with the Mortgage Indebtedness at present against their farms and their homes. 2. The Increase in Consumption will of necessity make a greater demand for services and that will produce wages to help settle these debts. 3. The Debt Adjustment Act will be amended to prevent hasty foreclosures on all property and adequately to meet the requirements of all classes of debtors. 4. Later, as prosperity returns under Social Credit, Interest-Free Loans may be granted to liquidate or refund the present interest-bearing mortgages. (b) The Municipal and the Provincial Debts. 1. Bonds could be offered to our citizens to liquidate this indebtedness at a lower rate of interest. 2. This would decrease the amount of taxes levied in proportion to the success of this proposition.

3. THE PROBLEM OF UNEMPLOYMENT

(a) Social Credit at once removes the demoralizing effect of Unemployment by the issuance of Monthly Dividends based on the Cultural Heritage of Citizenship. (b) The Increase in Consumption would of necessity result in increased employment. (c) The Issuance of Basic Dividends would retain our young people longer in schools of training and thus prevent them from entering the Labor Market. The Increase in Dividends for people who have reached the age of 50 would tend to remove older men from productive employment. Thus, there would be more employment for those who were better able to perform it. (*d*) Every sympathetic consideration will be extended to those in immediate need.

4. THE PROBLEM OF EDUCATION

(An Eighteenth Century System can never handle a Twentieth Century Problem)

(*a*) Our schools should at once be made to supply the training that the New Social Order demands. Up to the present the University requirements for an Academic preparation has predominated our Educational System. Only a small percentage of our students ever enter University. (*b*) Further attempts should be made to bring the various Provincial Educational Systems into greater harmony. (*c*) The Basic Monthly Dividends will at once remove the hindrances to any student proceeding along any line of instruction that appeals to him.

5. THE BASIC INDUSTRY—AGRICULTURE

(*a*) The Just Price for all products will remove the necessity of selling under the cost of production. (*b*) The Marketing of Agricultural and Dairy products must be assisted: 1. By taking definite steps to find export markets. 2. By pressing for lower and more equitable freight rates. 3. By seeking a revision of the system of grading farm products. 4. By attending regularly to the Market Roads. 5. By encouraging the feeding, breeding, and finishing of better livestock in Alberta. (*c*) The Development of the Industry should be encouraged in the following ways: 1. By a careful investigation of the irrigation projects of the Province. 2. By an aggressive policy of Noxious Weeds eradication. 3. By a survey and the formation of a definite policy regarding the Drought Area of Alberta. 4. By improving the regulations regarding grazing and hay leases. 5. By amending the Homestead Laws to make it possible for settlers to establish homes for themselves. 6. We are heartily in favor of assisting in the continuance of Rural School Fairs, and Boys' and Girls' Club Work within the Province.

6. THE PUBLIC HEALTH PROBLEM

(*a*) Definite action should immediately be taken to provide satisfactory health attention for the people in all parts of the Province, and any patient of a hospital should be permitted to secure any type of qualified, licensed practitioner he or she may desire. (*b*) We are favorable to the ultimate introduction of State Medicine into the Province.

7. THE ADMINISTRATION OF JUSTICE

(*a*) We favor the revision of the rules of court procedure, the reduction of costs, and the introduction of facilities for arbitration and conciliation. (*b*) We shall support the maintenance of Order and Law by means of an efficient Police Force.

8. LABOR, INDUSTRY AND COMMUNICATION

(*a*) We shall encourage the establishment of essential industries within our Province. (*b*) We favor a complete reorganization of the Alberta Government Telephone System for the purpose of making it efficient. (*c*) We will support and encourage an efficient inspection of all industries to see that all laws for the health, safety and payment of all labor and industry are safely guarded. (*d*) We favor the amendment of the present Compensation Act with a view to providing just compensation to all workers.

9. GENERAL REORGANIZATION

(*a*) Every Department of the Government needs to be reorganized and to be put on a business basis to eliminate the present enormous waste of taxpayers' money.

10. PLANNING

(*a*) A thorough survey of Alberta's productive resources and the relationship of these resources to domestic consumption requirements and export markets must be at once undertaken. (*b*) The methods of taxation must be brought under immediate consideration for revision and improvement. (*c*) The Social Credit Government when in power will pass legislation to the effect that candidates submit to the voters right of recall if they fail to carry out the proposals made prior to election.

Appendix II

THE PLATFORMS AND ATTITUDES OF THE U.F.A., LIBERAL, AND CONSERVATIVE PARTIES IN ALBERTA, 1935

PREMIER REID ISSUED the "Manifesto of the Alberta Government," the platform on which the U.F.A. conducted its campaign, on July 24, two days after his long-delayed announcement of the election. The Manifesto surveyed "the notable record of achievement" of the farmers' administration in many fields, outlined the social dividends being paid to the people of Alberta, and concluded by setting forth in sixteen clauses the further steps that were necessary for the realization of the ultimate objectives of the U.F.A. movement.

Replying to the challenge of the Social Credit movement, the government claimed that it had brought Alberta through the greatest depression in the world's history to better advantage than any other government anywhere. The general objective of the U.F.A. for the future was "to bring a sense of security into the lives of men and women, and to bring back to youth the vision of life as a great and worthwhile adventure." But, the Manifesto contended, there was no short-cut to this objective. Only Canada *as a whole* had sufficient sovereign power to try out any or all of the varied remedies being advocated. Alberta itself did not have sovereign power in any sphere where change was essential, nor was the province sufficiently self-contained to make a definite break with the rest of Canada. "The government," the Manifesto read, "is all for the objective, but the means to be adopted must commend themselves to the good sense of the people, and must be capable of being stated in terms that an ordinary reasonable person can understand. Surely this is the least we can expect of those who propose to revolutionize our whole economic and social structure."

The government, the Manifesto stated, was aware of the need for changing the economic and financial system. Its main function was to carry on existing essential services during the transition period. To this end the government had already taken the following steps:

The establishment by Legislative enactment of the fundamental principle that the man on the land is entitled out of his yearly production to sufficient to assure him of food, shelter, clothing and medical attention for himself and family, and the cost of carrying on his operations.

The utilization in Co-operation with our own Debt Adjustment machinery of the provisions of the Farmers' Creditors' Arrangement Act for the reduction of the principal and interest of farm debts, resulting in very many amicable adjustments and in reduction by the Board of Review totalling half a million dollars.

Legislative protection for home owners.

The payment of social dividends by the State in the course of the year to those who are unable, owing to conditions beyond their control, to provide themselves with the necessaries of life, as follows:

$1,286,000 to 6,200 persons for old age pensions;

$1,669,000 for the care of the sick;

$514,000 under the provisions of the Mothers Allowances' Act;

$5,123,000 for unemployment and farm relief;

Making a grand total of $8,591,000 from all sources.

The Manifesto maintained that, in addition to these important measures, the government had also given leadership in promoting health, institutional care, agriculture, and education up to the limit of its ability to do so.

The U.F.A. programme for the future was summarized as follows:

(1) The appointment of a Director of Youth Activities and the extension of the system of probation and follow-up for juvenile delinquents; (2) The extension of facilities for secondary education in rural districts, and the introduction of a new course of studies in the public and high schools so that the educational system may be more appropriate to the demands of the times; (3) The immediate reduction of the age at which old age pensions become payable from seventy to sixty; (4) A determined effort to introduce the principle of work for wages in connection with the relief and unemployment problem; (5) The recapture by Canada of the absolute control of the power to issue and regulate credit and currency; (6) The refunding of the public debt in co-operation with the Federal Government at rates of interest not exceeding three or three and one-half per cent; (7) The reduction of the rate of interest on private mortgages, and the fixing of a rate not in excess of five per cent; (8) The recognition by the Federal Government that unemployment, old age pensions, education and highways are problems of national importance and significance, and that more generous aid must be made available from Federal sources; (9) The development and extension of facilities for the marketing of all farm products, and the elimination of the unfair practices revealed in the report of the Price Spreads Commission; (10) The policy of assistance to settlers by way of breaking and advice and direction as to farming methods, and the re-location of settlers where necessary; (11) The application of the purpose of the Security Frauds Prevention Act to companies holding charters from the Dominion Government; (12) The evolving by a properly qualified commission of the changes necessary in our court procedure to simplify and speed up the procedure and reduce the costs of court proceedings so as to make our

courts accessible to everyone who has a legitimate right to enforce or wrong to redress on terms less onerous than at present; (13) The complete reconsideration of the tariff system on the premise that Canada's fiscal policies should be based on the selling of our agricultural products on the markets of the world rather than on building up an artificial eastern industrial structure without due consideration of the interests of the agricultural west; (14) Compensation by way of increased subsidies for the loss occasioned by the unequal incidence of the Federal tariff policies as between the Provinces of Canada; (15) Continuing to carry on its own investigations and to co-operate with the Federal authorities in their present enquiry into the whole of the activities connected with the production, the refining and the distribution of gasoline, distillates, and lubricating-oils, to the end that these commodities, which are so vital to our agricultural industry, shall be operated as public utilities. For the purposes of obtaining reliable and accurate data so that effective control can be applied to these industries, the Government proposes to establish a refinery in one of the oil fields of the Province; (16) Completion of the highway system, and the building up of our secondary roads, with the ultimate objective of a network of all-weather surfaced roads reaching into every community.

In concluding its appeal to the people for a renewal of confidence at the election the government asked them to examine its record in the light of the economic conditions prevailing during the previous five years, as well as in terms of the powers conferred upon the province by the B.N.A. Act.

From the viewpoint of Alberta's professional politicians, the real challengers of the U.F.A. were not the Social Crediters but the Liberals. Ever since 1932, when the Liberals had reorganized their party at a great convention in Edmonton, they had been ceaselessly attacking the government's record at public meetings and in the legislature. To build a platform that would appeal to the masses the Liberals had consulted people engaged in every industry. By correspondence, consultations, and conferences they had obtained opinions and suggestions for "a Reform Policy, a People's Policy, a Taxpayer's Policy" from farmers, ranchers, teachers, returned soldiers, the unemployed, coal miners, oil men, lumbermen, fishermen, merchants, manufacturers, and workers in every industry they could think of. The considered opinions of all these people were then consolidated into the platform on which the Liberals fought for power. This platform, they claimed, was different from any other that had been adopted by any political party in the province; it was specific, rather than general in character; and it was the expression of the people of Alberta rather than of professional politicians in a smoke-filled room. In submitting it to the electorate the Liberals invited further suggestions as to what the people thought would be good for their own districts and for the province as a whole. "The Liberal party," it was stated, "is asking you to join in giving Alberta a NEW START, A NEW DEAL."

To the Liberals, the prospects of victory seemed brighter than at any time since their defeat in 1921 by the U.F.A. The entry of the Social Credit movement into politics did not shake the confidence of their leaders. They felt that they had met the challenge of Aberhart's party by incorporating into the Liberal platform two planks dealing with Social Credit and monetary reform (see chapter VI, pages 153–4). They considered that their platform as a whole was sufficiently comprehensive to win the election.

Certainly, the Liberals approached the problems of Alberta on a wide front. They proposed no less than eighteen measures for the stimulation of agriculture, including the adjustment of excessive debts as to both principal and interest, the complete revision of taxation, and an energetic policy in securing working capital for agriculture at reduced rates of interest. They offered several proposals for the relief of the taxpayer, and promised that as long as the depression continued homes should not be lost through the owner's inability to pay debts or taxes. Their platform also included aggressive and enlightened policies regarding public health, education, ex-service men and their dependents, industry and labour, rural telephones, and legal reform.

The Liberals stressed the responsibility of the Federal Government for unemployment relief. But until the assumption of that responsibility by Ottawa, they promised (1) fair and adequate relief to those requiring it; (2) a work programme, instead of a dole system, for all unemployed who were able to work; and (3) support of the federal Liberal party in instituting a national system of unemployment insurance. They also pledged control of the credit of the province to preserve the financial stability of Alberta and to enable the province to meet its obligations while carrying on all necessary social services. Other planks included the improvement of the general administration of Alberta, the greater economic development of the province, and the abolition of tariffs on all implements used in primary production through the negotiation of a reciprocity treaty with the United States similar to that proposed in 1911. In the light of their platform the Liberals justly resented the charge, made repeatedly by Social Credit speakers, that they had nothing to offer the hard-pressed people of Alberta. Nor were they lacking in aggressiveness in the conduct of their campaign: it would be difficult to equal the energy which the Liberals displayed throughout the province during the election of 1935. Had that election been held a year earlier it is highly probable that they would have won it easily. The supreme error of the

Liberals consisted in underestimating the strength of the Social Credit movement, an error which led them to direct their major attack on the U.F.A.

The Conservatives announced a programme that was much less ambitious than that of the three other major parties. It was introduced by a statement of three general principles. They stood for (a) the maintenance of the British form of constitutional and parliamentary government; (b) the retention of existing institutions until they could be safely changed for the better; and (c) individual initiative and enterprise with government control to prevent exploitation and abuse. As the Conservatives had no real hope of winning the election they announced that they would co-operate with all who held, fundamentally, the same principles as themselves, but they were unequivocally opposed to Social Credit.

The twelve-point programme of the Conservatives included planks emphasizing retrenchment and efficiency in government, the restoration of credit and the investment of capital, the financing of education, and the maintenance of all existing social and public services. They proposed government control of production and distribution of fuel oil, insurance against hail and drought, and a comprehensive programme of permanent highways and market roads for farmers. Municipalities were to be relieved from all obligations in connection with unemployment relief. Other planks included a five-day week in all trades and industries; a minimum statutory rate for both men and women; collective bargaining in establishing rates of pay; reduced freight rates on primary products; and reduced tariffs on farm machinery. With their party in power at Ottawa, the Conservatives promised co-operation with the federal government in the operation of the Marketing Act, the Farmers' Creditors Arrangement Act, and with the legislation required to give effect to the findings of the Price Spreads and Mass Buying Commission, as well as with Prime Minister R. B. Bennett's Reform Programme. Obviously the Conservatives were much less willing to face the economic problems created in Alberta by the depression than were the U.F.A. or the Liberals. Nor did they display any great zeal, outside of Calgary and Edmonton, in the conduct of their election campaign. Resigned in advance to the prospect of winning only a handful of seats, D. M. Duggan, the Conservative leader, advertised his party not as the party of victory but as the party of co-operation. Yet he won the admiration of all who were opposed to Social Credit by his thoroughgoing refusal to compromise with that ideology in any form.

Appendix III

OUTLINE OF WILLIAM ABERHART'S *SOCIAL CREDIT MANUAL* (1935)

THE BLUE MANUAL began with a statement of its basic premise: "It is the duty of the state through its Government to organize its economic structure in such a way that no bona fide citizen, man, woman, or child, shall be allowed to suffer for lack of the bare necessities of food, clothing, and shelter, in the midst of plenty or abundance." The Province of Alberta, Aberhart insisted, was wealthy enough to implement this basic premise. Social Credit, however, was not based on any confiscation scheme; Social Credit recognized individual enterprise and individual ownership, but it would prevent "wildcat exploitation of the consumer through the medium of enormously excessive spreads in price for the purpose of giving exorbitant profits or paying high dividends on pyramids of watered stock." People with bank deposits or insurance policies with cash surrender value need not be alarmed: there would be no confiscation of these, nor would there be any interference with existing inheritance rights.

The economic disease of today, as Aberhart diagnosed it, was not due to over-production, and unemployment was merely a symptom, not a cause. Social Credit pointed out three great poisons at the root of the trouble: (1) the lack of purchasing power in the hands of the consumer; (2) wildcat profiteering (as revealed by investigation of the price spread), which had led to a decline in the value of the dollar; and (3) the retardation of the flow of credit through the maintenance of high rates of interest.

To understand Social Credit as a remedy it was necessary to grasp its four chief terms: cultural heritage, basic dividends, non-negotiable certificates, and the unearned increment. Cultural heritage implied that each consumer had the right to share in the production from the natural resources of the province. At the present time this great wealth was being selfishly manipulated and controlled "by one or more men known as the 'Fifty Big Shots of Canada.' "

The cultural heritage, as the property of all the *bona fide* citizens of Alberta, could only be made operative by the regular monthly issue of dividends sufficient to secure for the individual citizen the bare necessities of food, clothing, and shelter:

To enable each citizen to secure these bare necessities, each of them will receive a pass-book in which at the beginning of each month will be entered the basic dividend for that month, say $25.00. This is supposed to provide for the bare necessities of food, clothing and shelter for every bona fide citizen, whether he works or does not work, and he shall not be required to pay it back or work it out. The only stipulation will be that the recipient must co-operate in every way possible. Those who work will be given their salaries, wages, or commissions over and above the basic dividends. This would at once remove all relief and dole from our land and recover the morale of our people. Our bona fide consumers will at once have purchasing power amounting to $10,000,000 dividends, and probably in addition $20,000,000 salary, wages, and commission.

Basic dividend credit would be used by means of non-negotiable certificates issued in blank to each consumer.

These non-negotiable certificates were defined as "blank forms issued to each *bona fide* citizen to enable him to fill in the amount and signature, also the name of the recipient to whom he is transferring the credit." As such a certificate would be non-negotiable, the person receiving it would of necessity have to deposit it in a bank or provincial credit house. When this was done the issuer would be debited in his account and the recipient would be credited in his account. The recipient would then be able to issue another non-negotiable certificate of his own to pay his debts, and thus the circulation of credit would be possible. "It is very evident," wrote Aberhart, "to anyone who follows this thus far that this issuance of free dividends in order to prevent the province from continuously getting into debt, must be recovered in some scientific manner without introducing a huge tax scheme." This would be achieved by means of the "unearned increment."

Unearned increment was defined as that increment or increase in price of goods which is not earned by the owner or the producer of the goods. The term was well known to those who dealt in the buying or selling of land:

If a man sells a piece of property for more than he pays for it the Government claims rightly that he has an unearned increment and they proceed at once to tax him. However, this does not apply alone to land.
    A Coal Mine situated far from civilization or without transportation would be of little value to anyone except in so far as it could be used for his personal needs. If ten people lived near it, it would be more valuable. If a

thousand people were within reach of it, there would be that much greater demand for the coal, and, therefore, it would be a greater price. Thus the price of the coal above the cost of production is largely dependent upon the demand caused by the association of individuals in its immediate vicinity. Neither the owner nor the miner are responsible for this increased price. It is an unearned increment which accrues from the association of the people within the bounds of the land controlled by them. It sometimes goes by the name of price spread.

Aberhart's definition of the four key terms in Social Credit was followed by a general outline of his system under three heads: basic dividends, price control, and provision for the continuous flow of credit. In the section on basic dividends, it was suggested that children, as well as adults (for whom the promise of $25 monthly was reiterated), should receive monthly payments as follows: at sixteen years, $5; at seventeen– eighteen, $10; nineteen, $15; and twenty, $20 a month. Any who were handicapped physically or mentally should be given bonus dividend protection. It was also stipulated that these figures (which were merely illustrative) could be changed "at the end of any period to suit the standard of living then prevalent."

With regard to price control under Social Credit, Aberhart proposed that periodically a commission of experts from every sphere of life should assemble and decide upon a fair and just price for all goods and services used in the province.

This price must give the producer, importer, or distributor, a fair commission on turnover, and, at the same time, must not exploit the purchasing power of the consumer. Excessive profits will thus be eliminated. To help make consumption balance and control production a compensating price will be declared from time to time. This compensating price will be fixed according to the following formula:

$$\text{Market Price} = \frac{\text{Total Consumption}}{\text{Total Production}} \times \text{Just Price}$$

The difference between the Just Price and the Compensating price will be made up to the retailer or consumer much in the same way that the basic dividends are issued and recovered.

As credit was the life-blood of the state or community, Aberhart closed his exposition of Social Credit in the Blue Manual with an outline of his provisions for the continuous circulation of credit. All basic dividend credit and all salaries, wages, or incomes from whatever source, would have to be expended by the end of the year following their receipt. To encourage individual enterprise and to enable an individual to provide more adequately for the future, surplus credit might be used to purchase government bonds, maturing at a later date. All producers would be allowed temporary supervised credit. Direction should be given from time to time as to what products were most needed. To ensure adequate credit for the provision and distribution of goods, the state must be prepared to issue credit without interest to producers. "This would prevent hoarding," Aberhart concluded, "for the sake of making high interest."

Appendix IV

SUMMARY OF THE CASE OF THE ECONOMIC SAFETY LEAGUE AGAINST SOCIAL CREDIT, AS STATED IN *THE DANGERS OF DOUGLASISM* (1935)

1. The smooth running of our economic life and the progress of recovery from the depression depend on confidence. If Social Credit wins an electoral majority, confidence will disappear from business in Alberta.   2. Social Credit proposes to issue toy or make-believe money (which it calls credit) at the rate of $10,000,000 a month. It does not disclose any method by which this toy money can be given the same purchasing power as Canadian money. 3. The effect of issuing new money (or State House Credit) at this rate will be to raise prices, in terms of the toy money, at a constantly accelerating rate. The faster the toy money is spent, the faster prices will rise in terms of that money. Experience has shown over and over again that no attempt to enforce fixed prices or fixed wages can resist this tendency.   4. The intensive rise of prices hurts the weakest members of the community most. Wages and salaries are to be paid in toy-money. Only strongly organized groups can get their wages or salaries raised as fast as prices rise. When prices rise really fast, they can beat the printing press, that is, new toy money cannot be issued fast enough to meet the demand for it to pay the rising prices. This happened in Germany.   5. This rise in prices can only be avoided if the toy-money is withdrawn as fast as it is issued: i.e., at a rate of $10,000,000 a month at least. No people who have passed through a great inflation ever wish to do it again. The word "inflation" can create a panic in Austria or Germany. Under Social Credit the alternative to wild inflation is heavy taxation.   6. It is not possible to raise taxes in Alberta to this level and no reasonable plan has been produced by supporters of Social Credit for so doing.   7. Existing provincial taxes are about $15,000,000 a year. Dividend payments alone would require $120,000,000, which is eight times this revenue. This figure makes no allowance for cost of collection which would be high. To multiply the yield of taxes by eight requires the rates of taxation to be increased by much more than eight times; for if things are heavily taxed people buy less of them. 8. Mr. Aberhart himself admits the need for revenue, but does not show how it can be obtained. His attempts to do so are childish.   (*a*) Price spreads are to be taken by the Government—In 1933, Retail Sales were $112,000,000. How can anyone believe that these sales contained $120,000,000 in price spreads.—The total addition to the raw material and labor costs of Alberta manufactures was less than $15,000,000. Only a small fraction of this sum could constitute price spreads.—No tax can be levied on Alberta exports for

two reasons: (1) it would be illegal; (2) no one would buy the exports if the price were raised. (b) A turnover tax on wheat and its products is suggested amounting to 65 cents a bushel on wheat consumed in Alberta. The burden of such a tax is expected by Social Crediters to fall on consumers and to come out of their basic dividends. There is no reason in distributing dividends with one hand and collecting them again from the same people with the other. There would be a net wastage of the cost of collection. (c) Social Credit claims to be able to pay $120,000,000 a year with a much smaller sum (such as $10,000,000) if the toy-money is turned over fast enough. This is a crude fallacy. $120,000,000 a year can be paid with 10,000,000 dollar coins, notes, or even dollar-certificates if these are used over and over again (12 times a year is the example chosen). But the Government cannot use the dollars a second time till it gets them back from the public. The process of getting them back is called taxation.

To put our point in very simple words: A man can pay all his expenses (say $120) with the same $10 bill; but only if he gets it back time after time as wages for work done; or as a gift, or by selling something. In all, he will have earned the $120 which he pays. In the same way a government can pay $120,000,000 a year in dividends with $10,000,000 in money or credit; but only if it gets the money or credit back time after time by taxation. In the end, the annual taxation will have been $120,000,000. 9. Since continued inflation will make the toy-money valueless; and since the means for raising $120,000,000 a year are absurd, the whole Social Credit scheme is impracticable. It can be defended only by those who close their eyes to simple reasoning or those who are utterly cynical and reckless in what they say to electors. The religious atmosphere of Social Credit blinds people to these dangers.

Index

ABERHART, William: becomes premier of Alberta, 3; boyhood and education, 8–11; Ontario public school teacher, 11, 13; moves to Calgary, 11; career as teacher in Calgary, 13–14; attitudes of teachers to, 15–16, 19, 20; attitudes of students to, 16–17; techniques as principal, 17, 21–4; views on theory of evolution, 19; views on nebular hypothesis, 19n; early religious activities in Calgary, 24–6; relationships with Westbourne Baptist Church, 26–8, 30, 32, 37–9; develops Calgary Prophetic Bible Conference, 27–8; Biblical commentaries, 28; founds *Prophetic Voice*, 29; organizes Bible Institute study classes, 30; develops Bible Institute at Westbourne, 30; begins radio broadcasting, 31–2; organizes Radio Sunday School, 32; builds and attains control of Calgary Prophetic Bible Institute, 32–5, 37–9, 40; marriage, 40; physical characteristics of, 41; portraits of, 41; cultural, public, and recreational interests of, 41–3; player of and writer on chess, 43; abandons ambition to qualify as lawyer, 43; becomes aware of magnitude of depression of 1930's, 44–7; converted to Social Credit, 48–9; introduces Social Credit ideas into religious broadcasts, 51; begins weeknight lectures on Social Credit, 51; organizes first Social Credit study group, 52; publishes literature on Social Credit, 52–3; analysis of early writings and speeches on Social Credit, 53–8; summer speaking tours of Alberta, 59–61, 103–8, 307–11 *passim*; financial policy, 67; announces last address on Social Credit, 75; resigns as president of Social Credit movement, 76; rebuffed by Douglas, 78, 80; returns as president of Social Credit movement, 84, 85; appears before Agricultural Committee of Legislature, 87, 90–1; author of *The B.N.A. Act and Social Credit*, 93–4; visits leaders of Liberal and Conservative parties, 95, 111; contrasted with U.F.A. leaders, 96; launches "Man from Mars" series, 110–11; calls for One Hundred Honest Men, 112; host to U.F.A., 113–15; debates with U.F.A. leaders, 115–18; deliberates on political action, 119–23; demanded as leader, 128–9; addresses southern convention, 131–3; addresses northern convention, 134; attacked by Keys, 139–41; denounces U.F.A. contract with Douglas, 158; attitude to invitation of U.F.A. to submit Social Credit plan for Alberta, 160–3 *passim*; replies to Weir and Elliot, 165; relationship with Douglas, 168, 169, 171–80 *passim*; announces electoral candidates, 181–2; relationship to secondary leaders, 181–224 *passim*; characteristics as leader, 258–9; attitudes of people to, 259–68 *passim*; psychological shrewdness of, 263–5; functional penetration of U.F.A., 271–4; trains local leaders, 274–5; splits Alberta community, 283–8 *passim*; use of dramatization, 283, 343; opens election campaign, 290–1; criticized for mixing politics and religion, 293–6; pamphlet "What Would Social Credit Do For Us" analysed, 298–9; radio duel with Priestley, 299–301; accused of fomenting personal hostility to U.F.A. leaders, 302–3; accuses U.F.A. leaders of failure to understand